NEVER OUT of SEASON

NEVER OUT OF SEASON

A Timeless Guide
to Building Your Wealth

DAVID W. HUNTER

LOOKOUT FARM PUBLICATIONS

Pittsburgh

ISBN: 0-8191-8549-3

Grateful acknowledgment is made to the following for permission to
reprint previously published material:

Johnson's Charts, Inc.: Selected charts and graphs from the 1991
Johnson's Charts. Reprinted by permission of Johnson's Charts, Inc.

Salomon Bros.: Chart titled "The Asset Derby" from *Stocks Are Hot—
Collectibles Are Not*. Reprinted by permission of Salomon Bros.

Text design by Irving Perkins Associates

Manufactured in the United States of America

Printed on acid-free paper

3   5   7   9   10   8   6   4

To Pete, Sue, and Crock
With the hope that they can build on this foundation

Contents

Acknowledgments

WRITING THIS BOOK TOOK A CHUNK OF MY SPARE TIME FOR ALMOST two years. That is a good bit longer than I originally expected, since I knew about what I wanted to say and have given many one-hour talks with only ten minutes of preparation. But, I have a full-time job and several "*part-time*" jobs that keep me busy. The book would not be done, however, without the assistance of Marisa (MJ) Fera, who joined me a couple of years ago to develop and coordinate this book project, among other responsibilities. MJ, in her position as my associate, was instrumental throughout the project, demanding that I make the text and its concepts clear to her before they were included in the book, assisting in the research (especially all the charts and graphs you will be using), and the editing of the many drafts. Our primary aim in this book is to present those investing concepts in such a fashion that any *kid* of whatever age or financial status can understand them. Therefore, if you, the reader, understand what I am saying in this opus, you can thank MJ. I am grateful to her for all the time and effort she put into this book—and for putting up with me.

This book would not have gotten done so quickly without the help and patience of Sue Hartman. Sue did barrels of the word processing, but her real contribution was in taking care of all the other people in my full-time and part-time jobs—the vast majority of my clients and friends would rather talk with Sue than with me, a fact that surprises no one who knows me. Therefore, if you, the reader, enjoy this opus, you can thank Sue. I am grateful to her for her efforts—and for putting up with MJ and me.

Three other people also deserve individual thanks. Jim Frost edited the final drafts of the book over the last few months and knows what he is doing in the world of letters. Dennis Ciccone knows what he is doing in the world of books and was most helpful in getting this published. Chip Burke, a schoolteacher, came into my office to work part-time for two months and ended up having to read and comment on several chapters of the book. He also worked very hard on a mathematical equation, which we subsequently abandoned. Chip knows what he is doing in the world of baseball.

Aside from the individuals mentioned, there are whole groups of people to thank. My clients, for example, who are also my friends, have been very understanding. The time taken to write this book might otherwise have been used to solve some of their financial problems. On the other hand, if the book is helpful to them in understanding how I approach their problems, perhaps this trade-off will come out even in the long run. The people in my firm were also most understanding of the fact that I was fussing with this book and were nice enough to let me go ahead and do it. My family deserves even more credit, since writing the book took a good bit of time away from fixing the fences on the farm, a job marginally within my capabilities. Next year I will fix more fences.

Finally, I should probably even acknowledge the contribution of those who would normally play golf against me—it probably cost them some money. Those who would have been golf partners of mine should thank me for writing the book— it probably saved them some money.

PROLOGUE

A *Kid's* Book of Investment Policy

THE AIM OF THIS BOOK IS TO HELP YOU BETTER INVEST YOUR savings. Frankly, it will also save me time by providing my clients/friends with an understanding of how I approach their investment problems. About 30 years ago, I wrote a pamphlet titled "An Introduction to Investment Policy" so the Wharton School of Business would give me a certificate of merit and let me stay in class. The certificate was quickly lost, but the policy pamphlet was not. I inflicted it on potential and new clients for a few years. When I gave them the pamphlet, I found I did not have to talk so much, and they did not have to listen to me so much, a happy circumstance for both sides. After 30 years, I am trying again in a bit more detail, but I find, somewhat to my surprise, my basic approach has changed very little. Although I am in the autumn of my life (*early* autumn, of course!), I believe what someone once said: "Money is something that is never out of season."

As an individual, you are unique. Therefore, a good investment policy requires that you think about your particular situation. It requires that you establish your own practical goals by relating your financial situation and your aims to the investment world in a specific manner for a specific fit. This book presents various concepts and challenges to investing your savings well. What I want you to think about as you go through the book is how you fit the concepts I describe. If you are willing to take the time to make notes of your thoughts and reactions as you read this book, you will be well on your way to adopting and implementing your unique investment policy, a policy that will always be in season.

There are several concepts in this book which I strongly endorse and which are contrary to prevailing thought. These debatable ideas include:

1. No one can forecast the short-term stock market, but you can use the market fluctuations to your advantage.
2. A good investment policy comes from relating the individual to the investment world, not from using the investment world to dictate how each individual should be investing.
3. You should divide your portfolio of financial assets into groups based upon risk to principal.
4. The allocation of your financial assets to various types of investments should be consistent, varied only occasionally by the circumstances of your personal life but not by fluctuations in the markets.
5. You should keep your lendings conservative and short term, and take your risks with your ownership investments.
6. This business of investing is not an exact science, and you do not need mathematically precise approaches, fancy charts and graphs, or high-tech computer programs to be successful in the long term. The math neces-

sary to be a successful investor does not exceed the eighth-grade level.

7. Successful investing requires neither vast knowledge nor secret or fancy techniques to quick riches; rather, over time, a simple but unique investment approach utilizing stocks and bonds will help you attain reasonable goals.

You have probably bought books or toys for children that were labeled "for ages 4 to 7" or "ages 8 to 10." This book is for *kids* of all ages, for that childlike wonder, that openness to new ideas, enables us to shake off rigid ideas of investment orthodoxy and also to look inside ourselves. One of my theories is that we never really grow up. It is generally accepted that kids should have a lot of fun. I think older kids should also have a lot of fun. For me, and I hope for you, this business of investing is simply a complex extension of the games we played as children, although it is certainly more rewarding financially. Over a period of time, investing even beats playing shortstop for the Pittsburgh Pirates, which would have been my first choice as a career, at least for half my life. Good investors are always open to new ideas, and I encourage you to come up with different ideas to make your investing journey. The approach I have set forth is certainly not immutable. Although it has been worthwhile for me and many of my clients/friends, I still regard other approaches as worthwhile—especially if they work for you. Differing viewpoints provide much of the fun, so I welcome yours.

This book does not try to be sophisticated; rather, it tries to be understandable, because it is most important that you grasp its ideas and shape them to suit yourself. It will show you how to survey the economic landscape and your own backyard. *You* can analyze your *individual* needs. It will show you how to set realistic personal goals and to measure how far you have to go. It will show you ways to get there and how to plan your route. You will be able to structure a portfolio that meets your needs and goals, and manage your portfolio according to this *personal* design *first* and market conditions second. But, most of all, it will help you build the vehicle that will carry you there through all seasons—*your unique investment policy.* Okay, kids, let's get started!

NEVER OUT of SEASON

CHAPTER ONE

The World in Which We Live

IN FORMULATING YOUR INVESTMENT POLICY, I HAVE FOUND THAT IT is very important to relate your situation as an investor to the world in which you live. Therefore, understanding yourself financially as an individual or a family is only half the battle. If you are going to invest successfully over a period of time, you must have some awareness of this world to which you devote your savings. Further, it would please me if I leave you with the impression that we Americans are pretty lucky, that we investors are pretty important, and that we old kids are leaving you young kids some pretty formidable challenges.

In discussing investment policy with college students, for many years I usually started by defining money, inflation, and the various investment alternatives. Belatedly, however, I began to realize that most Americans—and my students in particular—had no clear understanding of America the Beautiful, of democracy and capitalism. We are free people, we are allowed to get rich, that much was understood. What was less clear was how the philosophical underpinnings of our nation

3

give rise to that freedom and the opportunity for a superb standard of living. I gradually learned from the students that we had not all taken the same political science and economics courses, assuming we had taken any. Some of us had only taken a course titled Civics, from which we learned how the government is supposed to work (but certainly not how it does work). Practical economics courses are still largely non-existent, at least those that pertain to our private enterprise system and how we ourselves relate to it. Yet, it is our political and economic world within which we develop our policy to invest and in which we ultimately invest our savings.

Each nation must have both a political system and an economic system. The function of a political system is to establish a government that passes rules and regulations allowing us to live together, it is hoped, in peace ("domestic tranquility") and for the betterment of all. Remember the Preamble to the Constitution? The function of an economic system is to provide as many goods and services as possible for the people.

We Americans all could profit from being more aware of our political system, so I'll spend a moment on it. We live in a democracy and elect our leaders through the vote of the people, a system that places the political power in the hands of the people (at least at election time). Perhaps more important, democracy implies the freedom of individuals to express themselves, both politically and economically, and certainly vocally. James Yard, one of the founders of the National Conference of Christians and Jews, expressed his thoughts on democracy as follows:

> Democracy is more than theory, it is not even a constitution or set of laws, democracy is the way you treat people—all people. It is a deep conviction of the value of personality and the eternal worth of the individual. Democracy cares about the everlasting rights of persons.

4

I like that. It tells me I am free, I am allowed to be opinionated, noisy, and do what I like as long as I do not hurt other people. In nondemocratic societies, the individual is not regarded highly enough to be considered as someone who can select those who govern. It is because we have such power as people that we have such rights as individuals. Remember the Bill of Rights?

Our economic system, called capitalism or the private enterprise system, is not well understood by most of us. The essence of private enterprise is the right of the individual to acquire assets, to be an owner, and even to become wealthy if that is one's good fortune. It is worth remembering that our democratically inspired Declaration of Independence did not promise happiness; it promised only the "pursuit of happiness." If we had a Declaration of Private Enterprise, it would not promise wealth; it would promise only the pursuit of wealth. We own our productive enterprises directly as individual shareholders or indirectly through pension plans, profit-sharing plans, or other institutions. We benefit as individuals, once again directly or indirectly, from the profits of these enterprises. We are allowed to be happy and to become wealthy.

From a philosophical standpoint, our economic system is far more fragile than our political system. We Americans almost unanimously endorse democracy. Even today, however, we debate our economic system. The alternative to our private enterprise system is clear: a collectivist economic system, such as socialism or communism, in which the government either owns our productive enterprises or dictates how such enterprises will operate and how the goods, services, and wealth will be distributed. The philosophy of a collectivist society is that the goods and services produced should be equitably distributed among the people, not on the basis of their contribution for producing them but on the basis that each person should receive the same reward or result.

5

Most of us capitalists endorse a system that provides equal opportunity for all but certainly rejects the concept of equal results. In other words, we want to be paid for our *efforts*, not simply receive the same pay as everybody else despite our efforts. Many of us may regret the fact that we have not achieved equal opportunity, but we do not see mandated equal results as a solution. Don't confuse democracy (one vote per person) with economics. In our view, the right of each individual to become economically successful itself makes a contribution to others by encouraging the successful person to invest capital in businesses that create new jobs as well as new or better products and services.

In periods when our economic system is performing poorly, for example, during the Great Depression of the 1930s, political advocates for changing the system pop up all across the country. If you are in San Francisco sometime (which you should be), visit Coit Tower, a picturesque tourist monument built as a make-work project during the pits of the depression. The murals inside Coit Tower, painted by unemployed artists, depict the worker as a husky, friendly hero and the business-man as a dour, unattractive character. Substantial numbers of Americans during that difficult period were very unhappy with American corporations, their managers, and even their shareholders. In such periods, the concept of socialism, having the government instead of individuals own our corporations, appeals to a substantial number of American voters.

Collectivism is still not dead, even as communism crumbles. Recently, Socialist International, a group representing 91 socialist political parties from around the world, met in New York City (at the Waldorf Astoria, of course). If you are as pleased as I am with the private enterprise system, it is worth bearing in mind that it can be changed to a collectivist system almost overnight at the ballot box. Even when our economy is doing wonderfully, there is no total agreement that the private enterprise system should be maintained. When was the last time you saw a movie in which the businessman was portrayed as the hero?

A lack of cohesiveness in our national economic system can be traced partially to our educational system. What did you learn in high school about how our economic system works, how to get a job, why you should save, or how you should invest your money? Chances are the answer is zero. Perhaps this is one reason our savings rate is so low. When I was in college, these questions were not explicitly addressed. If there was an underlying philosophical debate in my college days, it centered on our economic system and whether we should have a collectivist or a private enterprise economy. I remember clearly a course taught by Professor Colston Warne, who, by coincidence, was the founder of Consumers Union, which produces *Consumer Reports*. Professor Warne taught the course by acting as an advocate for each economic system ranging from fascism to communism. Our American private enterprise system was somewhere in the middle. Good course, but none of us left it with the conviction that we Americans had something unique and worth preserving. Philosophically, private enterprise is attacked because it is based on greed. It is also not very intellectually appealing.

The compelling case for private enterprise is that it works. Certainly, if you look at the goods and services produced by the United States, Japan, or West Germany, there is not much debate as to whether the private enterprise system works. What makes the system work? If we substitute the word *incentive* for greed, maybe we will find the key. What makes us get up in the morning and go to work? As an investor, what leads you to make a particular investment? Incentive. Whether we are working or investing, we have the incentive to win economically. We have the incentive to work hard, to think, to achieve, and to get paid for it. This is why you are important as an investor. You are providing the capital to an enterprise with the incentive of a good return to yourself, but, at the same time, you are providing the capital and the incentive to someone else to work for themselves and for you. Why does the collectivist economy not work? If you are going to receive the same goods and services or compensation as the guy next to you, who is doing nothing, why should you work so hard?

A couple of years ago, some Red Chinese steel managers visited Pittsburgh, presumably on a mission to learn something about how to produce more steel. Their steel company required 200,000 workers to produce as much steel as U.S. Steel does with 25,000 workers. I was invited to spend an hour with them and through an interpreter tried to answer their questions. If I had any response that surprised them, it was simply my recommendation that they figure out some way to give their workers an incentive to work. The thought that an individual might want some incremental reward for doing useful work appeared to be a new concept to them.

What is occurring in our political and economic systems is important to you and your standard of living, particularly if you are young enough to see the resolution of these historic conflicts. Capitalism is clearly winning the philosophical debate. In 1990, a headline appeared in the world-renowned *Pittsburgh Post-Gazette*—"Russia Turns to Capitalism." I never thought I would live long enough to witness the conclusion of the debate between the private enterprise system and the collectivist societies. Think of all those nations in the world that have been economically successful in the past 20 years—the United States, West Germany, Japan, etc.—and they are invariably capitalistic nations. Now think of those nations that have been unsuccessful economically over the past 20 years—the USSR, the Russian satellites, China, etc.— and they invariably have collectivist economies. We have

witnessed in Europe the capitulation of the collectivist economic societies and the recognition that the private enterprise
system, with its private ownership and greed/incentives, is
vastly superior in producing goods and services for people.

One aspect of our political and economic machinations not
commonly discussed might be helpful to you in thinking
about your investment policy. Not all of us capitalists with
strong opinions and similar backgrounds on political and
economic matters are, by any means, in identical philosophical camps. One of the contrasts I discovered in my brief
political endeavors was that some of us who did, in fact, take
the same courses in school ended up with different viewpoints on what is best for the nation. An interesting contrast is
between those like myself, who can be characterized as *people's capitalists*, versus what I will refer to as *corporate capitalists*. On matters such as tax policy, the people's capitalist is
generally advocating lower capital gains rates and/or supportive measures benefiting the individual investor, small companies, and risk-taking investments. The corporate capitalist
is generally supportive of policies—tax policies in particular—that permit lower tax rates or faster depreciation, both
of which have substantial impact on major companies.

In 1977, I had the privilege of breakfasting with Mike
Blumenthal, who as Secretary of the Treasury had joined
the Carter administration from the Bendix Corporation. What
we agreed on was that the economy was in the pits and
government tax policy changes were necessary not only to
balance the budget but also to get the economy off its duff.
His approach was very clear: Give corporations incentives
for making capital investments, such as rapid and liberal
depreciation schedules, and thereby reduce the governmental
burden on corporate America. However, we were miles apart
on how to solve the problems, for I strongly advocated a
reduced capital gains tax and those measures that would

stimulate individual American investors to begin to take risks with their savings. Now that Mr. Blumenthal has left both the government and Unisys and the economy is sagging, I suspect we could have the same breakfast and express the same disagreements. What we would agree on is our basic belief in the private enterprise system and that Congress is inept.

As a people's capitalist, it is not my contention that the profitability of major corporations is unimportant, for it certainly is, and it is far more important than most Americans believe. It is my contention, however, that when savings are channeled into smaller, faster-growing companies, we are more closely contributing to those factors most important to an economy: new products, new services, and more jobs. As you watch the debates in Washington, D.C., on spending and tax proposals, ask yourself which way the currents are moving and how they might affect your investment patterns.

People's capitalism will be the approach of the future, simply because we live in a democratic system and must have a large percentage of our voting populace understand, believe in, and endorse our economic system. Otherwise, the people will simply use the ballot box to change the whole system. I am an optimist as to how Americans respond when they understand what is going on. The problem is we are living in an increasingly complex society and understanding what is going on requires a consistently higher level of education.

The winning of the old philosophical debates brings all of us American kids, once again particularly you younger kids, a new set of challenges with enormous implications for both our investments and our future standard of living. Chief among these challenges is the fact that we Americans are for the first time faced with international economic competition as we move toward an economic *one world*. We certainly have some strong, competitive advantages. We have lived with a system of competition since our founding, and we have strong natural resources, great schools, advanced technologies, and a strong infrastructure, to list a few. We have also developed some competitive disadvantages. Without debating the pros and cons of these, I will mention a few. First, our government and our businesses have developed an adversarial position. Instead of unity, we have conflict between our political and our economic systems, which must compete against nations where government and business are working toward the same goals. Second, our system of justice, assuming we still have a system of justice and not just a judicial system, has become a competitive disadvantage. It is amazingly slothful, expensive, and capable of making terrible decisions. No matter how you view these debates, our government and our litigious society have added serious new increments in the cost structures of our businesses, making it more difficult for us to compete internationally. The goods and services produced by our economic system depend on our savings and the investment of these savings in productive enterprises (that is the importance of you, the investor). As I see the future competition, it will be based to a great extent on knowledge and effort, and I ask myself whether our school systems and families are adequately developing our young people to meet these challenges. These are tough questions for Americans, who have enjoyed having the largest piece of the world's economic pie for so long. I suspect that if we are to compete successfully in the future international economy, major segments of our population will have to endure a virtual cultural change. They will have to study, think, and work considerably harder than they have for generations.

Furthermore, our savings rate as a nation has never been very good, and it has been declining over the past couple of decades. Currently, it is less than 5% in the United States, or less than one-quarter of Japan's savings rate. Our savings provide the capital necessary for improving, building, and sustaining our productive resources. From a financial stand-point, running a nation, politically and economically, is somewhat akin to running a very large family—except that the government can postpone paying its debt. Critical to the future financial health and, therefore, the standard of living of our people as a whole is: (1) how much we save, and (2) how we invest those savings.

Government tax policies have a substantial impact on how investors both save and invest. Now, Congress has never promised that tax policies will be either consistent or eco-nomically beneficial. The only thing we can be sure of is that every time taxes change, the change will be labeled *reform.* To you, of course, the question becomes, what will be left after you pay your taxes and how will the government's new ap-proach dictate how you should invest your savings.

An example of a tax policy having an impact on our savings rate is the Individual Retirement Account (IRA). My early reaction to the inception of the IRA was that it was a gift from a grateful Republican administration to grateful Republican voters, who immediately took advantage of the tax break. Three or four years later, however, a vast number of Americans from all walks of life were using the tax benefits of an IRA to build retirement assets, and the nation's savings rate in-creased. Frankly, the implications of the IRA were much broader than Congress or most Americans perceived. A good many Americans are beneficiaries of pension or profit-sharing plans, but very few people have any involvement in the decision-making process regarding how these funds are in-vested. In setting up their own IRAs, however, Americans had to make some true capitalistic choices. The first, of course, was to create the savings and the second, most valuable exer-cise was that of deciding how the IRA money should be in-vested. With the IRA, we were well on the way toward educating a broad number of Americans in a capitalistic fashion. Isn't it a pity that the IRA was effectively *reformed* out of existence for most Americans.

One example of how tax policy influences our investment patterns, both individual investors and the nation as a whole, is the capital gains tax rate. In the mid-1970s, when the U.S. economy was flat on its tail and capital raising for small, growing enterprises was virtually nonexistent, capital gains tax rates were at their highest levels, and the incentive for investors to take risks to produce capital gains was also almost nonexistent. Furthermore, Jimmy Carter had run for office with an explicit program to increase capital gains taxes right up to the ordinary income rates. Based on the theory that a capital gains tax differential would stimulate financing for small, growing companies—the companies that produced the new jobs—and a study from Data Resources Inc., which indicated that the government would recover its lost revenues from the tax differentials within a five-year span, Congress actually reduced capital gains taxes substantially through the Tax Act of 1978.

Within a year, this country began its strongest period of risk-taking capital formation for small, growing companies and venture capital investments, thereby producing an expanding economy, a growth in jobs, and an increased prosperity for the nation. Within two years, the lost revenues to the government from the differential were restored, and Congressmen went home to win reelection by voicing their brilliant discovery that taxes could be reduced while actually increasing government revenues and providing a much-needed stimulus to the economy.

After the Tax Act of 1986, which unfortunately once again eliminated the capital gains tax differential, we Americans immediately became more conservative, the number of initial public offerings for small, growing companies peaked promptly and then substantially declined, and the number of

13

Americans devoting their savings to interest-bearing accounts increased enormously while those who assumed risks for growth and appreciation decreased enormously. Congress has never quite understood Abe Lincoln's admonition that "you don't make the poor richer by making the rich poorer." If you take away the incentives for workers to work, they will not work. If you take away the incentives for investors to incur risk, they will not incur risk.

I am not advocating that we use tax policy to protect the rich; I believe we should use tax policy to encourage the rich to take risks with their investments. In fact, a good tax policy will give a very broad-based number of people a feeling that they can win by taking risks with their savings. A Robin Hood approach in tax policy will not work for the betterment of all. When we create an environment in which people assume risks with their savings, we are using these savings to create new products, services, and jobs, which in turn will provide more tax revenues for the government. That's when we have a win/win government policy.

Fitting yourself, both philosophically and in practice, into this political and economic framework is a worthwhile place to start considering your investment policy. If I sound like a dedicated capitalist to you, I am. However, I admit that we have not yet created a world of equal opportunity. Nevertheless, as a substitute, we should not attempt to create a world of equal results through governmental redistribution of wealth. Having created a system motivated by incentives, we must certainly recognize that not everybody wins. Therefore, one of the concepts that more successful people are adopting is a feeling of responsibility to the less fortunate. I believe these programs to help people who need help are necessary but also more effective in the private sector than they are when administered by the government. Therefore, as you contemplate your investment approach, I suggest that you make one of your consistent *investments* a portion of your time and your money to help those who are less successful.

Our political and economic systems are intertwined, and together they provide the uniqueness of this country. In an increasingly complex world of international competition, our first problem is to gain an understanding of the issues, our strengths, and our needs. Some of our competitors seem to understand our system better than we do. Ask yourself what a foreign visitor to our country regards as the outstanding attribute of our political system, and I bet the answer is: "Freedom of the individual." Ask a foreign visitor what he regards as the outstanding attribute of our economic system, and I bet that he answers: "The opportunity for a high standard of living." This is why we are so lucky. The joy of political freedom combined with the opportunity for a high standard of living is the best possible world for the individualist and the investor, and we have it.

CHAPTER TWO

Economics 101

BEFORE WE BEGIN TO BUILD OUR INVESTMENT POLICY, LET'S SPEND a few more moments examining basic economic concepts. I will define the concepts, then provide my viewpoint. Compare your own viewpoint with mine. If you think along with me, my hope is that you will develop a feel for financial issues. Like most worthwhile efforts in life, personal investing requires setting goals and then devising a way to achieve them.

It is my belief that each of us has an individual pattern of handling our finances and that we Americans generally have a rather unsophisticated concept of money and savings. In our early education, we are given some idea of the sanctity of a dollar as a dollar, and we hear that "a penny saved is a penny earned." I understand a Boy Scout is still supposed to be thrifty, in addition to his other sterling attributes, but, after that, the concept is not developed much. Presumably, in our formative years, we are taught something at home about handling money, a questionable schooling when we consider that our parents probably never had a course in handling money either.

After we study Ben Franklin in Boy Scouts, we go to college with an increasing tendency to focus on how we will make a living or prepare for grad school. When I was in college, I felt that all the really smart kids majored in English and all the really dumb kids majored in history. I figured I was not in either group, so I majored in economics. In terms of helping me handle my financial affairs in later life, I might as well have majored in music. No respectable liberal arts college permits a mundane course in money management for the individual. Many of our young people, therefore, are taught how to make a good living, but are not taught how to manage themselves financially while they are making this good living. As a result, they become doctors or lawyers or even stockbrokers (if they can't do anything else), but they are not taught how to build their assets. Managing money, that is, how to save and how to invest, is a subject left either to instinct or the first good salesman who comes along.

I suspect that, unfortunately, what I have described is typical American financial training. We have some awareness that we should save and that we should invest those savings wisely, but we do not think much about it, let alone plan. Therefore, let's go back to the basics.

MONEY

In economics courses, *money* is defined very simply as a *medium of exchange*. Having some with you is convenient, so you can exchange it (buy something). We work for it, we use it to pay our bills, we invest it, but what we are really doing is exchanging it. We speak of people as having a lot of money, but what we are really saying is that they are wealthy. Cary Grant made a lot of money but reportedly never carried more than

$50 in cash. Maybe we can go to the bank and borrow a lot of money, but when we do, this borrowed money is not part of our savings and it does not make us any wealthier. If I asked you whether you would like to have a lot of money, you would say, "Sure," but what you really mean is that you would like to have a lot of savings and be wealthy. Let's quit thinking about money—it is not important unless you do not have any.

SAVINGS (THE NOUN)

In economics courses, *savings*, the noun, is defined as *deferred spending*. This definition implies that all the money we have will eventually be spent, if not by ourselves, then perhaps by our children, and almost certainly by our grandchildren. Those of us who have been taught to save do not like to think this is true, even though it probably is. The deferred-savings concept is an interesting one to consider for a moment because it introduces the time element in your investment policy. Have you seriously considered the period of time in which you are going to be investing your savings? For example, do you have a finite period of years before you retire? Or maybe you are designing your investment policy for your lifetime. How long is that? To help you answer this question, take a look at table 2.1. It is a simple life expectancy table, which will give you an idea of how long you are likely to live. An interesting couple of dates to keep in mind are how long you are expected to live and how long it is till you retire. The time period between the two will have investment implications for you.

If you think the questions I am raising about the time element in investing are simplistic, let me give you a couple of examples of major investment mistakes stemming directly from a lack of financial training made by enormous numbers of older Americans. One mistake many older Americans make

Table 2.1
LIFE EXPECTANCY

Present Age	Life Expectancy No. of Years Males	Females	Present Age	Life Expectancy No. of Years Males	Females	Present Age	Life Expectancy No. of Years Males	Females	Present Age	Life Expectancy No. of Years Males	Females
20	52.1	56.7	35	38.2	42.8	50	25.5	29.6	65	15.0	18.2
21	51.1	55.8	36	37.3	41.9	51	24.7	28.7	66	14.4	17.5
22	50.2	54.9	37	36.5	41.0	52	24.0	27.9	67	13.8	16.9
23	49.3	53.9	38	35.6	40.0	53	23.2	27.1	68	13.2	16.2
24	48.3	53.0	39	34.7	39.1	54	22.4	26.3	69	12.6	15.6
25	47.4	52.1	40	33.8	38.2	55	21.7	25.5	70	12.1	15.0
26	46.5	51.1	41	33.0	37.3	56	21.0	24.7	71	11.6	14.4
27	45.6	50.2	42	32.1	36.5	57	20.3	24.0	72	11.0	13.8
28	44.6	49.3	43	31.2	35.6	58	19.6	23.2	73	10.5	13.2
29	43.7	48.3	44	30.4	34.7	59	18.9	22.4	74	10.1	12.6
30	42.8	47.2	45	29.6	33.8	60	18.2	21.7	75	9.6	12.1
31	41.9	46.5	46	28.7	33.0	61	17.5	21.0	76	9.1	11.6
32	41.0	45.6	47	27.9	32.1	62	16.9	20.3	77	8.7	11.0
33	40.0	44.6	48	27.1	31.2	63	16.2	19.6	78	8.3	10.5
34	39.1	43.7	49	26.3	30.4	64	15.6	18.9	79	7.8	10.1
									80	7.5	9.6

SOURCE: Internal Revenue Code.

19

is to become very conservative in their investing when they retire, and then suffer from a decline in their standard of living as inflation erodes their savings' purchasing power and they live longer than they expected. The second mistake many senior Americans make stems from their belief that they should never invade principal. As a result, in order to maintain their income stream, they take greater and greater risks with investments to produce higher rates of return and end up losing substantial chunks of that principal.

Just pause for a moment and think about the time element for you in terms of your saving and your investing that comes from the concept of deferred spending.

WEALTH

Economically, wealth can be equated with savings, but it is worthwhile to think of what *wealthy* means to you. Can you put a dollar figure on it? My personal definition of wealthy is having enough money to do most everything you want to do. This definition varies the figure for each of us. When we were kids, I can remember my buddies and I expressing our desire to be rich like one of our friends, who seemed to be able to buy a Coke whenever he wanted and, therefore, was regarded as the rich kid in the neighborhood. As we grow older, wealthy becomes somewhat of a moving target even though we still have a tendency to attach some finite figure to it. Certainly, anybody with $1 million in my childhood days was almost unheard of. What seems like only a few years ago, there were about 20,000 millionaires in the United States. Very recently, I saw an article indicating that there are now 1 million millionaires in our country. Even in real dollars, that's a large increase. Apparently, being wealthy is a moving target nationally as well. Anyway, I figure that if we have enough money to do most everything we want, we are wealthy.

Emotionally, I think most Americans regard as wealthy all people who have more than they themselves. We do not think of ourselves as wealthy. Wealthy starts just above us. Some years ago at a speech in Chicago before a securities industry group, I made the mistake of referring to all of us present as "stinking rich." I suspect we had had one or two good years in a row at that time. My friend Tubby Burnham, who was then chairman of Drexel Burnham, and who *is* stinking rich, picked up on it immediately with the comment that he hadn't realized I was stinking rich. Of course, compared to Tubby, I'm not, and wasn't, so about all I could do was observe that being wealthy is somewhat of a relative thing. Since feeling wealthy is presumably a pleasant feeling, I suggest that if we set our standards just below where we are instead of just above, we'll all feel marginally wealthy all the time.

On one of my too frequent trips to New York, the Plaza Hotel gave me a copy of *Town & Country*—there wasn't a magazine that month with one of the Trumps on the cover. I happened to read an article titled "Golden Apple," which described the 25 blocks of Fifth Avenue characterized as the "spacious and elegant" places to live. A real estate brokerage firm had conducted a demographic study of the occupants in this area. Almost 85% of the people were in finance, law, or medicine. They produced an average annual income of $470,800. Guess what their average net worth was? Well, it was only $3.1 million, a figure that implies to me that they can't afford to live there, or at least they'd better hang onto their jobs for a while!

The interesting philosophical question for each of us is to consider the intertwining of our pursuit of happiness and our pursuit of wealth, and perhaps make sure that we are achieving happiness at the same time we are pursuing wealth. I have known a few people to whom there is almost a direct correlation between money and happiness. Therefore, happiness seems to revolve around getting more money. The best that can be said for this approach is that it does not lead to any confusions in goals. I am convinced that almost anyone who desires to be wealthier and is willing to make all the sacrifices necessary to do so, can be wealthier. Just before the crash of 1987, about 30% of the Harvard Business School graduates trooped off to New York City and the securities industry with the clear-cut goal of getting rich. What they got was a chance to live in New York City (a terrible place), ride the subway, and root for the Mets!

My generation had a tendency to be rather robotic in terms of wealth versus happiness. Too many of my friends are retiring as early as they can from jobs they really did not like to pursue happiness. Twenty-five years or so is a long time to spend doing something you do not enjoy. If you happen to have a job you truly love, even though it has low pay, you are probably better off than having a high-paying occupation that you abhor. One of the changes in the American culture from my generation to the next is that young people today do not have to be robots. Some of my friends do not like me talking to their offspring because I usually advocate that they quit their comfortable, miserable jobs and actively muddle toward an occupation that they thoroughly enjoy.

The correlation between wealth and happiness for most of us probably does not go very far up the money scale. Many might contend that, at the far end, being very, very wealthy leads to unhappiness. I am not sure that has to be so at all, although having many assets takes more time to manage well. Realize that being wealthy is usually a moving target for each of us and that it places more responsibilities upon us. Therefore, it is important to spend some time thinking about both the pursuit of happiness and the pursuit of wealth, how they fit together, and what responsibilities we take on as a result.

SAVING (THE VERB)

We all know what *saving* means. But really think about it. How does a person get wealthy? In terms of economics, the answer is easy: Create savings and invest your savings well. Some easy ways to create savings, of course, are to be born with it, marry it, or hit the lottery—all of which are statistically remote. For most of us, saving out of our income over a period of time is the only way to reach our goal of building wealth. Generally, young people have skinny balance sheets, and saving money thus has an enormous positive impact on their net worth.

Table 2.2, a convincing chart on the joys of saving, shows what $1,000 per year of savings will amount to over differing periods of years at differing rates of return. For example, if you save $1,000 a year for 20 years, and invest these savings to produce 12% per annum, all of a sudden (in 20 years) you'll have over $80,000. This is a rather compelling statistical case for being a saver.

Years ago at a securities industry convention, we were shown a 15-minute animated film called *The Richest Man in Babylon*. The theme is simple enough, and written at about the sixth-grade level, about right for us investment bankers and money managers. In ancient Babylon, the hero paid himself first every time he was paid, putting aside something like 10% out of every pay. With this disciplined approach to saving, he ended up being "the richest man in Babylon," and presumably happy. This was probably the most convincing movie the securities industry ever sponsored. It is also available in paperback and worth careful reading. You probably know somebody who has saved like this. I had a friend, a carpenter with a wife and two kids, who saved something from his pay every month. He never made a lot of money, but

Table 2.2
COMPOUND INTEREST
Investment of $1,000 per Year (Compounded Annually)

Rate %	5 Years Total Invested $5,000	10 Years Total Invested $10,000	15 Years Total Invested $15,000	20 Years Total Invested $20,000	25 Years Total Invested $25,000	30 Years Total Invested $30,000
2	5,308	11,169	17,639	24,783	32,671	41,379
3	5,468	11,808	19,157	27,676	38,553	49,003
4	5,633	12,486	20,825	30,969	43,312	58,328
5	5,802	13,207	22,657	34,719	50,113	70,761
6	5,975	13,972	24,673	38,992	58,156	83,802
7	6,153	14,784	26,888	43,865	67,676	101,073
8	6,336	15,645	29,324	49,423	78,954	122,346
9	6,523	16,560	32,003	55,765	92,324	148,575
10	6,716	17,531	34,950	63,002	108,182	180,943
11	6,913	18,561	38,190	71,265	126,999	220,913
12	7,115	19,654	41,754	80,699	149,334	270,292
13	7,322	20,815	45,672	91,470	175,850	331,315
14	7,535	22,044	49,980	103,769	207,333	406,737
15	7,754	23,350	54,718	117,810	244,712	499,957
16	7,977	24,733	59,925	133,841	289,088	615,161
17	8,207	26,120	65,649	152,139	341,762	757,503
18	8,442	27,755	71,939	173,021	404,272	933,318
19	8,683	29,404	78,850	196,847	478,431	1,150,387
20	8,930	31,150	86,442	224,026	566,377	1,418,258

SOURCE: Johnson's Charts 1991

he paid himself first and invested his savings well, com-pounded them well, and became *wealthy*.

Americans as a group, however, are not very good savers. As I mentioned before, we manage to save between 3% and 5% of our annual income. That is less than it was 20 years ago. The Japanese, on the other hand, have been saving 20% or more of their income for decades. When savings are reinvested, they have an enormously favorable impact on the economy of the nation. The important competitive questions are how much is saved and how these savings are invested.

One of my many unproven theories is that our personal pattern of saving is set at a very early age. Some of us are savers and some are spenders. An objective observer can usually tell which way we lean by the time we are age seven. From then on, we are only amending our behavior. Can you change your sav-ings pattern? If your response is yes and you intend to do it, the odds are overwhelmingly against you. But, with vigilance and commitment, you can overcome those odds.

Frankly, I do not know how our individual saving and spending patterns are established, because the variations even within the same family appear to be substantial. Presumably, each of our children has the same upbringing and yet their saving patterns differ greatly. I have seen this in my own urchins from an early age. There are three of them with pat-terns that seem to be as follows:

- FIRST URCH: You get money by working for it and you should do this, because eating well is important, but you should not work past the opening kickoff. Furthermore, spending should not be deferred.
- SECOND URCH: You get money by working for it and every-one should do this. Once you have some money, it's okay to give it away to others, but you should not spend much on yourself and you should save.

• THIRD URCH: You get money by working for it, but you should work for enjoyment, not money. You should also bear in mind, however, that money is nothing more than a medium of exchange and should be immediately exchanged for some material good, which may or may not last longer than a dollar bill.

Where do you fit into this question of saver versus spender? Do you see yourself in one of these patterns, or do you have another, different pattern? If you would like to change, can you do it? Since becoming wealthy involves creating savings and investing them well, let me throw out a few further observations on the psychological aspects of savers and spenders, and you relate them to yourself.

Good savers do not necessarily make good investors. Of course, neither do good spenders. Good savers, however, remain good savers under most economic conditions and almost never have a real financial problem. I have never met one who did. Sometimes I think that it does not even matter what good savers earn; they will save something under any economic conditions. Probably, this is because good savers generally require of themselves that they have the money before they buy something. You would think they would have greater peace of mind than good spenders, but that does not seem to be necessarily so. Since good spenders frequently spend before they have the money, they usually have a higher cost of living in the form of interest charges on their debts, but their peace of mind seems only to be disturbed when their spending gets completely out of hand. Most of us would like to save better than we do, but we do not seem to change much even when we take the oath, set up a budget, and try to live by it.

Remember, I am asking these questions with the hopes of building some practical goals. I think we can amend ourselves somewhat, but if we try to change ourselves completely, it probably will not work.

It is important to recognize what approach is practical for us and then adopt this approach wholeheartedly. I once had a client with a very clear, well-defined investment objective. Her husband had died and left her $3 million, and her objective was to spend the last dime on the day she died. About all I could do was show her a mortality table and give her some reasonable expectations of income while she lived. Her problem, of course, was that we did not know when she was going to die. At the rate she spent, however, there was a pretty good probability that the last dime would go before she did.

INFLATION

Most Americans learn early about inflation—by the time they are old enough to buy bubble gum for a couple of years. Certainly, we can remember our mothers lamenting the exorbitant prices of bacon and eggs at almost any point in our childhood. It is interesting that this idea of inflation always expresses a regret that prices are going up instead of a lament that the value of our money is going down. Keep in mind that it is not money that counts; it is the purchasing power of that money that is important. After we have learned either to make it or spend it, the most important concept of money is that it changes in value. Furthermore, it generally declines in value over time. The rate of inflation is worth keeping clearly in mind as a backdrop to both savings and investment. Our early training on the sanctity of the dollar and the relatively gradual rate of American inflation over the last 40 years makes us a little more sanguine about inflation than we should be.

Europeans seem to have a better concept of inflation than Americans. I will never forget a call from a foreign-born, well-educated client in the summer of 1974, a period of 12% inflation and a terrible stock market. His comment was: "Dave, you Americans are crazy."

I replied: "I know, but specifically how?"

His response was very telling: "For the first time in your lives you see inflation and you run out and put your money in the bank." What he was saying was that in a period of rapid inflation we Americans were more interested in protecting our dollars than our purchasing power.

Another very bright business school friend of mine was Czechoslovakian. He was about 12 years old in 1938 when the Germans rolled in. His father was killed, but his family had some money in the bank. At age 12, he took the family savings out of the bank and invested in the one material good purchasable in quantity—book matches. Inflation was so rampant that by converting his money to a material good, he saved his family's purchasing power and eventually bought his way to America.

Table 2.3 shows changes in the cost of living annually from 1938 through 1990. As you look at the figures, it is difficult to comprehend that South American countries have inflation rates of 50% to 100% a year. In Germany, after World War I, you could put enough money in the bank at the beginning of the year to buy a car and take the same amount out at the end of the year to buy a loaf of bread. Spend a little time with this table, kids. What it really shows is how much your assets had to increase at the end of one year, five years, or ten years to be as well off as you were at the start of the period.

It is somewhat comforting that since 1938 the U.S. cost of living increased as much as 10% in only four years. Unfortunately, the cost of living actually declined in only three years, each of them less than 2%. What really counts, of course, is what happens over a period of time. Even at our moderate rates of inflation, you can see from the chart that the cost of living increased 57% for the five years ending in 1982 or 129% for the ten years ending in 1982. Translated, this means that the American individual or family had to have 129% more money at the end of 1982 than ten years previously just to be as well off as before. It is in this context that we place the challenge to saving and investing. If we stay the same, we lose.

What rate of inflation per year would be acceptable to you for the rest of your life? What rate of inflation do you think you will have for the rest of your life? These are tough questions. Some people read bar charts better than they read figures. I worry enough about inflation to be a bit redundant and include the bar chart as table 2.4, which translates the same inflation figures annually and in five- and ten-year periods. Bar charts are good for watching waves. If you want to be scared, you can visualize the building of the next wave.

Back in 1979, I remember asking a group of students what inflation rate they would accept for the rest of their lives. Since the rate of inflation at that time was around 12%, the overwhelming consensus was that 8% per year for their lives would be satisfactory. Table 2.3 shows the mid-1980s had an average inflation rate of 4.3%. None of us, including economists, knows what will happen in the next decade. As one simplistic approach to this question, ask yourself how likely it is that our Congress will balance the budget and begin to reduce the national debt. When I ask myself this question, I end up wondering how bad inflation really could be over the next decade.

For the saver/investor, there is a very simple and handy guide to getting a feel for the ravages of inflation on your assets as well as a feel for the savings or investment results necessary to combat it. It's called the rule of 72. I have no idea why 72 is the magic number, but it is great for telling us how long it will take to double our money at various rates of return. I will give you four illustrations:

Table 2.3
U.S. COST OF LIVING
12/31/38–12/31/90

Year	Dec. Index 1982–84 = 100	% Yearly Change	5-Year Change	5-Year Average Rate of Inflation	10-Year Change	10-Year Average Rate of Inflation
1938	14.0	—	—	—	—	—
1939	13.9	– 0.5%	—	—	—	—
1940	14.1	1.0	—	—	—	—
1941	15.5	9.7	—	—	—	—
1942	16.9	9.3	—	—	—	—
1943	17.4	3.2	24.3%	4.5%	—	—
1944	17.8	2.1	27.5	5.0	—	—
1945	18.2	2.3	29.1	5.3	—	—
1946	21.5	18.2	39.1	6.8	—	—
1947	23.4	9.0	38.7	6.8	—	—
1948	24.1	2.7	38.1	6.7	71.7%	5.6%
1949	23.6	– 1.8	32.8	5.8	69.4	5.4
1950	25.0	5.8	37.4	6.6	77.5	5.9
1951	26.5	5.9	23.1	4.2	71.3	5.5
1952	26.7	0.9	14.0	2.7	58.1	4.7
1953	26.9	0.6	11.7	2.2	54.2	4.4
1954	26.7	– 0.5	13.1	2.5	50.3	4.2
1955	26.8	0.4	7.3	1.4	47.5	4.0
1956	27.6	2.9	4.3	0.9	28.4	2.5
1957	28.4	3.0	6.5	1.3	21.4	1.9
1958	28.9	1.8	7.7	1.5	20.2	1.9
1959	29.4	1.5	9.9	1.9	24.3	2.2
1960	29.8	1.5	11.1	2.1	19.2	1.8
1961	30.0	0.7	8.7	1.7	13.4	1.3
1962	30.4	1.2	6.8	1.3	13.8	1.3

30

Year						
1963	30.9	1.6	6.7	1.3	14.9	1.4
1964	31.2	1.2	6.4	1.3	16.9	1.6
1965	31.8	1.9	6.8	1.3	18.7	1.8
1966	32.9	3.4	9.7	1.9	19.2	1.8
1967	33.9	3.0	11.6	2.2	19.2	1.8
1968	35.5	4.7	15.0	2.8	22.7	2.1
1969	37.7	6.1	20.6	3.8	28.3	2.5
1970	39.7	5.5	24.8	4.5	33.4	2.9
1971	41.1	3.4	24.8	4.5	36.9	3.2
1972	42.5	3.4	25.3	4.6	39.7	3.4
1973	46.2	8.8	30.2	5.4	49.7	4.1
1974	51.9	12.2	37.6	6.6	66.0	5.2
1975	55.5	7.0	39.6	6.9	74.3	5.7
1976	58.2	4.8	41.6	7.2	76.8	5.9
1977	62.1	6.8	46.2	7.9	83.2	6.2
1978	67.7	9.0	46.5	7.9	90.7	6.7
1979	76.7	13.3	47.9	8.1	103.6	7.4
1980	86.2	12.4	55.4	9.2	117.0	8.1
1981	93.9	8.9	61.4	10.1	128.5	8.6
1982	97.6	3.9	57.2	9.5	129.8	8.7
1983	101.3	3.8	49.6	8.4	119.1	8.2
1984	105.3	4.0	33.3	5.9	103.1	7.3
1985	109.3	3.8	26.7	4.8	96.9	7.0
1986	110.5	1.1	17.6	3.3	90.0	6.6
1987	115.4	4.4	18.1	3.4	85.8	6.4
1988	120.6	4.4	19.1	3.6	78.1	5.9
1989	126.1	4.6	19.8	3.7	64.4	5.1
1990	133.8	6.1	22.4	4.1	55.2	4.5

SOURCE: Johnson's Charts 1991

31

Table 2.4
U.S. COST OF LIVING INCREASE
(Inflation: 1944–1990)

ANNUAL RATE
(Year by Year)

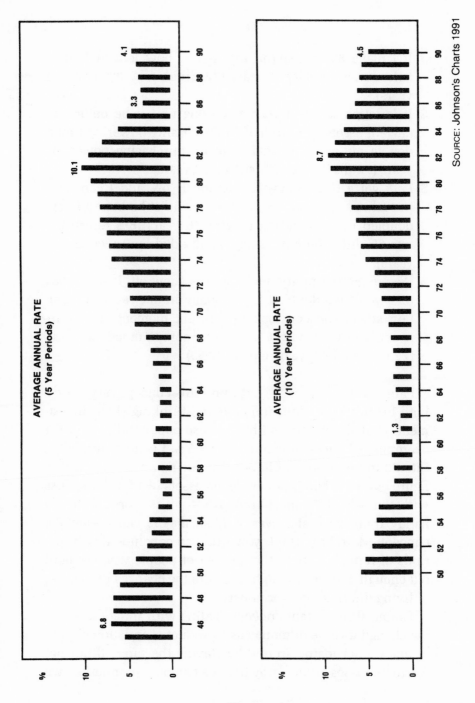

AVERAGE ANNUAL RATE
(5 Year Periods)

AVERAGE ANNUAL RATE
(10 Year Periods)

SOURCE: Johnson's Charts 1991

33

$ If I make 8% a year on my assets, how long will it be before they double? 9 years (72 divided by 8% equals 9 years).

$ If inflation is 6% a year, how long will it be before my current assets drop to half in purchasing power, or I must double my assets to maintain my purchasing power? 12 years (72 divided by 6% equals 12 years).

$ Let's get a little fancy. If inflation is 6% and I can compound my assets at 8%, how long will it be before I have doubled my purchasing power? 36 years (8% return minus 6% inflation equals 2%. 72 divided by 2% equals 36 years).

$ We are getting pretty good, so let's show off. If somebody tells you they doubled their money in six years in a certain stock, you can look very bright momentarily by responding, "Oh, you got 12%-a-year compounded, not bad." (72 divided by 6 years equals 12%.)

I am not much at math, but I find this concept very handy, both for thinking about inflation and thinking about investment results. Sometimes I have to use paper and pencil. For example, if I guess inflation will be 5%, I cannot divide 5% into 72 in my head, so I have to sit down and use a pencil to figure out that I had best double my assets in 14.4 years. Fuss with the rule of 72 until you have it—it is worth it. It is a handy framework and even English majors can master the concept. More important, you will also conclude that in periods of rapid inflation, the number of people who are both old enough and rich enough to ignore the changes in the cost of living diminishes enormously.

The most important concept dealing with inflation is that the changing value of money as a product of inflation simply means we are losing ground by staying the same. If our net worth increases annually by the exact amount of inflation, we are neither making progress nor losing. In this business of investing, we are winning (getting wealthier) if our net worth increases faster than the cost of living. Restful nights ensue.

INVESTMENT

When we think of *investment*, we usually think of stocks and bonds, real estate, and savings accounts. As a final bow to basic economics, we might also consider the fact that *savings equal investment.* According to this textbook principle, we invest all our savings. I had a little trouble with this in school and wondered how putting your money under the mattress could be considered an investment. Well, according to basic economics, it is. As an investment, it simply pays no return and perhaps is somewhat risky, particularly if someone else changes the bed.

Since this book is about investing, my aim here is simply to have you consider yourself for a moment as an investor in the broadest context. What rate of return would you be willing to accept for the next 10 or 20 years or whatever that time period is for which you are deferring your spendings? How does this relate to your guess on inflation over the same time period? How much risk are you willing to assume and how does that relate to your guess on rate of return? Needless to say, the higher the rate you pick, the more risk you have that you will not get it. The rule of 72 will tell you quickly how wealthy you will be at a future date if you invest your savings at different rates.

Look at table 2.5, which shows you how much money you will have if you start with $10,000 and apply your rate to it for 5, 10, or 20 years. It looks pretty good, doesn't it? If, for example, you pick 10%, you can see that your $10,000 will grow to $67,275 at the end of 20 years. If you pick a very high rate, you might consider that J. Paul Getty compounded his

Table 2.5
COMPOUND INTEREST
Investment of $10,000 (Compounded Annually)

Rate %	5 Years	10 Years	15 Years	20 Years	25 Years	30 Years
2	$11,041	$12,190	$ 13,459	$ 14,859	$ 16,406	$ 18,114
3	11,593	13,439	15,580	18,061	20,938	24,273
4	12,167	14,802	18,009	21,911	26,658	32,434
5	12,763	16,289	20,789	26,533	33,864	43,219
6	13,382	17,908	23,966	32,071	42,919	57,435
7	14,026	19,672	27,590	38,697	54,274	76,123
8	14,693	21,589	31,722	46,610	68,485	100,627
9	15,386	23,674	36,425	56,044	86,231	132,677
10	16,105	25,937	41,772	67,275	108,347	174,494
11	16,851	28,394	47,846	80,623	135,855	228,923
12	17,623	31,058	54,736	96,463	170,001	299,599
13	18,424	33,946	62,543	115,231	212,305	391,159
14	19,254	37,072	71,379	137,435	264,619	509,501
15	20,114	40,456	81,371	163,665	329,189	662,118
16	21,003	44,114	92,655	194,608	408,742	858,498
17	21,924	48,068	105,387	231,056	506,578	1,110,646
18	22,878	52,338	119,737	273,930	626,686	1,433,706
19	23,864	56,947	135,895	324,294	773,881	1,846,753
20	24,883	61,917	154,070	383,376	953,962	2,373,763

SOURCE: Johnson's Charts 1991

assets at only 17% annually. Of course, J. Paul lived a long time, longer than table 2.5 runs. If you like math, you could extend the table to 60 years, or you can just accept my word for the fact it comes out to over $1 billion.

When you looked up the figure that gave you $67,275 at the end of 20 years, did you figure out what to do about taxes as you went along? The compounding table requires that you compound the whole thing; you cannot spend any of the income, even for taxes. That can be a bit difficult for even a good saver. Therefore, if you figure you are going to have to pay taxes out of the principal or income, you might reduce your guess by a couple of percentage points or so to allow for taxes. Let's say you now guess 8%, which means that after 20 years instead of having $67,275 you will have $46,610. Still not bad.

Wait a minute, did you adjust for inflation? Good grief. Well, there are several ways to do this, including the rule of 72, of course, but a quick way is to subtract your guess on the inflation rate from your guess on rate of return (after you have already subtracted taxes if you are going to pay them out of this pot), and simply read the chart to see how much better off you will be in terms of real wealth. For example, if you thought you could do 10% as a rate of return but need 2% for taxes, you're at 8%. If you guessed 5% for inflation, you're at 3%. At 3% you will more than double your savings in 25 years—but that seems like a long time.

We should all recognize that *how* we acquire our savings has some pretty strong psychological impacts on our investment of these savings. High rates of return require the assumption of a fair degree of risk. If you work very hard to produce your savings in small increments, it is generally not very simple to become an aggressive investor. You might think about this for a moment and relate the question back to our consideration of the pursuit of happiness. If your tolerance for investment pain is low, your best alternative may be to be a good saver and a conservative investor.

Buck up, kids. As we think about these different concepts, I suspect that you are reaching the same conclusion I have— this business of managing our finances is a tough game. Thinking about ourselves relative to these various challenges, interrelationships, and trade-offs is not always a pleasant exercise, but it is a worthwhile step in establishing our own investment policy. We need some idea of our own goals; they have to be practical and realistic for us. The keys to economic well-being, however, are creating our savings and investing them well. The next time you are tempted to buy a get-rich-quick book, save your money and invest it.

CHAPTER THREE

Accounting 101

DO YOU KNOW HOW WEALTHY YOU ARE? I DO NOT MEAN GENERALLY;
I mean precisely. We all have a general idea, but if we are going
to invest well, we need rather specific numbers. Therefore,
my aim, a veritable dedicated mission, is to have you create
your personal balance sheet. Your balance sheet by definition
is a snapshot of your financial condition at a given point in
time—like today. It is a list of all your assets and all your
liabilities. If you have created your balance sheet correctly,
you can subtract your liabilities from your assets and determine your net worth—how wealthy you are. It is a very simple accounting formula:

Assets (what we own)
− Liabilities (what we owe)
Net worth (how wealthy we are)

If you happen to be among the vast majority of Americans
who have never actually sat down and created their own
balance sheet, their listing of assets and liabilities, I will help

you. As a matter of fact, I will spend four chapters (it is hoped, very brief) helping you, because we want to end up with a balance sheet that will be useful to you in establishing your investment policy and making financial decisions. Your balance sheet is the starting point, the focal point of your investment approach. If you have never made your balance sheet and I can convince you to do so, I will be happy for you.

Since I feel so strongly about it (I love a good balance sheet), let me convince you of the wonders and importance of creating your personal balance sheet. The conclusion is, of course, that you will be a happier, wealthier person for doing so—if not at the moment, certainly later on.

Let me count the ways:

— Listing our assets and our liabilities tells us precisely where we are financially at this moment. At least we are mentally out of the fog and know with certainty what our financial situation is.
— Our balance sheet will be the foundation for improving ourselves financially. It is the basis on which we will plan.
— If you happen to use a financial adviser, he or she certainly has to know where you are currently, if you expect help on getting wealthier. Rare is the client who walks into my office and hands me a completed portfolio breakdown in such a fashion that we can immediately discuss alternative courses of action. The reverse is usually true. I have had clients with whom I spent the first six months of our association—part-time, thankfully—trying to determine exactly what the person's financial situation was. Sometimes this was a happy process. One client disclosed in our first meeting that she had $15,000 to invest, implying that this was about all the money she had in the world. A few months

40

later we both had a clear picture of her balance sheet, which showed a net worth of well over $300,000.

— If your balance sheet is the only financial record you keep and you revise it occasionally, the comparison of your new one with the old one will tell you whether you are getting richer or poorer. All you have to do is compare this year's net worth with last year's (you might adjust for inflation, of course). It's a scorecard.

— Making up our balance sheet occasionally provides us with a psychological stimulus to improve our net worth. Periodic balance sheets can be an incentive to save, or at least to spend enough time with our financial affairs to improve our investment position.

— It is very likely, once you have done your balance sheet, you will discover assets with which you should do something. Frankly, I almost always discover something I should not have bought in the first place (and, therefore, something I probably should get rid of).

— Your balance sheet is useful at income tax time, since practically all your financial assets and liabilities have some kind of tax implication. A quick check of your balance sheet will tell you if you forgot to include the $43.78 income you received on that savings account you started five years ago and have since neglected. Therefore, if you create a balance sheet, you will reduce the likelihood of going to jail.

Now, if you have never done this exercise, I will help you with your first balance sheet. We will make it as of the last day of this month, whatever this month is. In the future I suggest you use the dates June 30 and December 31. We could do it today, but we will wait till the end of the month, after payday, and before the bills come in, so your net worth will look better. As you know, I would like you to do your balance sheet twice a year, but I will settle for once a year in the future if you are dedicated to financial indigence. Before we start, let me give you a further note of encouragement. After you have done the first balance sheet, making them in the future gets to be a much easier process.

As a first step, and the only step for this chapter, take a look at table 3.1, which shows a long list of assets and liabilities. I present these only to jog your memory as to what some of your assets or liabilities may be. At the outset, you can scratch out all the ones you know you don't have and simply put down some estimates as to the money values of both assets and liabilities that you do have. My list is certainly not an all-inclusive one, so you may even think of assets or liabilities (assets, I hope) that you have, which I have not listed. Once you begin this process, put this fascinating book aside and calculate all your assets and liabilities precisely. For the moment, at least, forget all your small physical assets, your material goods. Concentrate on the financial assets and liabilities and, if you like, very large physical assets like your home. The poorer you are the easier this should be and maybe the more important it is, especially if you want to quit being poor. The richer you are the harder it will be, but you will ultimately make some good decisions as a product of it. I don't care which you are. Just do it!

Having come this far, you can now subtract the total of your liabilities from the total of your assets to determine your net worth. If your net worth comes out to be less than zero, you're broke. Your investment policy, therefore, will be simply to figure out how to pay some of your debts so you can get back to zero and then increase your net worth from there.

If your net worth turns out to be more than you expected, congratulations. You're wealthier than you thought!

Table 3.1
LIST OF ASSETS AND LIABILITIES

Assets

Liquid assets
  Cash and checking account(s)
  Savings account(s)
  Money market funds
  Life insurance cash values
  U.S. savings bonds
  Brokerage accounts cash/credit balance(s)
  Other
    Total liquid assets
Marketable investments
  Certificates of deposit
  Municipal bonds
  Corporate bonds
  Mutual funds
  Common stocks
  Other
    Total marketable investments
Nonmarketable investments
  Business interests
  Investment real estate
  Pension accounts
  Profit-sharing accounts
  Thrift plan accounts
  IRA and other retirement plan accounts
  Tax-sheltered investments
  Other
    Total nonmarketable investments
Personal real estate
  Residence
  Vacation home
    Total personal real estate
Other personal assets
  Auto(s)
  Boat(s)
  Furs and jewelry
  Collections, hobbies, etc.
  Furniture and household accessories
  Other personal property
    Total other personal assets
      Total assets

Table 3.1 (*continued*)
LIST OF ASSETS AND LIABILITIES

Liabilities

Current liabilities
    Charge accounts, credit card charges, and other bills payable
    Installment credit and other short-term loans
    Unusual tax liabilities
      Total current liabilities
Long-term liabilities
    Mortgage notes on personal real estate
    Mortgage notes on investment real estate
    Bank loans
    Margin loans
    Life insurance policy loans
    Other
      Total long-term liabilities
        Total liabilities

        Family net worth
        Total liabilities and family net worth

CHAPTER FOUR

Lenders and Owners

SO FAR IN LIFE, I HAVE DISCOVERED ONLY TWO WAYS TO INVEST savings. The first is to lend them and the second is to use them to acquire ownership. Sounds pretty simple, doesn't it? So why would I dedicate a chapter to such a simple concept? The answer is equally simple: Too many people do not seem to care whether they lend or own; nor do they understand the implications of each, or else they believe that only one of the two ways is worth doing. In this chapter, we will see why lending and owning are *both* worth doing but for substantially different reasons.

A couple of years ago, a bright college kid, searching for a third way to invest, suggested *education* as an investment, with the implication that he would put it on his balance sheet. I am so much in favor of education that he stopped me for a moment before I could cynically respond that, in his case, the tuition was consumed and not invested. If he had insisted on *capitalizing* his education by putting it on his balance sheet and not on his resumé, I would have suggested that he list it under the heading of ownership, since I could not imagine anyone giving him his money back, never mind interest on his investment! So, we are still left with just lending and owning.

Let's discuss lending first. When we lend our money, we are essentially making a contract with the borrower, either directly or indirectly, in which the borrower promises to pay a set rate of return on our investment, until a finite date in the future at which time the lender receives his money back. The lender gets no more and no less than the contract specifies. We could make a long list of different fashions in which we make loans. We make a loan to the bank when we open a checking account or savings account. When we buy a bond, we are directly or indirectly making a loan to the institution that issued the bond. The borrower (or, debtor) can be a corporation, the U.S. government, a municipality, a federal agency, a bank, or even one of your buddies. Sometimes I think there are almost as many ways to make loans as there are ways to spend money.

The United States has historically been a nation of lenders. We dedicate the vast majority of our savings to lendings and almost all our liabilities are created by somebody lending us money. When someone lends us money, we have the same obligations as any of the borrowers I listed above: We pay a set rate of return for at least some period of time, and we promise to repay the face amount of the loan to the lender.

Though we like to think of our lendings as safe, they are certainly not without risk, most frequently when we think we have snared a high rate of return. There are two basic risks in lending: (1) credit risk, and (2) interest rate risk. Both of these risks should be kept clearly in mind when you buy a bond or make any type of loan.

Credit risk is the risk that we will not receive our interest payments or get our principal back from the borrower. It is a well-recognized risk and we Americans have rightfully always worried about it, especially recently.

The second risk of lending, interest rate risk, stems from the fact that interest rates change during the period that we own the loan or bond, causing the market value of our loan to fluctuate while the loan is outstanding. Frankly, unlike credit risk, most Americans do not clearly recognize the impact that interest rate risk can have on the value of their fixed income investments. Therefore, worry about it for the moment and I will get back to it a little later.

Acquiring ownership is usually a little more complicated than lending. In contrast to a loan, when you are an owner, nobody promises you anything. You are not promised that you will get a set rate of return (corporations are not legally required to pay you a dividend), and nobody promises to repay your money on any particular date in the future. To a great extent, owners get what is left over after the lenders have been paid. This can be a good situation or a much worse one if the company is really in trouble. In the bankruptcy arena, one of the many aspects about the court system that amazes me is why the common stock shareholders, the owners, get anything in a bankruptcy when the lenders have not gotten everything to which they are entitled. The cynical answer, of course, is because these legal machinations are settled by our court system.

Before we get into the details of the wonders of ownership, I would like you to do a little mental exercise. Take a look at the list of assets and liabilities in your balance sheet, which you whipped right off as a product of reading the last chapter, and divide the list of items into either *lendings* or *ownership.* What percentage of your assets represents lendings and what percentage ownership? In the next chapter, we will break down ownership into more detailed categories. First, let's explore the kinds of ownership that exist in our world.

I have discovered only three ways in which to acquire ownership as an investment. The first is to invest in (not consume) material goods. The second is to acquire ownership of real estate. The third way is to buy common stocks. We will briefly discuss each type of ownership.

MATERIAL GOODS

We consume most of the material goods we purchase, and when we do, we are not making an investment of our savings. Each of us can certainly justify a pleasing purchase with the observation that the price was so good it was a worthwhile *investment*. The fact is, however, that we spent the money. As I have mentioned, we Americans spend more than 95% of our income. We are good consumers and lousy savers. We all know a few people, however, who actually invest substantial portions of their savings in material goods, frequently with the idea of enjoying the asset, but primarily with the aim of having these goods appreciate in value.

For a moment, why don't we think of someone we know who does material goods investing very well. Certainly, a lot of us did a better job of buying baseball cards or postage stamps when we were kids than we do buying material goods as adults. The biggest threats to us kids, of course, were our mothers, who threw away these appreciating assets while filling the attic with worthless copies of the *National Geographic*. Incidentally, I had a good mother, who left my cards alone. *I* am the one who lost my 1935 Arky Vaughan card.

I am sure you can think of some friends who own some valuable antiques. In the little New England town in which my wife grew up, an ex-high-school teacher has become a rather renowned expert on American antiques. I am not about to advise him how to invest his money; he does it quite well already. Essentially, he acquires ownership of a material good at an attractive price and either maintains his ownership as it appreciates or he sells it. When he sells it, it is generally at an even more attractive price.

How about art? Another friend of mine who ran a very successful Wall Street securities firm, attended his first art auction at Sotheby's in London some years ago in search of an entertaining evening. He had one, and he bought a painting. Subsequently, he went to a couple of auctions a year because they were fun. He recently told me that he had made far more money buying Impressionist paintings than he had ever made from his investments on Wall Street. Pretty good material goods investing.

Now, for most of us, these illustrations on material goods investing are somewhat unique. Many of us *collect* certain items, but the value of our material goods generally has little impact on our balance sheet or on our investment process. I do not want you to use our discussion of physical assets as an excuse for not doing your financial balance sheet. My suggestion, therefore, is that most of us can forget about material goods as important items on our semiannual balance sheet. Unless we are serious collectors or in a material goods business, the existence of these assets is not going to have much influence on our investment policy or strategy. You make your own judgment, but I generally just pretend my material goods are worthless. If our physical assets survive the onslaught of our children, we can figure that the grandbrats will finish them off.

REAL ESTATE

Real estate is a second approach to acquiring ownership as an investment. As a matter of fact, if someone were to ask me what successful investment a very substantial number of Americans have made in the last 25 years, I would say it has been the purchase of their own home. They may have bought the home as a place to live and not with an orientation toward appreciation, but, nevertheless, substantial appreciation in

49

value occurred over time for many homeowners. Furthermore, since most Americans cannot afford to pay for homes immediately in one lump sum, we leverage this ownership asset through a mortgage, frequently inspired by the tax deductibility of the interest, and thereby produce an excellent return on our original equity over a period of years. Despite the recent difficulties in the real estate market, I have a favorable leaning toward home ownership. First, even if the home does not appreciate, paying off the monthly mortgage can be a forced savings that many people otherwise would not make. Second, once we own our homes, most of us spend some of our income improving them. To whatever extent these improvements add an increment of value to our home, they too may be a variety of *forced* savings.

Good real estate investments require a fair amount of both expertise and time, neither of which is readily available to the small investor. In addition, many require a constant investment of money, if only for taxes. Some accounting-minded investors are bothered by the fact that real estate investments frequently cannot be valued precisely. To others, the lack of precision is a comfort. Certainly, liquidity can be a problem. I am a good example of some of the problems. I live on a farm, which I foremost regard as home, so I am likely never to sell it and realize its underlying value or the profit on its appreciation. Something is always going wrong, so it requires a constant infusion of capital for upkeep. The farm has a fair amount of surplus land, which in theory could be sold as one or more lots, but it requires too much work to keep clear—let alone make attractive to a buyer. I suspect the appreciation, assuming there is some, will be realized by the grandbrats at the very first moment they are in a position to liquidate.

COMMON STOCKS

The third way to acquire ownership—buying common stocks—is more central to the theme of this book than those mentioned above. It also is one subject about which I am supposed to know something. Therefore, I will defer my comments for a later chapter (chapter 14).

When I am talking to college students, I describe these three means of ownership. Then, I frequently take a survey and ask the class which of these avenues of investment they would select if I were to give each of them $100,000 and a choice of only one type of ownership. Interestingly enough, the class always selects whichever of the three ownership approaches has performed the best in the previous year or so. If common stocks happen to be bubbling at the moment, they will look at me as if I had asked a really stupid question considering my occupation. My own answer is that I would select the one that best suited my personal long-term needs and the one in which my financial adviser or I had the most expertise.

CHAPTER FIVE

Classifying Assets

STAY WITH ME, KIDS, WE ARE ALMOST HOME IN THIS ACCOUNTING
and balance sheet business. I am going to complicate it only
one more step. I am assuming, of course, that you used that
long list of assets and liabilities in chapter 3 to at least get a
handle on where you are at the moment and that you have now
divided your assets into lendings and ownership.

Now, I think you will agree with me that simply listing all
our assets under either lendings or ownings is a little simplistic. Certainly, we can think of lendings that are quite risky,
and we can think of ownership investments that are quite
conservative. A concept that I find very useful is to divide our
balance sheet into four groups, not just two, and to list our
assets in a logical fashion based on the *degree of risk to
principal*. A four-way breakdown of our assets covers about
95% of us normal investors quite adequately and basing it on
risk to principal allows us to see where we are financially in
order to simplify sound decision making.

Take a look at table 5.1, which I regard as the most important visual aid in this opus, and let me tell you how and why I have created it as I have. Incidentally, don't ignore it as we go along because we are going to use this table as we discuss various aspects of investment policy and the ways to get financially healthier and wealthier.

As you can see, in table 5.1, I not only divided the balance sheet into lendings and ownership, I also included three groups of ownership, even though all the asset divisions include common stocks. The basic idea, of course, is that each of these four groups of investments in descending order involves more risk and, it is hoped, more reward.

Now, you might correct me right off and ask me why I put your home at the bottom when it certainly is not the riskiest thing you own. I would agree. However, I put the home at the bottom in a separate category called *Miscellaneous* because it generally will not figure prominently in investment decisions other than the question of whether or not we should pay off our mortgage or borrow against the equity. Frankly, my approach is conditioned by the fact that I work with the financial portfolios of my clients, and I am, therefore, interested in the first four categories and not interested in the details of the improvements to the garage. Different people may use various balance sheet formats for their portfolio breakdowns, particularly people who invest heavily in material goods or real estate.

If you sneak a peak over to the right-hand side of table 5.1, you will see that I subtotaled the financial assets and the percentages of total assets within each group (excluding the home and any personal physical assets you might want to put on your balance sheet). For most of us, this portfolio breakdown is the part of the balance sheet we work with in our financial planning.

Let's play with this a little bit more. You will notice that almost all the lendings are categorized as Group I. Everything

Table 5.1
FINANCIAL BALANCE SHEET OR PORTFOLIO BREAKDOWN

Shares	Security Description	Cost	Market Value	Total	%
	Lendings				
	Group I				
	Cash			$ 5,000	
	Money market			40,000	
	Savings account			25,000	
	Life insurance cash value			15,000	
	Profit-sharing acct. (½ in C.D. and bonds)			150,000	
$20,000	U.S. Treas. note 7.4% due 12/1/96	98.50	100	20,000	
$25,000	Penn. State Univ. 6.2%, due 10/15/00	100	95	23,750	
	Thrift Plan Acct. (Credit Union, C.D.)			56,250	
	Subtotal:			**335,000**	
	Less: Liabilities—$10,000 (Credit cards)			−10,000	
	Bank loans—$40,000			−40,000	
	Total:			**$ 285,000**	36%
	Ownership				
	Group II				
1,000	Mutual fund (Conservative stocks)	$ 10	$ 10	$ 10,000	
200	Bell Atlantic	40	50	10,000	
	Total:			**$ 20,000**	2%

54

				Amount	%
Group III					
700	IBM	$ 60	$100	$ 70,000	
1,000	Mobil	35	50	50,000	
1,000	Johnson & Johnson	40	60	60,000	
1,200	American Home Products	25	50	60,000	
1,500	General Electric	40	40	60,000	
	Profit-sharing acct. (½ in high-grade growth stocks)			150,000	
	Total:			**$ 450,000**	**56%**
Group IV					
500	Legent Corp	$ 3	$ 20	$ 10,000	
800	Waste Management	10	25	20,000	
$20,000	ABC junk bond 14% due 1/1/2008	100	50	10,000	
500	Respironics	12	20	10,000	
	Total:			**$ 50,000**	**6%**
	Total Financial Balance Sheet			**$ 805,000**	**100%**

Miscellaneous

Personal residence		$ 180,000
Less: Mortgage $50,000		−50,000
Vacation home		100,000
Total:		**$ 230,000**
Total Net Worth:		**$1,035,000**

in Group I has a set maturity and an established interest rate. Cash, for example, if it is in a checking account, has a maturity of any time you want it and, generally, a low interest rate. The money market fund *comes due* every day and changes the interest rate every day. The municipal bond and the U.S. Treasury note that I included in the portfolio come due in 1995 and the year 2000, respectively. Notice also that I included the cash surrender value of the life insurance, not the face amount of the policy. The cash surrender value is the current realizable value. You must die to get the face amount of the policy—not worth it.

I divided the ownership section into three parts: Group II, Group III, and Group IV. This is an arbitrary division on my part, but one that is important and very useful in terms of investment policy, and one with which I think you will agree. You will learn to classify your own investments according to risk, perhaps not by a rigid formula, but by your perception of risk. Remember, the basic aim in setting up this portfolio breakdown as I have is to list the assets in descending order based on the degree of risk to the principal. All common stocks do not have the same degree of risk, and they can be conveniently classified as conservative (such as telephone companies), as high-grade blue-chip or growth stocks (such as Johnson & Johnson), or as more speculative or aggressive growth investments (such as Legent). You might say, well, what about a very, very speculative stock or a so-called penny stock? I would agree that it should be listed in your portfolio breakdown. Therefore, you could add Groups V and VI and get down to a lottery ticket in Group VII or Group VIII. The reason I contend that four groups are probably enough is that after Group IV you are not doing aggressive investing. You are gambling, and the odds are very strong that you will lose. I would further contend that any success you have after Group IV will be largely a matter of good luck.

This four-way breakdown of assets allows me to work toward an allocation of assets for virtually all my clients. Notice that I computed a subtotal for Groups I through IV, and I calculated my percentage relationships in the portfolio based on the financial assets. This system allows me to use the groups above Miscellaneous in this balance sheet as a financial planning tool or a financial portfolio breakdown with which I can plan and work more readily. Therefore, if you have material goods that you definitely want to include in your own personal balance sheet, I certainly do not object. I just suggest that you put them down under the Miscellaneous section, so we can work with the financial assets.

With each of these four groups, I have an investment strategy, and I am, therefore, able to characterize the assets that I place in each group.

GROUP I—LENDINGS

My aim in this section of the portfolio is, above all, to protect my principal. Therefore, I want as little volatility in this section as possible with a secondary aim of producing a reasonable income. This section invariably consists entirely of cash, cash equivalents, and debt securities. Theoretically, we could have an ownership investment in this category, but, in reality, I cannot think of any common stocks that are so stable that I would classify them in the group. Further, although I would include most lendings and debt securities in this group, I can think of plenty of bonds that are not stable enough to include in Group I. For example, if you look at table 5.1, you will notice that I included a junk bond, on which the investor has a pretty good loss, as part of Group IV, on the theory that it has become a very speculative holding. Or I might buy a decent bond with a long maturity, with the aim of producing a profit on the bond from a decline in interest rates, and I would include it in Group II or Group III. As another example, in a period of high interest rates, I might buy a 30-year bond in a good telephone company, which is selling well below par because of high interest rates. I would be buying it to produce a profit by having interest rates decline and my bond move upward toward par. I would not include this bond in Group I because its price volatility will be greater than my requirements for Group I. My aim would be to have the bond appreciate, not to have the price stay the same.

GROUP II—CONSERVATIVE STOCKS

In my view, a Group II security is generally a very high-grade conservative common stock. It is ownership in a business that is basically defensive in nature. We expect the price fluctuations to be considerably less than the fluctuations in the Standard & Poor's Indexes or the Dow Jones Averages—utilities, for example. A few years ago, I felt that many of our better food companies and banks fit into this Group II category. Many of these companies were selling at about seven times earnings and yielding 7%. Then food companies began to grow faster, appreciating in price substantially, and began selling at much higher price-earnings (P-E) ratios. The P-E ratio compares the market price for the stock with the earnings per share of the company. At the moment, therefore, these stocks are not as defensive as they used to be, and I would drop most of the better-known food companies down to Group III. On the other hand, banks began to take very substantial risks, many of which did not work out very well. Their write-offs have increased, their earnings have suffered, and at the moment we might drop a lot of banks all the way down to Group IV.

Aside from the point that Group II stocks are intended to be conservative, remember that a company you buy at one point may move into another group because of either its price action or the company's performance. A good food stock at 7 times earnings is a lot more conservative than a good food stock at 16 times earnings. If either price or business conditions change the basic nature of the investment, you change the ranking you have given it in your balance sheet.

GROUP III—HIGH-GRADE COMMON STOCKS

The aim of Group III investments might be characterized as a *balanced offense*. We are no longer primarily concerned with protecting our principal. Our goal is to produce profits in a reasonable and measured fashion.

Group III generally consists of high-grade growth stocks and blue-chip companies. You will recognize the names in our model portfolio. They are not conservative enough to be Group II stocks, and they are certainly not as aggressive as Group IV stocks. Yet, if a smaller company is very strong financially, and has a steady earnings record as well as an excellent position in its industry, I include it in Group III.

Note that in this particular model portfolio, the family has a substantial investment in a profit-sharing plan. In classifying this plan, I studied the holdings of the plan just enough to realize that about half the money was invested in high-grade debt securities and the other half in high-grade common stocks. Therefore, I split the profit-sharing plan in two. You will see $150,000 under Group I representing the lendings, and $150,000 in Group III representing the high-grade stocks.

Most real estate and material goods investments fall into Group III or Group IV. It is certainly possible to have a real estate investment that has the quality of a Group II common stock, but I cannot think of any that would be descriptive to you. We could, however, visualize many real estate transactions that are very blue chip in nature and merit a Group III rating.

GROUP IV—AGGRESSIVE-GROWTH STOCKS

The objective of Group IV investments is almost exclusively appreciation in value. This group generally consists of smaller companies, considered by many to be more speculative investments. Since our classifications are done by risk to principal, we could very well have a sizable company in Group IV simply because this particular company's stock does not merit inclusion in the higher-quality groups of the portfolio. Examples are major industrial companies or banks that hit very difficult times and, therefore, became more speculative. Owning Chrysler is a lot different from owning General Electric.

Most material goods probably belong in this section. Think of the price action of even a van Gogh over a period of time, and you could regard it as a very valuable but speculative investment.

These divisions are certainly debatable. Nobody tells you when you buy a stock precisely where it fits and that it should be classified as a Group II, III, or IV. Some years ago a mechanism called *beta* was developed, which measures historical stock fluctuations with the intention of giving investors some idea as to whether their stock moves slower or faster than, or about the same as, the stock market as a whole. The stock market presumably has a beta of 1.0. Thus, faster-moving stocks have betas in excess of 1.0 and slower-moving stocks have betas less than 1.0, for example, .6. A company with a high beta normally fits in Group IV, and a company with a very low beta normally fits in Group II or Group III. Keep in mind, the beta measurement does not tell you how this company will perform in the future; it simply gives an indication of what might be expected in the near future as to the movement of the price of the company's stock.

As we move down from Group I through Group IV, we can

see that we are generally increasing our risk and, it is hoped, our rewards. This risk/reward relationship is basic to investing. There is no rule that says you will receive greater rewards by assuming greater risk, but at least we can get the idea that we are looking for greater rewards. Presumably, if we are operating well, our Group I's will sit quietly and do nothing but produce a reasonable income. Group II's should be relatively quiet, particularly in down markets. It is a delight when a Group II stock becomes a Group III over a period of time by showing that it can increase its earnings and become more of a growth stock (e.g., food companies). It is also nice when your original investment in a Group IV stock is justified by consistent growth in earnings and stature, which leads you to consider moving the stock from Group IV into Group III. The concept is simply that the fortunes of a company and its stock do change over a period of time, and the basic nature of an individual investment, therefore, changes sometimes for the better and sometimes for the worse.

It is not very important to debate the group into which a particular company should be classified, but it is important to do your balance sheet with this four-way portfolio breakdown in mind and determine what percentage of your assets are in each group. Needless to say, kids, we will come back to these percentage relationships.

CHAPTER SIX

Pay Your Debts

YOU KIDS JUST KNEW THAT AT SOME POINT YOU WERE GOING TO have to listen to a five-minute lecture on paying your debts, otherwise known as eliminating your liabilities. You knew it, you just *knew* it! Five minutes seems reasonable to me.

The first thing to remember about any debts you have is that they are an absolute claim or obligation against everything you own. To illustrate this concept, I want you to review table 5.1 and find the liabilities section. You will notice that I put two of the debts in Group I as deductions from the assets in that group. I do not care whether you incur the debt to buy a car, fix up the front porch, or take a well-deserved vacation. If you owe the money, the obligation is as strong for you to pay your debts as it is for the U.S. Treasury to pay its debts. Therefore, you should show your debts against the highest-ranking assets you have—your lendings in Group I. If I put my debts right up there at the top of my balance sheet against my most stable assets, I see them pretty quickly when I do my balance sheet, and it makes me think about them.

Thus, looking right square and smart at our liabilities near the top of our balance sheet every six months leads us very quickly to the consideration of paying the debt as an economic trade-off. This is the second concept I would like to have you consider relative to your debts. To my lender, I, as the borrower, may be anything from a good risk to a junk-bond risk, but I am certainly not as good as the U.S. Treasury, which can always print money. My creditor will, therefore, charge me for the degree of risk that he thinks I deserve. He is also going to charge me for all the paperwork and time to make me the loan. He may even like me, but he is lending to me to make money. If I keep my liabilities right up at the top of my balance sheet, I can recognize the trade-offs that exist for me in terms of what I get for lending my money and what I pay for borrowing it. If the rate of interest on a debt is greater than that which you earn on a cash investment, such as a money market, there is no question you are better off paying off the debt. If, for example, you have a large credit card balance at 17% interest—a common rate—and your money market is only earning 8%, pay off the balance. You will be far ahead. In table 5.1, for example, I suggest that this family think of using a chunk of their money market fund to pay off a corresponding chunk of their liabilities. There may be some unique reason for not doing so, but all across the United States people borrow chunks of money at the same time they lend money, and the *spread* is generally against them.

I am willing to compromise on home mortgage debt simply because, as I said, most Americans cannot afford to buy homes outright, and as I already inferred, I am generally in favor of home ownership. In table 5.1, you can see that I put the home mortgage liability against the home at the bottom of the balance sheet. Congress implies they share my view by allowing us to deduct the interest on our home mortgage but not on our consumer installment debts. Well, maybe they do not share this view, but they sure know that there are millions of noisy Americans with home mortgages who are already mad at Congress. At least they are smart enough to know they do not need a whole group of voters who are even madder.

Relative to your debts, the least you can do is to do your math. A couple of very simple math exercises are applicable primarily to you young kids, who have a reputation of being the instant-gratification generation. I have seen a lot of sizable purchases that might not be characterized as necessities made with borrowed money, sometimes because they "really got a bargain." As you are getting the bargain, you might sit down for a moment and add all the interest you will pay while you are enjoying the bargain, and you may come to the conclusion that you have a fairly expensive gratification.

By now, you have correctly inferred that I am pretty dead set against liabilities and believe it is generally an excellent investment to pay them off. In fairness, I should say that this is one of those points on which many experts and I disagree, and they have a case. I have heard many smart kids say that the way to become successful and wealthy is to borrow as much money as you can and produce an inordinate rate of return on these borrowings. They point out this country is such a nation of lenders (and borrowers) that we really are not charged enough for our borrowings. Conversely, of course, we do not get enough interest on our lendings, a point with which I agree. In any event, the prodigious borrower contends that other people's money is cheap to obtain in the United States, a point with which I also agree. The conclusion, however, that we should therefore use other people's money for investing is where we part company.

When I came into the securities business, the vast majority of the clients in our firm used margin accounts. They borrowed money to buy stocks. A few years ago, I did a little study of margin accounts and found that borrowers who were able to buy more stock through leveraging actually did worse in their performance than people who bought less stock and paid cash for it. Assuming this is true, *why* is it true? Well, I attribute it largely to the psychological pressures that come from owing money as well as owning fluctuating stocks. When the stock market is declining precipitously, the person with a margin account feels the pressure of the debt. This pressure will build until he or she takes the loss instead of waiting for the market to go back up. The investor, therefore, has a tendency to sell low. When the market is going up, the margin account investor becomes convinced of the wisdom in borrowing money to buy stocks. He then borrows more money and buys more stock while riding the euphoria of a bull market. He, therefore, has a tendency to buy high. My conclusion is that the psychological pressure of owing money increases the already natural tendency of an individual to buy high and sell low in stock market cycles.

Just as we each have inclinations toward being a spender or a saver, we each have a psychological tolerance for debt, and I think it is worthwhile to consider your own. The concept that people who have sizable debts are uncomfortable with them is not necessarily valid. Some of us certainly are, but I know plenty of people who have no problem leading their lives with a good slug of debt.

I will describe my own psychological makeup, not because it's perfect, but as a framework for evaluating yourself. As an investor, I incur a good bit of risk, measured risk I hope. Occasionally, I borrow a chunk of money when I find I want to make an investment that must be done promptly, and I do not want to sell something immediately to make this investment. Once I incur the debt, I am very conscious of it. Yes, I know I can equate it to the investment I made using the borrowed money, but I also know it is an obligation against everything I have. Therefore, I have a tendency to pay off this debt a lot faster than is necessary. As a risk-taking investor, it allows me to tell myself that I really own this stock. It may go from $50 to $5, but I own it and nobody is going to tell me I have to sell it. I find this is an enormous comfort in down markets, and it permits me the mental freedom to make aggressive investments at points when the stock market is indicating that the world is about to end, which it usually does not. It also allows me to do one thing in this world that I am very good at and enjoy thoroughly—sleep.

Now, let me contrast this approach with that of a person who advocates a judicious use of debt. This person believes in himself and his security selection enough to risk more than his own money on the investment. This does not mean that he is financially unstable. Certainly, he can live with it psychologically and may sleep even better than I do, although that is unlikely. His contention is that he makes substantially better returns from his investment than I do. During pleasant periods in the stock market, he is right; he does produce more appreciation. If he is well disciplined, he can certainly use the debt to augment his performance and pay it down as his stocks appreciate. However, my approach makes me look better on the downside, and my claim is that I can, as a product of my approach, be an aggressive buyer at very low points in the market and make up for his better performance during the good periods. With his debt as a burden, he cannot be an aggressive purchaser in bad periods because he does not have the financial capability at that point to do so. This is the kind of debate that could last all night. The important question is what kind of person are you?

Understanding what kind of attitude you have toward debt is very important. Whatever your attitude, do your math. Look at the trade-offs. However, if you are a good spender, have a high tolerance for debt and a skinny balance sheet, you must be a whale of a good sleeper!

CHAPTER SEVEN

Advanced Accounting

YOU ARE DOING GREAT, KIDS. I PROMISED YOU THAT IF YOU DID YOUR balance sheet, I would let you go outdoors and play. Therefore, if you know very well you are not going to do any more accounting than we have already done, this chapter, which explains profit and loss (P & L) statements and how to create budgets, is optional reading and you can skip to chapter 8. This chapter is suggested reading for those who feel this record-keeping subject is worth a couple of hours a month and not just every six months. However, if you are among those who have real trouble living within your income and do not already have a very good system, it is required reading.

Our P & L statement is the record that tells us how we are doing financially as we go merrily along between balance sheets. An analogy to illustrate the difference between the two might be that a balance sheet is the box score at the end of the game, and the P & L statement is a video of the game itself. The P & L statement, a record of income and expenses, tells us each month whether we are operating profitably or losing money. As I mentioned, the changes in our balance sheets from one period to another will reflect how we are doing, so we can come pretty close to measuring profitability from our balance sheets. It could well be, however, that our investments are appreciating at the same time we are operating in the red, so our lack of profitability can be disguised on our balance sheets by the appreciation of our assets. The reverse is also true. So your P & L statement, which gives you a truer picture of how you are operating, can be very important to understanding your financial fitness.

Savers are far more inclined to keep track of their income and expenses than *spenders*. Some years ago, a lady came to see me and told me she had $1,000 to invest. Her husband was a very successful doctor and had been for a number of years. When we got into the question of the family's financial balance sheet, however, it turned out that she was exactly right; she merely had $1,000 to invest. Her husband had probably earned at least $1 million in the previous ten years, and they had spent $999,000 of that $1 million. Our association ended when I concluded a brief lecture with the observation that with a little effort they could probably find something on which they could spend the last $1,000.

Moreover, some small percentage of people actually *like* keeping records. Grown-up kids who liked baseball when they were younger kids frequently are better at P & Ls than most people, because statistics are part of the lifeblood of the true baseball fan. Some kids, of course, never convert from baseball records to income and expense records. Keeping P & Ls through the new software available today is great exercise for computer kids.

If we can learn so much from our balance sheet, why should we keep records of our income and expenses? Well, for those who file complicated tax returns, such records are far better than throwing your slips in a drawer. The better answer, however, is the fact that when we keep track of expenses, the records have some impact psychologically on how we spend money. I strongly suggest income and expense records for young people on tight budgets. Many people feel they are being very careful with their money when, in fact, they are frittering away small amounts they would save if they knew how much they frittered every month. As reinforcement for the importance of saving even small amounts over time, take another look at tables 2.2 and 2.5 to remind yourself how rich you can be if you save a little and compound successfully. This is not meant to be a lecture because I fritter, too. The fact remains, however, that keeping track of income and expenses will have a favorable impact on most of us that may not even be perceptible while it is occurring.

Keeping track of our income and expenses is not as difficult a task as it appears to be before we actually do it. You can buy little record books in most good stationery or business-supply stores. Most of these are designed with large numbers of people in mind but not with you specifically in mind. If you look at a few models, however, you may find one that fits you nicely. However, making up your own is not very difficult. You may have to experiment with it for a month or two to set up the system that works best for you, but if you get into the habit, you will find it rather easy.

To help you set up your own personalized income and expense form, take a look at table 7.1, an enormous list of income and expense items, many of which you will, I hope, never incur. Don't be frightened. Just scratch out all the items that do not pertain to you or lump them together, so that you can put them under one heading. For example, lump Gas, Electric, and Water/sewer all under the heading of Utilities. The aim is to come down to a manageable number of categories for all your expenses.

Now, take a squint at table 7.2, which uses nothing more

Table 7.1
LIST OF MONTHLY INCOME AND EXPENSES

	Income
1	Salary
2	Salary—spouse
3	Child support
4	Alimony
5	Dividend income
6	Interest income
7	Notes/loans receivable
8	Mortgages receivable
9	Trust income
10	Pension income
11	Other income
	Total Income
	Expenses
1	Moving expenses
2	Employee business expense
3	IRA
4	IRA—spouse
5	KEOGH
6	KEOGH—spouse
7	Interest penalties
8	Alimony payments
9	Federal income tax
10	State income tax
11	Local income tax
12	Other withholdings

Table 7.1 (*continued*)
LIST OF MONTHLY INCOME AND EXPENSES

13	Social security
14	Property tax
15	Charitable contributions
16	Union dues
17	Financial services
18	Bank charges
19	Rent
20	Mortgage principal
21	Mortgage interest
22	Second-home principal
23	Second-home interest
24	Other interest
25	Homeowner's insurance
26	Auto insurance
27	Health insurance
28	Life insurance
29	Disability insurance
30	Liability insurance
31	Other insurance
32	Home repair
33	Auto repair
34	Auto expense
35	Licenses
36	Auto loans
37	Other loans
38	Charge cards
39	Savings

Table 7.1 (*continued*)
LIST OF MONTHLY INCOME AND EXPENSES

	Expenses (*continued*)
40	Investments
41	Child support
42	Child care
43	Care for other dependents
44	Domestic help
45	Doctors
46	Dentists
47	Medical—prescriptions
48	Medical—other
49	Electricity
50	Gas
51	Water/sewer
52	Trash removal
53	Miscellaneous utilities
54	Telephone
55	Gifts
56	Food—at home
57	Food—out
58	Clothing
59	Cleaning/laundry
60	Personal care
61	Pet care
62	Entertainment
63	Vacations
64	Hobbies/recreation

Table 7.1 (*continued*)
LIST OF MONTHLY INCOME AND EXPENSES

65	Books/magazines/newspapers
66	Education
67	Allowances
68	Appliances
	Total Expenses

than a columnar pad, to design your own income and expense form. For clarity, I have broken it into two parts for this book. After wasting a couple of sheets during experimentation, you can probably design one of these for each month, customize it with your own expense categories from table 7.1, and it will suit you perfectly.

For most of us, our income items are not very numerous, and we can simply list our income each month from various sources. I put this at the lower-left section of the monthly ledger in table 7.2.

Our expenses, however, generally fall into two categories:

1. Those we incur monthly, which require only one payment per month. You can see some of these on the lower-right side of the monthly ledger. One figure a month will generally do it.
2. Those we incur sporadically or even daily during the month. That is why we need the columns with our own particular headings in the daily-expense ledger. Fill in the amounts each day as you incur these expenses.

At the end of each month you can give your adding machine about a 15-minute workout to determine whether you are profitable or unprofitable for the month. If you are unprofitable every month and do not have a fat balance sheet, you can at

Table 7.2
INCOME AND EXPENSE WORKSHEET

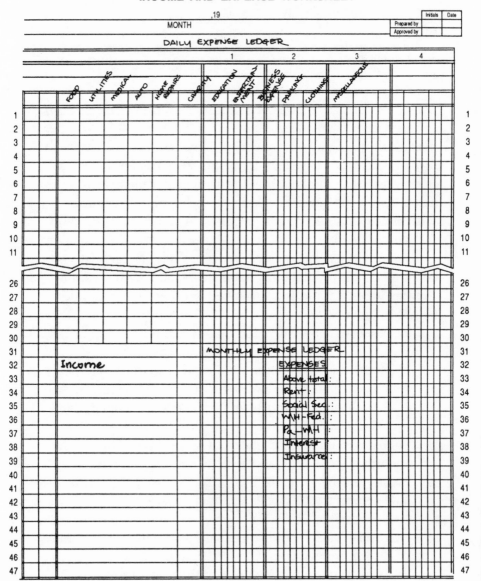

least infer you have a problem and maybe have a pretty good idea what the size of your problem is.

After you finish your income and expense sheet each month, I suggest you spend two more minutes simply thinking about your income versus your expenses. For people who have never done this exercise, this appears to be a lot of work, and one of questionable merit. My contention is, however, that the total time and devotion to this activity will be about five minutes a day and that if you allow it to become a habit, it will become both painless and rewarding. If you are one of those people who spends small amounts daily, for candy bars, newspapers, etc., then simply estimate these things at $1 to $2 per day and put it on your P & L this way—so you do not have to keep track of every dime.

There is one final step worth mentioning to those many individuals who have a tight financial situation or to those few individuals who happen to enjoy record keeping. I recommend that you take the next accounting step beyond the income and expense level: Create a budget. It is prudent of me to recommend it, but frankly, I am not about to do it myself. I will confess to you that, aside from having some awareness of future sizable expenditures, I have just never been able to put up with the fuss of doing a detailed budget. I support and admire those who receive the psychological and financial benefits that flow from budgeting and living by the budget. If this seems to be a strange attitude from a financial adviser, I further confess that although I characterize my clients/friends as *spenders* or *savers*, I avoid intruding very far into their P & L statements unless they ask for some guidance. I am supposed to make sure the balance sheet is invested well, not take away the joys of *frittering* money. That part is up to you.

CHAPTER EIGHT

Great Expectations

LISTEN UP, KIDS; THIS CHAPTER IS IMPORTANT. AS YOU WILL RE-
call, my opening sentence in this opus was: "The essence of
an investment policy is to relate the situation of the investor
to the world in which we live." Well, "the world in which we
live" is full of inflation. To combat its effects, investors can
employ stocks and bonds, and other vehicles to invest their
money. I hope this chapter will give you a better understanding of what you can expect from your investments and how
you might set your investment goals.

My impression of the average American's viewpoint on
inflation, bonds, and stocks is this: Inflation is always with us
and gradually erodes the purchasing power of our savings;
bonds are generally good, safe investments for producing income but not very satisfactory in fighting inflation; stocks,
over a period of time, may be better investments than bonds,
but they are certainly risky. Now, these impressions are fine as
far as they go, but I want you to have a somewhat deeper
understanding of each and how they might interrelate as you
develop your all-season investment policy.

To have a little fun, we will pretend you are in a contest. Your entry blank, which must be turned in tomorrow, reads as follows:

Mrs. Greatworth is leaving the country for a round-the-world vacation that will last exactly ten years. She wants you, and several other contestants, to invest $100,000 for her while she is gone. She is an extremely conservative investor who abhors risk and simply wants to maintain the purchasing power she already has—and Mrs. Greatworth has so much money already that she does not need her investments to appreciate faster than inflation. If you make too much money, you lose. You have taken too much risk. In this contest, any income produced by your investment will be spent, and no taxes apply, so your sole objective is to ensure that the principal keeps pace with the purchasing power changes over the next ten years, as measured by the consumer price index (CPI). Whoever comes closest at the end of ten years to matching the original purchasing power of Mrs. Greatworth's $100,000 wins the contest. Your entry must be filed tomorrow.

How would you invest the $100,000?

We will pretend it is a good prize, let's say $1 million. Mrs. Greatworth and I will settle for a general answer. Make a tentative answer now.

Let's think of some of the factors that we might consider before we finalize your entry blank. I will raise some questions and you give your answers as we go. Then, I will add a little bit of history and perhaps some logic to each question and give you my answer. If you want to keep this book ten years, you can drop me a note and tell me how wrong I was.

QUESTION ONE: What will the average inflation rate be over the next ten years?

Write your guess in this blank: _____ %.

If history would help you with this guess, go back to table 2.3 (page 30). In the third column, you will see the annual cost of living increase each year since 1939. You will notice there were only three years, none since 1954, in which the cost of living *decreased*. There were also only three years in which inflation hit double-digit figures. In the last three or four years, it's been in the 4½% range. Slide your eye over to the last column on table 2.3 and note the ten-year average rate for the previous decade, which might narrow your guess a bit. It may also make you yearn for those good old days in the late 1950s and early 1960s when the average rate was under 2%.

In this contest, you are allowed to apply political studies, economic models, tea leaves, or whatever you like to arrive at your inflation forecast. I will keep my studies simple, since this is a ten-year period and I am still planning next week. My guess is that we are just finishing a period of lower-than-normal inflation. We have had an ample supply of most basic commodities, such as oil, and generally enjoyed a period of peace, which certainly does not cost as much as war. On the other hand, we are now faced with the problems of paying for an enormous level of debt, including the necessity of bailing out the S&Ls and maybe even a bunch of banks. I would be somewhat more optimistic about inflation if I could see any signs that Congress intends to become more responsible in handling the nation's budget and tax questions. Since this opus is not an economics textbook, however, I just guess 5.9% annually for the 1990s and hope that my guess is high.

QUESTION TWO: Based on your inflation guess, how much will the $100,000 have to appreciate to have the same purchasing power in ten years?

My guess is I will have to end up with $ _____ to hold the purchasing power.

You can compute this answer exactly, but I know you won't.

Therefore, you can do a little practice with the rule of 72 and come pretty close. If you guess 7.2% on inflation, you can divide that into the magic number 72 and conclude that you must precisely double the $100,000 in ten years to win the contest. A second way is to find the ten-year average rate of inflation in table 2.3 that comes closest to your guess and then move one column to the left. It will show you by what percentage you must increase the $100,000 to win the contest. For example, if your guess is 6.6% for inflation, you will note that that is the rate for the decade ending in 1986, and the column to the left shows you would have to increase the principal by 90%—to $190,000—to hit your figure.

I've been teasing you. There is a very simple way to translate your inflation expectation into a dollar figure ten years hence. Just go back to table 2.5 (page 36), which shows $10,000 compounded at different rates over ten years. Add a zero to the figure you see, and you will know precisely the amount of your target. Pause for a moment and consider your guess on inflation and the ramifications for your investment policy. Unless your inflation guess is very low, *you will be forced to take risks to protect the purchasing power of your savings.* The faster the rate of inflation, the more risk you have to take. Clearly, inflation presents you with a severe challenge in investing your savings.

QUESTION THREE: What rate of appreciation do you expect from your lendings (your fixed income investments)?

I expect my lendings to appreciate at _____ % annually.

Remember, don't count interest income. Mrs. Greatworth is spending all her income—we set that rule for the contest. Your primary lending vehicles, savings accounts and bonds, are contracts in which the borrower promises to repay your principal, not your purchasing power.

If your guess on inflation in the 1990s was anywhere close

to mine, I suspect your answer to this question should be zero; no appreciation from bonds. If your guess on inflation was very low, you could probably aim for some appreciation by buying very long-term bonds and figuring that interest rates will decline as inflation declines, thereby giving you a bit of appreciation on your bonds.

One thing we learned from the 1980s is that buying bonds can be a very risky enterprise. There are plenty of investors across the country, including financial institutions, who wish today that their net change in principal on their lending activities for the 1980s had been zero.

A few of you will think of a sneaky way to win the contest by buying a ten-year zero % coupon bond with a yield to maturity roughly identical to your guess on the inflation rate. In case you are not familiar with zeros, they are bonds that pay no interest but are sold, both originally and subsequently, at a discount to their face value. Owners make their interest through the appreciation that occurs from the point of purchase until the maturity date. This investment might be the most conservative way to try to win the contest, but Mrs. Greatworth might be a little unhappy with you for producing no income and having her pay taxes over the years.

Personally, this lending question is the one I can answer with certainty. My target in terms of capital appreciation from my fixed income investments will be zero and that is exactly what I expect to produce. I will buy ten-year bonds at par and have them come due the day the contest ends, with no gain or loss. (Preferably, I would buy five-year bonds twice during the contest.)

You will note by now that this investing game is getting tougher. If our inflation guess is 5% or 6%, and we have to produce appreciation of $60,000 to $80,000, and we probably cannot get any of it by lending our money, it becomes a pretty tough game. Therefore, we have to take risks, we have to become owners if we are going to fight inflation successfully.

QUESTION FOUR: What ownership investments do you want to make?

I plan to invest in the ownership of _____ stocks and/or _____ real estate and/or _____ material goods.

I do not want to inhibit you in any way from winning the prize, so if you have a favorite alternative that will produce the appreciation we need, you are all set.

Back to history for context. Turn to table 8.1, which shows the investment performance of various alternatives over the last 20-, 10-, 5-, and 1-year periods. Note it is for the period ending June 1, 1991. Also note that these returns include dividend and interest income, so you must adjust stocks down 3% or 4% for dividends, bonds down 7% or 8% for interest, and wipe out the return on U.S. Treasury bills.

Table 8.1 surprises me a bit. House prices seem to be about as close as any of the alternatives in staying near the inflation rate shown at the bottom of the chart. If we bought a $100,000 house, however, once again the sponsor might get a little upset because she received no income and has had to pay annual real estate taxes. Farm land also disappointed me by being no better than the inflation rate for the 20-year period and considerably worse in shorter periods. Much as I love them, those amber waves of grain have not done much for a decade.

Some material goods investment may appreciate greatly in the 1990s, but most of us better stick with stocks, even after deducting dividends, because their performance is more reliable. I don't think I want to buy an old master painting, and I am not sure I would know a Chinese ceramic if I saw one.

QUESTION FIVE: What appreciation, if any, will occur in the Dow Jones Industrial Average (DJIA) or the Standard & Poor's 500 Stock Index (the S&P 500) through the 1990s?

I guess that the total appreciation of the DJIA or the S&P 500 will be ____ % in the 1990s.

To me, this is the toughest question in the contest unless

Table 8.1
THE ASSET DERBY

Asset Category	Investment Performance[1]			
	20 Years	10 Years	5 Years	1 Year
Old master paintings	12.3%	15.8%	23.4%	6.5%
Stocks	11.6	16.0	13.3	11.8
Chinese ceramics	11.6	8.1	15.1	3.6
Gold	11.5	− 2.9	1.0	− 0.7
Diamonds	10.5	6.4	10.2	0.0
Stamps	10.0	− 0.7	− 2.4	− 7.7
Bonds	9.4	15.2	9.7	13.2
Oil	8.9	− 5.9	8.5	20.7
Treasury bills (3 month)	8.6	8.8	7.0	7.1
House prices	7.3	4.4	4.6	4.7
Farmland (U.S.)	6.3	− 1.8	1.3	2.1
Silver	5.0	− 9.3	− 4.8	−18.9
Foreign exchange	4.5	3.8	5.4	0.2
Consumer Price Index	*6.3%*	*4.3%*	*4.5%*	*5.0%*

[1] Compound annual return (including dividend or interest income, if any) for periods ended June 1, 1991.

SOURCE: Salomon Bros.

you happen to be a whiz at some kind of material goods investing and, therefore, do not have to answer it. The likelihood of continued inflation, the inability of lendings to hedge it, and our material goods constraints together would force most of us to agree that we have to assume some risk through common stock investing in order to win the contest.

Take a look at table 8.2, the DJIA over the last 65 years, and table 8.3, the S&P 500 over the last 65 years. Spend a few minutes with them. We don't have to get our entry form in until tomorrow, so study the tables to give yourself a concept of history. Although you may be fascinated with these tables, keep in mind what we are trying to do: get a feel for the historical movement in high-grade stock prices over an extended period of time and where we are at the beginning of 1991. Then, relate these historical results to the challenge of inflation.

Some would contend, not without reason, that the DJIA, with only 30 stocks, is not broad enough to be a truly good stock market indicator. Furthermore, it is not immutable. In the 25 years from 1964 through 1989, there is some contrast between those stocks that were dropped from the DJIA and those that were added (see page 88).

Would you not agree that the DJIA gets upgraded over a period of time by its change in composition?

I will make my observations on the S&P 500 (table 8.3), since it is a bit broader with 500 stocks. This table is loaded with historical stock market information, and you will be able to form some useful impressions.

Let's first take a look at a long period of time, from 1926 to 1990. At the bottom, you will notice that the consumer price increase was 647%, while earnings and dividends increased over 1,600%. That is encouraging. Year-end prices increased even more—2,498%. Inflation was bad, but earnings and dividends substantially more than made up for it, and stock prices

Table 8.2
DOW JONES INDUSTRIAL AVERAGE
65-Year Performance
(1926–1990)

Year	Market				Earnings	Dividends	Annual Total Return	Year-end Yield	Year-end P/E Multiple	Book Value	Consumer Price Index 1982-84 = 100
	High	Low	Close	Annual Change							
1925	—	—	156.66		—				—	—	17.9
1926	166.64	135.20	157.20	0.3	11.39	5.54	3.9	3.51	13.8	75.2	17.7
1927	202.40	152.73	202.40	28.8	8.72	6.04	32.6	2.98	23.2	77.9	17.3
1928	300.00	191.33	300.00	48.2	15.97	9.76	53.0	3.25	18.8	84.1	17.1
1929	381.17	198.69	248.48	-17.2	19.94	12.75	-12.9	5.13	12.5	91.3	17.2
1930	294.04	157.51	164.58	-33.8	11.02	11.13	-29.3	6.76	14.9	91.2	16.1
1931	194.36	73.79	77.90	-52.7	4.09	8.40	-47.6	10.78	19.1	86.9	14.6
1932	88.78	41.22	59.93	-23.1	(.51)	4.62	-17.1	7.71	*	81.8	13.1
1933	108.67	50.16	99.90	66.7	2.11	3.40	72.4	3.40	47.4	80.5	13.1
1934	110.74	85.51	104.04	4.1	3.91	3.66	7.8	3.52	26.6	80.7	13.4
1935	148.44	96.71	144.13	38.5	6.34	4.55	42.9	3.16	22.7	82.50	13.8
1936	184.90	143.11	179.90	24.8	10.07	7.05	29.7	3.92	17.9	85.55	14.0
1937	194.40	113.64	120.85	-32.8	11.49	8.78	-27.9	7.27	10.5	88.30	14.4
1938	158.41	98.95	154.76	28.1	6.01	4.98	32.2	3.22	25.8	87.13	14.0
1939	155.92	121.44	150.25	-2.9	9.11	6.11	1.0	4.07	16.5	95.58	13.9
1940	152.80	111.84	131.13	-12.7	10.92	7.06	-8.0	5.38	12.0	98.75	14.1
1941	133.59	106.34	110.96	-15.4	11.64	7.59	-9.6	6.84	9.5	102.33	15.5
1942	119.71	92.92	119.40	7.6	9.22	6.40	13.4	5.36	13.0	107.50	16.9
1943	145.82	119.26	135.89	13.8	9.74	6.30	19.1	4.64	14.0	113.03	17.4
1944	152.53	134.22	152.32	12.1	10.07	6.57	16.9	4.31	15.1	118.33	17.8
1945	195.82	151.35	192.91	26.6	10.56	6.69	31.0	3.47	18.3	122.74	18.2
1946	212.50	163.12	177.20	-8.1	13.63	7.50	-4.3	4.23	13.0	131.40	21.5
1947	186.85	163.21	181.16	2.2	18.80	9.21	7.4	5.08	9.6	149.08	23.4
1948	193.16	165.39	177.30	-2.1	23.07	11.50	4.2	6.49	7.7	159.67	24.1
1949	200.52	161.60	200.13	12.9	23.54	12.79	20.1	6.39	8.5	170.12	23.6
1950	235.47	196.81	235.41	17.6	30.70	16.13	25.7	6.85	7.7	194.19	25.0
1951	276.37	238.99	269.23	14.4	26.59	16.34	21.3	6.07	10.1	202.60	26.5
1952	292.00	256.35	291.90	8.4	24.78	15.48	14.2	5.30	11.8	213.39	26.7
1953	293.79	255.49	289.90	-3.8	27.23	16.11	4.8	5.56	10.7	244.26	26.9
1954	404.39	279.87	404.39	39.5	28.18	17.47	45.5	4.32	14.4	248.96	26.7
1955	488.40	388.20	488.40	20.8	35.78	21.58	26.1	4.41	13.7	271.77	26.8
1956	521.05	462.35	499.47	2.3	33.34	22.99	7.0	4.60	15.0	284.78	27.6
1957	520.77	419.79	435.69	-12.8	36.08	21.61	-8.4	4.96	12.1	298.69	28.4
1958	583.65	436.89	583.65	34.0	27.95	20.00	38.6	3.43	20.9	310.97	28.9
1959	679.36	574.46	679.36	16.4	34.31	19.38	19.7	2.85	19.8	339.02	29.4

Year										
1960	685.47	566.05	615.89	- 9.3	32.21	20.46	- 6.3	3.32	19.1	369.87	29.8
1961	734.91	610.25	731.14	18.7	31.91	21.28	21.1	2.91	22.9	385.82	30.0
1962	726.01	535.76	652.10	-10.8	36.43	22.09	- 7.8	3.39	17.9	400.97	30.4
1963	767.21	646.79	762.95	17.0	41.21	23.20	20.6	3.04	18.5	425.90	30.9
1964	891.71	766.08	874.13	14.6	46.43	25.38	17.9	2.09	16.5	417.39	31.2
1965	969.26	840.59	969.26	10.9	53.67	28.61	14.1	2.95	18.1	453.27	31.8
1966	995.15	744.32	785.69	-18.9	57.68	31.89	-15.7	4.06	13.6	475.92	32.9
1967	943.08	786.41	905.11	15.2	53.87	30.19	19.0	3.34	16.8	476.50	33.9
1968	985.21	825.13	943.75	4.3	57.89	31.34	7.7	3.32	16.3	521.08	35.5
1969	968.85	769.93	800.35	-15.2	57.02	33.90	-11.6	4.24	14.0	542.25	37.7
1970	842.00	631.16	838.92	4.8	51.02	31.53	8.8	3.76	16.4	573.15	39.7
1971	950.82	797.97	890.20	6.1	55.09	30.86	9.8	3.47	16.2	607.61	41.1
1972	1,036.27	889.15	1,020.02	14.6	67.11	32.27	18.2	3.16	15.2	642.87	42.5
1973	1,051.70	788.31	850.86	-16.6	86.17	35.33	-13.1	4.15	9.9	690.23	46.2
1974	891.66	577.60	616.24	-27.6	99.04	37.72	-23.1	6.12	6.2	746.95	51.9
1975	881.81	632.00	852.41	38.3	75.66	37.46	44.4	4.39	11.3	783.61	55.5
1976	1,014.79	858.70	1,004.65	17.9	96.72	41.40	22.7	4.12	10.4	798.20	58.2
1977	999.80	800.85	831.17	-17.3	89.10	45.84	-12.7	5.52	9.3	841.76	62.1
1978	906.44	742.72	805.01	- 3.1	112.79	48.52	2.7	6.03	7.1	890.69	67.7
1979	897.61	796.67	838.74	4.2	124.46	50.98	10.5	6.08	6.7	859.41	76.7
1980	1,000.20	759.98	963.99	14.9	121.86	54.36	21.3	5.64	7.9	928.50	86.2
1981	1,024.05	824.01	875.00	- 9.2	113.71	56.22	- 3.4	6.43	7.7	975.59	93.9
1982	1,070.55	776.92	1,046.54	19.6	9.15	54.14	25.8	5.17	*	881.51	97.6
1983	1,287.20	1,027.00	1,258.64	20.3	72.45	56.33	25.7	4.48	17.4	888.21	101.3
1984	1,286.60	1,086.60	1,211.57	- 3.7	113.58	60.63	1.1	5.00	10.7	916.70	105.3
1985	1,553.10	1,176.79	1,546.67	27.7	96.11	62.03	32.8	4.01	16.1	944.97	109.3
1986	1,955.57	1,502.29	1,895.95	22.6	115.59	67.04	26.9	3.54	16.4	986.48	110.5
1987	2,722.42	1,738.74	1,938.83	2.3	133.05	71.20	6.0	3.67	14.6	1,008.95	115.4
1988	2,183.50	1,879.14	2,168.57	11.8	215.46	79.53	16.0	3.67	10.1	1,075.47	120.6
1989	2,791.41	2,144.64	2,753.20	27.0	221.48	103.00	31.7	3.74	12.4	1,276.14	126.1
1990	2,999.75	2,365.10	2,633.66	- 4.3	172.05	103.70	- 0.6	3.94	15.3	1,340.00E	133.8
Increase 1926-1990	+1,700%	+1,649%	+1,581%	—	+1,411%	+1,772%	—	—	—	+1,682%	+647%

E Estimated.
* Not meaningful.
NOTE: Book values are based on net tangible assets per share.
All data are adjusted to a basis consistent with the average.

85

Table 8.3
STANDARD & POOR'S 500 STOCK INDEX
65-Year Performance
(1926–1990)

Year	High	Low	Close	Annual Change	Dividend	Year-End Yield	Annual Total Return	5-Year Average Rate of Return	Earnings	Year-End P-E Ratio	Consumer Price Index 1982-84 = 100	CPI % Annual Change
1925	—	—	12.71	—	—	—	—	—	—	—	17.9	—
1926	13.66	10.93	13.49	6.1%	.69	5.08%	11.6%	—	1.24	10.88	17.7	−1.5
1927	17.71	13.18	17.71	31.3	.77	4.34	37.0	—	1.11	15.91	17.3	−2.1
1928	24.35	16.95	24.35	37.5	.85	3.51	42.3	—	1.38	17.64	17.1	−1.0
1929	31.92	17.66	21.45	−11.9	.97	4.53	−7.9	—	1.61	13.32	17.2	0.1
1930	25.92	14.44	14.34	−28.5	.98	6.37	−24.4	—	.97	15.81	16.1	−6.0
1931	18.17	7.72	8.12	−47.1	.82	10.07	−41.7	−3.9%	.61	13.31	14.6	−9.5
1932	9.31	4.40	6.89	−15.1	.50	7.26	−9.0	−8.1	.41	16.60	13.1	−10.3
1933	12.20	5.53	10.10	46.6	.44	4.38	53.0	−7.5	.44	22.95	13.1	0.5
1934	11.82	8.36	9.50	−5.9	.45	4.75	−1.5	−6.9	.49	19.39	13.4	2.0
1935	13.46	8.06	13.43	41.4	.47	3.53	46.3	3.2	.76	17.67	13.8	3.0
1936	17.69	13.40	17.18	27.9	.72	4.19	33.3	21.7	1.02	16.84	14.0	1.2
1937	18.68	10.17	10.55	−38.6	.80	7.62	−33.9	14.2	1.13	9.34	14.4	3.1
1938	13.79	8.50	13.21	25.2	.51	3.87	30.0	10.5	.64	20.64	14.0	−2.8
1939	13.23	10.18	12.49	−5.5	.62	4.94	−0.8	10.7	.90	13.88	13.9	−0.5
1940	12.77	8.99	10.58	−15.3	.67	6.34	−9.9	0.5	1.05	10.08	14.1	1.0
1941	10.86	8.37	8.69	−17.9	.71	8.19	−11.2	−5.7	1.16	7.49	15.5	9.7
1942	9.77	7.47	9.77	12.4	.59	5.99	19.2	4.2	1.03	9.49	16.9	9.3
1943	12.64	9.84	11.67	19.4	.61	5.25	25.7	3.5	.94	12.41	17.4	3.2
1944	13.29	11.56	13.28	13.8	.64	4.83	19.3	7.4	.93	14.28	17.8	2.1
1945	17.68	13.21	17.36	30.7	.66	3.81	36.2	17.8	.96	18.08	18.2	2.3
1946	19.25	14.12	15.30	−11.9	.71	4.61	−7.8	18.7	1.06	14.43	21.5	18.2
1947	16.20	13.71	15.30	0.0	.84	5.52	5.5	15.9	1.61	9.50	23.4	9.0
1948	17.06	13.84	15.20	−0.1	.93	6.14	5.4	11.9	2.29	6.64	24.1	2.7
1949	16.79	13.55	16.76	10.3	1.14	6.79	17.8	11.6	2.32	7.22	23.6	−1.8
1950	20.43	16.65	20.41	21.8	1.47	7.20	30.5	9.5	2.84	7.19	25.0	5.8
1951	23.85	20.69	23.77	16.5	1.41	5.93	23.4	16.1	2.44	9.74	26.5	5.9
1952	26.59	23.09	26.57	11.8	1.41	5.29	17.7	18.7	2.40	11.07	26.7	0.9
1953	26.66	22.71	24.81	−6.6	1.45	5.84	−1.2	17.1	2.51	9.88	26.9	0.6
1954	35.98	24.80	35.98	45.0	1.54	4.28	51.2	23.1	2.77	12.99	26.7	−0.5
1955	46.41	34.58	45.48	26.4	1.64	3.61	31.0	23.2	3.62	12.56	26.8	0.4
1956	49.74	43.11	46.67	2.6	1.74	3.73	6.4	19.6	3.41	13.69	27.6	2.9
1957	49.13	38.98	39.99	−14.3	1.79	4.48	−10.5	13.3	3.37	11.87	28.4	3.0
1958	55.21	40.33	55.21	38.1	1.75	3.17	42.4	21.8	2.89	19.10	28.9	1.8
1959	60.71	53.58	59.89	8.5	1.83	3.06	11.8	14.7	3.39	17.67	29.4	1.5

Year											
1960	60.39	52.30	55.85	− 6.7	1.95	3.35	− 3.5	7.9	3.27	17.77	29.8	1.5
1961	72.64	57.57	71.55	28.1	2.02	2.82	31.7	12.6	3.19	22.43	30.0	0.7
1962	71.13	52.32	63.10	−11.8	2.13	3.38	− 8.8	13.3	3.67	17.19	30.4	1.2
1963	75.02	62.69	75.02	18.9	2.28	3.04	22.5	9.9	4.02	18.66	30.9	1.6
1964	86.28	75.43	84.75	13.0	2.50	2.95	16.3	10.8	4.55	18.63	31.2	1.2
1965	92.63	81.60	92.43	9.1	2.72	2.94	12.3	14.2	5.19	17.81	31.8	1.9
1966	94.06	73.20	80.33	−13.1	2.87	3.57	−10.0	5.6	5.55	14.47	32.9	3.4
1967	97.59	80.38	96.47	20.1	2.92	3.03	23.7	12.2	5.33	18.10	33.9	3.0
1968	108.37	87.72	103.86	7.7	3.07	2.96	10.8	10.0	5.76	18.03	35.5	4.7
1969	106.16	89.20	92.06	−11.4	3.16	3.43	− 8.3	4.9	5.78	15.93	37.7	6.1
1970	93.46	69.29	92.15	0.1	3.14	3.41	3.5	3.2	5.13	17.96	39.7	5.5
1971	104.77	90.16	102.09	10.8	3.07	3.01	14.1	8.2	5.70	17.91	41.1	3.4
1972	119.12	101.67	118.05	15.6	3.15	2.67	18.7	7.3	6.42	18.39	42.5	3.4
1973	120.24	92.16	97.55	−17.4	3.38	3.46	−14.5	1.9	8.16	11.95	46.2	8.8
1974	99.80	62.28	68.56	−29.7	3.60	5.25	−26.0	− 2.2	8.89	7.71	51.9	12.2
1975	95.61	70.04	90.19	31.5	3.68	4.08	36.9	3.2	7.96	11.33	55.5	7.0
1976	107.83	90.90	107.46	19.1	4.05	3.77	23.6	4.9	9.91	10.84	58.2	4.8
1977	107.00	90.71	95.10	−11.5	4.67	4.91	− 7.2	− 0.1	10.89	8.70	62.1	6.8
1978	106.99	86.90	96.11	1.1	5.07	5.28	6.4	4.3	12.33	7.79	67.7	9.0
1979	111.27	96.13	107.94	12.3	5.65	5.23	18.2	14.6	14.86	7.25	76.7	13.3
1980	140.52	98.22	135.76	25.8	6.16	4.54	31.5	13.8	14.82	9.19	86.2	12.4
1981	138.12	112.77	122.55	− 9.7	6.63	5.41	− 4.9	7.9	15.36	8.12	93.9	8.9
1982	143.02	102.42	140.64	14.8	6.87	4.88	20.4	13.6	12.64	11.12	97.6	3.9
1983	172.65	138.34	164.93	17.3	7.09	4.30	22.3	16.8	14.03	11.76	101.3	3.8
1984	169.28	147.82	167.24	1.4	7.53	4.50	6.0	14.3	16.64	10.05	105.3	4.0
1985	212.02	163.68	211.28	26.3	7.90	3.74	31.1	14.2	14.61	14.46	109.3	3.8
1986	254.00	203.49	242.17	14.6	8.28	3.42	18.5	19.4	14.43	16.72	110.5	1.1
1987	336.77	223.92	247.08	2.0	8.81	3.57	5.7	16.3	17.50	14.12	115.4	4.4
1988	283.66	242.63	277.72	12.4	9.73	3.50	16.3	15.1	23.76	11.69	120.6	4.4
1989	359.80	275.31	353.40	27.3	11.05	3.13	31.2	20.2	22.90	15.43	126.1	4.6
1990	368.95	295.46	330.22	− 6.6	12.10	3.66	− 3.1	13.1	21.60 (e)	15.29	133.8	6.1
Increase 1926-1990	+2,601%	+2,603%	+2,498%	—	+1,654%	—	—	—	+1,642%	—	+647%	—

(e) estimated

Compounded Annual Rates of Return

5 Years	1986-1990	13.1	20 Years	1971-1990	10.9	40 Years	1951-1990	11.5
10 Years	1981-1990	13.7	25 Years	1966-1990	9.1	50 Years	1941-1990	11.8
15 Years	1976-1990	13.7	30 Years	1961-1990	10.2	65 Years	1926-1990	10.0

Source: Johnson's Charts 1991

87

Table 8.4
THE CHANGING DOW

Stocks Dropped Since 1964	Stocks Added Since 1964
Chrysler	Philip Morris
Esmark	McDonald's
American Brands	Coca-Cola
Johns-Manville	Merck
Owens-Illinois	American Express
International Nickel	Boeing
Anaconda	Minnesota Mining & Manufacturing
General Foods	IBM
Navistar	Caterpillar
Primerica	Disney
USX	J. P. Morgan

did even better. At the bottom of the table, you can see that over the 65-year period the compound annual rate of return of the S&P 500 was 10%, a conclusion that is in the same ballpark as most other long-term studies of stock prices. For our purposes, we can at least agree that it has not been necessary to have anything like 100% of our assets in common stocks to fight inflation.

To keep you on table 8.3, we might take a little closer look at the last ten years, a period in which the S&P 500 increased almost two and one-half times, from 135 at the end of 1980 to 330 at the end of 1990. This was a great period for common stock investors, since the inflation rate dropped off substantially during the 1980s. Let's go a little deeper. The dividend rate almost doubled during the 1980s, but dividends presumably come from earnings and earnings increased only about 50%. Obviously, if stock prices increased almost two and one-half times, while dividends were almost doubling and earnings were increasing only 50%, the stockholder was doing better than his company. The more worrisome fact, therefore, is in the P-E ratio column, which shows that from the end of

1979 to the end of 1989, the P-E ratio of the S&P 500 more than doubles from 7.25 to 15.43 times the earnings. Remember, the P-E ratio is the most commonly used analytical tool in stock selection.

This background should dampen optimistic forecasts for stock prices in the 1990s. Certainly, it would be nice if the consumer price index continued to decline, but we are going into the 1990s at a rate of 4.6% instead of 12%. If you look over historic year-end P-E ratios on table 8.3, it is pretty hard to conclude that it will double again and reach 30 times earnings at the end of the 1990s. It, therefore, appears that more of the gains in the 1990s from common stocks are going to have to come from earnings and dividends rather than increasing P-E ratios and reduced inflation.

I have inferred that common stock investment is likely to exaggerate changes in the cost of living over a period of time. Now, we might move from history and spend a moment on the logic of this occurrence by remembering that the purchase of common stock is actually nothing more than the purchase of a proportionate share of ownership in a company. Therefore, we own our share of the physical assets of the company, its inventories, its plant and equipment—everything that the company owns—and a share of its liabilities. The values reflected on the balance sheet of the company are historical and, in an inflationary world, adjusting the book value of our stock to current values can be a satisfying exercise. Most companies—but not all—are able to produce somewhat higher earnings as a product of inflation than they otherwise would. For one thing, we stockholders may well be the beneficiary of inventory profits. Second, most companies have at least some element of fixed costs in their P & L statements, which work to their benefit during a period when they can raise the selling prices of their products. Third, most of our companies have leverage in the form of debt in their balance sheets, which has a tendency to work for the company in an inflationary world. Spend a moment thinking about a particular company and what happens to it in an inflationary environment. Rapidly changing rates of inflation, however, can present real problems for business. As a businessman, my hope for inflation in the 1990s is that the rate will remain at least stable, whatever the rate is.

Back to the contest. I will give you my entry: I guess that common stocks will not perform as well in the 1990s as they did in the 1980s, but I also guess that they will appreciate more than the rate of inflation. I will spare you the qualitative reasoning and simply guess that 60% in common stocks and 40% in lendings are a reasonable approach for the entry form.

Having filed my entry, I will leave the game for a decade, but it would not displease me if you now have the impression that protecting your purchasing power over a period of time can be a tough challenge and requires the use of a fair degree of ownership. At times, this game is very, very hard. The DJIA closed 1964 at 874.13 and 1981 at 875.00, a gain of less than a point in 17 years! Not a bad case for studying Chinese ceramics.

If our sponsor had been a saver instead of a spender and let us reinvest income, the game would have been substantially easier. If you save all your income, you may be able to be conservative and still keep up with inflation. Of course, the assumptions are that you do not spend any of your income and you do not even pay taxes on it. Those are not easy assumptions, but you can see how the saver has an enormous advantage.

I designed these exercises not with the idea of convincing you to become a more conservative or a more aggressive investor but with the idea of providing you with a better context in which to evaluate what kind of investor you are and possibly what kind of investor you would like to be. It is statistically unlikely that the 1990s will turn out as either you or I forecast, but my hope is that you now have a better framework for "the world in which we live."

It is useful to create a mental framework for inflation and the challenges of investing your assets. The concepts and interrelationships between inflation, lending, and ownership are important enough to reiterate some of the conclusions we have considered for your framework. We invest for the future and generally to protect or augment the purchasing power of our assets. As a result, the rate of inflation has a substantial impact on our investments over a period of time. During the 1980s, the rate of inflation declined enormously in this country, but the threat of worsening inflation is as strong as the prospect for further improvement. Against this background, we have the inability of the lending approach, our bond buying, to fight inflation unless we are dedicated savers and forgo the pleasures of using the income from our lendings. This leads to the unfortunate necessity of taking risks to increase our assets and in turn to maintain our purchasing power. Thus, we look to ownership as our approach to fight inflation. The first question we must consider is what type of ownership. Certain unusual material goods investments have done very well, but some of the more common approaches have been disappointing. Selecting a material goods or real estate niche can, therefore, be a speculative approach. Common stocks are probably as forecastable a means of addressing the ownership question as we can find. Both the historical and qualitative cases for common stocks indicate that they have been, and should continue to be, good investments in an inflationary world. Nevertheless, there have been protracted periods in which stocks have done poorly, and we enter the 1990s after a decade of rather outstanding results. Therefore, as a note of caution, we might bear in mind that future results in common stock investing could well require consistently better records of corporate earnings and dividends.

CHAPTER NINE

You, Wonderful You

YOU ARE UNIQUE AND YOUR INVESTMENT POLICY SHOULD BE uniquely suited to you. From your balance sheet, you know your financial situation quantitatively, you have some awareness of your saving/spending patterns, and you now have some feel for what you can expect from different investments. Each of us has distinct financial needs that we should consider as we build our investment policy, so let's think about you *qualitatively* for a few minutes.

Portfolio managers who do not know you personally are handicapped in helping to solve your financial problems. We have all read articles that suggest in general terms a certain investment approach of the moment, for example, we should be 20% in cash, 40% in bonds, and 40% in stocks. Maybe the writer should be 40% in stocks and bonds and 20% in cash, or maybe his kids should be, but how does he know what either you or I should be? I want to be where I should be for me, and I want you to be where you should be for you. For example, at one time I was a private in the army with a wife and two kids, making $132 a month. Years before, my grand-father had been kind enough to set up a small trust for me, which the bank trustee invested 100% in tax-free bonds. Certainly, income was a serious subject for me and my young family, but, in our zero-tax-bracket situation, there was no need for it to be tax free. Obviously, the bank trustee had never met me.

Probably no one can identify all the qualitative factors that relate to you and your investment policy as well as you can, but I can mention a few of the obvious factors and let you think about your own situation. Of course, you may be more than just *you*. You may be part of a whole family and two or three generations may be involved in your thinking. If you are part of a family, talking about these subjects for a few minutes at the dinner table is not a bad approach. Mid-January is a good time for this, since most of us do not have much to talk about at the dinner table then. Only two cities in the nation will be represented at the Super Bowl, so all the rest of us can talk about something else. Furthermore, in mid-January you should have finished your year-end balance sheet, and there is plenty of time left in the year to do something about it.

Let's get the unpleasant subjects out of the way first and make a list of those—it is hoped, few—events that could have very serious financial implications for the family. *Who produces the income for this sumptuous meal, and what happens to the rest of the group if something happens to those who provide this income? What if they die or become incapacitated? What other terrible event could occur with enormous financial implications? What if one of us hits somebody with a car or somebody is very seriously injured coming up the front steps?* Well, we cannot buy insurance against all the terrible things that can happen in life, but we can buy insurance against most of the terrible financial things that can happen to us. My basic philosophy on insurance is to buy it for those events that can really have enormously adverse financial impacts on us, whether it is life insurance, health insurance, car insurance, or personal liability insurance. Forget about the little things like your dented right-front fender.

In today's world, your individual or family situation can vary greatly. I understand we now live in a world in which only 10% of American families have the male as the breadwinner taking care of the spouse, who does the housework and raises the children. What was once regarded as the typical American family is not typical anymore. What do we want to protect through insurance? Obviously, our assets and our income. Once we have anticipated terrible financial events, we can think about how to insure against them. The answers will vary, from the extreme of those who must dedicate all their savings to life insurance to the other extreme of those who, in the event their spouse dies, can return to wealthy parents. I would emphasize two points. First, your insurance program should be as unique and specific as your investment policy. Second, if all your annual savings must be dedicated to averting economic tragedies, then insurance is the place to spend them, and you can quit worrying about what stock to buy for a while.

Fortunately, you will find that some insurance, for example, personal liability, is still a minor budget item. You will also find that there are many different approaches to such a common need as life insurance. I am not as opposed to life insurance which builds permanent values as are most people in the securities industry. Stockbrokers frequently advocate buying the cheapest kind of life insurance and investing the difference. Frankly, many people I know who do buy cheap insurance blow the difference. I hope you will be so successful that what you spend on life insurance will become a minor budget item as time goes by, and you will probably be glad you bought some insurance with permanent values.

Next, you might have a lively discussion on the subject of *financial goals* and let each member of the group throw in his two cents' worth. You might divide these goals into *long term* and *short term*, since most of us may make some sizable expenditures in the near future. In the context of a lifetime, getting the kids through college may be one interim goal, albeit an important one. As a married PFC in the army, I could afford to do little more than have kids, which run about a dollar a pound in the army. The ultimate result was three kids, who barely qualified for America's most expensive colleges, all at roughly the same time. Needless to say, the situation led to a little pencil pushing in advance. There is no rule against using pencil and pad as you discuss some of these challenges, even at the dinner table.

Talking about long- and short-term goals can be fun, but then the question comes up as to how realistic these goals are and how we can actually attain them. Therefore, I will mention a few considerations common to all of us. You should consider each factor and how you believe it should affect *your* investment policy.

Your *age* and *health* can give you some idea of your *life expectancy*, which helps indicate how aggressively or conservatively you invest your assets. You might take another glance at table 2.1 (page 19) in case you cannot remember how long you are supposed to live. You might then relate your own life expectancy to *how long you expect to work and produce income*, assuming you do. Through this simple exercise, you will gain some feel for the practicality of your longer-term goals. For your discussion, I will also offer this thought: Younger people have a tendency to get too aggressive too soon and older people have a tendency to get too conservative too soon.

In my family, all of us who are over 39 consider ourselves to be only 39 and, therefore, at a good age to be aggressive. If retirement is a strong goal for you within a decade or so, I recommend that you use that pencil and pad to do a little calculation of your income at the point you retire and relate it to the inflation rate between now and then. (We'll do some calculating together in a moment.)

Another factor to which not enough people pay enough attention is the *nature of their occupation* and the *stability of their income*. Too many of my friends worked for large corporations, had good jobs, and found themselves unexpectedly out of work as a product of what happened within the corporation. As another illustration, I suggest that a healthy, tenured schoolteacher with a high certainty of stable income and a growing pension plan can have a considerably more aggressive investment policy than a commissioned salesman in a cyclical industry. Measure your own situation relative to the question of income stability as well as the amount of income needed.

The *size of your net worth* unquestionably should have an impact on your investment policy. If you do not have much, it gets a little serious when you lose some. If you have a bunch, it allows you more freedom to assume a higher level of risk. I will throw in a couple of observations. People who have always had a lot of money are sometimes too conservative in their investments because they are afraid of losing it and don't know what the world is like without it. People who have started from modest beginnings and built a fortune can frequently invest more aggressively because they know they were just as happy before they had a bunch. Another observation is that savers, if they know themselves well, can assume more risk and presumably reap more rewards simply because they know they will rebuild their assets if they lose some of them. In many cases, however, the savers tend to be overly conservative investors, maybe because they worked hard to be savers and do not want to lose it.

The next point to discuss might be the income you want to generate from your investments and when you want to generate it. Americans often do not distinguish between *want and need in the production of income.* Americans like income, whether they need it or not, and do not seem to grasp the trade-off, which is to give up appreciation. Sometimes I think Americans are happier if they are getting 7% income a year with no appreciation from their investments than they are if they get only 3¹/₂% every year while their assets are doubling every five years. My suggestion on income is to figure out what you *really* need from your investments and, once you have that covered, forget income and concentrate on long-term goals, such as building your net worth. Of course, future income can be a very strong long-term goal. Retirement planning is a great subject on which to do some income calculations combined with your life expectancy and time left to build assets before you retire. Figure out how long you are likely to live and how long you are likely to work. Then, figure out what your social security and pension benefits will be and what income you will need from your investments. Then, go back to those inflation tables and make adjustments in all your figures for inflation between now and when you retire, and now and when you die. Unless you are really old and rich, this is a very worthy exercise and you are silly not to do it. I suspect for many of us these figures could provide a pretty good incentive to save.

Next, you might discuss *your tax situation* and how it should impact your investment policy. For most of us, what we can or should do to reduce or control tax payments is more of a short-term strategy than part of the basic policy. Nevertheless, there are mechanisms for deferring income and tax strategies that can be used successfully in our investing. Only

Congress seems to ignore how tax policy influences our investing. We all hate to pay taxes, but sometimes we allow taxes to have too much rather than too little impact on our investment approach.

After dinner in front of the fire, you might discuss *your own psychological approach toward the assumption of risk versus reward*, your tolerance for pain versus your desire for gain. Your personal comfort with an investment such as an aggressive common stock should be a major factor in your policy and one that you should and can consider better than anyone else. Some people can handle every quantitative and qualitative factor, reach the logical conclusion that they should be quite aggressive in their investment policy, and then are simply unable to handle this psychologically. If a stock goes down a whole point in a day, it is really bothersome to some. Others can go through the crash of '87 with the reaction that it was sort of interesting. For example, not one but three of my little-old-lady clients called me within a couple of days after the October 1987 debacle. I asked them how they were and they said they were fine; each had called just to make sure I was fine. Good tough kids.

One of my theories relating to investment policy might be easier to understand for those of us who are older kids. After a certain point in life, maybe about halfway, a good many of us settle into a certain standard of living with which we are largely content. We do not change our life-style very much, and many of us really do not *want* to change our life-styles. This *pattern of living* has a certain annual cost to it, almost a fixed cost with an inflation adjustment and perhaps a small annual increment for a new extravagance like some new club we decide to join. If we have reached this point in life, we can use the awareness of the annual cost of this pattern to judge how we really want to model our investments for our future and perhaps that of our offspring.

98

Undoubtedly, you have factors in your personal financial situation that I have not raised that are important to you. My aim is not to tell you how you should think about these things but simply to make sure you do think about them. If more than one generation is involved, these discussions are likely to be more complex but perhaps more valuable. Table 9.1 contains a summary of the personal factors we have discussed so far in this book. You should review this list and consider whether each of these factors should lead you to be more aggressive or conservative than you are at the moment.

Table 9.1
SUMMARY OF PERSONAL FACTORS

I. Balance sheet/net worth factors
   A. Size of your net worth
   B. Classification of your major assets
   C. Your tax situation
II. Income factors
   A. Adequacy of your current income
   B. Nature of your occupation
   C. Stability and expectancy of your current income
   D. Wants vs. needs for investment income
   E. Your tax situation (again)
III. Insurance factors
   A. Insurance on income producer
      1. Life insurance
      2. Disability insurance
   B. Insurance on other terrible financial events
      1. Health insurance
      2. Liability insurance
      3. Auto insurance
      4. Property, casualty, and fire insurance
IV. Life habits and standard of living factors
   A. Your age
   B. Your health
   C. Your life expectancy
   D. Your risk tolerance
   E. Saver vs. spender
   F. Cost of your life-style

Table 9.1 (*continued*)
SUMMARY OF PERSONAL FACTORS

V. Additional factors

_____

_____

_____

_____

_____

_____

_____

_____

_____

_____

CHAPTER TEN

Setting Your Investment Policy

WE ARE GOING THROUGH THIS PROCESS SO THAT YOU WILL BE ABLE to design and understand your investment plan. Parts of your plan could be described as short-term financial strategies. Examples of short-term strategies include buying a certain kind of insurance policy, withdrawing some of your money market fund to pay off your current debts, or paying for an impending college bill. Most of these decisions can be handled with a little thought and a few calculations to make intelligent trade-offs. Without getting too wrapped up in semantics, I will refer to your *investment policy* as that part of your plan that involves longer-term strategies and is generally more permanent in nature, i.e., how you invest your savings for your future major goals.

If there is a central aim from the establishment of your policy, it should be to allocate your assets among the investment alternatives we have discussed in such a way as to attain these longer-term, presumably practical goals you have established. Certainly, your policy will contain some strategies for each investment alternative, but *the focal point of an invest-ment policy is asset allocation based primarily on the bal-ance of risk to principal versus reward.*

The number of individuals who have come into my office over the last 30 years and told me they have seriously consid-ered their own personal situation in the context of the exter-nal world and, therefore, can present me with a clear-cut investment policy is exactly zero. This is not a complaint on my part, because helping people establish their policies is frequently how I can help them best. Therefore, we can do it together. Establishing the policy is the part of this investment process in which my client/friend should have a viewpoint, give input, and make decisions. We then end up with an agreement that becomes his guideline as well as mine. Most frequently, however, the new client is presenting me with a sum of money at the same time I am trying to learn as much as I can about his situation. Incidentally, the most difficult factor for me to understand is usually the psychological background or makeup of the client, which can have an enormous impact on his policy and his resultant asset allocation.

Let me tell you how important I think this subject is. If you happened to be an institution with an enormous amount of money, such as a pension plan, the establishment of a policy that culminates in an asset allocation is probably 85% to 95% of the total investment challenge. For a typical individual, it is probably 50% of the investment challenge. Why the differ-ence? An institution with a very large sum of money cannot easily differentiate itself over a period of time through security selection. Large institutions have so much money to be diver-sified over such a limited universe of security selections that the asset allocation between fixed income investments and Groups II and III will be the dominant factor in the fund's performance. Individuals with limited sums of money have much more flexibility and can make individual investments that have substantial impacts on their portfolios including the substantial upside advantage that can be produced by utilizing Group IV investments. As a result, it is my conviction that the establishment of the investment policy and asset allocation for the individual or family is an extremely important part of the investment battle, although it is only half the battle. The selection of securities to implement the policy is the other half.

As a guide for you in establishing your own asset allocation, let me give you what I will call my middle-American model, a reasonably conservative case. You will recognize the scenario from the inflation-hedging contest you have already completed. I have amended that contest only to add a little flesh and blood to the situation and to complicate it by using the four groups of investments we discussed earlier instead of simply fixed income investments versus common stocks. It is hoped you can amend this model to suit your own situation.

This is a family of four with the kids fairly well grown. The father has an occupation with reasonable income prospects, a 20- or 30-year life expectancy, and decent health. The kids are in school, but the income constraints are not overwhelming, because one spouse has a decent, reasonably secure job and the other spouse provides income from a part-time job. Their financial net worth is $100,000, which they have saved. They own their home, which still has a small mortgage at an attractive rate of interest, but they have no other debts. They are not about to inherit a bundle, and they have worked hard to accumulate these savings.

Financially, their characteristics and psychology follow:

$ They have never owned many stocks.
$ They are conservative, but they are aware of inflation and know that they must look ahead to preserve their purchasing power for retirement.
$ They know their fixed income investments are not fighting inflation.
$ They conclude that what they really want to do over the

next ten years or so is to be as *safe* as possible while protecting their purchasing power. (Remember this challenge?)

With these objectives in mind, I might suggest an investment policy that is reflected in the following asset allocation:

Group   I—Fixed income   40%
Group II—Defensive blue-chip common stock   10%
Group III—High-grade growth and blue-chip stocks 50%
Group IV—Aggressive growth or speculative stocks   0%

My reasoning for this asset allocation is that our historical analysis, developed in chapter 8, indicates that we can keep up with inflation if we have 40% to 60% of our assets in high-grade common stocks. We do not need to buy smaller or speculative companies to do this. Our historical background uses the DJIA and the S&P 500, neither of which contains many speculative stocks.

The small percentage invested in Group II reflects the fact that the wild and woolly 1980s left us with few conservative stocks available to buy. Group II stocks are by nature somewhat like surrogates for fixed income investments. To get a feel for this, take a quick look at table 10.1, which compares the Dow Jones Utility Index with the Dow Jones Industrial Average with the Consumer Price Index (CPI), and you can see that hedging inflation with utility stocks would have required an enormous percentage of the portfolio.

I use the middle-American model as a guide and suggest that you tilt these percentages to fit your own situation. If, for example, you have more faith in ownership and common stocks, and your situation permits it, move part of that 40% in fixed income investments down to Groups II, III, and even IV. Change some of my assumptions on the family, and then adjust the asset allocations accordingly. If there is a very strong income need, I might move part of Group III up to Group I. If the family had some confidence in smaller companies, I might have to move part of Group III down to Group IV. As we change the assumptions for the family, we change the asset allocations.

Let me give you a couple of extreme examples from the conservative middle-American model. At one end, a widow with limited assets, a reasonable life expectancy, and a need for maximum income may never get past Group I. As a matter of fact, in a case with limited assets and a strong income need, an old-fashioned annuity may be the most applicable investment. With an annuity, the widow is making a contractual arrangement with an insurance company which, in exchange for a lump-sum investment, agrees to return a set amount of her principal and interest every year for as long as she lives.

At the other extreme is the happy situation of the person with plenty of money, plenty of income, long and successful experience with aggressive investing, and the psychological ability or even proclivity to assume risk and maximize appreciation. In this case, the distribution of assets might look as follows:

Group I	20%
Group II	0%
Group III	40%
Group IV	40%

Some of you more aggressive kids will look at this and say, "Why do we have 20% in the fixed income section if our objective is to go for it?" I will develop my viewpoint a little later on, but a quick answer to your question is that we want to have some money available to buy common stocks when the market goes down.

Now, you try some percentage allocations for yourself. You know the two extremes, a total fixed income orientation or an

Table 10.1
DJUA/DJIA/CPI
(1929–1990)

Year	Dow Jones Utilities Stock Average	Dow Jones Industrial Average	CPI
Year	Close	Close	1982–84 = 100
1929	88.27	248.48	17.2
1930	60.80	164.58	16.1
1931	31.41	77.90	14.6
1932	27.50	59.93	13.1
1933	23.29	99.90	13.1
1934	17.80	104.04	13.4
1935	29.55	144.13	13.8
1936	34.83	179.90	14.0
1937	20.35	120.85	14.4
1938	23.02	154.76	14.0
1939	25.58	150.25	13.9
1940	19.85	131.13	14.1
1941	14.02	110.96	15.5
1942	14.54	119.40	16.9
1943	21.87	135.89	17.4
1944	26.37	152.32	17.8
1945	38.13	192.91	18.2
1946	37.27	177.20	21.5
1947	33.40	181.16	23.4
1948	33.55	177.30	24.1
1949	41.29	200.13	23.6
1950	40.98	235.41	25.0
1951	47.22	269.23	26.5
1952	52.60	291.90	26.7
1953	52.04	289.90	26.9
1954	62.47	404.39	26.7
1955	64.16	488.40	26.8
1956	68.54	499.47	27.6
1957	68.58	435.69	28.4
1958	91.00	583.65	28.9
1959	87.83	679.36	29.4
1960	100.02	615.89	29.8
1961	129.16	731.14	30.0
1962	129.23	652.10	30.4
1963	138.99	762.95	30.9

Table 10.1 (continued)
DJUA/DJIA/CPI
(1929–1990)

Year	Dow Jones Utilities Stock Average	Dow Jones Industrial Average	CPI
Year	Close	Close	1982–84 = 100
1964	155.17	874.18	31.2
1965	152.63	969.26	31.8
1966	136.18	785.69	32.9
1967	127.91	905.11	33.9
1968	137.17	913.75	35.5
1969	110.08	800.35	37.7
1970	121.84	838.92	39.7
1971	117.75	890.20	41.1
1972	119.50	1020.02	42.5
1973	89.37	850.86	46.2
1974	68.76	616.24	51.9
1975	83.65	852.41	55.5
1976	108.38	1004.65	58.2
1977	111.28	831.17	62.1
1978	98.24	805.01	67.7
1979	106.60	838.74	76.7
1980	114.42	963.99	86.2
1981	109.02	875.00	93.9
1982	119.46	1046.54	97.6
1983	131.84	1258.64	101.3
1984	149.52	1211.57	105.3
1985	174.81	1546.67	109.3
1986	206.01	1895.95	110.5
1987	175.08	1938.83	115.4
1988	186.28	2168.57	120.6
1989	235.04	2753.80	126.1
1990	209.70	2633.66	133.8

aggressive posture with 80% in Group III and Group IV. You also have some idea from the conservative model what it takes to fight inflation. Where should you be relative to the model and to the extremes? Think about all your personal qualitative factors. Go back to your balance sheet and see where you are in terms of Groups I through IV. Are you too conservative or too aggressive? In terms of what you know at the moment, put a percentage beside each of the four groups that you think best fits you. If you do all this, and decide where you want to be, you have developed the basics of your investment policy and the resultant asset allocations. Congratulations!

Before I let you go, let me throw out a few further thoughts on your policy. The percentages we established here in these few minutes may be tentative, but the ones you make at the end of the book you should make with conviction. What happens tomorrow and the next day will weaken your resolve. If the market goes up, you will want more stocks, and if it goes down, you will want less. Therefore, I want you to promise yourself that once you have firmly decided what your asset allocation is you will live by it.

Have I implied that we are never allowed to change our approach? I hope not. The second pledge I ask you to make is that if you change your policy, it will be as a product of changes in your own situation and not changes in the outside world. Your policy is a reflection of you, your aims, your situation. If there are dramatic changes in your family, your occupation, your health, etc., you may have to shift your policy equally dramatically. You should promise yourself, however, that external events, such as swings in the stock market, changes in interest rates, war in the Middle East, etc., will not lead you to change your adopted allocations. The biggest mistake I find people making with their asset allocation is to change their percentages as a reflection of the external world and end up selling stocks at the bottom of market swings and buying them at the top. Therefore, I repeat: Your investment policy should fit you, with minor changes, in all seasons, for many years, and should only change as a product of internal changes (changes in your world) and not because of changes in the external world.

CHAPTER ELEVEN

Getting Where You Want to Be

If you have gotten this far, kids, you are doing great, especially if you completed the exercises. At this point, you
should have at least a tentative asset allocation among Groups
I through IV, reflecting your financial situation and goals.

The obvious question in implementing your asset allocation is how to deal with the difference between where you are
(your current balance sheet) and where you want to be (your
brand-new investment policy). Well, the first step, of course,
is to compute the amounts of money or values that you want
to move from one group to another. If you are currently all
Group I, for example, you can compute how much you want to
move into each of the other sections. These are your guidelines, and I will try to give you a few thoughts on how you
might do this.

As an adjunct to your basic policy, you might, at this point,
consider how many different stocks you want to have in a
particular group. You are now addressing the question of
diversification, a subject that has strong implications for your

future performance in much the same fashion as your asset allocation. Assume for the moment that your asset allocation suggests $25,000 in Group I, $15,000 in Group II, $50,000 in Group III, and $10,000 in Group IV, a total of $100,000 in the portfolio. How many different stocks do you want to have? 5? 10? 20? Once you answer this question, you will be able to conclude that a *normal* investment for you in a particular company is a certain amount of money. In the above illustration, for example, you might have 3 investments in Group II, 10 investments in Group III, and 2 investments in Group IV, a total of 15 stocks with a total investment of $75,000. A normal investment for you, therefore, would be approximately $5,000 per company. This is your guideline for the amount to be invested in a stock you like and decide to buy.

From your own balance sheet, I want you to take this step and compute your normal investment per company, but I will give you a few thoughts before you make a decision. The more stocks you have, the more likely you will act in a fashion coincident with the DJIA and the S&P 500, that is, the more likely you are to act like the market as a whole. The fewer stocks you have, the more likely you are to act in a unique fashion with the impact of your individual securities being greater on your portfolio. Some of the more prominent work in the field of financial economics has centered on this question over the last 20 years, including the three American Nobel Prize winners of 1990. All of us enjoy the concept of reducing risk without giving up potential appreciation, a most difficult exercise. For our purposes, having a few rather simple generalities probably suffices. If hedging inflation is a primary objective, we would probably endorse a rather broad diversification and avoid the risk that our narrow portfolio acts in a contrary fashion to all those DJIA and S&P 500 charts we have studied. It would be a very painful realization in ten years to find that inflation had doubled our cost of living, the DJIA had tripled, and our four or five stocks had not done anything. This is an interesting question for you—to what degree do you *want* to act like the market? If you happen to believe you or your adviser is pretty darn good at stock selections and you can handle the discomfort of wider vicissitudes, you might be willing to assume the risks attendant with having rather few stocks. Using the illustration above, you might have only one Group II investment, three or four Group III investments, and one Group IV investment. In a portfolio like this, you had best make few errors in stock selection.

I frequently use a concept on diversification that might be useful to you if you decide to use Group IV stocks. Recognizing that these investments are substantially more of a risk than the blue chips above, I frequently amend my concept of a normal investment in Group IV to make it somewhat less. For example, in the case I gave, if $5,000 were a normal investment for Group II or Group III, I might regard a normal investment in Group IV for this client to be only $2,500, what we might call one-half of a normal. The hope, of course, is that these stocks will appreciate faster and grow up to be as big as their blue-chip cousins, maybe even become one.

As you address your normal investment question, you might bear in mind the tendency I notice in those of us who are getting older and/or wealthier to build up a larger number of securities in our portfolios whether we mean to or not. Over the years, many of us have bought a few things that have worked pretty well, and we do not want to incur taxes by selling them, even when we find something we like better. When I do my balance sheet every six months, I invariably see a couple of items that I know I would not buy today, but I do not want to sell. Frankly, I am emotionally attached to the companies that have done very well. I also emotionally reject sending tax money to the government. If you were to make the brilliant statement that emotion is the enemy of performance, I would probably agree with you and keep holding those good companies anyway. We older kids have a tendency to have broader butts, bulkier balance sheets (fatter?), and more varied investments.

One of the difficult implementation questions is how rapidly you should try to move from where you are to where you want to be. If the gulf between the two is wide, this can be a rather difficult process. Under certain circumstances, of course, it could be done in a day by using mutual funds to substitute for the four groups with which we work. The personal factors of the individual or family have a great deal to do with how rapidly a substantial change in approach is implemented. With one of my clients, it took me three years to implement her policy and get her where she wanted to be. The portfolio was relatively small, and the situation a very sensitive one, because there was no likelihood of restoring assets if we lost money at the outset. Fortunately, the client was patient. Another problem for me at times is to have enough good stocks to buy to fill an individual portfolio. This is the point at which the investment policy decisions have to meld with the security selection decisions. Frankly, I seldom find I have enough individual companies I want to buy to move very quickly from an all-cash position to a fully invested one if the portfolio is of any size. The exception to the concept of having your buying or selling mode dictate your course of action is when you are basically in a buying mode, but you own a particular stock that you feel is a loser and should be sold. My suggestion is that you go ahead and sell it, recognizing that you are still underinvested in the equity area and that the sale will increase the pressure on you to be in an even stronger buying mode. With this exception, the important idea is to let your asset allocation make you aware of which way you are going and to keep moving in that direction. The question, therefore, of how to fulfill your asset allocation is another subjective judgment to work out with your financial adviser. Generally speaking, I would rather move more slowly than more rapidly.

No matter how substantial the distance between where you are and where your policy tells you to be, and no matter how fast you move to close this gap, the important concept in implementing your policy is that your asset allocation dictates the direction in which you should be aiming. At any one point, aside from the purchase or sale of a particular stock within one of the groups, we will be in one of three modes: buying stocks, selling stocks, or doing nothing. We can use our asset allocation to eliminate either the idea of buying or the idea of selling. If your percentage relationships in your portfolio change and tell you that you should be buying stocks in Group III, you can pretty much scratch the idea of selling and simply concern yourself with when to stop doing nothing and decide what stock you should buy at what price.

I have been talking as if all you kids are sitting on fixed income investments without enough equities. What if you are loaded with stocks and you have decided as a matter of your policy to build up your fixed income section? This can be even tougher since capital gains taxes are frequently involved and you have a real winner that is ten times normal in your portfolio. Once again, knowing you are in a selling mode and having an idea of your normal will be a help. Chances are, every stock you hold is not wonderful; chances are also good that you can do a little shaving on some of your larger holdings to work toward your objective. Take your time and use your judgment.

Putting your plan in place is not always easy, particularly if there is a sizable gap between where you are at the moment and where your investment policy indicates you should be. Your policy itself, however, will give you the first guideline telling you whether you are in a buying or selling mode. The second step is to compute the figure for a normal investment in one company, so you will not be fussing around wondering how much to buy when you or your adviser find something you should buy. The third step, deciding how fast to close the gap to get where you want to be, is a judgment call going all the way back to some of those qualitative factors of your particular situation we previously discussed. Follow these steps with care, and, even if it is at a measured pace, you will eventually get where you want to be.

CHAPTER TWELVE

Making Money

LET'S PRETEND THAT AT THIS VERY MOMENT, YOU ARE PERFECT, AN opinion you might want to keep to yourself. You have established your asset allocations, you have implemented your policy by buying or selling some stocks or bonds, and you have ended up exactly where you want to be. Unfortunately, so far you have not made any money. As a matter of fact, you may have spent some with your friendly broker or sent some to Uncle Sam in getting where you want to be, but you certainly have not made any money. Making money is a reasonable aim of investing.

As briefly as I can, and using as little math as possible, I will describe one of the two ways that I find I can make money by investing in stocks over a period of time.

Before I get very far, let me emphasize two important concepts that I try to remember at all times. The first is that I cannot forecast the stock market. I do not know which way it will go, and I do not know anybody who does. The second is that, based upon my asset allocation model, I will be in one of

three modes relative to stocks—buying, because my ownership areas are too low; selling, because my ownership areas
are too high; or doing nothing. I am very good at doing nothing, as are most of my clients, a point made occasionally by
my confreres in the brokerage business.

Let's look at these two points together. When I'm asked
what mode I'm in, I'm looking to buy stocks when my fixed
income section is too high, not when I think the market is
going up. I'm in a selling mode when my common stock
percentages are too high, not when I think the market is going
down. In this manner, I admit that I do not know what the
market will do, but I know what I will do when it changes
dramatically either way. I know I will lose some money if the
market declines by 30% or 40%, but I also know my asset
allocation will put me in a buying mode. Equally important,
perhaps, is the fact that it certainly will keep me from selling
after the market has declined.

To illustrate these concepts, let's do some pretending. Start
by pretending that your portfolio is $100,000 and your asset
allocation is very simple: 25% in fixed—good, quiet fixed—
and 75% in aggressive common stocks that move 50% faster
than the market as a whole (a beta of 1.5). For you, this is
perfect, you aggressive, little monster. I will take you through
a series of market movements and show you how your asset
allocation model should make you behave and what results
you might obtain.

1. We will start by pretending the DJIA is at 2400 and we
   start off *perfect*, which gives us:

$ 25,000 Fixed (25%)
+ $ 75,000 Stock (75%)
$100,000 Total

2. Now we will pretend the DJIA goes from 2400 to 1600, a drop of 33%. Our stocks are not basically better or worse than the market; they simply move faster because of the higher beta, and so we will pretend they go down 50%. On this sad day, our portfolio is as follows:

$25,000 Fixed (40%)
+ $37,500 Stocks (60%)
$62,500 Total

3. At this point, you are discouraged and very unhappy with me, and probably believe the market will go lower—and it might. You will note, however, that your percentage in stocks, because of the decline, is now only 60%. Therefore, your asset allocation tells us we must restore our percentages and put about $9,000 into stocks (getting them back to 75%), much against your will and better judgment. Even worse, you have to raise the $9,000 from Group I, your best-performing group, one endorsed by Ben Franklin, your grandmother, and most Americans. This puts your portfolio as follows:

$16,000 Fixed (25%)
+ $46,500 Stocks (75%)
$62,500 Total

4. Lo and behold, much to our mutual surprise, the market turns around and goes back up to where it started. All the stocks that you have owned also double and go back up to where they started. We will even pretend that every single security in the market went right back where it started. This assumption will keep you from trying to do this mathematically, which is very frustrating because it requires higher math, well beyond eighth

grade, and therefore certainly beyond the scope of both the writer and this book. The lovely fact is you now have a profit on the stocks you bought at the bottom, since they are also fast-moving stocks and they also doubled, giving you a $9,000 profit, from beginning to end, while the DJIA has done nothing. At this point, you are only mildly unhappy with me and your portfolio is as follows:

$ 16,000 Fixed (15%)
+ $ 93,000 Stocks (85%)
$109,000 Total

5. Because your common stocks appreciated as the market returned to our 2400 starting point, you must adjust your percentages again, even though in your mind common stocks are looking a lot better. Therefore, you shift $11,000 to restore your percentage relationships:

$ 27,000 Fixed (25%)
+ $ 82,000 Stocks (75%)
$109,000 Total

6. This time you are wrong, and the DJIA goes up to 3000. At this point, you are pretty happy with stocks, although you are very unhappy with me again, because I had you do some selling when the market was 2400. Once the DJIA reaches 3000, your fast-moving stocks will give you the following portfolio breakdown:

$ 27,000 Fixed (19%)
+ $113,000 Stocks (81%)
$140,000 Total

The world is bright, but once again you are less than 25% in Group I, which mandates that you be in the selling mode. As much as you like stocks at this point, you do move about $8,000 from the stock section to the fixed income section. Here is where you are:

$$\begin{array}{l} \$\ 35,000 \text{ Fixed (25\%)} \\ +\ \underline{\$105,000 \text{ Stocks (75\%)}} \\ \$140,000 \text{ Total} \end{array}$$

7. We will now pretend the DJIA goes back to 2400, right where it started in the first place. Your fast-moving stocks go down even faster, and you end this up-and-down process as follows:

$$\begin{array}{l} \$\ 35,000 \text{ Fixed (32\%)} \\ +\ \underline{\$\ 75,000 \text{ Equity (68\%)}} \\ \$110,000 \text{ Total} \end{array}$$

We will stop there because the DJIA is right where it started and we have gone both ways. With a total of approximately $110,000, we have beaten the DJIA by 10%. We made no market forecasts and even had rather lousy timing on one or two of our transactions. You are still mad at me, but you are richer by 10%.

How often we can augment our performance by moving our portfolio in this no-brainer fashion, which substitutes mechanics for forecasting, is very hard to tell. It depends on the movements of the stock market. The more often and violent the swings in the DJIA, the better it should work for us. If the DJIA just sits very steadily or trades within a very narrow range for a protracted period of time, the less often this approach will work for you. You can look over tables 8.2 and 8.3 (see pages 84 and 86) showing the DJIA and the S&P 500 levels over 64 years and get some feel for what you could expect historically. The more I rely on my asset allocation model, the more I eliminate psychological and emotional factors, and the more contrarian I become when I am feeling particularly contrary.

In using this fixed asset allocation approach, conviction is most necessary at the extremes of market movements. If we get an extended down market and you have already made one adjustment by buying stocks, it gets even harder psychologically—and eventually more profitable—to buy more stocks again six or eight months later when the market is down further. The reverse is true on the upside. The higher stock prices go, the more people believe they will continue to go higher. The psychological resistance to selling becomes stronger.

For me, it is easier to make my adjustments when the market is on its way down, because I am basically an equity-oriented person. Therefore, I enjoy buying stocks more than I like selling stocks. For most people, the reverse is true. They find it harder to buy when the market is down than to sell when the market is up.

This may be an appropriate time to endorse the concept of *dollar cost averaging*, a concept widely advertised by mutual funds, which calls for the investment of fixed amounts of money over a period of time, say $100 a month, that will buy more shares when the market is down and fewer shares when the market is up. If you are using mutual funds to fill your investment policy, this type of program is extremely worthwhile. If you are unfamiliar with the mathematical advantages of it and think it fits you, make one phone call to your friendly investment adviser, who will send you an illustration on virtually any mutual fund you can mention. Generally speaking, I seldom try to dollar cost average with individual common stocks for two reasons: (1) It is difficult to invest smaller fixed sums in individual stocks; and (2) the likelihood of being totally wrong on an individual stock is much greater than it is with a mutual fund. The concept, however, is excellent.

The basic allocation approach I suggest is certainly not my invention. As a matter of fact, back in the 1920s, some prominent institutions tried a somewhat similar approach called *formula planning* with their investments. Most of these early efforts of reacting to the market instead of forecasting it had the problem of reducing the common stock section to zero as the market moved up instead of simply restoring the stock section to an agreed-upon percentage allocation. In other words, those administering the plan decided at a time when the DJIA was at 50, that if it got to 100, they would cut the percentage in stocks from 50% to 25%. Further, if the DJIA ever got as high as 200, they decided in advance that the market would be way too high and the stock section should be eliminated. As a result, many of these institutions were entirely out of the stock market halfway through the Roaring Twenties. They missed a chunk of the bull market, abandoned the formula-planning approach, and paid higher prices to get some of their good stocks back, all just in time to catch the crash of '29.

More recently, however, the approach I am suggesting worked very well in the minicrash of '87. By October 19, Crash Day, the DJIA had lost something like a third of its value in a two-week period. At a point like this, you generally do not have to study your portfolio breakdown to determine that you are under your common stock allocation and therefore in a buying mode. Just for fun a month ago, I looked over my brokerage slips from October 20 and found that I had made 40 purchases and one sale. Apparently, somebody with a normal psyche had called when I was out to lunch (I ain't missin' lunch for no minicrash). There is no question in my mind that the convictions that I could not forecast the market and that asset allocation should be my guide were responsible for the decision to make the purchases and thereby benefit from the market recovery.

For those of you who feel cowed by the institutions, let me just say that they have a tendency to behave just like ordinary people. I am the token broker on the investment policy board of a charitable pension fund. In the mid-1980s, we were fortunate to have a good chairman, who made us take the oath that the normal relationship would be 40% fixed and 60% equities. Unfortunately, by 1987, he had shifted jobs and left town, as most sound bank trust officers do occasionally. In our first two meetings in 1987, our percentage in stocks was over 60% and got to about 70% by our July meeting. The consensus was that we were perhaps a little heavy in stocks, but the world was bright and the outlook was good. Therefore, we did not sell. Well, after the crash, we were only 50% in stocks. At that point, the prevailing view was that our percentage in stocks was perhaps a little low and we should eventually buy more stocks, but this was certainly no time to do anything about it. Therefore, we did not buy. Our committee was forecasting. I remember one guy's comment in response to my urgings to buy: "Deep down, I know you're right, but I just can't do it."

In 1989, when brokers could not find much else to sell to their clients, we had a spat of offerings in *tactical asset allocation funds*. Outstanding professional managers were to change the makeup of the funds, and the percentages in stocks and bonds and money market funds or whatever were going to be good in the near future, based upon their forecasts of market movements. If the stock market was hot, they were going to have a high percentage of their assets in common stocks, and vice versa with bonds. They varied the percentage relationships instead of restoring them each time to the agreed-upon allocations. Well, by mid-June of 1990, the *Wall Street Journal* published an article pointing out how poorly the "tactical asset allocation funds" had done relative to the market. Apparently, it had not taken much longer than a year to decide that there had to be some better answer to all our prayers than having the experts forecast the stock market's direction.

The toughest question relative to this personalized fixed asset allocation approach is how often we should adjust our portfolio. Unfortunately, no bell goes off and tells you when you should make an adjustment. There is no fixed rule. Obviously, it would be wonderful for both you and your broker if the market were to swing up and down about 50% every month or so, but it won't. In the illustration I used, I made the market swings rather dramatic and also used common stocks with high betas. It is probably a good idea for you to adopt a simple guideline for yourself, perhaps mandating an adjustment in your portfolio when your stock or fixed income sections get as much as 10% out of line. You can make the approach a little fancier by using the percentage relationships, not just between stocks and bonds but between all four groups in your portfolio, if you are using all four groups. The size of your portfolio and other qualitative factors will influence your decision to set points at which your asset allocation should be readjusted. One of the important aspects of the approach, however, is that the wrong bell does not go off on market movements. If nothing else, this system will prevent you from responding to the fear bell when you should be responding to the greed bell.

This system is the only one I know to make an unpredictable stock market work for you. It takes conviction and it takes patience, but I find these to be more easily attainable attributes than the ability to see the future. If you can beat the DJIA by 2% or 3% annually, even with mediocre security selection, you have a pretty good start toward excellent investment performance.

CHAPTER THIRTEEN

Fixed Income Investing

I'M NOT GOING TO TELL YOU EVERYTHING I KNOW ABOUT BUYING fixed income investments or, to put it another way, lending your money. If I did, this chapter might run three or four pages longer than it does, more than most of you could stand. Briefly, we will face together the challenges of fixed income investing.

Much of the investment world is divided into bond people and stock people. The two meet frequently when they are dealing with portfolios, but otherwise they do not communicate much. I am a stock person, and a good bond person might rightly say that we stock people should not talk about bonds. Except for establishing the policy aspects of a portfolio, I am content to let my bond experts do the specific bond selections in implementing client policies.

Because I am a stock person, I may have a bias against bonds. Generally speaking, I do not think we get paid enough for lending our money. Whether we are talking about U.S. Treasuries or junk bonds, our interest rates both historically and currently have not been high enough to compensate for the risks we assume when we lend. I blame this feeling on the fact that we Americans have been and still are a nation of lenders, who like a good level of income whether we need it or not. You might point out that, in the long term, rates are set by supply and demand. Fine. I just think the suppliers of funds generally do not ask for enough interest from the demanders for funds, considering the risks. Oddly enough, foreign investors also seem to disagree with me. I recently saw some figures on foreign investment in the United States, which showed that foreigners own 21% of our debt securities but only 6% of our equity securities.

As a corollary, I believe that when we do try to get a higher return for lending, we incur even greater than proportionate risks. Junk bonds illustrate the point. Needless to say, as a stock person, I want to take my risks in the ownership section of the portfolio. Also needless to say, I would make a lousy banker—I would make very few loans.

As a framework for this chapter, I will provide my viewpoints on fixed income investing; then, give you some historical information, with the understanding that you should amend my approach to build your own fixed income policy. In some ways, the building of the fixed income section of your portfolio is a simple process. The first question to ask yourself is whether taxable bonds, such as U.S. Treasuries, or tax-free bonds, such as municipal bonds, are best suited to your portfolio. The decision as to which of the two types is appropriate for you is based upon your tax situation. A quick way to determine this is to compare the current Treasury yield (taxable) with a high-grade municipal bond (tax-free) having a similar maturity, apply your applicable tax rates (use local and state as well as federal taxes in your calculation) to the Treasury yield, and compare the after-tax yield of the two approaches. People in higher tax brackets are almost always beneficiaries of the incremental after-tax return provided by municipal bonds. The degree to which this relative attractiveness of tax-free over taxable bonds exists at any point in time does vary, but it is virtually always in favor of tax-frees for the higher income taxpayer. This is the first step in my approach to constructing your fixed income policy. The remaining conclusions are applicable to either tax-free or taxable bond buyers.

The most important objective in fixed income investing should be the safety of your principal. Losing money in your lending section is an investment sin. An intelligent investor may occasionally speculate on a high return from lending, but these investments should be carried in Groups II, III, or IV, not in Group I. With this objective in mind, I design Group I to produce a reasonable, not a high, rate of return.

Next, the two risks of lending—credit risk and interest rate risk—should be carefully avoided. To do so, the fixed income section (Group I) of my portfolios usually consists of high-grade bonds with reasonably short maturities. The price for avoiding risk is to give up a little income, a price that most investors would be wise to pay. For investors who absolutely require higher levels of income, it is a far-smarter approach to get a reasonable return and consume a measured amount of principal annually than it is to take the risks of producing a higher income and lose a chunk of principal occasionally. For somewhat different reasons, which I will mention shortly, my approach is as applicable to aggressive investors as it is to conservative investors.

Finally, I implement my approach for a large investor by building a *ladder* of maturities and having a reasonably equal number of bonds come due in each of the next several years, no more than ten, giving an average maturity of five years or less, for the bond portfolio. For smaller investors, I recommend a reasonably equal number of bonds, due in two, four, and six years, for example. That's my approach to fixed income investing—and it's set in stone!

Now, let's look at the historical income production or rates of return investors have received on bonds. Just income—no gains, no losses, and no price fluctuations. In the first column of table 13.1, you will see the annual income return for a group of high-grade corporate bonds in each year since 1950. These figures are based on Standard & Poor's Corporate Bond Index. They are good quality bonds, AA ratings or better, with maturities averaging 20 years. These bonds are taxable and have historically paid more than the equivalent maturities in U.S. Treasuries, simply because AA corporate bonds have to return more than Treasuries to attract investors. You can see that the average return of these bonds has been close to 7% over the years.

Since I must pay taxes on these bonds before I spend the income, I computed an adjustment to the rate of return by assuming that this investor had to pay one-third of his income to federal, state, and local governments annually. Therefore, the second column on table 13.1 is the annual return after taxes for this investor. I should mention that if I were using municipal bonds instead of these taxable corporate bonds for the high-tax-bracket investor, the result in this column would be a little bit better than the 4.658% return that it shows, maybe 1% better. I also might point out that if your tax bracket is considerably less than my assumption, these taxable bonds would accordingly be more attractive to you.

Stay with me. As you might have guessed, the most disturbing factor in lending is that old bugaboo, inflation. Therefore, I included the third column of table 13.1, showing the inflation rate during each of these years, so you could compare it with the after-tax income figure in the second column. Finally, in the last column, I computed the after-tax and after-inflation return produced in each year. You knew I would.

You can draw some rather frightening conclusions from this table, the first being the fact that the average net annual income from 1950 through 1990 using this investment approach came to approximately one-third of 1% in real dollars! Wow! Another conclusion is that you would have had to save

Table 13.1
ANNUAL INCOME RETURN
HIGH-GRADE CORPORATE BONDS VS. INFLATION

Year	Annual Income High-Grade Corporate Bonds	Annual Income Tax-Effected Corporate Bonds	Inflation Rate	After-Tax & Inflation Real Return
1950	2.6%	1.73%	5.8%	−4.07%
1951	3.1	2.07	5.9	−3.83
1952	3.0	2.00	0.9	1.10
1953	3.1	2.07	0.6	1.47
1954	2.9	1.93	−0.5	2.43
1955	3.1	2.07	0.4	1.67
1956	3.4	2.27	2.9	−0.63
1957	3.7	2.47	3.0	−0.53
1958	4.1	2.73	1.8	0.93
1959	4.6	3.07	1.5	1.57
1960	4.4	2.93	1.5	1.43
1961	4.4	2.93	0.7	2.23
1962	4.2	2.80	1.2	1.60
1963	4.4	2.93	1.6	1.33
1964	4.4	2.93	1.2	1.73
1965	4.7	3.13	1.9	1.23
1966	5.3	3.54	3.4	0.14
1967	6.9	4.60	3.0	1.60
1968	6.5	4.34	4.7	−0.36
1969	7.8	5.20	6.1	−0.90
1970	7.4	4.94	5.5	−0.56
1971	7.1	4.74	3.4	1.34
1972	7.2	4.80	3.4	1.40
1973	7.7	5.14	8.8	−3.66
1974	8.6	5.74	12.2	−6.46
1975	8.6	5.74	7.0	−1.26
1976	7.8	5.20	4.8	0.40
1977	8.4	5.60	6.8	−1.20
1978	9.2	6.14	9.0	−2.86
1979	10.6	7.07	13.3	−6.23
1980	12.4	8.27	12.4	−4.13

Table 13.1 (*continued*)
ANNUAL INCOME RETURN
HIGH-GRADE CORPORATE BONDS VS. INFLATION

Year	Annual Income High-Grade Corporate Bonds	Annual Income Tax-Effected Corporate Bonds	Inflation Rate	After-Tax & Inflation Real Return
1981	14.5%	9.67%	8.9%	0.77%
1982	11.2	7.47	3.9	3.57
1983	12.3	8.20	3.8	4.40
1984	12.0	8.00	4.0	4.00
1985	10.1	6.74	3.8	2.94
1986	9.1	6.07	1.1	4.97
1987	9.9	6.60	4.4	2.20
1988	9.9	6.60	4.4	2.20
1989	8.8	5.87	4.6	1.27
1990	9.1	6.07	6.1	0.03
Average	7.04	4.70	4.37	0.33

virtually all your income if you were using lending as a means of trying to protect your purchasing power. That is a tough one to swallow, since we lend our money to receive income and would not be allowed to spend any of it. A corollary would be that virtually everything we spend out of this income is in one sense a consumption of our purchasing power principal. In any event, you would have to be a whale of a saver to get rich by lending.

Remember that, in table 13.1, I excluded price fluctuations on your principal and tried to look only at income from lending. Now, let's bring in the impact of market price changes. In table 13.2, in the second column, you will see the annual return in each year since 1926, which includes both income and appreciation or depreciation, for the same kind of corporate bonds we were looking at in the previous example, before tax and before inflation. For those of you who like looking at

Table 13.2
STOCKS, BONDS, TREASURY BILLS, AND INFLATION

For the 65-year period 1926–1990, compound annual returns, with all income reinvested were:

Consumer price index	3.1%	Government bonds	4.7
Treasury bills	3.7	Corporate bonds	5.2
		Common stocks	10.0

ANNUAL PERCENTAGE RETURN INCLUDING INCOME

Year	S&P 500	Corp. Bonds	Gov't. Bonds	T-Bills	Consumers Price Index
1926	11.6	7.4	7.8	3.3	-1.5
1927	37.5	7.4	8.9	3.1	-2.0
1928	43.6	2.8	0.1	3.2	-1.0
1929	-8.4	3.3	3.4	4.8	0.2
1930	-24.9	8.0	4.7	2.3	-6.1
1931	-43.3	-1.8	-5.3	1.1	-9.5
1932	-8.1	10.8	16.9	1.0	-10.3
1933	53.9	10.4	-0.1	0.2	0.5
1934	-1.4	13.9	10.0	0.2	2.0
1935	47.6	9.6	5.0	0.2	2.9
1936	34.0	6.8	7.5	0.2	1.2
1937	-35.0	2.7	0.2	0.3	3.1
1938	31.1	6.1	5.5	0.0	-2.7
1939	-0.4	4.0	6.0	0.0	-0.5
1940	-9.8	3.4	6.1	0.0	1.0
1941	-11.6	2.7	0.9	0.1	9.7
1942	20.3	2.6	3.2	0.2	9.3
1943	25.9	2.8	2.1	0.3	3.2
1944	19.7	4.7	2.9	0.3	2.2
1945	36.4	4.1	10.7	0.3	2.2
1946	-8.1	1.7	-0.1	0.4	18.1
1947	5.7	-2.3	-2.6	0.5	9.0
1948	5.5	4.1	3.4	0.8	2.8
1949	18.8	3.3	6.4	1.1	-1.9
1950	31.7	2.1	0.0	1.2	5.8
1951	24.0	-2.7	-3.9	1.5	5.9
1952	18.4	3.5	1.2	1.7	0.9
1953	-1.0	3.4	3.6	1.8	0.6
1954	52.6	5.4	7.2	0.9	-0.5
1955	31.6	0.5	-1.3	1.5	0.3

Year					
1956	6.6	-6.8	-5.6	2.5	2.9
1957	-10.8	8.7	7.5	3.1	3.1
1958	43.4	-2.2	-6.1	1.6	1.8
1959	12.0	-1.0	-2.3	3.0	1.5
1960	0.5	9.1	13.8	2.6	1.5
1961	26.8	4.8	1.0	2.4	0.7
1962	-8.7	7.9	6.9	2.7	1.3
1963	22.7	2.2	1.2	3.2	1.7
1964	16.4	4.8	3.5	3.5	1.2
1965	12.3	-0.4	0.7	3.9	2.0
1966	-10.1	0.2	3.6	4.9	3.3
1967	23.9	-4.9	-9.2	4.3	3.1
1968	11.1	2.6	-0.3	5.3	4.7
1969	-8.5	-8.1	-5.1	6.5	6.1
1970	4.0	18.4	12.1	6.6	5.5
1971	14.3	11.0	13.2	4.4	3.3
1972	18.9	7.3	5.7	4.1	3.4
1973	-14.8	1.1	0.9	6.9	8.8
1974	-26.5	-3.0	3.4	7.9	12.2
1975	37.3	14.6	9.1	5.8	7.0
1976	23.6	18.6	17.5	5.1	4.8
1977	-7.4	1.7	1.3	5.2	6.8
1978	6.5	-0.1	-1.1	7.1	9.0
1979	18.5	-4.2	-0.9	10.0	13.3
1980	32.5	-2.6	-3.0	11.4	12.4
1981	-4.9	-1.0	1.9	14.7	8.9
1982	20.4	48.5	49.5	10.7	3.9
1983	22.3	1.1	-1.5	8.6	3.8
1984	6.0	16.4	15.4	9.6	4.0
1985	31.1	30.9	35.0	7.8	3.8
1986	18.5	19.9	25.6	6.2	1.1
1987	5.3	-0.3	-5.2	5.5	4.4
1988	16.3	10.7	8.7	6.4	4.4
1989	31.2	16.2	21.5	8.4	4.6
1990	-3.1	6.8	5.3	7.8	6.1

SOURCES: Ibbotson Associates, Standard & Poor's, Salomon Brothers.

Johnson's Charts 1991

131

these tables, you can see that column three gives the annual percentage return, including income, for government bonds, and column four shows short-term Treasury bills. I might say that these figures are largely supported by extensive and authoritative studies done by various research firms over the years. If you spend a little time with table 13.2, I think you will agree that the aura of stability for bonds that comes from looking at the income-only table (table 13.1) dissipates when we see the annual price fluctuations of long-term bonds. These tables should impress upon you the fact that there is plenty of risk in buying even high-quality, long-term bonds.

It will not surprise me if you consider my comments of caution to be a bit extreme. We Americans have a tendency to believe what is happening at the moment will continue, and our current thinking is colored by the fact that the 1980s were a benevolent period for bond investors because interest rates and the inflation rate declined from historically high levels. The inflation rate over the last decade dropped to almost one-third of its previously double-digit levels, and interest rates gradually declined through most of the decade. Thus, these years were the best possible time to be investing in bonds. It would be a little optimistic to forecast the 1990s as a period in which we can produce the same levels of lending results we enjoyed recently because interest rates are at such low historical levels that it will be difficult to improve upon them.

Many years ago a popular investment policy concept was that investors should go from common stocks into long-term bonds when they believed the stock market was too high. My contention is that you should move somewhat from the stock market to short-term, high-grade bonds when your portfolio tells you the stock market is high. Notice the two differences. I am not forecasting the market; I am using my portfolio guidelines and I am certainly not going from common stocks to long-term bonds. The year 1969 provided a good lesson to the practitioners of the old theory. The DJIA was near 1000 at the end of 1968, and I can remember a few seasoned sages shifting their portfolios from corporate stocks to corporate bonds. Well, they were half-right. The stock market declined sharply in 1969, but so did corporate bonds. Bondholders received 7.8% in income but lost over 15% of their principal in 1969 as inflation accelerated. A period of rising inflation is generally not very healthy for stocks, but it is certainly very unhealthy for bonds.

Now that we see clearly what wonderful rates of return we get from lending, let's return to those two lending risks I mentioned way back in chapter 4—credit risk and interest rate risk. Credit risk, the risk that we will not be paid our principal and interest, is well recognized by Americans and easy to avoid. One easy way to avoid it, of course, is to lend our money so that it is guaranteed by the federal government, which has spent the last decade or so guaranteeing every financial institution in the nation at the expense of the next generation. The second easy way to avoid credit risk, and one I recommend you watch carefully, is to refer to the rating agencies and keep your lendings in the AA or AAA categories. Generally speaking, either of these approaches will avoid credit risk. I might add that another point in favor of short maturity bonds is that institutions in today's world often move from a AAA to a BBB in a rather short period of time. A short maturity offers some defense against a deteriorating credit.

The second risk—interest rate risk—is that the value of your bonds will decline as interest rates move up. The degree of this risk is ignored by many Americans who feel they have a *safe* bond because it is of high quality. Table 13.3 demonstrates how much the market value of your bond will drop as interest rates increase. For example, an 8%, 15-year bond will lose 8.1% of its value if interest rates rise by 1%, and from the second table we can see that the same 8%, 15-year bond will

Table 13.3
INTEREST RATES AND BOND PRICES

1. Price changes for bonds when interest rates
rise or fall by one percentage point:

YEARS TO MATURITY	8% COUPON IF RATES		10% COUPON IF RATES		12% COUPON IF RATES	
	RISE	FALL	RISE	FALL	RISE	FALL
1	−0.9%	+1.0%	−0.9%	+0.9%	−0.9%	+0.9%
2	−1.8	+1.8	−1.8	+1.8	−1.7	+1.8
3	−2.6	+2.7	−2.5	+2.6	−2.4	+2.5
4	−3.3	+3.4	−3.2	+3.3	−3.0	+3.2
5	−4.0	+4.2	−3.8	+4.0	−3.6	+3.8
10	−6.5	+7.1	−6.0	+6.5	−5.5	+6.0
15	−8.1	+9.2	−7.3	+8.1	−6.5	+7.3
20	−9.2	+10.7	−8.0	+9.2	−7.1	+8.0
30	−10.3	+12.5	−8.7	+10.3	−7.5	+8.7

2. Price changes for bonds when interest rates
rise or fall by two percentage points:

YEARS TO MATURITY	8% COUPON IF RATES		10% COUPON IF RATES		12% COUPON IF RATES	
	RISE	FALL	RISE	FALL	RISE	FALL
1	−1.9%	+1.9%	−1.8%	+1.9%	−1.8%	+1.9%
2	−3.6	+3.7	−3.5	+3.6	−3.4	+3.6
3	−5.1	+5.4	−4.9	+5.2	−4.8	+5.1
4	−6.5	+7.0	−6.2	+6.7	−6.0	+6.5
5	−7.7	+8.5	−7.4	+8.1	−7.0	+7.7
10	−12.5	+14.9	−11.5	+13.6	−10.6	+12.5
15	−15.4	+19.6	−13.8	+17.3	−12.4	+15.4
20	−17.2	+23.1	−15.1	+19.8	−13.3	+17.2
30	−18.9	+27.7	−16.2	+22.6	−14.0	+18.9

3. Price changes for bonds when interest rates rise or fall by four percentage points:

YEARS TO MATURITY	8% COUPON IF RATES		10% COUPON IF RATES		12% COUPON IF RATES	
	RISE	FALL	RISE	FALL	RISE	FALL
1	-3.7%	+3.9%	-3.6%	+3.8%	-3.6%	+3.8%
2	-6.9	+7.6	-6.8	+7.4	-6.6	+7.3
3	-9.8	+11.2	-9.5	+10.8	-9.3	+10.5
4	-12.4	+14.7	-11.9	+14.0	-11.5	+13.5
5	-14.7	+18.0	-14.1	+17.1	-13.4	+16.2
10	-22.9	+32.7	-21.2	+29.8	-19.6	+27.2
15	-27.5	+44.8	-24.8	+39.2	-22.5	+34.6
20	-30.1	+54.7	-26.7	+46.2	-23.9	+39.6
30	-32.3	+69.5	-28.1	+55.4	-24.8	+45.3

Johnson's Charts 1991

SOURCE: Journal of the American Association of Individual Investors.

lose 15.4% of its value if interest rates increase by 2%. This happens as the market price of your bonds adjusts to the changes in interest rates. The next time you think of buying a long-term bond, even of the highest quality, pull out this chart and ask yourself whether the degree of risk you are assuming is offset by the incremental return you will receive. One bad year in the bond market can take away your incremental return for years to come.

Now, you might point out how much your bond can *appreciate* when interest rates come down. Unfortunately, bond buying is not fully a two-way street, because most bonds clearly state that the bond can be redeemed (called) by the issuer at a price near par. If interest rates come down, you have a pretty good chance of having that good-looking bond refinanced or called. Therefore, you get a little bit of the profit and the problem of reinvesting at lower rates of return. I point this out not to discourage you from buying bonds with nearby call features. I am simply recommending that you have the call features in mind when you are buying a bond and calculate the yield to call as well as yield to maturity. Try to buy bonds with which you will be happy if they are called and even happier if they are not.

The important message here, however, is how much the market value of your principal can be eroded by an increase in interest rates. In smaller portfolios, therefore, I try to build a ladder of maturities in the two- to seven-year range, and in large portfolios, I seldom go beyond ten-year maturities. In a larger account, if I have some bonds coming due in each of the next ten years, my average maturity will only be about five years, certainly a tolerable risk for a sizable portfolio.

Despite my preaching, many of you are not going to want your lendings to be both high grade and short in maturity. You are going to want to take advantage of your guess/forecast that interest rates will come down and therefore *lock-in* what seem to be high rates of return. My suggestion is that when you do assume these incremental risks, take the bond out of Group I in your portfolio and move it down to Group II. If you buy a low-quality, long bond, I suggest you move it even further down to Group III or even Group IV, since it can have a fluctuation every bit as great as a stock. A junk bond, for example, which you may think is attractive as a speculation because of its inordinately high rate of return, you might take all the way down to Group IV, where you have your aggressive stocks. Even as a stock person, I feel these temptations at points of high interest rates and low bond prices. As a stock person, however, I also find that during these same periods, common stocks are also down, and I end up buying a stock instead.

Their vague understanding of these lending risks leads Americans to adopt some dubious fixed income investing practices. One practice is to use municipal bond mutual funds to produce a high rate of return and still be *safe*. Before you buy a municipal bond fund, take a look at the maturities of the bonds in that fund and recognize that interest rate risk is not eliminated by having 100 long bonds instead of 1 or 2. Incidentally, you might also take a look at the costs and fees of using this approach. A second error made by a great number of older people is to try to replace the high income from a maturing bond at a point when interest rates are low. Sure enough, to retain the income levels, they either stretch the maturities or reduce the quality of their bond. Do not do it. A third practice of many bond investors has been wonderful for brokerage firms. For some number of years during periods of rising interest rates, almost annually in November and December, investors would *swap* their municipal bonds and incur losses to offset their common stock gains. Seldom was this done to avoid risk. Over a period of time, this is almost a sure way to reduce the effectiveness of the fixed income section of your portfolio. I remember calling this practice "the broker's reward for being wrong in the first place."

After mentioning all these worrisome aspects of fixed income investing, you might assume that I use few bonds in portfolios. Quite the opposite. I use fixed income investments in virtually all my portfolios, and most of these are bonds in one form or another. For conservative investors who absolutely need high current income, bonds can at least provide a measured and higher current return on our investment than common stocks. Second, some of us conservative kids have reached an age where we do not necessarily try to keep up with inflation, let alone beat it. These worrisome aspects of bonds are more easily avoided than the worrisome aspects of common stocks. It is simply a matter of tailoring the investment policy to fit the individual.

If your fixed income policy should be centered, as I suggest, on high-grade bonds with short maturities, what does this mean to the aggressive investor who wants to increase his wealth? In the previous chapter, I described the only way I know to make money from fluctuations in the stock market— having my asset allocation dictate the purchase of common stocks (Groups II, III, and IV) when the stock market goes down and I have lost money in stocks. Now, to do this successfully, the Group I section of my portfolio must be stable. If I take substantial risks in my lendings, there is every likelihood that the value of my bond section (Group I) will decline almost as far as my common stocks during an adverse period. Therefore, in a difficult time, with an aggressive Group I, I am losing money throughout my portfolio, not just in the equity section, and there is not enough percentage change in the different groups for me to reallocate my assets. They are all lower. As an aggressive investor, therefore, I want my Group I investments to be my harbor from stormy seas and a source of funds when my common stocks decline substantially. This is the strongest reason I know for the aggressive investor to adopt a conservative fixed income policy, keeping his maturities short and his quality high. He wants the price stability and the resultant liquidity for the opportunity periods in the stock market.

I find that a good many people to whom municipal bonds are applicable have a distrust or lack of understanding of the municipal market that prevents them from investing as well as they could. Certainly, if we are buying reasonably short-term bonds, the Standard & Poor's and Moody ratings of AA and AAA can give you comfort. I might observe that the market for municipal bonds in many states, including Pennsylvania, is not necessarily a very efficient one. Therefore, if you have a good bond adviser, you can occasionally take advantage of incremental returns without incurring incremental risks. Bonds selling at substantial discounts or premiums frequently offer a somewhat better return than bonds selling at par. Banks are a major force in most municipal markets. They have an affinity for bonds selling at or near par if for no other reason than to avoid explaining to their clients why they are not getting much return on their discount bonds or how they are *losing* part of their principal by buying premium bonds (they are getting their principal back from the high return while they hold the bond). The fact is that either discount or premium bonds can be more attractive than bonds selling at par. Some years ago, I had a good friend who was a whiz on Pennsylvania municipal bonds. We would, of course, debate the merits of stocks versus bonds, which led to no change in either position, the normal outcome of most investing debates. We lived in an inflationary world, but he was so good at buying bonds in that inefficient market, that he almost made up for it. If you do not have a friend with these capabilities, stick to the ratings as your quality guidelines. With good quality and short maturities, you will keep your Group I stable and have funds readily available for buying in a down stock market.

I have a suspicion that the material I have presented to you on bond returns and risks is a little disheartening, one of those bothersome concepts of which we are vaguely aware but would rather not face. As a result, almost all of us have been tempted from time to time by the brokerage ads in the Sunday papers—the ones with stars beside what looks like a very good rate of return. The ad may even describe these bonds as *guaranteed* by some entity or even by the federal government. Well, every time you get tempted to buy either a long bond or a lower quality bond, just sit down and figure out how much the incremental after-tax return will affect your standard of living. If you perform this little calculation, you might save yourself a few worrisome moments in your fixed income investing.

CHAPTER FOURTEEN

Common Stock Investing

ANYTIME ANYBODY TALKS ABOUT THE FACTS OF COMMON STOCK investing, they should confess that it is only their opinion—especially me. But, it is a fact that common stock investing is, for me, the most challenging aspect of investing. Everything we've talked about up to this point is relatively pedestrian. I hope the book so far contains a bit of common sense, a viewpoint of history, and a smidgen of logic. Even in fixed income investing, my major thrust is low key: prevent errors, play defense, don't get beat up lending your money. The primary goal of common stock investing, however, is to play offense, to make money. As I said before, for the individual investor, this business of common stock selection can be as much as 50% of the investment and intellectual challenge, so if there is any section of this book that should be fun, this is it.

Because my focus in this book is primarily on investment policy, not individual common stock selection, in this chapter I will confine myself to those areas of stock selection that are most meaningful in terms of policy. I will discuss first general concepts applicable to all common stock investing and then address each of the three groups into which I divide the common stock world. I hope you can fit this approach to yourself and gain some insight as to how to implement your own investment policy.

GENERAL COMMON STOCK CONCEPTS

I frequently use modern art appreciation as an analogy to common stock selection. It is an easy analogy for me, since I know nothing about modern art. If 20 of us clods took an introductory course in modern art appreciation, the teacher would presumably give us some guidelines and explain the techniques the artists used. Likewise, an introductory course in securities analysis would explain how to use such tools as cash flow, price-earnings (P-E) ratios, yields, book values, and growth rates. If we worked hard, even those of us students with little skill would pass the art course. Certainly, those with ninth-grade math skills willing to apply themselves could pass the equivalent securities analysis course. After the art course, if the teacher took us to the annual Carnegie International Modern Art Exhibit, I believe only one, two, or perhaps none of the class would be able to look at a particular painting, say it's terrific, and somehow know it truly is. There is a vast difference between learning the mechanics of analysis and being able to recognize greatness. The same is true in common stock selection, and one's ability to make good stock selections is largely indiscernible at the outset, even if the numerical analysis has been properly performed. Over the years, gifted students will find, perhaps to their own surprise, that they are often correct in their selections. Securities selection is not an art. It's *art appreciation*. The art is the company itself, just as the picture at the Carnegie is the art. The stock picker recognizes the art, prices it, and tries to extend its value into the future.

Much has been said about the impact of computers on the business of security selection, using quantitative analysis to select securities. I regard the computer as helpful, but in the long term and at the critical points, quantitative analysis alone will not do the job. Good stock selection over time is more qualitative and subjective, a liberal arts rather than a mathematical exercise.

A few years ago, I was invited to listen to the head of a major research firm, which had invested enormous sums in computer research. He probably does not remember saying this, but his comment was: "Life is a discounted cash flow analysis." I laughed. Even applying the phrase to a single stock, let alone life itself, is a little heady for me. Sometimes I think we have spent so much money on computers that we *have* to use them. I am reminded of the old saw about giving a four year old a hammer—he begins to think everything in the house is a nail. The computer is able to do mountains of mechanical work, and for that it is very helpful. Perhaps it could be programmed to pass introductory art appreciation, but it has not yet been invited to be a judge at the Carnegie art exhibit.

When you buy stock in a particular company, it is helpful to recognize the two influences on your stock's price performance while you own it. One will be the gyrations of the stock market; the second will be the results of the company. As a rule of thumb, I would say the stock market will have the greater influence on the stock price in the short term, and the results of the company will have the greater influence on the stock price in the long term.

The fact that there will be two influences on the price of a stock you own is an important concept to keep in mind. I fervently believe that no one can forecast the short-term stock market. Even today, this is to some people the most disturbing, heretical, and debatable concept I mention in this book. I say *short term* because I am among those who feel the stock market will have an upward movement over an extended period of time, from the gradual growth of American businesses, if nothing else. That is about as much as I will forecast. Of all the people I have known who have done extremely well investing in common stocks, no one had a short-term market forecast as their focal approach. As a matter of fact, I believe that any success from market forecasting comes from being a contrarian, not a member of the majority. Years ago, economists concluded their year-end speeches about the economy with a market forecast—the part that everybody really came to hear. However, the forecasts were so bad that they impinged on the credibility of the economists' basic work. As a result, they all stopped doing the market forecast (and, therefore, lost a chunk of their audience).

Twenty-five years ago, my belief was a lot more heretical than it is today. If you read the savants of security analysis today, you will find very few if any articles on how to predict the stock market. Those of you who have been around for a while might see the same trend in our daily business reading material, like the *Wall Street Journal*, where, in the short term, the dart throwers outperform the professional stock pickers frequently. The only people I know who have profited handsomely by forecasting the stock market are those who write market forecast letters and sell them for $200 a year to pigeons across the nation.

The fact that we do not know where the market is going does not eliminate some useful market information. We are allowed to know whether stocks are historically high or historically low and whether P-E ratios are historically high or historically low. We are allowed to know where the market is at the moment and where it has been. Fortunately, the conviction that we do not know which way it will go allows us to make our asset allocation approach work better. We are allowed to know what we will do, buy or sell, when the market does whatever it is going to do. I find that telling yourself what

144

you will do far in advance helps you psychologically to act when the market has dropped or risen substantially. I know right now that if the market drops 25% in the next six months, I will be buying what I hope are temporarily wilted flowers at lower prices.

I only know three groups of people who do extremely well in common stock investing and two of these groups are not very big. The first group consists of those few people who generally own one stock, usually because they work for the company, and the company does very well over a period of time. They hold the stock because it is their company, they show their loyalty by holding the stock, or maybe they do not even know they can sell it. You could call this a no-brainer approach, but some of them love that stock, and, in some cases, they should.

This is an appropriate time for an additional word about diversification. One of the hackneyed expressions in the securities business is: "You should not have all your eggs in one basket." Try telling that to a guy who has made $50 million on his stock in a small computer company. As I previously mentioned, I believe diversification should stem from the aims of the individual investor, but there is also a point to be made from the experience of these people who made a bundle on one stock. It is simply that they allowed themselves to do it. The one-stock holders had the faith and perseverance to allow a winner to really win by not selling it. Too many of us sell a stock too soon and do not permit it to make us enough money over time by becoming a great company. In North Carolina 20 or so years ago, a few neighbors invested in a small supermarket chain, which became very successful. A bunch of them held on because they knew the company and the management. One of these investors sold when his profits bought him a new riding lawn mower. It is now colloquially known as the $3 million lawn mower. I understand it is still working well.

The second group of winners is the largest. It is all the people across the country who try to select stocks in good companies and do not shift around very much. They let the good companies work and grow. Some of these people will occasionally sell a stock when they do not think it is going to do very well or buy one when they think it will do well. Over a period of time, they have differing results, but they are successful investors. Most of these people own common stocks through both good and bad times in the market. What differentiates people in this group from each other in terms of their investment performance is frequently the long-term results of the companies they own. Some of them, however, consistently own better stocks than other people, and you should try to be among them.

This leads me to the *growth-stock theory*, the most commonly accepted approach to producing good common stock investment results over a period of time, and the one that I heartily endorse. This theory concentrates on buying companies with sales and earnings that generally increase at better than an average rate. Those of us who endorse the growth-stock theory are concentrating on cash flow and earnings per share, both now and in the future, for the company we buy. We, therefore, study companies in the belief that the future earnings results of these companies are somewhat forecastable even if the overall stock market is not. Years ago, David L. Babson did a very simple little study contrasting ten popular income stocks with ten popular growth stocks. Forgetting about the price appreciation from the growth stocks versus the others, the study showed that by the end of ten years, the growth stocks were actually producing more in dividends than the income stocks. I liked that little study. The work we do studying a particular growth stock is focused on the question of future earnings. We learn as much as we can about the company and decide what we think this year's earnings will be, what next year's earnings will be, and how likely it is that earnings will continue to trend upward in future years.

Unfortunately, the work we do in studying a company and forecasting earnings does not eliminate the element of risk that comes from fluctuations in the market itself. Take another minute with tables 8.2 and 8.3 (see pages 84 and 86), which show the price performance of the Dow Jones and S&P 500 averages over the years. The earnings over the last decade, if you will recall, increased rather nicely, but not nearly as nicely as the averages themselves. You will notice again that the P-E ratio for the Dow closed at over 15 times earnings in 1990, double what it was ten years earlier. As I write, we have had a pleasant stock market in 1991, and this average is currently in the area of 20 times estimated earnings. Obviously, this has been a favorable stock market environment for shareholders, and, almost equally obviously, it can go the other way. The growth-stock investor, therefore, is hoping to find a company that will increase its earnings substantially in a reasonably short period of time and that the market influence on the stock will not be strongly negative. If I can buy stock in a company that grows its earnings at 20% a year, I will double my money in 3.6 years (the rule of 72) as long as there is no change in the P-E ratio. Of course, growth-stock purchasers would like to be right on their earnings forecast and also benefit from market influence. On the other hand, they realize they are still winners if there is no adverse impact from the outside market influence. As a matter of fact, if our earnings growth is strong enough, we may actually be a winner with an adverse market impact. If all my stocks have the same P-E ratios in five years as they have today, my appreciation should be directly related to the increase in the earnings of my companies. This is the influence of the company on my stock price, the one I really want.

You might quickly point out that we have to pay more in

terms of higher P-E ratios to buy the high-grade growth stocks with strong and consistent earnings records. You would be right, and this is one of the risks that you have to take into account using the growth-stock theory. A helpful exercise I use is to calculate how long it might be before a particular company produces earnings per share that will make my purchase price very reasonable. If I have to pay 20 times earnings for a particular stock, I try to figure out how long it will be before the company doubles its earnings, so that my initial price becomes only 10 times earnings. If the answer is five or six years, my purchase is pretty speculative. The growth stocks that attract me are ones where the period to achieve a conservative initial cost, such as 10 times earnings, seems reasonably short, say two or three years, and the certainty of these higher earnings materializing is rather good. A lovely growth stock, therefore, is a company that you believe has a high certainty of increasing its earnings at an excellent rate, say 20%, and that you are able to buy for a very reasonable price, say 10 times earnings. Do not hesitate to give me your suggestions of any companies you know like this that I should consider.

Whether we mean to or not, each of us involved in this stock selection business builds up certain personal standards in the selection process, which gradually become almost instinctive through constant use. We are looking at growth rates and the probability of the company attaining them, P-E ratios, and other analytical tools, some of which we looked at in table 8.2. After a while, I do not think we change these approaches much, certainly we don't change them as rapidly as the market changes. In my own case, I find that as the market goes up and the stocks I am coveting become more expensive, I have a harder time buying them. Everything seems expensive. When the market has had a strong period, I worry more about the stocks I own getting too expensive. The reverse is true on the downside, because then there seem to be more companies selling at prices that I regard as attractive. I suspect what is happening is that my analytical approaches and standards are not changing as fast as the market. If I am accustomed to paying 15 times earnings for a 10% growth rate, and the market moves up to a point where it is 20 times earnings for a 10% growth rate, most stocks will seem unattractive to me because my mind has not adjusted to the new world as fast as the market. This intellectual lag can be very helpful over a period of time since it makes stocks seem more expensive when they are high and cheaper and more attractive when they are low.

We believers in the growth-stock theory occasionally make it sound too easy. The idea is that we simply buy a good growth company, and even if we are wrong in our market timing, the company's earnings will bail us out and make us right. It is worth keeping in mind that the theory is dependent on future earnings, which do not always materialize. When forecasting earnings, we certainly make judgments. Accounting procedures permit management to have quite an influence on even currently reported earnings, so the first question to ask ourselves before we forecast next year's earnings is what the current earnings of the company we are studying really are. Second, we might consider the *quality* of earnings, how sustainable the earnings are from year to year or whether this business is susceptible to many surprises. A third question I ask myself in studying a company has to do with the growth rate. What has the growth rate of earnings been and what is it likely to be? Most fast-growing companies have a tendency to slow down as they grow. The danger in buying growth stocks, therefore, is that we will pay too high a price for a company in which the earnings growth slows down or stops. If I buy what I think is a lovely stock today, and the market starts going to pot tomorrow, I fully expect my lovely stock to wilt with the

149

rest of the garden. This is market influence, so it won't bother me much, since I did not buy it for tomorrow anyway. As the quarterly earnings reports come out, however, and the earnings turn out to be a lot less than I expected, I am in trouble. When our judgment is wrong on a growth stock, the opportunity to lose money abounds.

The third group who do well investing in common stocks is a rather small group of capable analysts who study companies in great detail and buy stocks frequently not well recognized by, or interesting to, most of us investors. These people use the so-called value approach to common stock selection, one I wish I had the time and intellect to use more frequently. The approach generally requires a very in-depth analysis of the company by very patient investors who buy their stocks on the basis of price relative to intrinsic values, balance-sheet assets, unrecognized future-earnings capabilities, and other similar values. These holdings can be very frustrating in bull markets, because these stocks are frequently overlooked by the market both ways—they may not go down when the market goes down, but they also have a tendency not to go up when the market goes up. Over a period of time, however, value investors can produce excellent results, partly because their in-depth analysis allows them to buy at attractive prices without as much downside exposure as occurs occasionally with a growth stock.

One small company I keep buying will probably earn a dollar a share this year, generally sells between $6 and $7 a share, and has a $6 book value. Its earnings have increased by 10% to 15% in each of the last five years. Furthermore, the company could be earning $2 a share in another four or five years. I have seen one research report on this company in the last three years. I regard myself as analytical, patient, and a *value* investor. So far, the market regards me as wrong.

Over the years, two approaches to common stock analysis

seem to have developed, whether the ultimate aim is a value investment or a growth-stock investment. One approach is called the *top-down approach*; the second is called the *bottoms-up approach*. The top-down approach suggests that we start with what might be called global economics, work down to industries or sectors, and finally down to companies with the idea of selecting the best company in a particular area. The bottoms-up approach suggests that we look deeply at a particular company, get to know that company well enough to acquire conviction on its value, and, therefore, what might happen to its stock. It is a little embarrassing to admit that I am not quite sure which group, if either, I fit. If the top-down approach requires that I forecast the market, I will not be accepted in that group. If the bottoms-up approach requires that I do not try to relate the particular company to its economic environment, that group would not accept me either.

Let me suggest an approach on this selection problem that has been enormously helpful to me for years. Back in the late 1950s, I had the good fortune to spend some time with a fellow from Boston named Horace Nichols (Nick), who has been retired for some time but was absolutely one of the best security analysts I have ever met. At that time, the professional managers of sizable sums were still allocating a certain percentage of their portfolios to various industries—the chemicals, the rails, the steels, etc. What Nick and I concluded, or he did and I adopted, was that the external environment in which a company operated had very important impacts on the results of the company. This external environment, however, was not necessarily a function of an easily categorized industry. What we wanted to look at were companies that were beneficiaries and not victims of very strong and consistent economic trends, trends that cut through the economy well beyond particular industries. If we could identify these trends, we could ask ourselves whether a particular company was a beneficiary or a victim of the pertinent trends influencing its business, and thereby buy companies with a favorable economic environment to produce outstanding results. You could work from the top down or the bottom up. In other words, you could look at a particular company and then ask yourself, what is the economic environment in which this company operates? Is it a beneficiary or a victim? From the top down, you could look first at what trends were strong and consistent in the country. In the 1950s, for example, Americans were working shorter hours with longer vacations and being paid at rates that gave them a much higher degree of discretionary spending. Using the trends approach, Walt Disney looked better than Bethlehem Steel because the economic trends were working well for Disney and against Bethlehem Steel.

Some of the trends beginning in the 1950s have become obvious today. Think about women in the work force (Liz Claiborne), America's health kick (the drug companies), the demographics of the aged (the drug companies, again), the internationalization of our markets (Reuters Holdings, in the financial area). When you think about the impact of external trends on different companies, it becomes obvious that the Penn. Central was a wreck waiting to happen as soon as we built the Pennsylvania Turnpike and our national highway system.

We now live in a world of dinks and oinks and yuppies and aarps and lawyers and cockroaches, and they create the external environments within which our companies operate. One of my favorite clients years ago was an elderly lady who went to Kaufmann's Department Store, not to buy things—"she didn't need a thing"—but to watch what the other women were buying. Therefore, she bought Revlon in the 1950s, at a time when women were consistently applying pounds of makeup per face per year, instead of U.S. Steel, into which the professional investors were still putting 5% of their portfolios. My message here is that when you read an annual report or research report, or whatever you read about a company that interests you, ask yourself what strong economic trends influence this company and whether this company is a beneficiary or a victim of these trends. You do not have to be a professional securities analyst to ask yourself these questions. As a matter of fact, some of your best security analysis might be done in a grocery or department store.

What I have said above does not preclude the very desirable goal of knowing as much as you possibly can about a company you are thinking of buying, one you own now, or one you are thinking of selling. Understanding your company and reflecting on its economic environment are both worthy exercises in evaluating and forecasting the company's long-term influence on its stock price. If you are involved in your own common stock selection and investing a chunk of your savings, you might think of giving the effort as much time as you take to buy a lawn mower. One of my own rules, which I occasionally break, usually to my regret, is that I should understand the company's products and business very clearly before I buy the stock. In an increasingly technical and scientific world, this little rule is not always as easy to follow as it sounds. I can't expect you to spend as much time as you would in buying a car, but spend a little time thinking about the company. Despite my advice, I will confess that I generally learn more about a company after I have owned it a while than I had learned before I bought it. Fortunately, there is no rule against continuing to learn.

Let me give you one more important reason for knowing as much about your company as you can. Knowledge helps give us conviction, and conviction helps move us away from the psychological norm, otherwise known as the *herd*. If you know your company well and you are pleased with how your company is doing, the fact that the stock market and the price for your stock is currently going down rapidly just does not bother you as much. If your company, and its stock, however, is nothing more to you than a price in the *Wall Street Journal*, you are very likely to join the herd, selling low and buying high.

Textbooks on common stock selection are almost bound to recognize management as a critical ingredient in the success of a company, and certainly we have plenty of books from Peter Drucker and others suggesting successful management approaches. We all know management is important, and we all spend time evaluating them. But, would you rather have a good management in a lousy industry or a lousy management in a good industry? Fortunately, you don't have to answer the question. What we are usually looking for is a good company in a good business with a good management. Friends keep sending me books on this subject with the faint hope they will improve my approach toward evaluating managements. In appreciation I skim the books. My approach toward management is about as subjective as you can get—the most important ingredient being whether I actually like the managers as people. Yes, I want to know whether they are interested in increasing shareholders' value, and how they are going to increase it, but if I really don't like them as people, I probably won't buy their stock anyway. Aside from liking them personally, I am very interested in learning what their fellow employees think of them and whether the people seem to enjoy working at the company. How's that for sophistication?

All of us who have followed the progression of management books over the years have a theory as to how management should run its business. Going back a few decades, management has moved from the *jungle fighter* to the *organization man* to the *gamesman*. All those management texts seem to make sense to me at the time I read them, and then a year or so later we get a new and better theory. So that you can have a little fun about ten years from now, I submit my forecast that the top-flight managements of the 1990s will adopt an approach called *participatory management*. Management will get a lot of direction on how to run the company from the people who work there. More specifically, managements will have enough self-confidence to expose their ideas to people up and down the ladder, and employees, in turn, will have enough confidence in management to express their own ideas to the managers. This will certainly flatten out the organizational chart when the fourth guys down on the current chart will talk to the CEOs and tell them how to run their business. The CEOs, for a change, will have to listen to how they have been screwing up, but they will make better decisions as a product of it.

An uncommon recommendation relative to stock selection is that you engage in a certain amount of self-study. I suspect that it takes some time and experience to know yourself and to have some awareness of your capabilities and/or lack thereof, but the knowledge is certainly worth the effort. For example, I personally seem to enjoy down markets a good bit more than most people. This is helpful to me, because it allows me to buy more stock in a good company if the adverse price activity is simply a result of a short-term market decline and the company I like is doing as well as or better than I expected. Unfortunately, I also have a surfeit of pride that keeps me from recognizing my errors as promptly as I should and curing them accordingly, by selling the stock. Like most people, I have periods of months or years in which I feel I can shoot six in a row from midcourt and have them all swish right through. At other times, I feel I can't make a lay-up. If you are the same, don't get discouraged. One of the questions I ask myself continually as I get older is whether I am adjusting and changing enough or whether I am simply getting more conservative as most people do when they get older. Maybe we should become more conservative as we get older. I have taken the oath, however, that I will keep taking risks and keep playing the game as long as I can. Therefore, Hunter kids, I will probably blow your inheritance, so plan accordingly.

If you enjoy the subject of common stock selection, and don't leave it entirely to your investment adviser, let me suggest a few books with which you can spend anywhere from a little to an enormous amount of time:

— Graham, Benjamin, and Dodd, David, L. *Security Analysis: Principles and Techniques.* 4th rev. ed. New York: McGraw-Hill, 1988. Benjamin Graham is properly known as the Father of Financial Analysis. The first edition was published in 1934. My copy is the third edition (1951). To the casual student, this book is heavy, so I would suggest you spend a little time with it at the beginning and the end of your self-study course.

— Graham, Benjamin. *The Intelligent Investor: A Book of Practical Counsel.* Rev. ed. New York: Harper & Row, 1985. This is Graham's second classic. Much easier reading and a good place to start for the serious student.

— Fisher, Philip A. *Common Stocks and Uncommon Profits.* Rev. ed. New York: Harper & Row, 1984. This book originally came out in 1958, at a time when I was trying to put a structure or framework on my own approach toward common stock investing. It had enormous impact on me and my thinking. It is still worth reading today.

— Ellis, Charles D. *Investment Policy.* Homewood, Ill.: Dow Jones–Irwin, 1985. This is a short but excellent book on investment policy for an institution or an investor with a very large sum of money. If Ellis had written a similar book for the individual investor, he would have saved me a lot of time.

— Lynch, Peter S. with Rothchild, John. *One Up on Wall Street: How to Use What You Already Know to Make Money in the Market*. New York: Simon & Schuster, 1989. The amazing thing about Lynch is that he did so very well with so much money to manage. At first blush, the book seems shallow and glib, but it's deep enough to be read two or three times.

— Ellis, Charles D., ed. *Classics, An Investors Anthology*. Homewood, Ill.: Dow Jones–Irwin, 1989. A collection of writings on investment subjects dating back to 1929, this is my favorite book on the history of investment policy and security selection. For people who really enjoy this subject, it's great. *Classics II* (1991) has now been published, but I have not had time to read it.

GROUP II—THE CAUTIOUS OFFENSE

If Group II doesn't ring a bell, go back to table 5.1 (page 54), our balance sheet, and notice that I included the telephone company and a very conservative common stock fund as Group IIs. Group II implies that it is possible to acquire ownership, buy a stock, and yet be reasonably conservative while doing so. The aim of this section of the portfolio is to be quiet, that is, to go down slowly while the rest of the stock market is going down rapidly, and to make a profit. Notice that I put making a profit as the secondary, not the primary, aim. I don't think we should ever buy a stock unless we expect to make a profit; there is simply too much inherent risk in ownership to expose yourself without expecting to make a profit. In Group II stock investing, however, the approach is simply that I want the stocks to behave better in down markets, and this aim is somewhat stronger than the aim of expecting a substantial profit.

What I consider to be Group II stocks are those companies engaged in a very basic business with the demand for their product quite stable and inelastic, a virtual necessity, and little altered by an economic recession (e.g., utilities, telephone companies). Most people equate Group II stocks with high-income production, but, remember, you can have high-income stocks with all the risk of Group IVs and plenty of them are that risky. Incidentally, years ago common stocks yielded more than bonds, and it was almost unanimously considered proper that they should do so. After all, there was risk in common stocks and not in bonds. The fallacy, of course, was that in the long term stocks could appreciate and bonds would mature. My, how the world has changed: We now get 8% on our bonds and only 3% on our stocks.

When I look at Group II's recent history, I smile at my own naïveté. As recently as the early 1980s, I would have included in Group II most electric utilities, a good number of our telephone companies, quite a few of our best-known food companies, and what I thought to be quiet, conservatively run banks. Certainly, we could have, and still can, included a quiet common stock mutual fund. These all appealed to me as attractive approaches to ownership for people with conservative investment policies or for people who were pretty scared by this stock market business or required a higher level of current income.

Now we can see what occurred with these companies during the 1980s and how they differed from my expectations. The electric utilities perhaps were not too surprising. To a certain extent, they are, by nature, surrogates for fixed income investments and live in a regulated environment. If anything surprised me about the utilities over the last 10 or 15 years, it is probably how willing the regulatory bodies have been to permit some utilities to become financially unsound. I never would have guessed the number of utilities that would have some financial difficulty leading to dividend cuts as we have seen in the last 10 or 15 years. Surprising to me on the upside were two of the groups—telephone companies and food companies. The *quiet* telephone companies have produced terrific earnings and are now regarded more as growth stocks. We *little old ladies* look pretty smart in retrospect. The food companies that, in the early 1980s, were selling at seven times earnings and 7% yields also began to be regarded as growth stocks. Some of the best, like Nabisco and General Foods, were gobbled up by other companies at prices that once again made us little old ladies look pretty smart. The opposite occurred with the *quiet* banks. What we discovered recently is that there do not seem to be any quiet banks: All the quiet banks have been making aggressive loans in less-developed countries like Texas and in real estate developments where people don't want to live or work. If there is something to be learned from these surprises, it appears to me that Group IIs, over a period of time, can move both ways a good bit faster than I expected.

At the moment, it is very difficult to find stocks that I truly consider Group IIs. I am looking for companies in defensive industries with low betas that sell at reasonable P-E ratios and generate a decent dividend. Perhaps I should look more at some balanced (bonds and blue-chip stocks) or conservative common stock mutual funds as functional equivalents for Group II stocks.

While we are discussing the Group II area, let me throw in another irritating concept, the subject of buying stocks for income. With perhaps a little hyperbole, I take the position that, if you can afford to, you should forget about dividends. If I were to generalize on the investing errors I have made over the years, the largest category by far would be titled Attempts to Get Inordinately Good Current Return. The same generalities that apply to the junk-bond trap could be applied to conservative common stock investing, that is, that the measure of a stock over a period of time should be more related to its total return, appreciation plus dividends. Too many investors pay too much attention to only the current dividend.

Worth considering in this regard is the origin of a dividend. A company produces earnings over the period of a year, and a board of directors presumably makes a decision to retain a certain portion of those earnings and to pay the shareholders a dividend with a portion of those earnings. Now, a rapidly growing company has a great need and use for funds, and will characteristically lead the board to the decision that they should retain the earnings and benefit the shareholders best by reinvesting in the company. If the dividend is a very large percentage of the earnings, the implication is that the board has studied the company and concluded that the company does not have superb uses for the earnings. We cannot ignore the elements of consistency and continuity in dividend policies that strongly impact on the board's decision. Nevertheless, when we leave our retained earnings in the company, they still belong to us shareholders, and when we get them in cash, we pay taxes on them. If you need a useful guide in terms of your own actions, the next time you look at a company and are attracted by the size of its dividend, do a little calculation and figure out how much the incremental return over a normal dividend rate will improve your standard of living. In most cases, the added income will not change your life-style.

Find me some good Group IIs. I have a lot of little old lady friends, some of whom are 35-year-old men, and the number of companies I carry in Group II has been shrinking constantly for a decade.

GROUP III—THE BALANCED OFFENSE

Group III is the bulwark of most common stock portfolios. It consists of the type of companies you see listed in the DJIA and in the S&P 500, that is, the blue-chip, well-known companies and the high-grade growth stocks. The aim of the investor with Group III is not to play defense; it is what you might call a balanced offense. The primary aim for most of us, of course, is to do a lot better than the rate of inflation over a period of time. Look at the DJIA chart in table 8.2, because these are blue-chip, mostly Group III stocks. Look at it and compare it with the inflation rate. It does not include income, like the bond charts. How well high-grade growth stocks have hedged inflation is clearly demonstrated by tables 8.2 and 8.3, so if these relationships did not sink in, go back and spend another ten minutes with the tables. If necessary, read chapter 8 again. Frankly, being human, our aim is usually greater than just beating inflation: We want our good stocks to go up a lot and we do not want to own the ones that go down a lot.

Most of the general common stock concepts I have expressed apply very strongly to Group III selections. You can use the growth-stock theory or the value-stock approach and you can go top down or bottoms up. Since Group III includes most of the better-known corporations in the United States from Abbott Labs to Xerox, it is a very large group, and for most of us it is helpful to categorize or classify these companies. For example, you may have a tendency toward high-grade growth stocks or cyclical heavy-industry stocks. Peter Lynch, in *One Up on Wall Street*, does a good job at segmenting Group IIIs when he talks about "stalwarts" and "fast growers" and "turnarounds" and "slow growers." Some analysts are better at certain areas than others. I have never done very well at "cyclicals" or "turnarounds," so I try to avoid them. Occasionally, though, I take the plunge. To borrow one of Warren Buffett's analogies, I have a "toad" in my portfolio that I have "kissed" for three years without it showing any signs of ever becoming a princess. The stock is analytically fascinating, but it still remains a toad. More recently, Buffett gave us some further wise advice relative to our own capabilities when he made the comment that he had done better avoiding "dragons" than slaying them.

One theory espoused by some analysts is the so-called efficient-market theory, which contends that all the public information available on a company is reflected in the current stock price. Therefore, the market price each day is the appropriate price for the stock and only new information on the company should alter relative price action. I presume from this that you could just decide from the betas how much risk you want to take to build your portfolio and end your analysis.

A second intellectual approach is the so-called random-walk theory, which implies we will all come out the same in our stock selection over an extended period of time.

I do not subscribe to either of these theories, especially for individual investors. I advocate that we do a great deal of homework on individual companies, their financial measurements and prospects, and virtually no work on forecasting the general direction of the stock market. I agree that the market for major companies, reflecting the enormous amount of research work that is done today, is more *efficient* than it was years ago. To shed some light on the subject, I included table 14.1, which shows the monetary change in the 30 Dow Industrials from the beginning of 1981 through the end of 1990. Take a moment to look at it.

It should be obvious, even to the random-walkers, that it sure mattered *which* stocks you owned, given the wide difference in performance. Still, this was a remarkably prosperous

Table 14.1
DOW JONES INDUSTRIAL STOCKS

The results in market value of $10,000 invested for ten years in each of 30 Dow Jones Industrial stocks on January 1, 1981, exclusive of dividend income. The total investment in the 30 stocks was $300,000.

	Market Value 12/31/90
Philip Morris	$ 95,727
Coca-Cola	83,596
Merck	63,628
McDonald's	60,491
Procter & Gamble	50,309
Woolworth	48,889
Westinghouse Electric	38,482
General Electric	37,469
Boeing	34,706
AT&T	33,611
Minnesota Mining & Manufacturing	29,068
Du Pont	26,250
Exxon	25,674
International Paper	25,476
American Express	20,497
Alcoa	19,329
IBM	16,648
Sears, Roebuck	16,639
United Technologies	15,697
General Motors	15,278
Primerica	15,062
Chevron	14,598
Eastman Kodak	13,427
Texaco	12,604
USX	12,323
Goodyear	11,797
Union Carbide	9,776
Allied Signal	7,470
Bethlehem Steel	5,592
Navistar	878
Total:	**$861,091**

time for the stock market generally, so for balance, and your reading pleasure, I added table 14.2, which shows the prices for the 30 Dow Industrials in the ten years ending December 31, 1974. This shows that you can hold a lot of well-known companies for ten years and not make any money (27 out of 30 during this decade), but it still mattered plenty which ones you owned. I had so much fun looking at these charts that I included table 14.3, which shows the ten years from 1974 through 1983. I suspect you can use these tables to conclude anything you would like about Group III investing, but I will simply say that it makes a lot of difference what you own for a decade. Interestingly, only two companies, General Electric and Exxon, appeared in the top half of the 30 Dow stocks in each of the three decades.

I play a little game every time I see charts like these. I draw a line between the top 15 and the bottom 15 and see how many of the top 15 I have in client portfolios versus the bottom 15. Then I try to figure out why. Personally, I have discovered only two broad techniques that I believe will keep most of my selections in the top 15 stocks over a decade. I mentioned both previously, but they bear repeating: (1) Try to learn as much as you can about the company; and (2) think about it in its broader context, the external environment, and whether it is working for or against the company.

One of the nice things I discovered about Wall Street research is that it is generally free to an individual. An analyst works very hard on a research report, manages to talk a few people in his own firm into reading it, but is absolutely delighted when someone like myself actually wants to read a copy. In the securities business, it is a lot better to be able to recognize good work than actually be able to do it. It is also a lot easier. If someone asked me how many times I think I have been the first person to have a very creative and successful stock selection idea, my answer would be once. The stock

Table 14.2
DOW JONES INDUSTRIAL STOCKS

The results in market value of $10,000 invested for ten years in each of 30 Dow Jones Industrial stocks on January 1, 1965, exclusive of dividend income. The total investment in the 30 stocks was $300,000.

	Market Value 12/31/74
Procter & Gamble	$ 20,000
Eastman Kodak	18,159
International Paper	10,916
Esmark	9,654
American Brands	9,133
United Aircraft	7,471
Sears, Roebuck	7,466
U.S. Steel	7,451
Johns-Manville	7,290
Alcoa	7,287
Exxon	7,171
General Electric	7,158
Bethlehem Steel	7,083
American Can Company	6,744
Standard Oil of California	6,686
AT&T	6,538
Union Carbide	6,516
Owens-Illinois	6,459
International Nickel	6,399
Allied Chemical	5,833
Goodyear	5,692
International Harvester	5,223
Anaconda	5,168
Texaco	4,765
Westinghouse Electric	4,706
General Foods	4,434
Du Pont	3,830
Woolworth	3,394
General Motors	3,142
Chrysler	1,189
Total:	**$212,957**

Table 14.3
DOW JONES INDUSTRIAL STOCKS

The results in market value of $10,000 invested for ten years in each of 30 Dow Jones Industrial stocks on January 1, 1974, exclusive of dividend income. The total investment in the 30 stocks was $300,000.

	Market Value 12/31/83
United Technologies	$ 61,053
American Brands	36,744
Owens-Illinois	24,211
General Foods	21,632
Westinghouse Electric	21,576
Goodyear	19,918
Standard Oil of California	19,786
IBM	19,776
Woolworth	19,116
General Electric	18,611
American Can Company	18,564
Alcoa	18,505
Union Carbide	18,388
General Motors	16,125
Exxon	15,883
Procter & Gamble	12,364
AT&T	12,269
Texaco	12,213
U.S. Steel	12,110
Allied Corporation	11,378
International Paper	11,346
Merck	11,192
Minnesota Mining & Manufacturing	10,577
Du Pont	9,811
Sears, Roebuck	9,252
Bethlehem Steel	8,636
Manville Corporation	6,667
Eastman Kodak	6,563
International Harvester	4,466
Inco	4,149
Total:	**$492,881**

increased six times over a two- or three-year period. The crazy thing is I picked the wrong one of the two stocks I was considering at the time; the other one did better longer. Every other good idea I have ever had was borrowed from somebody else.

GROUP IV—THE AGGRESSIVE OFFENSE

Before I say anything about my favorite investment area, Group IV, let me repeat very clearly that you do not absolutely require Group IV common stocks to balance a portfolio, fight inflation, or produce reasonable rates of return over a period of years. A good portfolio does not necessarily have to go below Group III.

The aim of Group IV stocks is very simple—to make a large amount of money! Almost all the investments I make in Group IV stocks are in smaller companies that I want to see grow rapidly and have their stock prices at least track their growth rates. Since I suggested that your division of assets be on the basis of quality or safety of principal, I also include in Group IV sizable companies that are *turnarounds* and speculative enough so that they simply do not qualify to be Group IIIs.

The approach toward selecting Group IVs differs little from buying a high-grade growth stock or a good value stock except that it is easier. Smaller companies with narrower product lines are a lot more easily understood than most of our major industrial concerns. As a matter of fact, that is one thing I am looking for in Group IV, a company that is a leader in a particular niche or narrow industry, with distinctive products and perhaps new products that will allow them to grow faster than most larger businesses.

Because the smaller companies are less well researched and frequently *underowned* by institutions, you are more likely to find a lower P-E ratio compared to the growth rate. Be aware that the reverse can also be true: P-E ratios of Group IVs are occasionally very high, far beyond those that pertain to the blue-chip, growth-stock area. Certainly, Group IVs lend themselves to the question I mentioned previously: How long will it be before the price I pay now is reasonable? If I have to pay 20 times earnings for that pretty little company that is currently growing at 20% a year, it will be 3.6 years before my cost basis becomes 10 times earnings. That can well be long enough, since the earnings just might not grow 20% annually.

Incidentally, if a company or its stock seems pretty risky to you but you still find it very attractive, simply make a smaller-than-normal investment in the company. As I mentioned previously, there is nothing wrong with building a concept like half-normal into your investment policy.

Group IVs are also a great area for finding *value* investments as well as growth stocks. The research reports may be few in number. If you read the writings of the great security analysts over the last 20 or 30 years (starting with Benjamin Graham, of course), you might believe that what good analysts are all looking for is a great company, the *supercompany*. The idea is to buy a stock and have the company perform beautifully almost year after year. Recognizing companies like this early in their growth periods is certainly not easy, but it is a worthy quest. The analytical trade-off, of course, is the fact that we make more errors in buying smaller, rapidly growing companies. Group IV errors can be pretty expensive. They are not all supercompanies.

As you consider Group IV stocks and your own investment policy, it might be helpful for you to divide the group into large companies and small companies. The larger companies that I include in Group IV have a speculative aspect to them, a quality deficiency, which provides too much risk to include the stocks in Group III. A typical example is a large company that hits very adverse circumstances and becomes speculative enough to drop from Group II or III to Group IV. Many of these companies are then characterized as speculative turnaround situations.

My comment that Group IV investments are not necessary to achieve very satisfactory investment results in no way should discourage conservative investors from buying Group IV stocks once they have the financial stability to do so. Some years ago, I attended the annual meeting of a small software company, a meeting mostly attended by young analytical types who I am sure understood more about the products of this company than I. The stock had performed very well, and it was a real pleasure to see two of my little-old-lady clients (who were literally little old ladies) sitting in the back row of the meeting with big smiles on their faces.

GROUP V—THE LONG BOMB

What is a Group V stock? Well, I define a Group V stock, and also Groups VI, VII, and VIII, as common stocks in which there is so much risk that they really do not make good investment sense. A lottery ticket might be a good Group VIII. Do people occasionally make money from these types of investments? Absolutely. Somebody wins lotteries, but more money flows into lotteries than flows out to investors. Certainly, a few of these companies start out as very speculative and gradually work their way to become enormously successful enterprises over a period of years. The point is that many investment possibilities are more likely to be poor investments than good investments and the odds are therefore against the individual investor. I admit, however, that a capable securities analyst can occasionally look at what many of us consider to be a Group V or VI and recognize it as an attractive Group IV because of a unique knowledge of the

169

company or the business. I frequently think of a case where a venture capitalist invested some years ago in a genetic engineering company and eventually made a sale of such size that his gain was noted in the newspapers. This was more than luck, but I also admit that had I been offered the stock at the outset, there is no way I would have bought it. Therefore, having outstanding analytical capabilities and judgment can allow certain investors to assume more intelligent and greater risk than others.

Keep in mind, too, that companies can move both ways in your portfolio. I have a couple of Group Vs that started as Group IVs and worked their way down through poor performance. Most people who engage in Group V common stock investing are simply interested in *making a killing*, buying low-priced stocks or following unfounded rumors or tips. If you find yourself intrigued or tempted by very speculative investments, promise you will do one exercise. Find the total number of shares outstanding and multiply that times the price of the stock to determine the total market value of the company. Now, compare that figure with this year's, last year's, or even next year's sales and earnings to see how expensive this company really is.

If, by chance, you have kissed quite a few "toads" and none of them has turned into a princess (or prince), one possible conclusion is that you are not much good at kissing toads. Remember, to be successful there is no requirement that you kiss any toads, and certainly there is no rule that says you have to kiss all the toads.

After all this discussion on buying a stock, you might well ask the question of when should you sell a stock. I will suggest a few guidelines. Some successful investors employ set rules for guiding both their buying and selling of individual stocks. Illustration: "If it goes down 15% after you bought it, sell it." Personally, I am not much for firm rules on selling. As a matter of fact, some of the old Wall Street expressions, such as "no tree grows to the sky" or "water seeks its own level," may be mildly humorous, but they are not much in the way of guidance. Certainly, if our policy dictates it, we have to sell something; so the question is which of my stocks do I sell? An easy answer with a fair amount of validity is to sell your losers. Swallow your pride, do not wait for it to get back where it started, sell it. When we buy a stock, we normally have expectations for the company to do certain wonderful things for us, such as produce good earnings. When these wonderful things do not happen, their absence raises a red flag. When our analysis is wrong, we should think about selling the stock. Do not think about selling the stock if the company is doing fine and the market simply declines. In good markets we occasionally get lucky and our errors are concealed by the ebullience of the market. Our stock has appreciated but think about selling it anyway. Certainly, our capital gains tax is an incentive to eliminate our clunkers. The one period during the year when my clients are happy with my errors is when they are doing their income taxes. It is interesting that we refer to our errors as *tax losses*. You do not hear many people talk about *tax gains*. In any event, an important control is to keep one stock from ruining your performance. Sell your errors before they get serious.

Over a period of time, try to understand your own psychological makeup and adjust for it in both buying and selling. Personally, I wish I were better at selling. Prices for good stocks seem to go a lot higher than I think they should, so my own problem with selling is not getting rid of the clunkers but selling too soon on the upside. Strangely enough, I think as I get older my time horizon or my patience seems to get longer rather than shorter. Therefore, I tell myself that I am getting better at selling because I do less of it than I used to. I try to remember what Philip Fisher said when he would sell a very successful company: "Almost never."

If this business of investing well is a function of having a good, consistent investment policy and selecting good common stocks, I certainly picked the easier of the two subjects by concentrating on investment policy. What we can learn about individual security selection is endless, and I recognize that I only scratched the surface in this chapter. As Christy Mathewson, the great pitcher, said, "I'd rather be lucky than good," but he practiced a lot. As the story goes, when he was a kid, he cut a hole in the barn door and threw baseballs at it by the hour. For most people, the task of selecting individual stocks is best left to the professional. What you can do, however, is to make sure you know where your securities fit into your investment policy, and certainly each of us can develop a sensitivity to economic trends—at least we can know what is going on in the supermarkets and malls of America.

CHAPTER FIFTEEN

Myths and Fears

IT IS FASHIONABLE IN BOOKS OF THIS TYPE TO HAVE A CHAPTER titled "Things You Should Not Do" or "Mistakes Investors Make." Even Philip Fisher in his classic, *Common Stocks and Uncommon Profits*, had a chapter titled "Five Don'ts for Investors" followed by another one titled "Five More Don'ts for Investors." At least once a year I see a don't-do list in some publication. I cannot remember ever reading one with which I had a major disagreement. Therefore, the next time you see one, I suggest you spend a few minutes with it.

Instead of writing a list of things you should not do, however, I would rather address some of the prevalent investing myths and fears that seem to bother a large number of individuals and try to give you some comfort about the very pervasive fear that you do not know very much about this investing business.

It used to bother me years ago that I did not know very much, so I read a lot and studied different approaches to the stock market and investing—but I was still bothered. My first comfort came after a few years when I realized that most everybody else involved in this investing business did not know very much either. This is an endless and vast subject. The second comfort came with the realization that if I knew a good bit about a few things, it was better than knowing a little bit about a lot of things, and that knowing a good bit about a few things was enough to get by.

One of the most prominent fears centers around the idea that *they*, the institutions and professional money managers with unique knowledge or information, make all the money and the individual investor is, therefore, at a great disadvantage. About all you have to do to dismiss this myth is take a look at the lackluster performance of most institutional investors over a period of years. Frankly, I do not expect the major institutions to perform outstandingly well simply because they have so much money to invest that they are almost precluded from being creative in stock selection. Peter Lynch at Fidelity was an aberration by performing well with ever-increasing sums of money. My perception is that many long-term clients of most institutions are reasonably happy by now if their institution keeps up with the market averages. Most do not. To me, the most surprising aspect of institutional managers is how frequently they turn over their portfolios. If they were individual investors, they could be accused of churning their own accounts. As a matter of fact, if my clients turned over their portfolios as frequently as the average institutional investor, I would be the wealthiest guy in the Pittsburgh jail.

A second area of concern about institutions involves their use of momentarily popular strategies with which the layman has no affinity or understanding. This creates in the individual investor a fair degree of fear of the unknown. When you think, however, of the motives behind some of the popular strategies employed by large institutional investors, they appear to be designed more to prohibit terrible performance

174

than to promote good performance. For example, we employ *hedging* when we are not sure what we are doing; we use *indexing* when we want to come out about the same as others; we buy *portfolio insurance* so we won't get clobbered. It seems that institutional investors have almost given up on extraordinary performance. Furthermore, the fiduciaries behind the institutions spend millions of dollars a year employing performance-measurement analysts with the primary incentive of protecting their fiduciary butts, and seemingly a secondary incentive to move money around from places that are about to perform better to places where they are about to quit performing well.

Certainly, in recent years the computer-based institutional activity of *program trading* has led the individual investor to question his own sophistication and ability to compete. Most of my friends in the securities industry dislike program trading because it leads to excessive volatility in the market, thereby disturbing individual investors and giving them the feeling that they are at a disadvantage to the institution. Somewhat secretly, I am in the opposite camp. In fighting for their eighths and quarters, if the institutions sent the market up and down 50% every month or so, my approach toward asset allocation should allow me to be a beneficiary and not a victim of their machinations. If some institution has managed to use computer program trading to perform outstandingly well, I have not as yet seen those results published.

A third category of investor concerns stems from an almost wavelike feeling that you as an investor *have to* or *should* invest in a momentarily fashionable and *profitable* investment vehicle. Many of these I put under the category of What Brokers Are Selling This Year. Years ago, when things were quiet in the securities business, you could put your feet up on the desk, relax, and recognize the firm was not going to be very profitable for a while. In recent years, however, most major firms have hired creative geniuses to produce new *products* for their brokers to sell during quiet periods. You do not have to be very old to remember when it was very fashionable to trade options or buy option income funds. Further, I do not even have to have 10% of my money in Europe or 10% of my money in the Pacific Rim to sleep well. You could make a long list of what was *the thing to do* in any given year over the last decade. As a matter of fact, if I had done everything in my clients' portfolios that I either had to or should have done, there would be no room for a good common stock.

A fascinating aspect of the 1980s was how creative the investment community got in the fixed income section of a portfolio. Junk bonds, for example, were designed to attract buyers by offering a very high rate of current return, which, in most cases, proved to be too low a rate of current return considering the risks. Institutional investors bought most of these. At the moment, some of these institutions are using the standard American approach of suing the creators of the bonds for their losses instead of admitting that they violated their fiduciary duties to the funds they were managing when they bought the junk in the first place. If my cynicism is showing, let me quickly suggest that not all junk bonds were necessarily bad investments. Furthermore, at the other end of the fixed income spectrum, the investment community invented the zero-coupon bond, which as previously mentioned promised to pay the investor nothing (but appealed to many as the saver's approach to building an estate by totally forgoing the pleasures of income). You buy a zero-coupon bond at a substantial discount and it increases in value to its face amount at the time of maturity. In certain portfolios, zeros can be pretty good fixed income investments.

One of my major criticisms of almost all us investors (including institutions, many individuals, and even corporate management) is that our time horizons for investing are too short rather than too long. The members of the next generation are not the only ones who expect instant gratification. This human failing gets translated into a substantial number of our popular *products*. You buy a stock option, for example, on an excellent company, but your option frequently expires before the company can do for you in the short term what it could do for you over time.

The daily gyrations of the stock market itself have a tendency to keep us overly concerned with a short time frame. If you are among those who watch your stocks go up and down daily, if not more frequently, why not admit to yourself that you are wasting your time and simply check your stock prices every couple of weeks. Now, what do you do if you own a stock priced at $60 and some bad news comes out causing the stock to drop six points? Before you join the crowd selling the stock, simply ask yourself whether that particular event was really worth 10% of the value of your company. It is the emotional market reactions of this nature that give some credence to the old Wall Street saying, "Buy on bad news, and sell on good."

Short selling, usually a short-term trading mechanism, involves selling a stock that we do not own with the expectation of buying it back later at a lower price to produce our profit. This type of investing strategy is not the psychological norm for most of us Americans. When we think of making a profit, we think of buying something low and having it rocket upward. Certainly, there are people who are psychologically, as well as analytically, capable of being good short sellers. Personally, I am a natural optimist, so I do not engage in short selling. I tell myself that managements are hired by shareholders to improve companies, not make them worse, and it is the responsibility of the board of directors to do something about it if management is not solving the company's problems.

Occasionally, experts as well as vast numbers of the public

seem to get hung up on certain types of securities. For example, as well known as they are, mutual funds, in my mind, are neither good nor bad investment vehicles in themselves. They can certainly be used, instead of individual securities, to attain the investing objectives of a great number of individual investors. The important consideration, of course, is to select the fund that fits what you are trying to do with the money and to choose the management that will do it for you. Probably worth mentioning in the context of investment policy is the fact that most mutual funds are well diversified, and this diversification has a moderating effect on the price movement of the fund. This leads me, on occasion, to rank a particular fund one group higher in our asset allocation model than I would each of the individual stocks within the fund. A very blue-chip stock fund, for example, even one laced liberally with high-grade growth stocks, could be regarded as a Group II investment because of the moderating effect on price movement by the diversification offered by the fund (the whole bunch of high-grade Group IIIs might equal a Group II holding).

The stock-option contracts previously mentioned are other examples of generic types of security that are not necessarily good nor bad investment vehicles in themselves. In this example, however, they are applicable only to a narrow number of qualified investors and generally, once again, for short periods of time. With stock options, historically, too many small investors assumed a great deal of short-term risk and paid the price for it.

The same kind of generic labeling is occasionally applied to *convertible securities*. Convertibles are bonds or preferred stocks that can be exchanged into common stock if the common appreciates in price enough to make the conversion attractive. Now, I do not know why you would buy a convertible bond just because it is convertible into common, especially in a company you do not like. Convertibles are simply hybrid

178

securities that require a little mathematical exercise before you decide you would rather buy the convertible bond of an attractive company rather than the common stock or instead of just a bond. Do the mathematics, compare the yields, figure the premium, know precisely why you are buying the convertible bond instead of the common. It is all eighth-grade stuff, so I won't bore you with it. Just do it. In addition, watch out for call features if you pay a premium for the bond. An unexpected call can be a quick way to pay a high price for the common stock.

Do not worry about not knowing it all. You do not have to know it all. Furthermore, you as an individual can compete very successfully with *them*, the *big kids* of the investment world. Spend more time thinking about and improving your own capabilities and limitations, and spend no time worrying about the institutional investors. Our greatest fear is probably the fear of the unknown. Well, in the investment world, a lot of the unknown is not worth knowing. You might wish you were better at cyclical-stock selection, but you do not have to invest much in cyclical stocks to be successful in investing. Personally, I wish I were better at turnaround situations, but I can live without them. In fact, you might even get all the way through your life without ever understanding a gold-indexed *bear* bond or owning a Eurodollar future—certainly I will.

CHAPTER SIXTEEN

When You Get Rich

THE BEAUTY OF DEMOCRACY IS THAT IT PROVIDES FREEDOM TO THE individual. We have an obligation to ourselves to express this freedom in a unique and individual way, in both our opinions and our investments. One of the few joys of getting older is that we care less about what other people think of us and perhaps more about what they really think. I find myself not caring much anymore who somebody is (I can't remember their names anyway), but it seems more and more important whether I enjoy them, even in brief encounters, talking with them and exchanging ideas. I encourage you to express your point of view on most any subject. In my family, having a strong viewpoint with very little knowledge of the subject goes back at least a generation or two.

The pursuit of happiness is more important than the pursuit of wealth. I have known a few people for whom the correlation between the two is very strong and I feel a little sorry for them. This business of investing should be fun and to many people it isn't. I have known a few people who spend entirely too much time on it without being happy with the results. There is something to the theory of benign neglect, because I think many investors do better by not fussing too much with their stocks. If you own a good company, reading the quarterly reports in many cases is probably enough.

As I mentioned, investing is something like a complicated kid's game that you are allowed to keep playing when you grow up. My viewpoint is certainly not shared by everyone. Some people just hate spending time with their investments. Knowing your tolerance or enjoyment for time spent on your own investments is worthy, something like staying within your own limitations. Certainly, plenty of financial advisers/brokers are willing to help. Frankly, if I had to pick only one trait for a financial adviser, it wouldn't be brains; it would be empathy. I think a good adviser has a feeling for a client/friend and helps translate and implement this individual's investment policy.

The primary aim of this book is educational. If you happened to learn something, it would make me happy. I strongly believe that education is the only solution to our problems in an increasingly complex society. It is the only means of protecting our democratic and capitalistic privileges, which, in turn, allows us the opportunity to enjoy a good standard of living. Fortunately, we can always keep learning. Keeping informed is the only way to stay ahead and win in our society. Unfortunately, without the education to deal with this complex world, many people are unable to win. It certainly makes advising young people easy: Find something you enjoy (happiness) and become very good at it (education) in order to compete successfully and be a winner. The most difficult aspect of education for me is not to arrive at a conclusion but to appreciate the other person's perspective. You, particularly you young kids, are supposed to give me that. Oddly enough, I welcome your rejection of some of my ideas, so I submit them with the hope that you will challenge them, amend them, and improve them. It would be great fun for me to sit down with a half-dozen of you who have read this book and have you tell me where I am wrong.

Once you get rich, the question you must deal with becomes what to do with all the money. I have discovered only two good uses for money after we have paid the basic necessities of life (including cable TV, of course): Reinvest it or give it away. When you buy stock in good growing companies, you are contributing capital that, combined with the efforts of the employees, helps the company to grow and to provide the goods and services that, in turn, increase the standard of living of everyone who buys them. If the company's products or services are worthwhile, are cheaper or better, and the company makes a profit, continues to grow, and provides more jobs, then it is fulfilling my concept of social investing. We should learn the company's viewpoints on social policy questions, and the shareholders should approve of them or voice their objections. You should remember that by being an investor in a company with decent products or services, you are sponsoring something economically worthwhile. For me, the most fun of all is investing in a smaller company and watching it grow and succeed. I take the pledge that I will not become too conservative as I get older and stop investing in smaller companies. Too many successful businessmen do that much too early in their lives.

The second good use for excess money is to give it away. In this competitive, capitalistic society, some of us are fortunate enough to be winners, but, obviously, some are unfortunate enough to be losers. In today's world, the question is not whether or not we will take care of the unfortunate; it is whether it should be done in the public or the private sector. The public sector involves the federal, state, and local governments, through taxation, with competing interest groups

182

attempting to administer aid to those who need it. I think most of you will agree with me, after you think about it for a bit, that we are much more efficient and effective in providing such aid in the private sector directly through individual volunteers without the red tape and enormously expensive bureaucratic government programs. In any event, the satisfaction you feel in achieving material success is small in comparison to the joy of being able to help others less financially able than yourself to win in our capitalistic world of opportunities. If we can give back both time and money to those less fortunate, we will be expressing our individualism, our freedom, our ideals, and maybe even take a step toward our pursuit of happiness.

College students must sacrifice none of their idealism to be successful in their careers or their investments. It is a myth to think otherwise. The most successful businessmen and investors I have known have had a very high degree of ethics and idealism. I am not saying that your high personal standards will not occasionally cost you money or cause you discomfort. They are almost bound to do so. Therefore, you will have troubles along the way. For what it's worth, the only two solutions I found that help when you're in trouble are to work harder and to help somebody else.

I am not sure that investing and making lots of money is all that important in the larger scheme of things. A few years ago I gave a one-hour-a-week course at an inner-city high school because I was feeling a little out of touch with the next generation. I seem to excel at getting good nonpaying jobs. One day, being unprepared, I asked them to do the work. I wanted them to define *success* and I put the key words on the blackboard. Very quickly, we had *money, power, position, fame,* etc., but then they began to mix in *happiness, good health, challenge,* and a few more different kinds of words. After half an hour or so, I suggested they look at all the words we had written and try to put them together in a pattern. What they then decided was there are two kinds of success: an external success and an internal success. The external success included the words like *money* and *power*, and the internal success included words like *happiness* and a *feeling of well-being*. Finally, they decided that internal success was considerably more important than external success. I gave the whole class an A that day.

INDEX

great escapes

NEW ENGLAND

Great Escapes

Weekend Getaways

Nature Hideaways

Day Trips

Easy Planning

Best Places to Visit

Felicity Long

NEW ENGLAND

The Countryman Press • Woodstock, Vermont

We welcome your comments and suggestions. Please contact Editor,
The Countryman Press, P.O. Box 748, Woodstock, Vermont 05091,
or e-mail countrymanpress@wwnorton.com.

Great Escapes: New England

ISBN 978-0-88150-868-0

Map by Paul Woodward, © The Countryman Press
Book design by Bodenweber Design
Text composition by Chelsea Cloeter

Published by The Countryman Press
P.O. Box 748
Woodstock, Vermont 05091

Distributed by W. W. Norton & Company, Inc.
500 Fifth Avenue
New York, NY 10110

Printed in the United States of America

10 9 8 7 6 5 4 3 2 1

ACKNOWLEDGMENTS

There is something magical about New England, and I have always believed that the urgency of the changing seasons has something to do with that. How much more beautiful is a sparkling spring day exploding with the first flowers of the season when thrown into relief by the hard winter that came just before? The joy and challenge of embarking on this book provided the opportunity to revisit some of my favorite haunts and to explore new ones, all the while trying to convey that sense of magic. Lucky for me, I had help in that quest. Special thanks to my husband, Chris, and my travel buddies, Avis Pinkos and Carole Moore, for sharing their love of New England with me during our innumerable *Thelma and Louise* road trips. Thanks also to Joan Law and her husband, Tingey Sewall, for their hospitality in the Berkshires and for their in-depth knowledge of the region. Author John Galluzzo offered his invaluable time and knowledge about Nantasket Beach in Hull, while ranger Donald Cann, also a writer, shared his love of the Boston Harbor Islands with me. Many thanks to the Weintraub family and to Eric Hager for showing me the lesser-known side of Martha's Vineyard. Thanks also to Lisa Gunville for her hospitality in Shawnee Peak and for her wonderful insights into this lovely, evolving area. I want to give a special shout-out to my kids, Cole, Shane, and Chloe, whose love of skiing revived my passion for the sport and got me onto the slopes of just about every ski area in New England in the last 10 years. Yes, we ski in the Rockies, too, but we have had some of our best ski days right here, closer to home. Thanks also to Shane for his beautiful photos of Martha's Vineyard, which grace that chapter. I also want to express my appreciation to the representatives of the various New England visitors' bureaus, many of whom did backflips to help me find bits of arcane information about their areas, and some of whom even took me on personal tours of their favorite lookouts, taverns, and scenic vistas.

Whether this is your first trip to New England or your hundredth, I hope this book will inspire you to get to know our beautiful region even more.

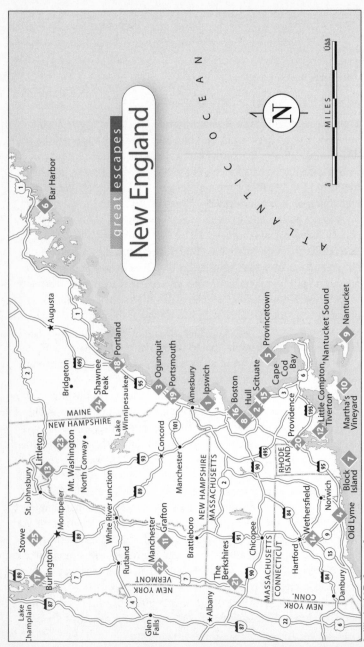

great escapes

New England

Paul Woodward, © The Countryman Press

CONTENTS

Part Five: Mountain Escapes

INTRODUCTION

There are a lot of features to love about New England; size is not one of them. We don't have the tallest ski mountains, the highest ocean waves, or vast prairie lands as far as the eye can see. What we do have are more charming towns, villages, beaches, and ski areas than we could cram into a book twice this size, many within an hour or two of Boston. Willing to venture a little farther? Vermont's appealing blend of rural charm and yuppie splendor, Maine's rocky coast and pictur-esque islands, and Connecticut's beachy state parks are chock-full of activities—both high adrenaline and low key—that can fill a few days, or even a few hours. And because nobody does the change of the sea-sons like we do, we've incorporated some tips to put you in the right place at the right time.

Foodies can follow their noses through the region, dining on every-thing from lobster roll sandwiches on toasted hot dog rolls and fried clams served with mounds of onion rings to quahog chowder and microbrews. Nor is dining out in Boston the uninspiring, staid affair it used to be. Big-name chefs are vying for the attention of trendy young residents and visitors alike, and good old-fashioned Yankee pot roast and Indian pudding have given way to fusion and ethnic fare as well as fresh interpretations of old regional favorites.

And as much as we love Beantown, Boston is the not the only game in town for visitors who like their adventures with an urban twist. Port-land, Maine; Portsmouth, New Hampshire; and Providence, Rhode Island are among the cities undergoing a renaissance from conserva-tive also-rans to hot destinations in their own right.

To help save you time as you navigate the beauties of this region—not to mention, steer you toward some out-of-way places most tourists haven't discovered yet—we have included 25 or so of our favorite escapes to point you in the right direction.

When planning your escape, be aware that prices of accommodations and restaurant meals in New England vary dramatically by season. A seaside hotel might triple its rates in summer, while prices at a mountain resort will likely spike during fall foliage season. Keep in mind, also, that even the priciest ski hotels will probably offer ski-and-stay packages that combine discounted rooms with lift tickets. Those deals are less likely to be available during school vacation weeks and holidays.

The price of fresh seafood—particularly lobster and clams—also rises and falls from year to year and season to season. In the summer of 2009, for example, lobster sold for a remarkably low $5 a pound retail, but we have seen it at more than twice that in previous years. Most restaurants use the term "Market Price" on their menus, with the understanding that diners will ask before ordering.

BEACH
ESCAPES

1 • CRANE'S BEACH, IPSWICH, AND ESSEX, MASSACHUSETTS

About 28 miles from Boston on the North Shore

Devotees of Boston's North Shore are justifiably proud of Crane's Beach in Ipswich, whose spectacular sand dunes and thriving flora and fauna give Cape Cod a run for its money.

The beach offers 4 miles of white sandy beach and an astonishing 1,000-plus acres of dunes and salt marshes. Because of the fragility of the dunes, conservation is crucial here, but that doesn't mean visitors can't explore the area to their hearts' content. Boardwalks and 7 miles of trails snake through the dunes, allowing walkers to immerse themselves in a variety of habitats. Keep an eye out for intriguing plants along the way, as well as birds including egrets, terns, and herons.

If your idea of a perfect day at the beach is more about snoozing and swimming, you can do that here, but plan to arrive early on good-weather days to avoid having to wait for a parking place. Unlike many Massachusetts beaches, nonresidents can park here for $22 a carload on weekends and holidays; $15 weekdays from Memorial Day to Labor Day. Pay half-price after 3 PM or bike or stroll in for $2 anytime.

Facilities include showers, picnic tables, lifeguards, a store, and facilities for visitors with physical challenges. Don't miss the annual Sand Blast sand castle building competition in August.

Visitors who want an eyepopping view of the beach without getting sand between their toes can opt to spend the day at **Castle Hill** at the Crane Estate (978-356-8540, www.craneestate.org), which has been part of the history of Ipswich since the mid-1600s. Various important families lived at the Brown Cottage on Castle Hill, but it was the construction of the Great House in the early 20th century by industrial magnate Richard Crane in 1910 that put the estate on the map. Originally built as a summer home for Crane's wife, the mansion on the hill was once an Italianate palazzo, but Crane tore it down and had it rebuilt as a 59-room English Stuart mansion to suit his wife's evolving tastes. Eventually the estate grew to a whopping 3,500 acres, including a sprinkling of islands in Essex Bay and 1,000 acres of beach and dunes, which have since been turned over to the local Trustees of Reservations.

The Great House, which dominates the hill, rivals the estates in Newport, Rhode Island, and contains murals, period furnishings, and faux marble woodwork in the bathrooms. If you don't have

Russell Farm, Ipswich

Estuary at Crane's Beach

time for a tour of the interior (the house is open seasonally for guided tours), the grounds alone are worth the price of admission. Check out the circular Rose Garden and the formal Italian Garden, which looks like a Roman Odeon containing ornamental flowers, matching teahouses, and a fountain. Other highlights include the Farm Complex with its preserved barns and stables; the log cabin site, which was once a family playhouse; and the half-mile Grand Allée that sweeps from the Great House toward the sea. The Castle Hill grounds are open daily from 8 AM to sunset with all sorts of special events that take place in summer, from concerts to a July 4th extravaganza.

Choate Island and Crane's Beach are notable not only for their scenic beauty but also for their more recent history as film locations. Several movies have been filmed there, including the 1968 version of *The Thomas Crown Affair* with Steve McQueen and Faye Dunaway, portions of *The Witches of Eastwick* with Jack Nicholson, and *The Crucible*, with Daniel Day-Lewis and Winona Ryder, about the Salem witch trials.

▋▋▋▋ GETTING THERE (AND GETTING AROUND)

From Boston, take Route 95 North to Route 1 North, then turn right onto Ipswich Road and follow the signs to the end of Argilla Road. You can also take the train to Ipswich from Boston's North Station and travel to the beach and local historic sites on the **Ipswich Essex Explorer Bus** (www.ipswich essexexplorer.com), which runs on weekends in summer.

Once there, unless you opt for the Explorer, you'll need a car to fully see the sights, and be prepared for traffic in high season.

▮▮▮▮ WHAT TO SEE

The town of Ipswich is known for having more "first period" houses—that is, homes that date from before 1725—than anywhere else in the country. Stop by the **Ipswich Visitors Center** (36 South Main St.; 978-356-8540) for an audio walking tour or just go on your own to visit two of the most famous antique houses, the **Whipple House Museum**, which dates from 1677, and the **Heard House Museum** from 1800, which boasts paintings by Arthur Wesley Dow. The houses, on the corner of Rtes 1A and 133 (www .ipswichmuseum.org) are open for tours Wednesdays through Sundays May through October.

Adjacent to the free Essex Marina parking lot, just a few miles from Ipswich along Route 133 East, stop at the **Essex Shipbuilding Museum** (66 Main St.; 978-768-7541; www.essexship buildingmuseum.org) for a look at maritime artifacts and interactive exhibitions that describe the town's once-thriving industry. A working shipyard, where visitors can watch wooden ships being made using the techniques used some 300 years ago, is adjacent to the museum.

About a block away from the marina is the **Essex First Congregational Church**, which boasts a bell crafted by Paul Revere in 1798. Locals insist the bell rings in a perfect C sharp.

Art lovers can spend an hour or two at **Cogswell's Grant** (60 Spring St., Essex; 978-768-3632), an 18th-century farmhouse that showcases a collection of American folk art assembled by Bertram and Nina Fletcher Little. The collection includes everything from painted furniture and hooked rugs to wooden decoys and naïve paintings.

▮▮▮▮ WHAT TO DO

Winter visitors can cross-country ski at **Appleton Farms** (219 County Road, Ipswich; 978-356-5728; www.appletonfarms.org) on paths that double as hiking and bridle paths in warm-weather months. There are also guided tours and orienteering classes available year-round.

Canoe or kayak to **Choate**

Crane Estate,
Ipswich

Island, once inhabited by hogs but now the home of deer, otter, coyote, and a dazzling variety of birdlife. The island is distinguishable from the other four in the estuary because of its thick forest of blue spruce trees, planted by Richard Crane to give the island more aesthetic appeal. There are miles of hiking trails on the island, or take a guided kayak tour offered by the **Massachusetts Audubon Society** (978-887-9264; www.massaudubon .org) or **Essex River Basin Adventures** (1 Main St., Essex; 978-768-3722; www.erba.com), which also operates moonlight tours to Crane's Beach.

Explore the salt marshes and estuary adjacent to Crane's Beach via an **Essex River Cruise** (800-748-3706, 978-768-6981; www .essexcruises.com). Cruises depart three times a day from the marina in **Essex**, and Sunday morning Coffee & Muffin and evening cocktail versions of the river cruises also are available. The one-and-a-half-hour narrated journey, which runs May through October, takes place on the *Essex River Queen II*, an enclosed riverboat with bench seating and a restroom onboard. The vessel is piloted by U.S. Coast Guard–certified guides who are part historians and part naturalists. Instead of corny jokes and inane patter, the captains bring the scenery in the estuary to life with anecdotes about the Crane family, the ecosystem of the islands and Crane's Beach, and the area's rich history. The captain will also help passengers spot the birds that make their homes among the salt marshes.

As compelling as the historical and natural attractions are in Essex, save time for a stroll through the more than 35 shops

Fried clams aren't the only seafood delicacy in Essex County. Lobster was once so common that it was used as bait to attract cod and haddock, and was served so often to local prisoners that they launched a formal rebellion to ban it from their diet. Nowadays, visitors can apply for the right to put in 10 pots to catch lobsters for their own personal consumption.

that either sell or restore antiques. Designed to appeal to serious antique buffs and casual shoppers alike, the stores offer mostly high-end furnishings and objets d'art, but some of them also buy quality items, should you have Aunty Em's rolltop desk in your trunk. Since many of the antique shops are within walking distance of each other, nab a parking place on Main Street and take in as many as you have time for. A good place to start is the **White Elephant Shop** (32 Main St.; 888-768-7355, 978-768-6901; www.whiteelephantshop.com), a warren of rooms clogged with paintings, china, furniture, and books. The shop also operates a half-price outlet a mile north on Rt. 133 open weekends and Monday holidays year-round.

▪▪▪▪ WHERE TO STAY

The Inn at Castle Hill (978-412-2555; www.theinnatcastlehill .com) at Crane Estate is the latest incarnation of the Brown Cottage, now transformed into a B&B and tavern with plenty of Old World charm. Run by the Trustees of Reservations, the property has 10 rooms, each individually decorated and many offering views of the dunes at Crane's Beach or the salt marshes. Each room has its own bathroom, but you won't find TVs or telephones. From $175.

The **Ipswich Inn** (2 East St., Ipswich; 978-356-2431; www .ipswichinn.com) in the restored 1863 Robert Jordan house, offers Victorian charm in the historic center of Ipswich. Innkeepers Ray and Margaret Morley serve drinks by the fireplace in the living room or on the deck and whip up breakfast specials like homemade pancakes and granola. The seven-room property is within easy strolling distance of the town's most historic sites. There are seven rooms in all, with no minimum stay required. From $120.

Kaede (16 N. Main St.; Ipswich; 978-356-8000; www.kaedebb .com), in the restored Coburn

Home overlooking the town center, is an intriguing mix of New England charm and Japanese aesthetics. The 10-room Federal-style B&B building dates from the mid-19th century, and the accommodations range from traditional guest rooms to a Japanese room with tatami mats. From $110.

The **Whittier Motel** (120 County Rd., Ipswich; 978-356-5205; www.whittiermotel.com) is a small, no-frills 20-room property with kitchenettes and an outdoor swimming pool. Open year-round, the motel serves breakfast and has a cocktail lounge. From $110.

■■■■ WHERE TO CAMP

Black Bear Campground (54 Main St., Salisbury; 978-462-3183; www.blackbearcamping.com) is about 20 miles north of Ipswich and features two swimming pools, fireplaces, and a playground. $35.

■■■■ EATING OUT

Woodman's of Essex (Main St., Essex; 800-649-1773; www.woodmans.com) is usually considered the winner of the friendly rivalry between Ipswich and Essex about who has the best fried clams. For one thing, the restaurant's first owner, Lawrence "Chubby" Woodman, invented the dish more than 90 years ago, and the walls are papered with accolades the eatery has won in the intervening years. The no-frills atmosphere is part of the charm, so be prepared to stand in line to order—fried clams and boiled lobster are hands-down favorites—and then wait for your number to be called. Dishes are served up in cardboard boxes, and portions—especially if you order the all the fixings, including fried onion rings—are enormous. Or stop by any night in summer when lobsters are being boiled out front for a take-out treat or dinner under a tent by the water. Woodman's also hosts clambakes and as many as 700 catered functions a year. Market rate.

The **Clam Box of Ipswich** (246 High St., Ipswich; 978-356-9707) is a worthy contender for the title, claiming that although they didn't invent the fried clam platter, the company's motto is: "we believe we have perfected it." The restaurant has been in operation since the late 1930s, garnering its share of kudos and accolades along the way. Market rate.

■■■■ SPECIAL EVENTS

Late April: There are almost too many noted authors who lived in and wrote about this region to mention, but they include Robert Frost, T. S. Eliot, Nathaniel Hawthorne, and Harriet Beecher

Stowe. Find out more at the **Newburyport Literary Festival** (www.newburyportliteraryfestival.org), just north of Ipswich, where you can hobnob with such contemporary writers as Anita Shreve, Richard Bausch, and Elinor Lipman.

Early June to October: Explore the 25-plus historic sites throughout Essex County on 17th Century Saturdays (www.northofboston.org), when homes and businesses in buildings dating from 1625 to 1725 are open to the public.

Mid-June to November: The **Strawberry Festival** in mid-June, the **Peach Festival** in mid-August, and the **Apples and Wine Festival** in mid-November are just a few of the reasons to visit **Russell Orchards Farm and Winery** (978-356-5366; www.RussellOrchardsMa.com), on the road from Castle Hill toward the Ipswich town center. Free events include hayrides, live music, and locally produced treats to sample, and you can also pick your own berries in season. Visitors can stroll the barnyard to see the animals, sample fresh cider doughnuts, or shop for organic produce, from maple syrup and honey to baked goods and local wines.

▪▪▪▪ NEARBY

The 190-year-old **Topsfield Fair** on Route 1 (978-887-5000, www.topsfieldfair.org) is the oldest continuously operating county fair in the country. The annual event takes place every October and offers a retro mix of cooking, needlework, and flower contests. There is plenty of livestock are on hand as well, from rabbits and chickens to draft horses and oxen, and yes, there is a giant pumpkin weigh-off to get you in the mood for the winter holidays.

In summer, venture farther up the coast to **Newburyport** for a whale-watch dinner cruise (54 Merrimac St., 800-848-1111, www.newburyportwhalewatch.com) on Thursday nights from 7 PM to 9:30 PM with a buffet, music, and a cash bar. Or take the Merrimack Valley Regional Transit Authority Bus #51 to get to Plum Island from Newburyport.

▪▪▪▪ RESOURCES

Ipswich Visitor Information Center, 36 South Main St.; 978-356-8540; www.ipswichma.com/directory/visitors.asp

North of Boston Convention and Visitors Bureau, 7 Peabody Square; 978-977-7760; www.northofboston.org

2 • NANTASKET BEACH, HULL, MASSACHUSETTS

About 20 miles south of Boston

Time-crunched visitors to Boston who crave a day at the beach won't spend half their time in transit if they abandon thoughts of the Cape, where the rush-hour traffic heading south begins midday on Fridays in summer, and instead set their sights on Nantasket Beach in Hull. Because Hull is a narrow peninsula, this beach town is blessed with water views in just about any direction. That said, the place to be is on the public beach, which is more than three miles long and where on any given sunny day you'll see just about every type of beachgoer, from toddlers in heavy, sand-filled diapers to teens hanging out and seniors enjoying a stroll along the boardwalk. Because of its proximity to Beantown, Hull has a more urban vibe than many of the state's other beach towns, which means it's not the place to come for preppy shops and designer ice cream. But if sandy feet, fresh seafood, and a dose of New England history are on your list, Nantasket won't disappoint.

The Nantasket Beach Reservation (617-727-5290), which comprises 26 acres in all including the beach, is officially open from dawn to dusk year-round, and there are lifeguards present from late June to early September. Best of all—and this is a rarity in New England—there is plenty of parking at the beach, although during high tide, the water often reaches the retaining wall. An exception to keep in mind when snagging your beach real estate for the day is the section in front of the Red Parrot restaurant,

Paragon Carousel

which typically stays dry even at high tide.

Locals love to talk about the rich history of Hull, and with good reason. The town played a role during the Revolutionary War, and it made a splash as an early tourism destination for Bostonians looking to escape the gritty city. In 1905 a beachfront amusement park called Paragon Park opened to much fanfare, and subsequent generations made the trek from the city every weekend to take in the heady mix of beach, roller coasters, bumper cars, and cotton candy. Over time, the park lost its luster and was torn down in the mid-1980s, but the beloved **Paragon Carousel** (205 Nantasket Avenue; www.paragoncarousel.com) still operates daily in summer, holding pride of place front and center on the boardwalk.

You'll see just as many adults as children climbing aboard for a ride on the carousel, which boasts an eyepopping 1926 Wurlitzer band organ and dozens of lovingly restored horses. If you look closely at the top of the carousel, you'll see a series of ornate paintings including one that depicts Charles Lindbergh and his wife in period costume. Locals are serious about the preservation of the carousel, so much so that when it was on the

brink of being sold off in the mid-1980s and again a decade later, investors stepped in for the save at the 11th hour. Fund-raising efforts are ongoing, and townsfolk breathed a collective sigh of relief when the carousel was recently guaranteed a preservation grant. Spring for a ride, then stop for ice cream at **The Creamery** next door or stroll the boardwalk for fried dough sprinkled with powdered sugar (a highly caloric local speciality that tastes a lot better than it sounds), take-out pizza, or fried clams.

The boardwalk also contains other remnants of the town's carnival past, including a video arcade and mini golf next to the carousel, mixed in with a few surprisingly high-end restaurants that rival some of Boston's finest.

The centerpiece of the boardwalk is the Pavilion, a replica of the original structure from the 1800s, on the waterfront directly across from the carousel. Summer night band concerts and group dancing lessons are reminiscent of the days when our grandparents swayed to the sounds of big band music, and some days you may even see a couple or two unselfconsciously practicing their dance moves to those retro sounds.

It is not surprising that a beach town as historic and scenic as Hull would attract dozens of artists. One of the town's best known is watercolorist Elizabeth Trubia (www.elizabethtrubia.com), whose depictions of Hull reflect what the town once was and how it looks today. Another is Karen Flanagan (www.karenflanagan.com), whose beach and lighthouse scenes evoke the long, uncomplicated days of summer.

Photographers also are attracted to Hull, with its mix of the scenic and funky, including Richard Glackemeyer (www.richard glackemeyer.com), whose starkly colored work makes an interesting contrast to the more typical pastel seascapes.

▮▮▮▮ GETTING THERE (AND GETTING AROUND)

From Boston, take route 93 South to Route 3 South to exit 14, then follow Route 228 into Hull. Or hop on the water shuttle for direct, scenic service into Hull on weekdays (617-222-3200; www.mass port.com). The new Greenbush commuter rail line (www.mbta .com) also serves Nantasket Junction from Boston's South Station terminal. Either way, you'll want to take a taxi to the beach, especially if you're laden with picnic baskets and other gear.

If you want to see Fort Revere Park or some of the other historical sections of the city, however, you might want to consider driving or renting a car. The good news is that there is plenty of public and on-street parking.

▮▮▮▮ WHAT TO SEE

Fort Revere Park (Telegraph Hill in Hull Village) is a few miles from the boardwalk and an ideal place for visitors with a car to picnic. Wander through the ruins of a fort where soldiers fought and died trying to repel the British navy during the Revolutionary War. On summer weekends, there are concerts and plays in the old bunker, which overlooks some of the best views of the Boston skyline.

The **Boston Lighthouse** (Little Brewster Island) is just a mile offshore. The oldest staffed lighthouse in the country, the structure is still inhabited, and public tours are available in summer. The fort is also a great place to watch the Parade of Tall Ships that visits Boston Harbor every few years.

While driving back to the boardwalk from the fort, visitors will see numerous historic houses sprinkled in among the beach houses that dot the landscape. Take a drive up Allerton Hill, where the Pilgrims came ashore in the 1600s and where you can get some of the best views of the harbor. The **Hull Public Library** (Main St.; 781-925-2295) was once the summer home of Irish poet John Boyle O'Reilly, and various members of the Kennedy family summered and had houses in town.

The first **Town Hall** (old Hull Village) is now an active fire station, but visitors who come in winter can strap on a pair of skates and practice their figure eights on the frozen-over town green in back.

Nantasket Beach has seen more than its share of shipwrecks over the centuries, so much so that many attribute the birth of the Coast Guard to the rescue efforts used here. **The Hull Lifesaving Museum** (1117 Nantasket Ave.; 781-925-5433; www.lifesavingmuseum.org) brings that seafaring history to life year-round with interactive exhibits, films, and ships' logs.

■■■■ **WHAT TO DO**

Outdoor buffs can rent a kayak on the bay side via **Nantasket Kayak Rentals** (781-962-4899; www.nantasketkayaks.com), which uses a floating dock to make launching the kayaks easy even for beginners. The company also offers kayak fishing—complete with all the requisite gear—and guided two-and-a-half-hour eco tours of the Weir River Estuary, which is teeming with birdlife and shellfish beds.

Three times a week, the **Hull Lifesaving Museum** offers open-water rowing at Windmill Point, and while it's okay to just show up, staffers prefer that you call ahead. First-timers are encouraged to come on Saturday mornings and bring waterproof footwear.

Shopping along Nantasket Beach is mostly about T-shirts and inexpensive souvenirs, but a somewhat incongruous hot spot

Nantasket Beach

View of Boston Lighthouse from Ft. Revere

is **Johnny Cupcakes** (17 D Nantasket Rd.; 781-925-0700; www.johnnycupcakes.com), a homegrown company that sells limited-edition clothing festooned with images of cupcakes and packaged in bakery boxes. The brainchild of John Earl, the concept caught fire when young celebs began wearing the clothing at international A-list hot spots and in the media. The products are so in demand that it's not unusual to see fans waiting in line to buy new designs at JC's other two shops on Boston's Newbury Street and on Melrose Avenue in Los Angeles. Or walk just beyond the boardwalk to **Simply Irresistible** (305 Nantasket Ave.; 781-925-5858; www.simplyirresistiblehull.com) for a selection of whimsical fare for everyone from babies to brides.

It stands to reason that any town with as much beach as Nantasket would draw kite flyers like a magnet, and **Sea Side Kites** (293 Nantasket Ave.; 781-925-3277; www.seasidekites.com) is a great place to pick up some gear and meet other enthusiasts.

▮▮▮▮ WHERE TO STAY

Josephine's on (45 Salisbury St.; 617-803-9152; www.josephinesbandb.com) is a B&B that only looks old. In fact, the new property is a loving re-creation of the proprietor's childhood summer home, complete with home-cooked breakfast. The innkeeper is Ann Marie Kenny, who named the property after her grandmother, and the guest rooms are named for her mother and sisters. Rates range from $110.

The **Clarion Nantasket Beach Hotel & Spa** (45 Hull Shore Dr.; 781-925-4500; www.nantasketbeachhotel.com) hosts the town's annual Sand Castle competition. The property features fireplaces in the guest rooms and a first-rate restaurant, Raffael's, right in the lobby. From $119.

▮▮▮▮ EATING OUT

Jakes (50 George Washington Blvd.; 781-925-1024; www.jakesseafoods.com) is a local favorite for fresh seafood. The restaurant, which serves lunch and dinner, doesn't accept reservations, but the food is worth the wait. Closed in winter, Jakes offers bare-bones ambience, friendly but casual service, and serious seafood, from clams and lobster to a truly exceptional raw bar. You can also buy seafood to go—lobster meat, of course, as well as everything from bluefish to mussels and swordfish. Lobster and clams at market price. Chowder from $4, sandwiches from $10.

The Ocean Club (42A State Park Rd.; 781-925-3030; www

.oceanclubdining.com) serves a
lobster salad or a juicy burger on
a sunny outdoor patio overlooking the beach or indoors by floor-
to-ceiling windows. From $12.99.

Bridgemans Restaurant (145
Nantasket Ave.; 781-925-6336;
www.bridgemansrestaurant.com)
has the most chic and trendy
atmosphere in Hull, so much so
that you'll think you are on
Boston's Newbury Street. Stop in
for upscale fare, including risotto, calamari, and lobster panini,
served with an extensive wine list.
Entrées from $14 at lunch to $18.75
at dinner; half plates are available.

Caffe Tosca (15 North St.; 781-
740-9400; www.eatwellinc.com),
a few miles down 3A in Hingham,
is a more casual version of the
award-winning Tosca restaurant
across the street. The menu is
upscale Italian and includes
wood-fired pizza, arrosticini of
shrimp and hanger steak. From $9
for lunch; $16 for dinner, with half
plates available.

■ ■ ■ ■ SPECIAL EVENTS

Memorial Day to Labor Day: During the annual **Studio at the
Beach** (217 Nantasket Ave.; www
.hullartists.com) celebrations, the
boardwalk becomes an extended
outdoor studio showcasing the
works of some 60 South Shore
artists as part of the Hull Artists
Studio Connection. Visitors can
meet the artists, buy their artwork—ranging from paintings to
furniture and jewelry—or simply
enjoy looking. Other art-themed
events in Hull include a Fine Art
Flower Show in spring, Artists
Open Studios Weekend Tours in
July and October, and the Winter
Arts Festival over Thanksgiving
weekend.

July 4: Many beach communi-
ties in New England go wild on
the Fourth, but Hull is one of the
most popular spots, given its size
and relative proximity to Boston,
so come early to stake out a good
spot and be prepared for some
spectacular fireworks.

Mid-September: Although the
**Hull Endless Summer Waterfront
Festival** moniker is an exercise in
wishful thinking, this popular
weekend event is a reason in
itself to visit the beach town in
early fall. Local restaurants and
vendors take to the streets to sell
their wares on Nantasket Avenue,
all to the accompaniment of live
music and bustling crowds.

A highlight of the weekend is
the sand castle competition,
when professionals give demonstrations divulging their creative
secrets and locals compete to see
who can make the best castle. The
real fun is when spectators get to
stomp the castles into oblivion at
the close of the event, beating
the waves to the punch.

▮▮▮▮ NEARBY

One of the area's most beautiful parks, romantically named **World's End**, is in nearby Hingham (250 Martin's Lane; www.the trustees.org). The beauty of the reservation is especially poignant considering how close it came to being developed—at one point it was being eyed as a location for a nuclear power plant. Accessible from Hull by car or via a guided kayak tour from Nantasket Beach, World's End boasts miles of tree-lined walking trails overlooking the harbor and the Boston skyline. There are guided tours and even a summer solstice event in June, or visitors can simply grab a trail map and head out for the day—or a few hours—on their own.

▮▮▮▮ LIT LIFE

Local historian John Galluzzo is the keeper of the flame when it comes to Nantasket lore. President of the Fort Revere Park & Preservation Society and Executive Director of the U.S. Life-Saving Service Heritage Association, Galluzzo has written several very entertaining books on the area, including *Hull and Nantasket Beach, Then & Now*. For an in-depth look at the good, the bad, and the ugly in Hull's history, check out his work at bookstores, online, or at Simply Irresistible.

▮▮▮▮ RESOURCES

The Hull Nantasket Beach Chamber of Commerce; 781-925-9980; www.hullchamber.com

Hull Town Hall; 253 Atlantic Ave.; 781-925-2000

3 • OGUNQUIT, MAINE

About an hour and a half north of Boston

Maine is famous—and not always in a good way—for its wild, rocky coastline. Yes, the rough coast can be breathtakingly beautiful, but if a day at the beach is more what you had in mind, not every Maine beach will fit the bill. With its 3.5-mile sandy beach, Ogunquit in southern Maine will give you that quintessential beach experience, as well as a dose of the scenic charm for which New England is famous. For the time-starved (to paraphrase the old joke) you *can* get there from here. In fact, you can reach Ogunquit, a Native American word that means "beautiful place by the sea," in only about an hour and a half from Boston, but once there, you are guaranteed to feel a world away.

Ogunquit is also known for its shops and restaurants, but don't miss the many galleries that showcase original works by the local artists who live and work in the area.

The downside, of course, is that other tourists have discovered Ogunquit's charms, which means that you will be jockeying for space in high season. The solution? Time your visit for the shoulder seasons in spring and fall. Sure, a few of the stores might not be open, but you'll get a better table at the local restaurants and a lot friendlier service.

The influx of tourism in Ogunquit is an integral part of this beach town's history. The Native Americans who first inhabited this region enjoyed initial friendly dealings with the early English settlers, but that goodwill evaporated as the two groups struggled for ascendancy. The land was eventually given to loyalist British settlers, and the area remained relatively remote to outsiders until a bridge across the Ogunquit River was constructed in the late 19th century. Travelers took one look at the white, sandy beach—so different from the dramatic rocky cliffs that characterize this part of the coast—and it wasn't long before tourism became a force to reckoned with.

Town officials began to worry about the preservation of the beach—which some businesspeople wanted to turn into an amusement park—and the concept of conservation took hold long before "green travel" became popular. Judging from the pristine look of the beach today, despite the hordes of visitors who come in summer, their efforts are paying off.

▮▮▮▮ GETTING THERE (AND GETTING AROUND)

From Boston, the quickest route is to drive north on I-95 in Maine to exit 7, but for a more scenic route, consider taking on Route 1 farther south at Kittery and following the coastal road the rest of the way.

As you exit onto Shore Road from Route 1, your first goal should be to park in one of the town-operated lots that dot the village and beach areas or, if you are lucky, on the street. Once safely parked, you can get around easily by foot or trolley, operated by the **Ogunquit Trolley Company** (www.ogunquit trolley.com).

▮▮▮▮ WHAT TO SEE

Although tiny, **Perkins Cove** is lined with art galleries, shops, and seafood restaurants. The real charm, however, is its fishing-village setting, where you can watch the fishermen haul in their pots, while bird lovers will be mesmerized by the sight of dozens of varieties of birds swooping around the quaint wooden drawbridge. The view from the bridge is compelling, and you won't be alone watching the yachts, fishing boats, and sightseeing vessels navigate the waters below.

If a day at the beach is your goal, head to **Ogunquit Beach**, accessible from Beach Street. Although popular, the beach is just as appealing for beachcombers on the lookout for the perfect shell as it is for sunbathers dozing with a book or watching their toddlers romp and build sand castles. Or go where the locals go—to the smaller **Footbridge Beach** a little farther north along Route 1. If you forgot your gear, pick up a rental beach

View from Perkins Cove bridge

Woods to Goods in nearby York sells goods made by inmates of Maine's prisons

Historians credit Boston Brahmin Charles Woodbury for turning Ogunquit into an art colony, and some of the tiny shacks that once held the area's first artists are still there, having been lovingly renovated into guesthouses and inns for vacationers. Since then, big-name artists, such as Walt Kuhn and Edward Hopper, have been drawn to the area, alongside newcomers inspired by the natural beauty and clear light. The **Ogunquit Museum of American Art** (543 Shore Rd.; 207-646-4909; www.ogunquitmuseum.org) was founded in the early 1950s and still features hundreds of works by American painters and sculptors. On Tuesday nights, the museum also hosts theatrical and musical events, films, and talks. The Barn Gallery (1 Bourne Lane; 207-646-8400; www.barngallery.org) is a nonprofit center that features free exhibits as well as talks and workshops offered by members of the art association. The gallery also runs the annual Art Auction in August as well as the yearly Chamber Music Festival in June.

Private galleries include the **Beth Ellis Cove Gallery** (Perkins Cove Rd.; 207-646-7700; www.bellisart.com), in a house that looks out over Marginal Way, for plein air paintings and the **Stone Crop Gallery** (805 Shore Road, York; 207-361-4215; www.stonecropgallery.com), created by founder Grace Merrill in the 1920s using reclaimed materials from nearby barns and dilapidated houses and now housing the works of present-day owner and photographer Dana Berenson.

chair, umbrella, or boogie board at **Ogunquit Beach 'n Sport** (207-351-7840; www.ogtbeachn sport.com).

History buffs can take a break from the sun at the **Ogunquit Heritage Museum** (86 Obeds Lane; 207-646-0296; www .ogunquitheritagemuseum.org), a preserved 18th-century Cape dwelling that was originally the home of Captain James Winn. Today's visitors can learn about

the maritime history of the harbor area as well as the architecture of which the museum is a classic example.

Theater is big in Ogunquit, thanks to **Ogunquit Playhouse** (Rte. 1 S; 207-646-5511; www .ogunquitplayhouse.org), which has been in operation in various incarnations since the 1930s, performing big-name musicals in one of the most respected summer theater groups in the country. Shows tend to sell out, but tickets are available online as well as at the box office. You can also check out the **Booth Theater** (13 Beach St.; 207-646-8142; www.boothproductions.com) for summer repertory theater and community productions at the Betty Doon Motor Hotel, where you don't have to be a guest to enjoy the show.

▪▪▪▪ WHAT TO DO

Go **hiking** along **Marginal Way**, a 100-year-old, mile-and-a-half-long footpath that starts in Perkins Cove and wends its way along the cliffs that overlook the sea. This is an easy walk, and there are benches along the way where the footsore can rest and simply enjoy the view. Marginal Way is under conservation, with an eye to keeping it safe not only from the ravages of storms but also from the effects of the thousands of travelers who walk the path every year.

Climb aboard **Silverlining Sailing Cruises** (Perkins Cove; 207-646-9800; www.silverlining sailing.com), which operates short excursions on a 42-foot sloop, designed to appeal to novices and experts alike. There are cruises that set sail in the calm morning and late afternoon waters, as well as two two-hour outings for experienced sailors

who want the thrill of more challenging conditions, not to mention the best likelihood of a suntan. The last sail of the day at sunset is an opportunity to soak in the scenery before heading out in search of that perfect evening meal.

For a more active on-water experience, rent a kayak or join a guided kayak tour via **Excursions Sea Kayaking** (1740 US Rte 1, Cape Neddick; 207-363-0181; www.excursionsinmaine.com). The company, which provides instruction for novices, offers half-day tours as well as overnights for adventurers with fewer time constraints. The morning half-day program is a leisurely exploration of the coastline, beaches, and scenic lighthouses, while the multiday tours explore Casco Bay and include campfire dinners prepared by the guides, as well as all the necessary equipment. If time is short, try a two-hour tour via **World Within Sea Kayaking** (Ogunquit River Plantation, Rte. 1, Moody; 207-646-0455; www.worldwithin .com/tours.html).

If the scenic views have put you in a relaxed frame of mind, enjoy your yoga practice or try a spa treatment at **Sacred Movement: A Sanctuary for Yoga & Healing** (414 Main St.; 207-409-4216) or try Your Body Works Massage & Day Spa (24 Shore Road; 207-646-1322) for a respite from everyday cares.

Diehard golfers don't wait until summer to play the links at **Cape Neddick Country Club** (650 Shore Rd.; 207-361-2011; www .capeneddickgolf.com), where nonmembers are welcome, space permitting, but proper golf attire is required.

▌▌▌▌ WHERE TO STAY

The Grand Hotel (276 Shore Rd.; 207-646-1231, 800-806-1231; www.thegrandhotel.com) is a good choice if you want a two-room suite and a heated indoor pool, all within easy walking distance of the beach. From $69.

Meadowmere Resort (74 Main St.; 207-646-9661, 800-633-8718; www.meadowmere.com) offers summer getaway specials and inventive off-season packages, like the Maine Maple Weekend in March to experience the maple sugaring process firsthand. The property is a 10- to 15-minute

walk from the beach. From $65.

16 Beach Street (207-221-5329; www.16beachstreet.com) is a B&B in the town center, surrounded by shopping and restaurant venues and within a few minutes' walk from the beach and Marginal Way. From $110.

▌▌▌▌ WHERE TO CAMP

Beach Acres Campground (Rte. 1, Wells; 207-646-5612; www .beachacres.com) offers camp-sites less than a mile from the beach, as well as an on-site swimming pool and fireplaces, and you can reserve ahead online. $38 for a tent site.

▌▌▌▌ EATING OUT

Five-O Shore Road (50 Shore Rd.; 207-361-1100; www.five-oshore road.com) is frankly upscale, but the Mediterranean-inspired menu, which changes with the season, offers plenty of grilled entrées, plus a more casual lounge menu, all washed down with a variety of wines. Prix fixe

Marginal Way

If you like your New England towns a little funkier than Kennebunk or Ogunquit, take the short drive south on Route 1 to **York**, where you will find dozens of antique stores lining both sides of the street. As you continue along Route 1, you will come to **Woods to Goods** (www.woodstogoods.com), a quirky store that offers a selection of furniture, toys, and home decor items crafted by inmates of Maine's prisons. Farther down, **When Pigs Fly** (www.sendbread.com) sells loaves of artisanal bread, while **Stonewall Kitchen** (www.stonewall kitchen.com) offers a café and a huge assortment of kitchen gadgets, dipping sauces, and other goodies. York also has a sandy beach, a zoo/amusement park called **York's Wild Kingdom** (www .yorkzoo.com), and a stellar fried-clam shack with an unprepossessing exterior called **York's Best Seafood & Roast Beef** (Rte. 1; 207-439-3401), which serves Bailey's whole-belly clams from the mouth of the Scarborough River.

menus starting at $29.50; entrées from $23.

Arrows Restaurant (Berwick Rd.; www.arrowsrestaurant.com) offers a decadent tasting menu—parsnip crème brûlée, anyone?—that has received nods from *Gourmet* and *Bon Appetit* magazines. Three-course prix fixe dinner for $39.95; entrées from $41.

Barnacle Billy's (Perkins Cove; 207-646-5575, 800-866-5575; www.barnbilly.com) is a local favorite for lobster roll sandwiches. Market price.

Jackie's Too (Perkins Cove; 207-646-4444; www.jackiestoo .com) is another strong contender. You may have to make up your own mind to decide the winner. Market price.

Village Food Market (230 Main St.) is the place to go to grab a hunk of cheese and a bottle of your favorite wine for a low-key picnic at sunset.

■■■■ **SPECIAL EVENTS**

August: Summer visitors can also take in the **Annual Sidewalk Art Show and Sale** (207-646-2939), which takes over Ogunquit with the works of some 75 painters, sculptors, and photographers lining town streets and parking lots.

Late October: In the fall, locals don costumes and get out the pumpkins and horse-drawn wagons for a weekend festival called the **OgunquitFest**, which includes ghost tours, a scarecrow contest, and bonfires on the beach.

December: The annual **Christmas by the Sea Celebration** offers concerts, chowder competitions, and, of course, a visit from Santa.

February: And while we won't pretend that beach destinations have the same appeal in winter as in the warmer months, Ogunquit is not one of those beach towns that close up completely during the off-season. In fact, locals go all out with an annual **Mardi Gras** celebration, during which local restaurants chime in with celebratory menus, hat-making demonstrations, and a parade to crown a new king and queen every year.

▮▮▮▮ NEARBY

In the pretty-towns-of-Maine sweepstakes, **Kennebunkport** can give Ogunquit a run for its money. Fortunately, the two towns are so close together that you can easily combine them if you have a little extra time. A well-established summer resort for generations, Kennebunkport gained even greater notoriety as the vacation home of President George H. W. Bush and clan. The area has beautiful beaches and ample opportunity for boating, but there also are a number of festivals that lure visitors year-round. Food lovers should make note of the **Annual Arts in the Inns Festival** in June, described as "a pairing of palates and palettes," during which guest chefs and vintners offer a round of dinners and tastings that foodies can attend for a fee and by reserving ahead of time online.

While there, train buffs can check out the **Seashore Trolley Museum** (195 Log Cabin Rd.; 207-967-2712; www.trolleymuseum .org) with more than 250 trolleys and other transit vehicles from the United States and around the world. If you are looking to spend the night in Kennebunk, The **White Barn Inn** is a Relais & Chateaux property with an atmospheric main house and annex, as well as waterfront cottages for even more privacy. Save room for dinner, as the Inn boasts a selection of tasting menus served in the ultraromantic barn for which the property was named.

▮▮▮▮ RESOURCES

Ogunquit Chamber of Commerce, 36 Main St., Ogunquit; 207-646-2939; www.ogunquit.org

4 • OLD LYME, CONNECTICUT

On Long Island Sound and the Connecticut River, about 100 miles from New York and Boston

When it comes to New England beaches, Connecticut sometimes gets short shrift. But while the state's beaches may not be the first thing you think of, travelers dipping into New England from the south are missing out if they don't put Old Lyme on their radar.

Depending on what kind of day you have on your wish list—sand between your toes or bustling boardwalk—Old Lyme has several beaches to tempt you. In fact, the village of around 8,000 residents—not counting the summer crowd—boasts nearly 30 miles of coastline.

There are several beaches from which to choose, including two on Long Island Sound—**Sound View Beach** (Hartford & Swan Aves.), in town, and a long, pristine portion of **White Sand Beach**. Which one you choose will have something to do with how you plan to get there. You can park your car at the town lot or at one of several private lots for $10 per car on weekdays and $20 on weekends to access Sound View Beach, or you can catch a ride,

bike, or walk to White Sand Beach, which has sticker-only parking. You can also try for on-street parking, which is allowed in some areas, so just look for signs.

The beaches also have very different personalities, with Sound View being the best choice for music, drinks, and a boisterous atmosphere. There are cafés, restaurants, and even a vintage carousel, and don't be surprised if you see people arriving on motorcycles for a day in the sun.

Old Lyme Inn

White Sand draws families and locals looking for a more serene beach experience. Lifeguards staff the beach, and the sand stretches for miles in either direction. Or drive a few minutes down I-95 to East Lyme to **Rocky Neck State Park**, which boasts beautiful white sand beaches, walking trails, and picnic areas.

Like many of New England's seacoast towns, Old Lyme has its roots in the seafaring trade, thanks to its location at the junction of the Long Island Sound and the Connecticut River. In subsequent years, however, the town became known as an artists' colony, and some of the most famous masters of the American Impressionist school had their summer homes here. That legacy continues to this day, with a thriving art scene and enough galleries to keep a visitor busy for days.

The town itself is a charming mix of Federal and Colonial buildings, but a sprinkling of seafood shacks, working farms, and ocean drives keeps the scenery varied and interesting.

■■■■ GETTING THERE (AND GETTING AROUND)

Old Lyme is about 100 miles from Boston and New York off I-95 to Route 1.

The closest airport is Bradley International Airport, or you can take the train to Old Saybrook or New London (www.amtrak.com).

Once there, you can get walk around the town center on foot, but you will want a car to visit the farms and beaches. You can also get around by bicycle, but keep a wary eye on the traffic.

■■■■ WHAT TO SEE

The Florence Griswold Museum, (96 Lyme St.; 860-434-5542; www.florencegriswoldmuseum.org) is the centerpiece of the art scene in Old Lyme, partly because of its collections and pastoral setting and partly because of its unique history. Miss Florence, as she was known in the early 20th century, was the impoverished adult daughter of a sea captain who opened her beautiful family home to artists. Charmed by the rural setting, noted American Impressionists including Childe Hassam and Henry Ward Ranger became regulars, and soon a vibrant art colony was born. You can tour the house, which is chock-full of paintings and period furniture, and check out the adjacent Krieble Gallery, which houses rotating collections. The grounds, which adjoin the Lieutenant River, are breathtaking and still serve to inspire plein air painters and sculptors. If nature walks are more your thing, the museum leads guided tours of

While shopping in Old Lyme, you may come across baseball hats and T-shirts depicting a deer tick crossed out and sayings, such as "Ticked Off" and "Ticks Suck," emblazoned on them. Lyme disease is named for the towns of Lyme and Old Lyme, but deer ticks are prevalent in many parts of New England. Check out www.lymediseaseassociation.org for information on simple precautions you can take when out and about and on symptoms to be aware of, should you get bitten.

nearby preserves and farms and also offers painting sessions for kids and talks on landscaping and flower arranging for grown-ups.

The **Lyme Art Association** (90 Lyme St.; www.lymeartassociation.org) was founded by the early Lyme Colony artists and still mounts exhibitions featuring new and more established artists, including a core group of local painters. There are also classes and workshops in a wide range of mediums, and the association is in a beautiful, historic building.

One of the best-known galleries in town is **The Cooley Gallery** (25 Lyme St.; www.cooleygallery.com), which focuses on American paintings from the 19th century to the present, showcased in a restored carriage house. You can preview the gallery's inventory on its Web site, and the staff offers appraisal services.

You don't have to enter a gallery or museum to enjoy art in Old Lyme, however; take a stroll along Lyme Street to the **Gilbert Boro** gallery (80—1 Lyme St.). The artist displays his oversized, eye-catching works in his studio and in a sculpture garden that is open to the public.

In the Old Lyme Marketplace, go shopping at **The Bowerbird** (Halls Rd.), a store that prides itself on having something for everyone, from gourmet food items to fair trade accessories and inventive toys for the kids.

▮▮▮▮ WHAT TO DO

Drive along Route 156 to **Ferry Landing Park** at the end of Ferry Road at the mouth of the Connecticut River. Comprised of tidal wetlands, the park is the site of the Department of Environmental Protection, and there are tidal wetland conservation programs in progress here. There is plenty of free parking here, and you can stroll along the boardwalk overlooking the water or relax at one of the on-site benches or picnic tables.

Go **kayaking** on the Lieutenant River State Boat Ramp (Rte. 156 Bridge St.), which offers free parking in a tiny lot, free access to the river, and areas for fishing. You can also kayak at Rogers Lake (Grassy Hill Rd.), which has its own waterfront park and is stocked with rainbow trout. Or try a guided kayak tour with **CT Coastal Kayaking** (www.ctcoastal kayaking.com), which also has a fleet of rental kayaks.

Spend an afternoon at **McCulloch Farm Whippoorwill Morgans** (100 Whippoorwill Rd.; 860-434-7355, www.whippoorwill morgans.com), where owner Mary Jean Vasiloff allows visitors to hike for free through her scenic acreage and relax in the sun by her private lake. Call first and feel free to bring the kids—under supervision—and if they are not too busy, staff will show visitors around the Morgan horse barn and grounds.

For a completely different farm experience, take a drive to **Sankow's Beaver Brook Farm** (139 Beaver Brook Rd.; 860-434-2843, www.beaverbrookfarm .com), where you can visit the farm animals, buy artisanal cheeses and handcrafted woolens, and bring home takeaway meals of lamb curry stew

and white bean chili. You don't need to call ahead, and owner Suzanne Sankow is friendly to guests, although, because this is a working farm—rather than a petting zoo—animals are behind electric fences.

Follow the **Ice Cream Trail**, which runs through Mystic County. Two stops in Old Lyme are the **Hall Mark's Drive In** (see Eating Out) and the **Old Lyme Ice Cream Shoppe**, one of the area's best places to get homemade ice cream.

Strap on your hiking boots for an excursion along the **Deborah and Edward Ames Preserve** (103 Whippoorwill Rd.) for a 45-minute trek through woods and along a bog. Or explore the **Bartholomew Preserve** (Buttonball Rd.), on an easy trail that takes less than a half hour.

■ ■ ■ ■ WHERE TO STAY

Old Lyme Inn (85 Lyme St.; 860-434-2600; www.oldlymeinn.com) is across the street from the Florence Griswold Museum in the town center. Innkeepers Candy and Keith Green greet and interact with guests, and the furniture in the 13-room property is ultra-romantic, with period antiques and canopy beds. The Inn serves a complimentary continental breakfast and is pet friendly, but the real draw is the Friday night concert series on the outdoor terrace. Have dinner under the stars and listen to live music, which can range from jazz to American standards. From $135.

The Bee and Thistle Inn (100 Lyme St.; 860-434-1667) has only nine guest rooms, each tricked out with an upscale feel and run by innkeepers Linnea and David Rufo. The property has a spa with such treatments as Gentlemen's Indulgence and Layered Luxury, and a restaurant that has received nods for its romantic ambience. Reserve ahead for a prix fixe dinner Wednesdays through Saturdays or pop into the new martini bar in the Garden Porch Lounge. From $174.

▮▮▮▮ WHERE TO CAMP

Rocky Neck State Park is about ten minutes away in Niantic off I-95N on Long Island Sound. From $15.

▮▮▮▮ EATING OUT

Hall Mark's Drive In (113 Shore Rd.; 860-434-1998) serves up homemade ice cream, and the fried clams and lobster rolls are among the best around. Be prepared to wait in line for takeout, which you can eat inside with air-conditioning or at picnic tables around back within squinting view of the Long Island Sound. Sandwiches from $4.50; seafood market price.

Boom Restaurant (90 Halls Rd.) in the Old Lyme Marketplace is so popular among foodies that reservations are recommended. Try the Ahi tuna tartare or the sweet potato and walnut ravioli, but leave room for one of their award-winning desserts. Lunch from $5.50; $12.50 for dinner.

Lenny's on the Beach (88 Hartford Ave.; 860-598-4484) lives up to its name; this restaurant and bar is directly on Sound View Beach, with indoor and outdoor seating, loud music, and a menu full of burgers, beer-battered shrimp, and hot wings (priced at $.25 on rainy days.) From $3.50.

Cherrystones Restaurant (218

Farm in Old Lyme

White Sand Beach

Shore Rd.; 860-434-5686) has a raw bar with oysters, shrimp, and, of course, cherrystones, as well as sandwiches, tavern fare, and seafood and steak dinners. From $7.95 in the tavern; $17.95 for dinner entrées.

■■■■ SPECIAL EVENTS

Late May: The Old Lyme **Antique Car Show and Flea Market** (84 Lyme St.) at the Lyme Art Academy includes a Memorial Day Parade, complete with 25 of the top vintage cars.

Late June: Old Lyme's **Midsummer Arts Festival** at venues around town features concerts, informal buffet dinners, and art shows. There is even a dog show—winners and losers alike are rewarded just for showing up.

Mid-August: The **Hamburg Fair** (Rte. 156) at the Grange Fairgrounds is a fun, honky-tonk mixture of pony rides, craft booths, live music, and food concessions. There are clowns for the kids and Wild West reenactments and blacksmith demonstrations, as well as an ox pull and face painting for the kids.

■■■■ NEARBY

Old Lyme is in a cluster of charming villages, including Old Saybrook, Mystic, and Essex. Climb aboard the **Essex Clipper Dinner Train** (1 Railroad Ave.; 800-377-3987) for a four-course meal as you steam your way through the Connecticut River Valley. The train operates year-round, which makes it a great choice for leaf-peeping in the fall or seeing Santa and Mrs. Claus in winter. You can also try a train and river-boat combination ride. **Foxwoods** casino (39 Norwich-Westerly Rd., Ledyard) is more than a place to gamble. There are big-name entertainers, dining venues, a spa, and a golf course, all about 40 minutes from Old Lyme. The resort complex is owned by the Mashantucket Pequot Tribal Nation and offers three on-site hotels, including the MGM Grand.

■■■■ RESOURCES

Old Lyme Memorial Town Hall, 52 Lyme St.; 860-434-1605

5 • PROVINCETOWN, CAPE COD, MASSACHUSETTS

About 125 miles south of Boston, sandwiched between the Atlantic Ocean and Cape Cod Bay

If you are looking for a tranquil getaway, far from the traffic and zaniness of the summer tourist season, keep looking. In high season, Provincetown on the lower tip of Cape Cod is—not to put too fine a point on it—a zoo. Yes, the town is historic and, yes, it is charming—but tranquil, it's not. The population of about 3,000 swells to 50,000 or 60,000 in summer, and many of them congregate on Commercial St. Picture tourists and locals strolling busy streets as cyclists thread their way through the foot traffic and cars inch along beside you, and you get the idea.

All that said, Provincetown is well worth the hassle, particularly for travelers looking for a respite from the chain stores, franchise hotels, and routine ambience that increasingly characterizes much of our lives. There are some 25 miles or so of gorgeous beaches here, etched by wild dunes covered with acres of rosebushes, scrub oak, and tall grasses. The beaches form part of the **Cape Cod National Seashore,** which

was created in the early 1960s to preserve the fragile shoreline.

P-Town is also one of the country's top gay- and lesbian-friendly destinations for visitors as well as residents, and many of the area's businesses, including hotels and restaurants, are run by gay couples. This is a great family destination, with numerous activities on tap for children, and pets are not only welcome but also seem to be everywhere.

The offbeat identity P-Town enjoys today owes a debt to the artists, photographers, writers, and theater folk who began populating the area a century ago. In fact, this former fishing village bills itself as the oldest continuous art colony in the United States thanks to the half-dozen or so art schools that flourished here in the 1920s. The tiny, unadorned shacks sprinkled among the dunes—originally used by early versions of lifeguards—attracted the attention of artists and writers. Inspired by the surreal beauty of the dunes, many set up shop in the shacks and began cranking out some of their best works.

Authors Eugene O'Neill and Jack Kerouac, artists Mark Rothko and Willem de Kooning, and poet e.e. cummings are among the famous names who roughed it in the shacks over the years, braving the lack of running water and heat in the name of their art. Seventeen of the shacks are still in use today, and a few of those are rented out by the week to those seeking their inner muse.

▪▪▪▪ GETTING THERE (AND GETTING AROUND)

Provincetown is about a three-hour drive from Boston, but be aware that southbound traffic on Fridays and northbound on Sundays can be brutal. Take Route 93 South to Route 3 South to Route 6, then cross the Sagamore Bridge, which spans the Cape Cod Canal. The recent construction of the Sagamore Flyover, which replaced a confusing and cumbersome roundabout, has smoothed out the entrance to the Sagamore Bridge but didn't completely eliminate the bottleneck. The best advice is to avoid peak driving periods or, if that isn't possible, bring along an audiobook and give yourself extra time.

You can also hop on a high-speed ferry (200 Seaport Blvd., Boston; 877-783-3779; www.ma

fastferry.com) May through October or make the journey in 90 minutes via Boston Harbor Cruises (1 Long Wharf, Boston; www.bostonharborcruises.com). You can also fly from Boston on Cape Air (800-352-0714; www.flycapeair.com) in under a half hour.

If you drive, park in the first available lot you come to after exiting the highway, for unless your B&B has parking, you won't

Dune Shack

Portuguese Bakery P-Town

find any on Commercial Street. Walk or bike everywhere or flag down the town shuttle to get from beach to town.

■■■■ WHAT TO SEE

Explore the dunes and get within eyeball distance of the lonely shacks in a 4x4 via **Art's Dune Tours** (4 Standish St.; 800-894-1951, 508-487-1950; www.arts dunetours.com). Four to eight people at a time pile into enclosed vehicles and set out from the busy downtown to Race Point Beach, climbing up and down the sand dunes for an up-close-and-personal view of the eerie landscape. Friendly drivers are founts of knowledge about the shacks, local history, and the vegetation that holds the dunes together. You can take one of the scheduled hourly tours or go all out for a clambake dune tour or a sunset tour, the latter of which you will want to book ahead. You can even plan a wedding or commitment ceremony on the dunes, and the company will help you arrange the details.

Catch a panoramic view from the 255-foot-high observation deck of the **Pilgrim Monument** (1 High Pole Hill Rd.), which commemorates the "First Landing" of the Mayflower pilgrims in 1620 before they continued on to Plymouth. If the 116 steps to the top of the monument are too daunting, check out the museum at the ground floor.

If you have always wanted to see the view of the Cape from a lighthouse—there are more than a dozen lighthouses off Cape Cod—you can arrange an overnight at the lighthouse keeper's house at **Race Point Lighthouse** (508-487-9930; www.racepointlight house.net), but be aware that you will be bringing your own sheets, food, and libations. That said, the swimming and secluded nature walks along the beach are a highlight of the experience.

Provincetown's history as a thriving arts community lives on in its numerous galleries, as well as through the **Provincetown Art Association & Museum** (460 Commercial St.; 508-487-1750; www.paam.org), which hosts exhibitions, special events, and classes for would-be artists and spectators alike.

There also is a robust theater scene at the **Provincetown Theater** (238 Bradford St.; 508-487-9793, www.provincetown theater.com), where the New Provincetown Players continue the tradition set by founding members Eugene O'Neill and Tennessee Williams.

Or explore the spookier side of P-Town via **Provincetown Ghost Tours** (315 Commercial St.; 508-

487-4810; www.provincetown
ghosttours.com), where you can
choose between a creepy night
tour of the town or a guided
morning walk through the
cemeteries.

If you don't mind playing the
cheerful tourist, you can see the
sights, avoid getting run over,
and save your tired feet aboard a
40-minute **Provincetown Trolley
Tour** (37C Court St.; 508-487-
9483; www.provincetowntrolley
.com), which will take you along
Commercial Street, through part
of the National Seashore Park,
and through some of the most
historic neighborhoods where sea
captains once lived and plied
their trade, and where a few of
their houses still stand.

▪▪▪▪ WHAT TO DO

Bicycling is hugely popular in
Provincetown, and one look at
the limited parking in town
shows you why. Bring your own
bikes or rent one in town at one
of the many local outfitters, but
be aware that pedestrians have
the right of way here. Try **Ptown
Bikes** (42 Bradford St.; 508-487-
8735; www.ptownbikes.com) or
Gale Force Bikes (144 Bradford St.
Extension; 508-487-4849; www
.galeforcebikes.com), which sits
at the other end of town, just
steps from the bicycle trails at the
Cape Cod National Seashore.

Equipment ranges from comfortable touring bikes for visitors
who just want to putter around
the town, to off-road bikes and
even beach cruisers for visitors
with strong thigh muscles who
want to test their strength
against the 8 miles or so of paved
bike trails among the steep
dunes.

Pick up a self-guided map at
the entrance of **Beech Forest
Trail**, which wends through an
area teeming with birdlife. Or
stop by **Province Lands Visitor's
Center** for maps of the Pilgrim
Spring Trail, where you can follow
in the footsteps of early settlers.

For the ultimate in aerial views
of the beaches of Provincetown,
try a photo flightseeing tour at
Race Point Aviation (Provincetown Municipal Airport; 508-873-
2342; www.racepointaviation
.com). The flight for one to three
passengers makes the trip over
Cape Cod Bay in about 20 minutes, with a longer flight from
Provincetown to Chatham in
about an hour.

Book a whale-watch outing
through **Dolphin Fleet Whale
Watch of Provincetown** (307
Commercial St.; 508-240-3636;
www.whalewatch.com) and
explore the Cape Cod National
Seashore from the water. Cruises
are led by naturalists who not
only point out marine life and

other points of interest during the excursion but also fill passengers in on local conservation efforts and whale behaviors. The guides know where the whales are to be found, but passengers on a cruise that doesn't find one—an unlikely event—receive free tickets for another cruise.

Pick up a permit and drive onto **Race Point Beach,** one of two local beaches with lifeguards. You won't see too many surfers here (head to Eastham for that), but the scene is relatively serene and the dunes are spectacular. Or head to **Herring Cove Beach,** where nude sunbathing is not exactly sanctioned but not unheard of.

■ ■ ■ ■ WHERE TO STAY

The White Porch Inn (7 Johnson St.; 508-364-2549; www.white porchinn.com) opened in 2007. The property has only nine rooms and features a mix of contemporary decor along with such traditional elements as a carriage house and, as the name implies, a large front porch overlooking the Bay. All guest rooms have flat-screen TVs with DVD players, iPod docking stations, and Wi-Fi. Some have fireplaces, Jacuzzis and views of the Pilgrim Monument, the water, or the town. From about $165.

The **Carriage House** (Central

P-Town bikes

St.; 800-309-0248; www.the carriagehse.com) near the town center offers cozy, elegant guest rooms, and a hot tub and sauna, with flowers and champagne available for preorder. From about $125.

The Brass Key (67 Bradford St.; 800-309-0248; www.brasskey .com) is known for its restored period buildings organized around an infinity pool and terrace, as well as its location just off the main drag. From $120.

The Provincetown Inn (1 Commercial St.; 508-487-9500; www .provincetowninn.com) is a 100-room property surrounded on three sides by water. The rooms are standard with no frills, but the location is relatively serene—away from the crowds but within walking distance of the town center—and the property has its own private beach. The inn also provides a full-sized swimming pool, grills for outdoor cooking, and free parking. Rates include continental breakfast. From $69.

■■■■ WHERE TO CAMP

Dunes' Edge (Rte. 6; 508-487-9815; www.dunes-edge.com) campgrounds features 85 tent sites and 15 spaces for trailers. Open May through September, the campgrounds border the Cape Cod National Seashore and are within hiking and cycling distance of the beaches and town. From $40.

Horton's Camping Resort (71 South Highland Rd., N. Truro; 800-252-7705; http://hortons campingresort.com) nearby is a 40-acre campground in the middle of the Cape Cod National Seashore. Facilities include a store, Laundromat, and playground, as well as shuttle bus service to P-Town. From $32.

■■■■ EATING OUT

The Lobster Pot (321 Commercial St.; 508-487-0842; www.ptown lobsterpot.com) draws crowds, partly because of its location front and center in the heart of downtown and partly because of its cute if somewhat kitschy exterior. If you are craving steamed littleneck clams, sautéed squid, a boiled lobster plate, or fried clams with a side of fried onions, you won't be disappointed in the selections here, and you can look out over the water while you dine. From $16; market price for lobsters and clams.

The Mews Restaurant & Café (429 Commercial St.; 508-487-1500; www.mews.com) Overlooking the water, the Mews presents upscale ambience and menu items and is open year-round for dinner and Sunday brunch. Selections include raw oysters, sake miso salmon with baby bok choy and white chocolate crème brulee. Or opt for more casual fare, such as an Angus beef burger or a falafel in pita at the Café. From $16 at the restaurant; $11 at the Café.

Cafe Heaven (199 Commercial St.; 508-487-9639) serves all three meals, but most people like to tuck into the Eggs Benedict or fluffy pancakes at breakfast. From about $8.

Enzo (186 Commercial St.; 508-487-7555) serves brunch, lunch, and dinner. The menu veers toward Italian cuisine and seafood, including a raw bar, and other inducements include live music, skits, and even singalongs in the downstairs Grotto bar; views of the water; and free parking. Entrées from $16.

JD's Wood Fired Pizza (258 Commercial St.; 508-487-7776) isn't on the water side, but the outdoor second-story terrace overlooks the bustle of the main street as well as the Town Hall. Salads are served family-style, pizzas come in interesting varieties—such as Frutti de Mare topped with lobster, shrimp, and calamari and Quattro Stagione with eggplant, artichoke, prosciutto, and mushrooms. From about $10.

The Box Lunch (353 Commercial St.; 508-487-6026; www.box lunch.com, as well as other Cape locations) prepares takeaway meals, including lobster sandwiches and guacamole salads, in beach-ready packages that are easy to transport by bike. From $6.99 for a kid's sized lobster sandwich; made-to-order breakfasts from $4.25.

▮▮▮▮ SPECIAL EVENTS

Late June: One of the liveliest events in Provincetown is the annual **Portuguese Festival** (508-487-0500; www.province townportuguesefestival.com), which honors the Portuguese fishermen who were among the area's earliest settlers. The event includes big band concerts, art exhibitions, soup tastings, and the traditional Blessing of the Fleet.

Mid-August: The annual **Carnival Festival** (508-487-0500) celebrates the inclusivity for which P-Town is famous. Expect a wild scene, with King and Queen competitions, parade floats, and musical performances.

Mid-August: the **Provincetown Jazz Festival** (www.provincetown jazzfestival.org) is three-day event that draws a mix of vocal and instrumental jazz performers.

Late November: The **Lighting of the Pilgrim Monument** takes place every Thanksgiving Eve, and the lights stay on through New Year's Day.

Yes, the Red Sox are kings in New England (New Yorkers might want to keep their Yankee hats in the suitcase), but all visitors can put their rivalries aside and enjoy a rousing game of America's favorite pastime at the **Cape Cod Baseball League** (www.capecodbaseball .org). Games take place at venues throughout the Cape during the summer, with the highlight being the annual Cape League All-Star game sometime in July. Don't forget a tour of the Cape Cod Baseball League Hall of Fame exhibit—complete with baseball memorabilia and interactive programs—at **Heritage Museums & Gardens** in Sandwich (www.heritagemuseums.org).

▪▪▪▪ NEARBY

Try a wine tasting at the **Truro Winery of Cape Cod** (11 Shore Rd., North Truro; 508-487-6200; www.trurovineyardsofcapecod.com), where you can sample the local vintages and buy bottles to take home from the shop set in a renovated 19th-century farmhouse.

And if you can't get enough of **Cape Cod Potato Chips**, visit the factory in Hyannis (100 Breed's Hill Rd.; 888-881-CHIP; www.capecodchips.com) for a factory tour and free samples.

After the pilgrims left Provincetown, they stopped briefly in Eastham, where they encountered Native Americans for the first time. Now called **First Encounter Beach**, the site is especially popular at sunset, thanks to its calm waves and generous (but not free) parking.

Join a Discovery Cruise aboard **OceanQuest**, a marine research vessel at Woods Hole (Waterfront Park; 800-37-OCEAN; www.oceanquestonline.org). More than a sightseeing cruise, these 90-minute excursions, which operate in July and August, focus on the oceanography of the region, allowing participants to examine marine specimens, pull lobster traps, and pore over navigation equipment. Parking is virtually nonexistent in Woods Hole, so consider parking in Falmouth and hopping on the Whoosh Trolley (Falmouth Mall; 800-352-7155), which runs in summer.

▪▪▪▪ RESOURCES

Provincetown Chamber of Commerce Visitor Center, Commercial St.; 508-487-3424; www.ptownchamber.com

Province Lands Visitor Center, Race Point Rd.; 508-487-1256

ISLAND
ESCAPES

6 • BAR HARBOR AND LITTLE CRANBERRY ISLE, MAINE

About 260 miles north of Boston. Although it is technically on an island, Bar Harbor is accessible by car.

There is a reason Bar Harbor on the northern coast of Maine draws hordes of tourists. In addition to its charming streets, shops, and restaurants, the famous resort town has the added advantage of being surrounded by Acadia National Park and within shouting distance of several picturesque small islands offshore. Fans of ocean cruising will find that Bar Harbor is increasingly showing up on cruise ship itineraries of the East Coast, with some 70 ships calling into port every year.

The area, collectively known as Mt. Desert Island, appeals to nature buffs, foodies, and art lovers alike, thanks to a mix of lobster shacks, art galleries, hiking trails, and a whole menu of boating options. Ocean cruise ships, sailboats, and fishing vessels bob in the harbor on any given summer day, and if the crowds in town become overwhelming—and they can, especially in high season—you can climb aboard one of them for an island escape.

There are two Cranberry Isles—Great and Little, respectively—with **Little Cranberry** offering the most in terms of sights and ambience for visitors strapped for time. Also known as Islesford, the island has all of about 80 year-round residents. That number quadruples in summer with an influx of artists who rent houses for the season and display their wares in a smattering of galleries on the island. Potters, painters, and photographers are among those inspired by the island's remote beauty. They nurture its art colony, which has been thriving since the 1950s.

Unless you have made private arrangements in advance, accommodation options on the island—which measures about 400 acres—are minimal, but Little Cranberry is easy daytrip distance from Bar Harbor, where visitor digs range from B&Bs, motels, and camping to posh hotels and resorts.

Unlike Mt. Desert Island, the Cranberry Isles are accessible only by boat, and one of the easiest options for daytrippers is **Sea Princess Cruises** (207-276-5352; www.barharborcruises.com), which operates from May through October from Northeast Harbor. Keep an eye out for harbor seals and osprey nests as you pass by Bear Island Lighthouse and the dramatic cliffs that jut out of the waters of Somes Sound Fjord on the way to Islesford. In addition to day cruises, the company operates three-hour Sunset Dinner Cruises that include a meal at the island's dockside restaurant (see Eating Out).

As you disembark at Little Cranberry, the spirit of the island and its carefully guarded lifestyle become immediately apparent. The architecture is mostly white with green shutters, giving the whole island a nostalgic feel. Residents don't lock their doors, kids leave their bicycles unattended on the sidewalks as they run and play, and cars and trucks sport outdated license plates if any at all. Children attend the one tiny schoolhouse through elementary school, after which they decamp to the mainland for secondary education. Locals don't bat an eye to see a mother duckling and her chicks wander through one of the island's shops or chickens scratching around by the road.

All this rustic splendor only enhances the appeal of the island's art scene, and you don't have to go very far to find it. The islanders aren't much for street addresses, so if you want to find something, just ask.

■■■■ GETTING THERE (AND GETTING AROUND)

Bar Harbor is just over 250 miles— or about five hours by car—from Boston off I-95 to Route 1A to Route 3. The **Hancock County Airport** is less than 15 miles from town, and **Bangor Airport** is under an hour away.

You can reach Little Cranberry via a six-passenger water taxi (207-244-5724) that is also avail-

Cadillac Mountain as seen from Bar Harbor
VISITMAINE

able for excursions by prior reservation. Or take the **Cranberry Cove Ferry Service** (Harbor Ave.; 207-244-5882; www.downeast windjammer.com), which operates scheduled passenger ferry service from Southwest Harbor Upper Town Dock and Manset Cranberry Isles dock, or the **Beal & Bunker Mail Boat Ferry Service** (207-244-3575), which operates year-round from Northeast Harbor. You can bring your bicycle and even Fido, but leave the car at home. With the exception of the water taxi, you can buy your tickets onboard. Ferry tickets are good for stops at both Cranberry islands.

You can access the docks in Bar Harbor via the free **Island Explorer** (207-667-5796) bus, which links the piers to hotels, beaches, and attractions throughout Mt. Desert Island, including Acadia National Park.

▪▪▪▪ WHAT TO SEE

The **Islesford Artists Gallery** (207-244-3145; www.islesford artists.com), spitting distance from the Town Dock, showcases works by dozens of artists, some local and some from other parts of the state. The gallery is operated by islander Danny Fernald and his wife Katy, whose grandchildren are eighth- and ninth-generation islanders on both sides. The gallery generally deals with two-dimensional artwork—mostly landscapes—focusing on local artists and those who have ties to the island. Artists range from established painters to emerging talent.

Pottery enthusiasts can find a selection of handcrafted wares at Marion Bakers' **Islesford Pottery** (207-244-5686; www.marian bakerpottery.com), at the dock, which serves as a studio as well as a retail space where you can see the artists in action at the potter's wheel.

Art and history are entwined in the culture of the island, as witnessed by the exhibit at the **Islesford History Museum** (207-244-9224), an imposing brick building that you can reach by bearing left from the Town Dock. The museum traces the lives of the fishermen who braved the elements to make a life on the tiny island through such everyday 19th-century objects as a harpoon gun and a ship's clock, as well as a collection of ship models. The museum, which was built in the 1920s, also has a tiny bookstore and is open in season from mid-June through September. Visitors who want the benefit of a guide can book a ranger-led **Islesford Historical Cruise** through **Acadia National Park** (www.nps.gov) that includes a

*Islands off
the coast of
Bar Harbor*

*Downtown
Bar Harbor*

VISITMAINE

45-minute stop at the museum.

As with any small community, the local restaurant is more than just an eatery, but rather a hub of news and activity, and so it is with the **Islesford Dock Restaurant** (see Eating Out). The restaurant, which recently opened its own art gallery, is part of the dock complex that also includes Marion Baker's **Pottery Shop** and **Winters Work** gift shop, where you can buy everything from yarn and handmade soap to works by local artists.

▌▌▌▌ WHAT TO DO

Explore the island on foot or by bicycle (bring your own on the ferry). Make your way to the end of the main street to **Gilley Beach**, where you can find a perch on the rocks and admire the view of the Duck Islands. Or take the first right at the town beach and follow the road to the cemetery, where you will find a small memorial park with granite benches commemorating the

ships that have set to sea from the harbor. There are pathways to **Sand Beach** from the fields here, but to avoid trespassing, ask friendly locals for directions to the right of ways.

Explore the coast from the water in a two-person kayak via **Joy of Kayaking** (207-244-4309), run by Joy Sprague, the island postmistress. Sprague provides equipment and directions for a self-guided outing, as well as her cell phone number in case kayakers get tired and decide to pull up on a sandy coastal beach. Some of her favorite itineraries include hugging the south shore of the island, paddling out to **Crow Island**, or heading into **The Pool**, a tidal inlet at Great Cranberry, where you are likely to spot osprey and seals sunning themselves on rocks. More adventurous kayakers can make the mile-or-so trip to **Baker Island**, although Sprague is strict about nixing that route if the weather is iffy.

For a wider selection of kayak outfitters, head back to Bar Harbor, where the sea kayaking is said to be among the best in the world. Try **Aquaterra Sea Kayak Adventures** (1 West St.; 207-288-0007; www.aquaterra-adventures.com), where owner David Legere will arrange for guides and naturalists, or **Coastal Kayaking Tours** (48 Cottage St.; 207-288-9605), which runs guided tours of six tandem kayaks or fewer at a time and whose guides pride themselves on helping passengers spot such local wildlife as harbor seals and osprey. Tours range from half-day outings to three-day camping trips with experienced guides.

If marine life is more your thing, try **Bar Harbor Whale Watching Tours** (1 West St.; 207-288-2386; www.barharborwhales.com), which offers a whole menu of cruises aboard a 140-foot catamaran aimed at helping passengers spot whales, puffins, and seabirds in the bay. The company also offers tours aboard a lobster fishing boat, as well as lighthouse and park tours.

Visitors whose interest in lobsters goes beyond putting one on their dinner plate can book a two-hour trip on **Lulu Lobster Boat Ride** (56 West St.; 207-963-2341; www.lululobsterboat.com), where the captain will explain the history of the lobster industry and the steps fishermen take—such as tagging and releasing female breeders—to preserve the crop.

▪▪▪▪ WHERE TO STAY (LITTLE CRANBERRY)

Islesford House (207-244-0988) is a four-bedroom B&B near the Little Cranberry ferry dock behind the school. The property, which has recently been redecorated, is open from Memorial Day through Columbus Day. Rates include a continental breakfast, and dinner is available for an additional charge when the Islesford Dock Restaurant isn't open. $125.

▪▪▪▪ WHERE TO STAY (BAR HARBOR)

Bar Harbor Inn & Spa (Newport Dr.; 207-288-3351; www.bar harborinn.com), on the bay, features Old World decor, an outdoor pool, and affordable rates. From $79.

The Bar Harbor Motel (100 Eden St.; 207-288-3453; www.bar harbormotel.com) is within easy walking or biking distance of the Acadia National Park trails and

To examine marine life without getting wet, try the **Dive In Theater** (PO Box 870; 207-288-DIVE; www.divered.com), created by former Bar Harbor Master Eddie Monat—otherwise known as Diver Ed. The concept is that the captain dives to the ocean floor in Frenchman Bay with a camera, and his excavations are projected onto a screen on the boat. He then picks up whatever he can find down there—from sea cucumbers to starfish—for passengers to touch, before returning them to the ocean.

The *Margaret Todd* (207-288-4585; www.downeastwindjammer .com) is a four-masted schooner that operates several one-and-a-half to two-hour windjammer cruises a day for visitors who prefer a serene experience on a sailing vessel. Bring a picnic and choose from a morning or afternoon cruise, a sailing led by a nature ranger, or a leisurely sunset sail.

For an educational overview of the role of the lobster in Maine's ecosystem, visit the **Mount Desert Oceanarium** (Eden Rd.; 207-288-5005; www.theoceanarium.com), which also houses a lobster hatchery, museum, and marsh walk.

Walk under an enormous skeleton of a humpback whale at **The Bar Harbor Whale Museum** (52 West St.; 207-288-0288; www.bar harborwhalemuseum.org), a free, nonprofit center that promotes the study and appreciation of local marine life.

near the ferry dock to Nova Scotia. From $69.

The Bar Harbor Quality Inn (40 Kebo St.; 207-288-5403; www.qualityinn.com), within walking distance of the harbor, features an outdoor pool and free Wi-Fi. From about $179.

The Bass Cottage Inn (14 The Field; 207-288-1234; www.bass cottage.com) in central Bar Harbor is a good choice for a romantic getaway with its elegant, historic interiors and casual Adirondack chairs in the garden. From $185.

Cleftstone (92 Eden St.; 888-288-4951; www.cleftstone.com) is a cozy historic mansion within eight blocks of downtown and the water. Run by Bob and Anne Bahr, the property has some rooms with fireplaces. From $90.

■ ■ ■ ■ WHERE TO CAMP

Bar Harbor Camping Resorts (www.barharborcampingresorts

.com) operates several camp-grounds—Mt. Desert Narrows, Narrows Too, and Patten Pond—that offer sites on the ocean or lake. From $27.

▮▮▮▮ EATING OUT (LITTLE CRANBERRY)

Islesford Dock Restaurant (207-244-7494), run by Dan and Cynthia Lief, is right on the Little Cranberry dock. You can dig into a plate of Maine rock crab cakes and steamed mussels or try the Cranberry Isles Lobster or organic roast chicken. The restaurant is open for lunch and dinner; dinner only on Mondays. From $9.

Alley Way is a new lunch wagon open at the Little Cranberry ferry dock with fresh lobster rolls, bottled water, and snack food.

Little Cranberry Farmers Market on Main Street sells baked goods, fresh vegetables, jams and jellies, and other local products on Tuesdays and Fridays.

▮▮▮▮ EATING OUT (BAR HARBOR)

The Bar Harbor Club (111 West St.; 207-288-3351; www.barharbor club.com) in Bar Harbor cooks lobsters and steamers in a huge pot and serves them on a terrace overlooking the water. Market price.

Stewman's Lobster Pound (123 Eden St. or downtown on the wharf; 207-288-9723; www.stew manslobsterpound.com) offers a funkier take on the lobster feast. Opt for freshly steamed lobster, chowder, a frosty beer, and blueberry pie. Market price.

Guinness & Porcelli's (191 Main St.; 207-288-0030; www.guinness porcellis.com) is the place to go if you want to abandon seafood altogether and dine on upscale Italian cuisine with an Irish ambience. Oh, and they serve lobster. From $12.95.

Havana (318 Main St.; 207-288-CUBA; www.havanamaine .com) is an elegant Cuban restaurant downtown with a more urban vibe. From $18.

▮▮▮▮ NEARBY

Not everything in Bar Harbor is about water. Landlubbers can enjoy a number of stay-dry pursuits, one of the most popular of which is rock climbing. Even first timers can get in the act at a number of rock-climbing schools, such as **Acadia Mountain Guides** (198 Main St.; 207-288-8186; www.acadiamountain guides.com), which offers instruction for all skill levels in summer, and **Atlantic Climbing School** (67 Main St.; 207-288-2521; www.climbacadia.com) which includes a half-day Experience Course for newbies who just want to give the sport a try.

You can explore the nearly 45-mile network of **Carriage Roads**, built by John D. Rockefeller in the early 1900s in **Acadia National Park**, specifically for hikers and cyclists, as well as the horse-drawn carriages for which the trails are named. The roads, most of which are fairly low impact, are not open to motor vehicles, but you can reach access points via the **Island Explorer** bus, which allows passengers to bring their cycles along. In winter, many of the trails are open for cross-country skiing.

To experience the roads the old-fashioned way, book a one- or two-hour carriage ride at **Wildwood Stables** (Park Loop Rd.; 877-276-3622) inside the park, and be prepared to see a scenic vista around every corner.

The park offers great trails for hiking, most of which are fairly easy, but for more of a challenge, try the ¾-mile, nearly vertical **Beehive** off Park Look Road near Sand Beach, which features ladders for hikers to climb on their way to the summit.

For a guided hike, try **Downeast Nature Tours** (150 Knox Rd.; 207-288-8128; www.downeastnaturetours.com), which has a special focus on bird-watching. Owner Michael Good even runs an **Acadia Birding Festival** in June (www.acadia birdingfestival.com), which draws enthusiasts from far and wide. Even visitors who don't know a woodpecker from a hummingbird should keep an eye out for the majestic bald eagles, which are increasingly plentiful in the area and sometimes fly low, providing an up-close-and-personal view from the ground.

Time-strapped visitors who want to cover even more territory can consider driving the 20-mile **Park Loop Road** for some of the area's best views. Be sure to save time to hike the short trail on the top of **Cadillac Mountain**.

■ ■ ■ ■ LIT LIFE

The Cranberry Isles might be small, but their legacy extends beyond art into literature. One of the best-known local artists is **Ashley Bryan**, also a children's book author and folklorist. Winner of the 2009 Laura Ingalls Wilder Award, Bryan is also the recipient of the Coretta Scott King Award for Illustration and the Arbuthnot Prize for children's literature. Autographed copies of his books are available at **Sue Hill's Winters Work gift shop** on the dock.

Also noteworthy is children's author Rachel Field, who used Great Cranberry Isle as the setting for her Newbery Medal–winning book *Hitty, Her First Hundred*

Years. Published in 1929, the book tells the story of a wooden doll whose misadventures take her from her home in Maine to the streets of New York. Fans can trace some of the locations in the book to actual sites on the island, including the **Preble House**, home of Hitty's first owner, as well as watch a Hitty video and check out the collection of dolls at the **Great Cranberry Island** **Historical Museum** (Cranberry House; 207-244-7800). The museum is about ¼-mile from the ferry dock.

■ ■ ■ ■ RESOURCES

Acadia Welcome Center, 1201 Bar Harbor Rd. (before the bridge to Mt. Desert Island); 1 West St., on the pier (in season); www.bar harborinfo.com; 800-288-5103

7 • BLOCK ISLAND, RHODE ISLAND

This picturesque island 12 miles off the coast of Rhode Island is only accessible via boat, plane, or ferry.

Tiny Block Island, measuring only 3 by 7 miles, is as much characterized by what it doesn't have as by what it does. You won't see any fast-food outlets here, for example, or any franchise stores, and locals like to keep it that way. While there is a distinct upscale element, the ambience is low key with less of the frenetic activity that keeps Martha's Vineyard hopping in high season. You get the sense that the type-A folks who vacation here—and there are many—really do make an effort to turn off their Black-Berry devices on arrival.

Given the crescent shape of the island, there are plenty of vantage points from which to get those water views. In fact, there are 17 miles of beaches, some at the foot of dramatic bluffs, not to mention hundreds of inland waterways. Block Island is a boaters' paradise, and on any summer weekend there could be nearly 2,000 boats bobbing in the waters off the coast. You will also see plenty of kiteboarding, paddleboarding, and surfing on the island's various waterways.

There are also two harbors: **Old Harbor**, where the Point Judith and Newport ferries dock, and **New Harbor**, inland at the Great Salt Pond. Most day-trippers spend their days in the Old Harbor—essentially the only town on the island—where Victorian buildings house shops, art galleries, and restaurants. The Great Salt Pond, which is connected to the ocean by a manmade channel, serves as a popular spot for boaters, especially for those who have enough time to explore the less frequented areas away from the busy waterfront. You can

Staircase at Mohegan Bluffs

Don't miss the statue of **Rebecca at the Well** in the town center. Locals love to explain how the statue, which was erected during prohibition by the Women's Christian Temperance Union to depict a virtuous character from the Bible, resembles Hebe, an ancient Greek deity whose water jug would have been far more likely to contain wine. The statue is nonetheless a landmark, and don't be surprised if locals give directions using her as a starting point.

access Great Salt Pond from Old Harbor by foot in only about 15 or 20 minutes or bike the 2-mile route on a flat trail easy enough for families to navigate.

Taxi drivers will swear that there are 365 **freshwater ponds** on the island—enough for every day of the year—and while that exact number may be suspect, there are certainly hundreds sprinkled across the island. There are also acres of open land blanketed with wildflowers, all crisscrossed with more than 400 miles of stone walls. Not surprisingly, locals take conservation seriously here. Nearly half of the island is preserved open space, overseen by the Nature Conservancy, the Block Island Conservancy, and the Block Island Land Trust. The good news for visitors is that there are some 30+ miles of **interconnected trails** throughout the island that are just right for exploring the island on foot, either through leisurely strolls or all-day hikes.

The name Block Island derives from a Dutch explorer, Adrian Block, who came upon the island in the early 17th century, but earlier Native American inhabitants called it Manisses or Island of the Little God. Over the centuries, the island played a role in the history of New England, despite its diminutive size. During the Revolutionary War, colonials kept watch over British warships from an island observatory, and Ulysses S. Grant held court here during his presidency in the mid-19th century. By then tourism was in full swing on the island, with several hotels in operation, including Block Island's oldest, the **Spring House Hotel**, which is still open today (see Where to Stay). Captain Kidd is also said to have spent time on the island, spurring rumors that some of his treasure may be buried here. Others maintain that enjoying the view of the ocean from one of the white Adirondack chairs on the lawn of the Spring House Hotel is treasure enough. Just remember to turn off that phone.

▋▋▋▋ GETTING THERE (AND GETTING AROUND)

If you plan to bring your car, reserve your spot ahead on the **Block Island Ferry** (401-783-4613; www.blockislandferry.com), which runs all year from Point Judith—passengers can just walk on—or take the summer ferry from Newport. The **Block Island Hi-Speed Ferry**, which runs in season and takes only passengers, makes the trip from Point Judith in just a half hour. If you are traveling from New York, take the high-speed **Block Island Express** (860-444-4624; www.go blockisland.com), which makes the trip from New London, Connecticut, in an hour.

Commuter air service (800-243-2460) flies in and out of Block Island via New England Airlines from Westerly, Rhode Island.

There is no public transportation on Block Island, and since most visitors arrive without cars, you can get around by foot, bike, rented car, or taxi.

▋▋▋▋ WHAT TO SEE

The island is bracketed by two famous lighthouses, the **Southeast Lighthouse** perched on a cliff 150 feet above sea level, and **North Light** on Sandy Point. To see them both and get the lay of the land, consider an island **taxi tour**. Expect to pay about $55 for an hour-long tour, keeping in mind that every driver will offer his or her own slant on the island's history. There are stands in the Old Harbor or, if you are staying overnight, many taxi tour companies will fetch you from your hotel. Check out www.block islandinfo.com for a listing of providers.

Despite the lighthouses, there have been some memorable shipwrecks off the island, according to the Block Island Historical Society, and islanders in the 18th and 19th centuries became adept at rescuing survivors and making use of their cargo. The most recent wreck took place in 1939, when the oil tanker *Lightburne* went down near the Southeast Lighthouse, providing a popular spot for contemporary scuba divers who want to explore the wreckage.

If you have the time, however, probably the most satisfying way to experience Block Island is by foot or bicycle. **The Nature Conservancy** (401-466-2129) will provide information on hiking the Greenway Trails, which explode with daffodils and shad blooms—resembling white popcorn balls—in spring. Bikes are not allowed on the Greenway Trails, but you can park your bike at the access points and hike in on easy-to-navigate, well-marked trails. Or take a taxi to one of the lighthouses and walk back to the ferry dock, for an easy way to see the island on foot. The route back from North Light will take you past **Sachem Pond**, where sharp-eyed visitors might see turtles popping up their heads in summer. The pond has brackish water that freezes in winter, prompting intrepid locals to go iceboating on its surface after a cold spell.

One of the most famous sights on the island is **Mohegan Bluffs**, and with good reason. The dramatic, 150-foot cliffs descend to **Bluffs Beach** below via 142 steps—not enough to deter die-hard surfers eager to try out the much vaunted waves, but a bit much for the rest of us carrying armloads of beach paraphernalia. You can access the entrance to the bluffs at Payne's Overlook, which has ample bike parking and limited spaces for cars.

Most New England towns and resort areas worth their salt have historical sites and buildings to brag about, but Block Island's past goes back—way back—to prehistoric times when the island was formed by glaciers some 20,000 years ago. There are glacial depressions all over the island, accounting for the many ponds, but one that has remained dry is the enormous **Rodman's Hollow**, which has been preserved by a joint conservation effort of the Nature Conservancy and other conservation entities. There are two walking trails within the hollow, which is only about a mile from the sea.

Other popular routes for hikers

A local anecdote involves **Cow Cove** at Sandy Point, where the island's original settlers are said to have swum to shore with their cows in the 1600s. As the ocean isn't particularly calm here, the journey must have been a sight to see. Check out the names of those bovine-friendly settlers at Settlers' Rock in the cove.

include **Clay Head Hill Trail**, which wends from Corn Neck Road to the sea, and the **Hodge Family Preserve**, also off Corn Neck, which features walking paths to the ocean through a beautiful meadow. Nearby, test your wits against **The Labyrinth**, a stone maze whose ancient design is said to bestow peace upon those who make it to the center. If you come in from the airport, spend a few hours walking the carefully maintained **Enchanted Forest** trail, which is also part of the Greenway Trail system.

▪▪▪▪ WHAT TO DO

Mopeds are big on the island, and renters can find several outlets including **Aldo's Mopeds** (Chapel St.; 401-466-5018) and **Island Moped and Bikes** (Chapel St.; 401-466-2700). Or opt for leg power on a bicycle through **Seacrest Inn & Bicycle Rentals** (High St.; 401-466-2882) or **Old Harbor Bike Shop** (Water St.; 401-466-2029).

Indulge the wannabe seafarer in you and check out the **Block Island Maritime Institute** (Ocean Ave.; 401-466-7938) for information on the Great Sale Pond or opt for a cruise aboard **Ruling Passion Sailing Charters** (401-741-1926; www.rulingpassion.com), with excursions that range from early-bird outings to wine-and-cheese sunset cruises.

Water sports abound on Block Island, and there are several marinas where visitors can rent equipment. Try **Pond & Beyond** (401-466-5105) in New Harbor for a guided kayak tour or **Block Island Parasail** (401-864-2474) in the Old Harbor for parasailing and banana boat rides. You can also indulge your inner adventurer at **Diamondblue Kiteboarding & Surf Shop** (Bridgegate Square; 401-466-3145; www .diamondbluekiteboarding.net).

If you are the kind of traveler who would rather catch a fish than buy one, Block Island is the place to **go fishing**. You won't have to go far to find bass and bluefish, for example, and bigger game, like marlin and tuna, can be found farther out to sea. Finding a fishing boat with a reputable captain is as easy as wandering along the Old Harbor dock. Or, for fishing of another sort, try clamming at **Cormorant Cove** near Charlestown Beach on the island's west coast.

Perfect your tan. With 17 beaches competing for your attention, all of which are open to the public, finding the right one for you becomes an issue of access and your personal preferences. **Ballard's Beach**, close to the Old Harbor dock in front of

Ballard's Restaurant and Inn, is not the place to go to read a book or enjoy a quiet moment in the sun, but it does boast a happening scene with live music and a party vibe.

Or head north from the ferry dock toward **Crescent Beach**, which comprises a number of smaller beaches along the island's east coast. At **Fred Benson Town Beach**, for example, you will find families swimming under the watchful eye of lifeguards, as well as food outlets, beach chair rentals, and outlets to rent kayaks. At night, the beach also hosts live performances.

To get an up-close-and-personal view of exotic animals, including llamas, emu, yak, and even a zedonk—a cross between a zebra and a donkey—walk up from the ferry dock to **Justin Abrams' Farm** off Spring Street, where the admission is free and the animals are friendly.

■ ■ ■ ■ WHERE TO STAY

Block Island is the type of destination where repeat visitors rent houses by the week or even the summer or stay in B&Bs and guest cottages. The Tourism Council (see Resources) offers up-to-date listings of a wide range of offerings. If you prefer a hotel, there are several beautiful properties from which to choose, and be prepared to embrace the fact that most don't have air-conditioning or TVs.

The Atlantic Inn (High St.; 401-466-5883; www.atlanticinn .com), a 21-room Victorian property with croquet and horseshoes on the front lawn, is walking distance from the Old Harbor. Innkeepers Brad and Anne Marthens keep the antique furnishings, wraparound porch, and flower garden in top shape. From $165.

The 1661 Inn & Hotel Manisses (Spring St.; 401-466-2421; www .blockislandresorts.com) offers a range of accommodations, from rooms in the Inn to private cottages. Menus in the dining room are prepared using fresh local fish and herbs and produce from the garden behind the hotel next to **Justin Abrams' Farm** (see What to Do). The room rate includes a hearty breakfast and a Wine & Nibbles hour in the afternoons in high season. From $75 for the Hotel; $90 for the Inn.

The **Spring House Hotel** (Old Harbor; 800-234-9263 or 401-466-5844; www.springhousehotel .com) is the oldest property on the island, and its wraparound porch provides a vista from which to view the water and surrounding countryside. In summer, you can expect a full schedule of outdoor events, from wine dinners to live concerts. From $175.

The National Hotel (Water St.; 401-466-2901), a block or so from the ferry, is prominent on the skyline as the island comes into view. Listed on the National Register of Historic Places, the property is a good fit for visitors who want to be right in the middle of the action. From $99.

▪▪▪▪ EATING OUT

The hotels listed in Where to Stay have terrific restaurants, or try some of the choices below:

The Beachhead Restaurant (Corn Neck Rd.; 401-466-2249) is thronged with locals, but the food is worth the wait. Try the lobster ravioli or the sesame seared yellowfin tuna or a fresh salad from the garden. From $8.95; seafood market rate.

The Oar (221 Jobs Hill Rd.; 401-466-8820) overlooking Great Salt Pond is an insider's favorite for lobster rolls and burgers at great prices. The funky decor is also notable for, as you might have guessed, hundreds of oars hung from the ceiling. From about $14.

Bethany's Airport Diner (Center Rd.) is one of the few restaurants open year-round, and the fare is cooler than its name might imply. Menu items range from clam chowder to Jumbo Jet pancakes. From $3.99 for breakfast; $4.99 for lunch.

Mohegan Cafe & Brewery (Water St.; 401-466-5911) serves Tex-Mex, pad thai, and juicy burgers, all about a block from the ferry overlooking the water. From $8.95.

Rebecca's Seafood Restaurant (Water St.; 401-466-5411) specializes in seafood, but you can also get veggie sandwiches, wraps, and breakfast items. From $4.25 for lunch or dinner.

Winfield's (Corn Neck Rd.; 401-466-5856; www.winfields restaurant.net) serves up a high-

View from the ferry (National Hotel)

Justin Abrams' Farm

end fusion of European and Asian dishes, including lobster risotto and blackened beef tournedos, with a varied wine list. From $16.

▮▮▮▮ SPECIAL EVENTS

Late June: Watch the action on the water from a comfortable deck chair during **Block Island Race Week**, an annual weeklong event during which sailors pit their wits against Mother Nature and each other as they sail around the island.

June to October: For fresh produce and baked goods, visit the open-air **Farmers' Market** (100 Ocean Ave.) on Saturday mornings.

▮▮▮▮ NEARBY

Missed the ferry? Spend a day at the beach in Point Judith. Choose from **Roger Wheeler State Beach** near the ferry dock, which has plenty of parking, picnic tables, and other facilities. Or try **Scarborough State Beach** in nearby Narragansett, with showers, a boardwalk, and other amenities.

▮▮▮▮ RESOURCES

Block Island Tourism Council, 1 Water St.; 401-466-5200; www.blockislandinfo.com

Block Island Historical Society, Bridgegate Sq.; 401-466-2481

8 • BOSTON HARBOR ISLANDS, MASSACHUSETTS

Spectacle and Georges islands are accessible by ferry from Boston's Long Wharf and from the South Shore, with connections to the other islands.

Martha's Vineyard and Nantucket aren't the only visit-worthy islands off the coast of Massachusetts. Actually, there are 34 islands right in Boston Harbor, a fact that would probably astonish even residents of Beantown (who, if pressed, could probably name two or three). Some of them are so close that they are visible from the waterfront, which means that even visitors strapped for time can hit a few for the day and be back in time for dinner. The trick is to plan your visit according to your interests, as each island has its own personality and unique history.

Formed by glaciers during the last Ice Age, the islands make up part of the 50-square-mile **Boston Harbor Islands National Recreation Area.** Although the islands are managed by a partnership of government and nonprofit entities, the folks you are likely to see during your visit are park rangers and volunteers from the Friends of the Boston Harbor Islands. Rangers accompany the ferries from Boston Harbor and greet visitors as they arrive onshore—counting noses to make sure no one is left on the islands overnight who doesn't want to be (for information on which islands accept campers, see Where to Camp below).

Nowadays, sensitivity to the islands' ecosystems is evident everywhere, but this wasn't always the case. **Spectacle**

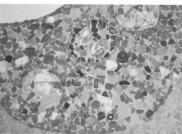

Georges Island from the ferry

Beach glass display, Spectacle Island

*View of Boston
from H.I. ferry*

Island, in particular, has become the darling of the green movement in the last few years in spite of—or more likely because of—its recent dramatic transformation. Until a few years ago the island was an eco-disaster, serving the good citizens of the Commonwealth as a convenient offshore dump. This indignity was especially galling considering that the island was populated for several thousand years by Native Americans, who used its resources with more reverence.

After the arrival of the European settlers—who gave the island its name because it was shaped like a pair of eyeglasses—things went quickly downhill. By the early 18th century, Bostonians with smallpox and other contagious diseases were quarantined here. A century later, Spectacle became notorious for its houses of gambling and prostitution. A horse-rendering plant—what we

used to call "the glue factory"—and finally a city garbage dump followed, leaving the island not only foul smelling, but also considerably larger than it had been, thanks to its mountains of garbage.

This ignominious past makes the present-day incarnation of Spectacle Island, now the hippest of the island chain, all the more sweet. The turnaround began with the Big Dig, a massive engineering project that sank Boston's Central Artery and repurposed the land above it (see our chapter on the **Rose Kennedy Greenway** for more on the Big Dig). Part of the project included the refurbishment of Spectacle Island, an undertaking that involved dumping literally millions of tons of dirt unearthed during the Dig onto the island, adding good topsoil and building a seawall to contain it. Eco-engineers then were enlisted to create walking paths, clear the beaches, and plant specific vegetation that would retard erosion.

The results are so spectacular that you may be tempted to spend your whole day here, but if time permits, many of the other Boston Harbor Islands are also worth visiting. Plot out your ferry schedule and set your sights on Georges, Bumpkin, Thompson, Grape, Peddocks, or Lovells Island to round out your day. Whichever ones you choose, remember to leave your bike and pets (except service dogs) at home and bring your camera and good walking shoes.

▌▌▌▌ GETTING THERE (AND GETTING AROUND)

Harbor Island Ferries (617-223-8666; www.bostonharborislands .org) leave from Boston's Long Wharf for Georges and Spectacle islands hourly from 9 AM to 5 PM Monday through Thursday and every half hour until 6 PM on weekends. Hang on to your ferry ticket for the interisland shuttle boat if you want to visit both islands.

Ferries also run in spring and fall on an abbreviated schedule. If you must drive—and we encourage you not to—the nearest public parking lots are near the New England Aquarium and Faneuil Hall. A much better bet is to take the subway (the T) to the Aquarium and follow the signs for the ferry to the kiosk on the north side of the Marriott Long Wharf hotel.

From the South Shore, ferries link Hull (see our chapter on Nantasket Beach), Hingham, and Quincy with Georges, Bumpkin,

Get spooked by the tale of the **Lady in Black**, Georges Island's favorite ghost story. According to legend, the wife of a Confederate prisoner at the Fort Warren prison during the Civil War rowed out to the island—on a dark and stormy night, of course—in a bold attempt to help her husband escape. The two were discovered, and the wife accidentally shot her husband in the ensuing scuffle. The woman wore black to her own hanging, and her ghost is said to still haunt the intricate corridors of the fort to this day. Anecdotes of guides enlisting volunteers to play the Lady in Black during tours are rampant and go a long way toward explaining the continued popularity of the tale.

Grape, Lovells, and Peddocks islands.

▪▪▪▪ WHAT TO SEE

The ferry from Boston's revitalized waterfront will likely bring you to **Spectacle Island** first (there is also a direct route to Georges Island), offering great views of the Boston skyline as you make the journey in only about 15 minutes. You will see the **Visitors Center** as you pull in, and this a great place to start. Videos and interactive displays show how the island changed over the centuries—at one point it was a proposed site for a nuclear power plant—into the recreational hotspot it is today. Because of the soil brought in from the Big Dig, the island now resembles a saddle more than a pair of glasses, but its contours are lovely and verdant with some 105 acres of trees and ground cover. There are two **beaches** flanking the visitors center, one for swimming (with showers and lifeguards) and the other for picking your way through sea glass, pottery shards, and other remnants of the island's history that continuously wash ashore.

Take the ferry from Boston or Spectacle Island to **Fort Warren** on **Georges Island,** a huge 19th-century National Historic Landmark that will make you think you are on a movie set. You only see a sliver of it from the ferry as you approach the island, but once you have walked past the redbrick building (now being renovated to become a welcome center), the sheer size of this huge fort will hit you. Join a ranger-led tour or grab a map and wander the ramparts, cavernous rooms, and spacious parade grounds on your own. The views of Boston and neighboring islands from the top are stellar, and from below you are likely to see young children acting out heroics as they romp on the grounds. The 40-plus-acre island also offers walking trails, open

European settlers used **Grape Island** for farming, and while you won't see any forts, there was some action of a sort during the Revolutionary War, when British naval vessels landed on the island in search of food and livestock, abetted by a friendly loyalist. Patriots on the mainland, including relatives of President John Adams, soon arrived to retaliate, and the British were sent packing after a scuffle.

Like Georges Island, **Peddocks Island** boasts an interesting history as an outpost against the British and as a military training facility through World War I. Fort Andrews, a Historical and Archeological Landmark, has been allowed to fall into dereliction, but if proposals to revitalize it come to pass, it could become part of a more robust visitors' experience.

fields, and places to picnic, as well as tidal pools along the shore teeming with sea critters.

Explore **Grape Island**, whose size depends on what time of day you get there: 54 acres at high tide and nearly double that when the tide is out. Wildlife takes precedence over humans here, with varieties of birds and wild plant life in abundance. Don't expect as much in the way of visitor amenities here, but many visitors love the island for its secluded beauty.

Visit the wonderfully named **Bumpkin Island**, one of the smallest in the group at only about 30 acres, which has undergone a number of incarnations since it was first inhabited by Native Americans and subsequently Colonial farmers. Over the years, the island was home to a 19th-century fish-drying and smelting company, a turn-of-the-century children's hospital, and a U.S. Naval base in World War I. The hospital burned down in 1945, leaving only a few intriguing ruins that leave an evocative presence on the network of trails that traverses the island. Nowadays you can visit the **Bumpkin Island Art Encampment**, a program of interactive installations that runs all summer on weekends. Recent examples include artists who constructed musical instruments from found objects, while another group flew gigantic, illuminated wings and dragonflies over the island at night.

Keep your eye out for the **Boston Lighthouse**, a historic lighthouse on Little Brewster Island that was once used to watch for British warships, or catch a view of the lighthouse from the ramparts on Georges Island.

Attend a **vintage baseball** game on Georges Island, when enthusiasts play according to mid-19th-century rules and in costume, sometimes roping in the rangers as opponents.

Only about 7 miles from Boston's coast, **Lovells Island** once had a sinister reputation as the site of several prominent shipwrecks. The survivors of a sunken passenger ship crawled to shore only to die on the inhospitable island. Lovers' Rock, where a couple is said to have died together after the storm, is still intact on the island, which now has a beach, picnic areas, and lovely dunes.

▌▌▌▌ WHAT TO DO

Go **kayaking** on Spectacle Island Mondays, Wednesdays, and Thursdays during July and August. Rangers will offer instruction and equipment to all skill levels aged 12 and up. The free half-hour outings are first-come, first-served. Free kayaking is also available on **Grape Island** Wednesdays, Thursdays, Saturdays, and Sundays in season.

Attend free **Dixie, Swing, and Jazz concerts** on Spectacle Island on Sunday afternoons in summer. Musicians play on the Visitor Center porch all afternoon, while the winds carry the sounds across the water.

Join a guided **Salt Marsh Walk** on **Thompson Island** Sundays in summer. The free hour-and-a-half tour departs from the Visitors Center and makes the rounds of the most interesting parts of this rugged island, which is owned by Outward Bound. Ranger-led tours on Georges Island are led by guides in Civil War costumes who get into the spirit of the day with period games and stories.

Take a free **ranger-led tour** of Spectacle Island or grab a map for a self-guided hike along the 2.5-mile trail that leads to the tallest point on the island. Here you can picnic, fly kites, or just enjoy the 360-degree views of the city and neighboring islands. Travelers with mobility issues can ride a stretch golf cart with a ranger to take the tour in comfort. Picnic tables are made of recycled materials and have extensions to accommodate wheelchairs.

See a play at the **Fort Warren Stage** on Georges Island Fridays in late June through late August. There are two performances daily, and there is no admission charge. Past performances have been *Folktales Near & Far*, *Twelfth Night*, and *The History and Adventures of Tom Thumb*.

▌▌▌▌ WHERE TO CAMP

Lovells, Bumpkin, and Grape Islands allow camping. Rangers are on hand to assign campsites, and reservations are required

(877-422-6762; www.reserve america.com). Facilities vary by island and are limited.

■■■■ EATING OUT

Jasper White's Summer Shack (www.summershackrestaurant .com) on Spectacle Island looks like a routine snack bar, but don't be fooled. You can get burgers and dogs here, but they are grilled to order on an outdoor grill, and other options range from award-winning lobster rolls and clam chowder to grilled veggie salads and sandwiches in baguettes. Seating is outdoors on picnic tables under a tent or on any of the picnic tables that dot the island along the hiking trails. Market price for lobster.

Summer Shack Clambake on Spectacle Island includes a sunset ferry ride from Boston Harbor and a clambake dinner with chowder, lobster, mussels, steamers, and corn, plus dessert. Clambakes take place every Thursday night from mid-June early September. From $56.

Georges Island Hot Dog & Ice Cream stand offers just the basics, but you can't beat the scenery at the on-island picnic areas.

■■■■ SPECIAL EVENTS

Mid-July: **Free Ferry Day** takes place one Friday a summer with

an eye to introducing people to islands they have only seen from the shore. For visitors, it's a great way to stretch your budget if the timing works with your schedule.

Late September: The annual **Boston Harbor Islands Regatta** (http://islandalliance.org /regatta.asp) is a 12-mile race open to sailors of all skill levels, followed by a round of parties for winners and also-rans.

■■■■ LIT LIFE

Fans of Dennis Lehane may be disappointed to find that, while he was inspired by the Boston Harbor Islands when choosing a setting for his novel *Shutter Island*, that particular island doesn't exist. Nor does the Ashecliffe Hospital for the Criminally Insane, which provides the backdrop for this thriller. The good news is that parts of the movie version of the book—directed by Martin Scorsese and starring Leonardo DiCaprio—were filmed on Peddocks Island.

For an in-depth look at the islands, you can't do better than *Discovering the Boston Harbor Islands; A Guide to the City's Hidden Shores* by Christopher Klein or *Boston Harbor* by Donald Cann and John Galluzzo.

9 • NANTUCKET, MASSACHUSETTS

Long and skinny—about 14 miles end to end—Nantucket is about 30 miles from the Massachusetts coast.

In real estate parlance, if Martha's Vineyard is the Millionaires' Club, then its sister island, Nantucket, is the Billionaires' Club, thanks to its increasingly posh ambience and high-end home prices. But while the exclusivity, high prices, and snobbish appeal do make up a part of the island's character, there is more here for the discerning visitor with an eye for history and scenic beauty to discover.

The name "Nantucket," which refers both to the island and to the town, means "far away island" in the language of the Wampanoag Native American tribe, its earliest known residents. The island's most popular nickname, however, is the "grey lady," because of the dense fog that so often shrouds the island and the weathered cedar shingles that grace many of the local structures. One look at its quiet streets lined with pre—Civil War architecture—some 800 buildings in all—and it is easy to see why the entire island has been placed on the National Register of Historic Districts.

If you squint at the gray buildings as they come into view from the ferry, it is not hard to imagine what the island must have been like in its early days of colonial settlement, when whaling was the lifeblood of Nantucket's economy. Whaling not only brought prosperity to the ship captains who built some of the finest homes along the harbor but also informed much of the island's culture before the chic shops and trendy restaurants began to encroach on its historic streets.

Even today Nantucket baskets adorned with scrimshaw are highly prized among collectors and astonishingly expensive. And while nowadays most boating in Nantucket waters is done for pleasure rather than fishing, gazing at the island from the water remains one of the best ways to see Nantucket in all its restrained beauty.

Many visitors don't realize that in addition to important architecture, Nantucket boasts a whopping 82 miles of beaches and moors, not to mention acres of cranberry bogs. Residents take land conservation very seriously, so much so that more than 40 percent of the island is protected from development by various entities, including the Nantucket Conservation Foundation and the Nantucket Land Bank. The good news is that much of this land is open to the public, which means that visitors are free to explore the island on foot or by bike knowing that the land and water are among the most pristine in the country.

One of the challenges of planning your visit is deciding when to go. A confirmed beach lover who really just wants to sprawl onto a beach towel and soak in the sun after a long hard winter is probably not going to find Mother Nature all that cooperative too early or late in the season. That said, keep in mind that the population of about 12,000 swells to about 55,000 in summer, which makes the off-season tempting to visitors looking for a more

serene—and less expensive—experience.

▮▮▮▮ GETTING THERE (AND GETTING AROUND)

Island hop to Nantucket via ferry from Hyannis via the **Steamship Authority** (508-477-8600; www .steamshipauthority.com). The traditional ferry ride takes about two and a quarter hours and is available year-round; the Fast Ferry takes an hour. Or try a Hy-Line ferry or high-speed catamaran ride board **Hy-Line Cruises** (508-778-2600; www.hy-line cruises.com), also from Hyannis. Reservations for the high-speed ferries are a good idea and required as far in advance as possible for visitors who want to bring a car.

You can also fly into Nantucket Memorial Airport (www .nantucketairport.com) via commercial flight or, should you have access to one, private plane.

Once on the island, transportation can be tricky, especially dur-

The new Shipwreck & Lifesaving Museum

Nantucket's Compass Rose

ing the off-season. In fine weather, bikes are a great resource, and you can certainly bring your car over on the ferry or rent one by the day or week. That said, the traffic is no fun, and most visitors prefer to leave their vehicles on the mainland. Be aware, however, that taxis are prohibitively expensive, so if you are planning an afternoon in 'Sconset from downtown, for example, be sure to pick up an NRTA shuttle schedule (www.shuttlenantucket.com) beforehand. The shuttle buses, which run from late May to early October, stop at Broad Street and Washington Street, or you can pick up a pass at 3 East Chestnut Street.

▪▪▪▪ WHAT TO SEE

Many of Nantucket's most rewarding outdoor pursuits are available in the shoulder season. **Bird-watching** is huge on the island, partly because of the annual migration pattern that passes the island twice a year and partly because there are uncommon bird species—such as the piping plover—living on the island. Check the schedule at the **Maria Mitchell Association** (www.mmo.org) for birding nature walks.

Three of the best-known historic mansions in Nantucket are called the **Three Bricks** (93–97 Main St.), so named for their imposing brick construction. They are not open for tours, but you won't be the only one tempted to stop for a photo op of their imposing exteriors. Another is the **Hadwen House** (96 Main St.), a surprisingly opulent building that boasts antique furniture, ornate wallpaper, and gilt picture frames. The house is maintained by the **Nantucket Historical Association**, and also opens its gardens to visitors. The Jethro Coffin House, known locally as the **Oldest House** (16 Sunset Hill Lane) is just that, dating from 1686 and the only remaining building from the original English settlers on the island. The house, which was restored in the 1990s, is open to the public in season, and also boasts an authentic kitchen garden.

If you are torn between museum hopping and exploring the island outdoors, try the new **Nantucket Shipwreck & Lifesaving Museum** (158 Polpis Rd.; 508-228-1885; www.nantucket shipwreck.org), open May to mid-October. You can take in the collection of vintage surfboards and island memorabilia, then join a guided tour (available Sundays) to the **Coskata-Coatue Wildlife Refuge** (107 Wauwinet Rd.; 508-228-0006) and its **Great Point Lighthouse**, in conjunction

The **Dreamland Theater** was an icon in Nantucket for years, and residents and repeat visitors mourn its passing. The good news is that, thanks to efforts by the Nantucket Dreamland Foundation, construction was slated to begin on an environmentally friendly rebuild in the fall of 2009. Earmarked to become a year-round cultural venue for film screenings and live music, dance and theatrical performances, the site has meanwhile been used as an outdoor space for movies and performances under the stars as well as a summer venue for the Sustainable Nantucket's Farmers and Artisans Market. For information on the project or details on how to donate, check out www.nantucketdreamland.org.

with the **Trustees of Reservations**. The refuge is home to 200-plus acres of wild dunes, red cedar trees, and maritime oak, much of which you can explore via 16 miles of trails. The Trustees also offer a range of naturalist-led guided tours on various days of the week themed around fishing and ecology.

Another favorite museum is the recently renovated **Whaling Museum** (13 Broad St.; 508-228-1894), with its gigantic, looming skeleton of a sperm whale—teeth and all—and restored mid-19th-century candle factory. Museum staff also lead guided tours of such famous local sites as the **Old Gaol** (15R Vestal St.), where miscreants were locked up to contemplate the error of their ways from 1806 to the 1930s.

■■■■ WHAT TO DO

The good news about cycling on Nantucket is that you don't have to be Lance Armstrong to handle the terrain, especially near town. There are about the more than 20 miles of paved paths, and hot spots to visit include the **Old Mill** (South Mill and Prospect Sts.), an incongruous 50-foot structure that dates from the 1740s and the oldest operating mill in the United States, and **Brant Point Lighthouse** (Easton St.; 508-228-2500), the second oldest in America and the first of Nantucket's three lighthouses. You can also bike to many of the island's beaches or just cruise through town for a leisurely look at the mansions, cafés, and shops that line the streets.

Most bike rental shops offer free delivery, as well as a variety

of tandem bikes and other accessories. Some also rent scooters
and four-wheel-drive Jeeps. Try
Nantucket Bike Shop (Steamboat
Wharf and Straight Wharf; 800-
770-3088), **Young's Bicycle
Shop** (6 Broad St.; 508-228-1151)
or **Easy Rider Bicycle Rentals** (65
Surfside Road; 508-325-2722) just
off the bike path. If you'd rather
avoid town traffic, pick up your
bike at **Island Bike Company** (25
Old South Rd.; 508-228-4070), on
the bike path outside town.

Hit the beach. There are many
on the island, from ocean beaches with big waves to the calm
waters of inland ponds. Many
local beaches are accessible via
shuttle bus in season, while others can be reached by bike. One
of the most popular is **Jetties
Beach** close to town on the north
shore, which has every visitor
amenity imaginable, from showers and take-out food to life-

guards and kayak rentals. **Dionis
Beach**, 3 miles from town off
Madaket Road, is another popular
north shore beach, thanks to its
calm waters and sheltering
dunes. If you like heavy surf,
head to **Surfside** beach on the
south shore, about 3 miles from
town off the bike path or accessible via shuttle. There are lifeguards on duty, as well as food
service and showers. To the west,
you can bike or take the shuttle
to **Madaket** beach, where locals
brave the robust surf or just stay
to watch the sunset.

From mid-June through mid-
October, you can set out on a
whale-watch cruise with **Shear-
water Excursions** (508-228-
7037) aboard a catamaran. The
staff is so confident that passengers will see whales that they
offer a free ticket for another
cruise if they don't. The company
also operates seal cruises to the

*Nantucket
Harbor*

outer island of Muskeget, where the local gray seals like to play in the surf.

Rent a kayak at **Sea Nantucket Kayak Rentals** (Francis St. Beach; 508-228-7499) or relax on an excursion via **Endeavor Sailing Excursions** (Straight Wharf; 508-228-5585; www.endeavorsailing .com), where the captain will share his knowledge of the island and let passengers lend a hand sailing. Excursions last from an hour to an hour-and-a-half, including one at sunset, and don't be surprised if a fiddler or storyteller enlivens the proceedings.

Hang 10 at **Nantucket sUrfari** (1 Essex Rd.; 508.228.1235; www .nantucketsurfari.com), where you can choose from private or group lessons or even weeklong camp to learn to surf or stand-up paddle surf. Try the three-hour tour, which includes pickup at your hotel, lessons on whichever beach fits your skill level and equipment rentals.

Expert and newbie fishermen and -women can pit their wits against striped bass, bluefish, and even shark with **Topspin Sportfishing Charters** (Straight Wharf; 508-228-7724; www .fishingnantucket.com), where outings on the 32-foot Albemarle range from two and a half hours to a full day. **Herbert T Sports**

Fishing (14 Straight Wharf; 508-228-6655) provides everything from lessons to equipment, and your catch will be cleaned and packaged to take home at journey's end. **Albacore Charters** (17 Straight Wharf; 508-228-5074; www.albacorecharters.com) offers two-and-a-half-hour to all-day private charters in a 35-foot sportfishing boat under the direction of Captain Bob DeCosta, a second-generation charter boat captain.

For an insider's view of the island, seasoned with plenty of anecdotes, let Gail Nickerson Johnson, a sixth-generation resident and local tour guide, show you her island via **Gail's Tours** (508-257-6557; www.nantucket .net/tours/gails/). Tours depart three times daily in season, and Gail will pick you up and drop you off anywhere on the island. Or try **Aras Tours** (508-221-6852; www.arastours.com), which includes Brant Point, 'Sconset, and the cranberry bogs in its hour-and-a-half excursions.

■■■■ WHERE TO STAY

The **White Elephant** (50 Easton St.; 508-228-2500; www.white elephanthotel.com), formerly a collection of cottages, has been transformed into an elegant, upscale resort with a luxurious spa. The property is within eyeball distance from the ferry dock, but hotel staff will meet you in a shuttle to transport you to reception. Or opt for the comforts of home at the new White Elephant Hotel Residences, one-, two- and three-bedroom cottages with fancy kitchens spiffed out with Sub-Zero refrigerators and Royal Doulton china. From $275 to $3,000.

The Wauwinet (120 Wauwinet Rd.; 508-228-0145; www.wauwinet.com), which belongs to the tony Relais & Châteaux chain, offers a luxe waterfront location and historic architecture that manages to be both upscale and unstuffy. Catch up on your reading in the sitting room by the fire or relax on the terrace outside overlooking the water. Although some 9 miles from town, the property transports guests back and forth via hotel shuttle and *Wauwinet Lady* ferry. From $380 to $1,450.

The **Century House** (10 Cliff Rd.; 508-228-0530; www.centuryhouse.com), one of the island's oldest guesthouses, won the International Restaurant & Hotel Award for Best of City in 2008. In operation for 175 years, the grand dame property on Cliff Road is within easy walking distance of the shops and restaurants in town. From $175 to $695.

The **Union Street Inn** (www

.unioninn.com) is a 12-room boutique property in a restored 1770 whaling captain's home just off Main Street. Decked out with upscale linens, authentic architectural details, and cooked-to-order breakfasts, the property has garnered a bouquet of kudos from *Boston* magazine and *Cape Cod Life*, to name a few. An ACK Getaway package includes accommodations, welcome bottle of sparkling wine, and a sunset cruise, from $239.

▌▌▌▌ EATING OUT

The Brotherhood of Thieves (23 Broad St.; 508.228.2551; www.brotherhoodofthieves.com), named for a 19th-century abolitionist pamphlet and preserved with period architectural details, is the place to go to tuck into Wellfleet oysters or a juicy burger. Be sure to ask for a seat downstairs in the historic portion of the restaurant, however, or you may find yourself in an anonymous upstairs room without a view. From about $10.

Cinco (5 Amelia Dr.; 508-325-5151; www.cinco5.com) serves up everything from sizzling tapas to porterhouse steaks, and the interior doubles as an art gallery. From $10.

Topper's at The Wauwinet (120 Wauwinet Rd.; 508-228-8768; www.toppersrestaurant.com) is a special-occasion splurge, but you won't soon forget the tasting menu, created by celebrity chef David Daniels. $185 per person (not including tax and gratuity) will buy you an evening of inventive small plates paired with wines selected by the sommelier.

The RopeWalk (Straight Wharf; 508-228-8886; www.theropewalk .com) is the first eatery you will come to as you exit the Hy-Line ferry. The menu includes the usual seafaring specials, from lobster rolls to calamari, but try starting your day here with hearty flapjacks or a Rise & Shine Omelet. From about $20.

Dune (20 Broad St.; 508-228-5550; www.dunenantucket.com) opened in 2009 with seasonal menus, a full array of cocktails, and chic modern decor. The restaurant is run by well-known chef Michael Getter. From $25.

American Seasons (80 Centre St.; 508-228-7111; www.american seasons.com) is a Zagat-rated restaurant with a big following and an in-town location. Snag a table on the terrace and peruse the wine list, which garnered a *Wine Spectator* Award of Excellence. From $23.

Cowboy's Meat Market & Deli (7 Bayberry Court; 508-228-8766; www.cowboysmeatmarket.com) whips up take-out sandwiches and meals, along with butcher items if your digs include a kitchen. $9.95 for sandwiches.

Beachside Bistro (17 Ocean Ave.; 508-257-4542; www.the summerhouse.com), one of the eateries at the posh Summer House inn and cottages, is the place to go to reward yourself for biking to 'Sconset. Enjoy an al fresco lunch overlooking the water or stay for dinner. From about $24.

▌▌▌▌ SPECIAL EVENTS

Late April: The annual **Daffodil Festival** has grown over time to become an unrestrained riot of festivities that pay homage to the rites of spring. The hot ticket is the **Annual Antique Car Parade,** where period automobiles festooned with daffodils snake through town to the enjoyment of passersby who line the streets. An **Annual Daffodil Tailgate Picnic** follows at 'Sconset village, where camera bugs won't be able to resist snapping shots of the quaint cottages. Other events during the festival include the **Daffodil Dog Parade,** which you can enjoy even if you don't have Fido with you, or the quirky **Daffy Hat Pageant.**

Mid-May: The annual **Nantucket Wine Festival** (www .nantucketwinefestival.com) draws some 100 participating wineries. Half the fun of the festival is the variety of venues, which include some of the island's most posh homes.

June & October: **Nantucket Restaurant Week** (www.nantucket restaurantweek.com) now takes place twice a year, giving visitors a chance to try some of the island's most exclusive eateries. The way it works is that diners pay from $25 to $45 for a three-course lunch or dinner, respectively, at restaurants that normally cost an arm and a leg.

Mid-August: Beachcombers can get creative or just watch the action at the annual **Sandcastle and Sculpture Day** at Jetties Beach, where they will find gentle surf and visitors' facilities all summer.

Late August through early September: The **Nantucket Arts Festival** (508-325-8588; www .nantucketartscouncil.org) brings together an eclectic mix of artists with exhibits that range from paintings and weaving to sculpture and gardening, as well as musical, theater, and dance performances.

Early-October: **Cranberry Festival**, hosted by the Nantucket Conservation Foundation, entertains visitors and locals of all ages with hayrides and food tastings.

Mid-October: The **Annual Chowder Contest** is the time when local restaurants woo the public with free samples in their bid for the title.

Late November through New Year's: Think there's nothing to do on Nantucket in winter? Yes, many of the restaurants and shops are closed, but locals get into the spirit of the season every year with the annual **Christmas Stroll**. There are decorated Christmas trees on every corner, house tours, theatrical and musical productions, and—of course—a very public visit from Santa.

▪▪▪▪ RESOURCES

Nantucket Island Chamber of Commerce, Zero Main Street; 508-228-1700; www.nantucket chamber.org

10 • MARTHA'S VINEYARD, MASSACHUSETTS

About 7 miles off the coast of Cape Cod

For generations the Vineyard managed to fly under the radar of the wider public despite being immensely popular among residents of the East Coast. Some arrivals owned second homes on the island, many were renters who came year after year, and others were day-trippers touring the island in hopes of catching a glimpse of a Kennedy or two. A few famous people lived on the island—among them the musician Carly Simon, the Pulitzer Prize—winning author William Styron, and the columnist Art Buchwald—but they were not of the Paris Hilton or Brad Pitt variety. In short, the Vineyard had an air of exclusivity about it that remained more or less constant for decades.

Fast-forward to the late 1990s when the former President Bill Clinton chose the island as his favorite annual vacation destination, followed in 2009 by President Barack Obama. The media scrutiny that followed has sent the destination's popularity into overdrive, casting an international spotlight on the tiny island that only has around 16,000 year-round residents.

That popularity can be a two-edged sword, so much so that

Edgartown lighthouse
SHANE HAGER

Fishing off Menemsha dock

Cottages in Campgrounds

SHANE HAGER

first-time visitors, particularly those who concentrate their time on the tiny streets in **Oak Bluffs** and **Vineyard Haven** near the ferry docks, can find themselves mired in a circus atmosphere that doesn't do justice to the overall ambience of this picturesque island.

One way to avoid the crowds is to time your visit for the shoulder seasons in spring and fall. While October may not be sunbathing weather, you can still walk, bike, and fly kites on the beaches and visit the towns free of the traffic that descends in July and August. But if you have your heart set on sunbathing, you can also find serenity of a sort on the Vineyard even in high season, if you know where to look.

▮▮▮▮ GETTING THERE (AND GETTING AROUND)

Take the ferry to Vineyard Haven or Oak Bluffs from Woods Hole, Falmouth, Hyannis or New Bedford, all in Massachusetts. Check the **Steamship Authority** (www.steamshipauthority.com) or try a **Hy-Line ferry** (www.hy-linecruises.com) for schedules and prices. Reserve weeks ahead (months in high season) if you plan to bring your car, and expect to pay around $150 passage fee. You can just walk on as a passenger or with your bike.

Buses (vineyardtransit.com) are available at the ferry dock to most points on the island, and taxis and bike rentals also are available. Or fly via Cape Air (www.flycapeair.com) from a number of gateways, including Boston and Providence. Amtrak offers year-round connections to the ferry piers via shuttle.

▮▮▮▮ WHAT TO SEE

Oak Bluffs boasts some of the most arresting architecture in the form of colorful wooden cottages with gingerbread trim that date from the Methodist summer camps of the mid-19th century, now called simply the **Camp-**

ground (508-693-0525; www.mv
cma.org). While the rest of the
crowds are jostling along Circuit
Avenue for a "Mud Pie" at **Mad
Martha's** (12 Circuit Ave.; 508-
693-9151) or an ice cream at **Ben
and Bill's Chocolate Emporium**
(20A Circuit Ave.; 508-548-7878),
you can walk past beautiful
Ocean Park—on the left as you
exit the ferry—and continue
inland into the heart of the
Campground. Cheerful cottages,
organized around the Tabernacle
in Trinity Park, seem to be in a
competition to see which one
boasts the most ornate trim and
the most riotous profusion of
flowers. There are **guided walking tours** on Tuesdays and Thursdays at 10 AM in July and August,
and summer events on the Campground green all season, including an annual flea market and
jazz and folk concerts.

One of the prettiest views from
Edgartown's harbor is of **Chap-
paquiddick**, a tiny island just off
the coast of the Vineyard. Get
even closer by hopping aboard
the **Chappy Ferry** (508-627-9427)
to explore the island firsthand.
The ride takes less than five minutes and costs a mere $4 round-
trip for pedestrians, $6 with a
bike and $12 with a car. While
there, you can kayak on Poucha
Pond, relax on East Beach, join a
Cape Pogue Lighthouse tour, or

enjoy the tranquil Mytoi Japanese
garden.

Watch glassblowers in action at
Martha's Vineyard Glassworks
(683 State Rd.; 508-693-6026),
where glassblowers demonstrate
the craft and sell their creations.

Strap on your walking shoes or
bike from Oak Bluffs along **East
Chop Drive** for a dose of instant
serenity as you take in the sight
of multimillion-dollar mansions
perched overlooking the sea.

For a glimpse of what the Vineyard might have looked like
before it was discovered by
tourists, take a ride "up island"
to **Menemsha's Dutcher Dock** in
Chilmark, which still retains the
look of a quaint fishing village.
There are a few shops to browse
in and eateries with some of the
best chowder and clams around,
but the real draw is the unob-
structed view of the fishing boats
as they bring in their heavy lobster pots and buckets of clams
onto the dock to be delivered to
the fish market for take home or
to be boiled and eaten on the
spot.

Stop in at the **Felix Neck
Wildlife Sanctuary** (Felix Neck
Dr.; 508-627-4850; www.mass
audubon.org), the Massachusetts
Audubon Society's 350-acre
refuge about 2 miles outside
Edgartown, where you can par-
ticipate in guided walks, explore

the network of trails on your own, or handle turtles, frogs, and crabs in the touch pool.

If your departing ferry leaves from Vineyard Haven, set aside time to wander in and out of the art galleries that line the streets, take in a play at the **Vineyard Playhouse** (24 Church St.), which operates year-round, or visit the **Carol Craven Gallery** (29 Breakdown Lane; 508-693-3535) or **Tisbury Antiques** (339 State Rd.; 508-693-8333), and be aware that most shops will ship their wares.

▌▌▌ WHAT TO DO

Explore the island by bicycle, either by bringing your own on the ferry or renting one on arrival. Some 26 miles of trails link all parts of the island, and the going is mostly flat and well marked, although it can be windy in some areas. Follow the bike paths along Beach Road to **Joseph A. Sylvia State Beach** on the way to Edgartown or continue on to State Beach, known as **Bend-in-the-Road Beach** to locals, overlooking Nantucket Sound.

Rent bikes at **Wheel Happy Bicycle Rentals** in Edgartown (Upper Main St., 508-627-5928) and **Martha's Vineyard Bikes** in Vineyard Haven (4 Lagoon Pond Rd., 508-693-6593) are just two

of the outlets where you can rent bikes and related equipment.

Grab for the brass ring on the **Flying Horses Carousel** (Oak Bluffs Ave.; 508-693-9481), the oldest operating platform carousel in the country. Open from Easter through Columbus Day, the carousel ride costs only $1.50, with a free second ride if you succeed in nabbing the brass ring.

One of the best ways to see the island is by boat, and rentals are available for just about any vessel you would want, from kayaks to sailing and windsurfing. Try **Winds Up** in Vineyard Haven (199 Beach Rd.; 508-693-4252; www .windsupmv.com), for example, or simply be a passenger on the **Sea Witch Sailing Charters** (508-631-6535; www.seawitchsailing charters.com), also in Vineyard Haven.

Spend a day at the 200-acre **FARM Institute** (Aero Ave.; 508-627-7007; www.farminstitute .org) for a close-up-and-personal visit to a working farm. You can help feed the animals, collect eggs, and work in the garden. In August you can challenge your sense of direction in the 5-acre corn maze and stay for a picnic lunch with fresh local produce.

Join the locals at **Edgartown's Memorial Wharf** in the evening as they "**jig for squid**," a messy

Visitors who just really want to spend a day at the beach will find a menu of beautiful sandy beaches on the Vineyard to suit a range of moods. Those who like big waves can test their mettle against the lively surf at the Pease's Point end of **South Beach**, which is also great for kite flying off-season. For a dose of culture, make your way to **Aquinnah**, formerly known as Gay Head, on the tip of the island. Renamed for the Wampanoag tribe, there are shops and an Aquinnah Cultural Center (Aquinnah Circle) here, as well as dramatic views of the Elizabethan Islands from the cliff. For a more secluded beach experience, although you will need either a car or a bicycle with good shocks, take the bumpy ride along Herring Creek Road to **Lake Tashmoo Beach** in Tisbury. You will see a few families with dogs and a parade of boats ranging from yachts to fishing dinghies.

but intriguing activity that involves popping a fluorescent jig lure onto a fishing line and watching as the squid that teem in the local waters spout their ink.

Despite its congestion in summer, a surprising amount of the Vineyard is still undeveloped, and while exploring the island, you will see a number of farms dotting the horizon, some of which encourage visitors. Try the **Island Alpaca Farm** (Pond Rd.; 508-693-5554; www.islandalpaca .com) for a tour or shop at the store for mittens or scarves.

Spend an afternoon on the Vineyard's longest pony ride (carts also are available) for a ride through **Nip-N-Tuck Farm** (38 Davis Look Rd.; 508-693-1449) in West Tisbury, which

boasts a menagerie of animals and a farm stand.

▌▌▌▌ WHERE TO STAY

The **Winnetu Inn** (31 Dunes Rd.; 978-443-1733; www.winnetu .com), the only resort hotel on South Beach, is 3 miles from Edgartown and offers a private path to South Beach. The comanager was the former executive chef at the Four Seasons Hotel Boston, and guests can sample his culinary wizardry at the on-site Lure restaurant. Guests also have access to the facilities at the adjacent Mattakesett Properties, with private tennis club and heated swimming pools. The property will arrange for rental bikes to be brought to you, or guests can take the free hotel

For all its tranquil charm, the Vineyard has inspired a number of mystery writers to set their stories on the Island. One of the best known is the Martha's Vineyard Mystery series by the late **Philip R. Craig**. Another favorite is the mystery series by **Linda Fairstein**, whose protagonist, Alexandra Cooper, splits her time between New York and Chilmark and spends her downtime swooning over local culinary specialties.

shuttle in and out of Edgartown's Main Street. The concierge will also book high-speed ferry passage from New Bedford and arrange for free ferry transfers to and from the resort. From $195.

Charlotte Inn (27 South Summer St.; 508-627-4751; www .charlotteinn.net) is an in-town splurge in the heart of Edgartown. Frankly posh, the circa 1860s Relais & Châteaux inn has sumptuous antique furnishings, fireplaces, and even a carriage house with private terraces and courtyards. From about $325.

The Madison Inn (18 Kennebec Ave.; 800-564-2760; www .madisoninnmv.com) among the cottages of Oak Bluffs, offers 14 recently renovated guest rooms near the ocean at modest rates. All rooms come with private bath, flat-screen TV, and air-conditioning, as well as free wireless Internet service and complimentary bottled water and snack baskets. From $79.

The Mansion House Inn (9 Main St.; 508-693-2200), in Vineyard Haven is an easy stroll from the ferry dock and offers great views of the harbor as well as one of the best day health clubs on the island. From $99.

The Narragansett House (46 Narragansett Ave.; 508-693-3627; www.narragansetthouse.com) offers a casual ambience and affordable prices within walking distance of Oak Bluffs. From $125.

■■■■ EATING OUT

The Black Dog Tavern (508-693-9223; www.theblackdog.com) in Vineyard Haven harbor is an institution most first timers feel obliged to visit and pay homage to. You can enjoy a great lunch or dinner, but the real treat is breakfast overlooking the water. There is also a bakery on Water Street and a café a mile west of town on State Road. Keep in mind that there are Black Dog retail stores all around the island, however, if all you really want is a T-shirt with the famous Black Dog logo. From about $7 for breakfast and lunch; $20 for dinner.

Linda Jean's Restaurant (25 Circuit Ave.; 508-693-4093) in Oak Bluffs serves home cooking with all the trimmings, including breakfast more or less all day. From under $10.

The Seafood Shanty (31 Dock St.; 508-627-8622) in Edgartown Harbor is a great choice for a lobster quesadilla or peel-and-eat shrimp, or try the new sushi raw bar. From about $15.

The Menemsha Fish Market (54 Bain Rd., Chilmark, 508-645-2282) not only sells some of the freshest fish around but also will cook it up for you to take home or eat on the spot. Try a cooked, split lobster with butter and lemon, a cup of chowder, a stuffed clam, and coleslaw, for example—bring your own chilled bottle of wine—and perch on the dock overlooking the water for a low-key version of al fresco dining. Market price.

The Bite (Menemsha Harbor, 508-645-9239; www.thebite menemsha.com) is a local fish shack where the delicious food—especially the takeaway fried clams—explains the long lines. Market price.

■■■■ SPECIAL EVENTS

July to late September: The free, annual **Vineyard Artisans Summer Fair** (West Tisbury Grange Hall), held Thursdays and Sundays, shows off local crafts, enlivened with music and food.

Late August: The annual **Illumination Night** at the Campground is named for the Chinese paper lanterns that are lit all night to mark the end of summer. A band concert adds music to the mood of the free event.

Mid-September: The Martha's Vineyard **International Film Festival** is a four-day event featuring feature and short films, as well as chats with producers and directors.

■■■■ RESOURCES

Martha's Vineyard Chamber of Commerce, PO Box 1698, Vineyard Haven, MA 02568; 508-693-0085 or 800-505-4815; www.mvy.com

VILLAGE
ESCAPES

11 • GRAFTON, VERMONT

About three hours north of Boston, just over two hours from Hartford

Just because a village is picture-postcard pretty doesn't mean that real people don't live there. In the case of tiny Grafton, Vermont, we're only talking about 600 or so residents, but on any given day you will see them going about their business—pushing strollers, buying milk at the general store, or popping into the Post Office—as if only half aware of the storybook setting around them. In fact, this knockout destination has been ready for its close-up ever since the mid-1960s, when Anheuser-Busch chose to use Main Street for those famous commercials depicting Clydesdale horses clopping through the snow. More recently Grafton was named one of the most beautiful towns in America by *USA Weekend*, and while all this attention is welcome, the trajectory that brought Grafton its present-day kudos has not always been an easy one.

In its heyday in the 1800s, life was good. Grafton residents made their living herding sheep and mining soapstone, and thanks to the town's location on a throughway between Boston and New York, business was robust and dependable. With the Great Depression and the advent of highways that bypassed the town, however, traffic began to fall off, and like many of its neighbors, Grafton began to fray around the edges. Enter Dean Mathey, a banker and philanthropist from Princeton, New Jersey, who nurtured fond memories of happy childhood summers with his aunt in Grafton and decided to help the town get back on its feet. In the early 1960s Mathey began the rejuvenating process by creating the Windham Foundation, and the ripple effect from that one act continues to grow outward to this day.

The first task was to refurbish the **Old Tavern** on Main Street, which opened in 1801 and is one of the oldest inns in America still in operation. Other business projects followed—most notably Grafton Ponds and Grafton Village Cheese Co. (both mentioned below)—and while the Foundation is proud of its work to promote the vitality of the village and protect its rural identity, members are quick to point out that they do not own or run the town. Far from being a living museum controlled by one entity, Grafton is a real place just like any other. It is just prettier than most.

■ ■ ■ ■ GETTING THERE (AND GETTING AROUND)

Plan on a good three hours from Boston and nearly five hours from New York to get to Grafton by car. From I-91, take Route 5 north to Route 121 and be prepared to navigate several miles of smooth but unpaved road. The nearest airports are Manchester-Boston Regional Airport, technically in Manchester, New Hampshire, about an hour away, and Burlington, Vermont.

Once in Grafton, park and walk through the tiny downtown but drive or cycle to Grafton Ponds.

■ ■ ■ ■ WHAT TO SEE

For a glimpse into the evolution of the village, stop in at the **Grafton Historical Society Museum** in the Stowell/Mead house (Main St.; 802-843-1010), which is open in summer through foliage season. Exhibits rotate from year to year and focus on re-creating scenes from daily life of previous centuries, using period furniture and everyday objects. In 2009,

for example, a key exhibit was a re-creation of the mid-19th-century Phelps Hotel, an elegant property of yore funded by proceeds from the Gold Rush. The permanent exhibitions include collections of objects fashioned from soapstone quarried in town, as well as antique quilts, toys, and tools. The museum is operated by the Grafton Historical Society, which also organizes educational

Grafton Ponds

Grafton Village Cheese Co.

SHANE HAGER

programs and publishes historical books.

Go around the corner to the
Grafton Blacksmith Shop
(School St.), where you can see
demonstrations of this lost art in
June through Columbus Day,
examine antique tools, or buy
souvenirs. In New England, the
oldest church in town frequently
dominates the town center. In
Grafton, there are two, across
from each other, the **Brick** and
White churches, just off Main
Street. Both were built in the
mid-19th century, and they share
a United Church of Christ minis-
ter, holding services in summer
and winter, respectively. The
imposing **Grafton Library** (204
Main St.) is also worth a look, as
is the **Grafton Village Store**
(802-843-2348), which was built
in the mid-19th century. Nearby
is the much-photographed **Kid-
der Hill Covered Bridge** just
south of town, which dates from
about 1870.

History buffs can wander several very old cemeteries in town
looking for markers commemorating soldiers who died in the
Revolutionary and Civil wars, or
they can visit the **Barrett House**,
now a vacation rental on Main
Street and part of **The Old
Tavern**, believed to have been a
stop along the Underground
Railroad.

This part of Vermont is known
for its rich minerals, marble, and
granite, and visitors can examine
some of the most spectacular
examples at the **Vermont Museum of Mining and Minerals** (55
Pleasant St.; 802-875-3562;
www.vtmmm.org). Exhibits at the
museum, which is open in summer and early fall, include a
model village made of local
stone. **DyakCraft** (802-869-1880;
www.dyakcraft.com) is the place
to find fiber art tools, including
hand spindles and crochet hooks,
as well as hand-dyed yarn. Call
ahead of time if you want to visit
the studio.

Go gallery hopping at **Gallery
North Star** (151 Townshend Rd.;
802-843-2465), in a 19th-century
home and full of paintings and
sculptures by dozens of New England artists. The **Hunter Art
Works** (Townshend Rd. adjacent
to the Old Tavern; 802-843-1440),
sells arty gifts, dispenses maps to
lost tourists, and is conveniently
located next to the Daniels Café
right in town center. Antique
lovers can visit the **Grafton Gath-
ering Place Antiques** (748 East-
man Rd.; 802-875-2309) for
country furniture and accessories
or **Sylvan Hill Antiques** (39
Pleasant St.; 802-875-3954),
where you'll find everything from
American and English furniture to
original art.

One of the best-known residents of Grafton was **Daisy Turner**, the daughter of freed slaves, who created recordings on which she tells the story of her ancestry.

More recently, the 1988 movie *Funny Farm* with Chevy Chase was filmed partly in town.

■■■■ WHAT TO DO

If your motives for visiting Grafton are focused on outdoor pursuits, the place to start is at the **Grafton Ponds Outdoor Center** (783 Townsend Rd.; 802-843-2400; www.graftonponds.com) operated by the Windham Foundation. Cross-country skiers love the 18 miles or so of groomed trails, and the snowmaking equipment helps ensure good conditions all season. Those who prefer ungroomed backcountry skiing will also find plenty of terrain to keep them busy.

Snowshoeing, an increasingly popular sport because it has virtually no learning curve, is available on nearly 10 miles of trails at Grafton Ponds, including four that were new in 2008/09. A beginner trail makes an easy loop near the base lodge, while the other three end up at a warming hut at the top of the hill. Quirky snowshoe tours are available all season, including a moonlight snowshoe tour that combines exercise with roasting s'mores

around a roaring bonfire. One of the most popular guided excursions is the **Wine & Cheese Snowshoe Tour** that rewards participants for their exertions with wine and local cheese afterward. Tours start from the base lodge at 1:30 PM, and advance reservations are required. An **Off the Beaten Path Snowshoe Tour** led by Pond director Bill Salmon takes small groups off groomed trails into the countryside for a personalized guided tour. The routes are tailored to suit the skill level of the participants, who will also learn about local flora and fauna en route.

You don't have to be a kid to enjoy **snowtubing** on the Ponds' 600-foot dedicated run, but be aware that you'll be lugging your rental tube up the hill without a lift. Another way to work off lunch is to strap on a pair of rental skates at the ice skating pond.

In summer, the Pond is just as appealing with some 2,000 acres of **mountain biking** and **hiking** trails for a range of fitness levels.

You can rent bikes and other equipment right from the base lodge and embark on a self-guided exploration or join a guided tour. Fans of road biking can join a leisurely guided ride with Kevin O'Donnell, the innkeeper of the Old Tavern, whose outings can range from short tours to long treks, depending on the mood of the group. The rides, which are open to everyone, usually depart at around 10 AM. For more amped-up cycling, try the new bike terrain park at the Ponds, which, while not overly intense, offers loops with man-made jumps and rollers for the young and young at heart.

First-time visitors to this part of Vermont are often surprised at the number of scenic rivers, ponds, and lakes there are, and one of the best ways to experience them is by **canoe** or **kayak**. Ponds staff will take participants out on guided half-day excursions on local waterways, creating the day's itinerary based on what the group wants to do. Lunch is included, and participants will learn about the area from the guides en route. A new hour-and-a-half fly-fishing clinic teaches participants the ins and outs of the sport and provides the accompanying gear.

The Nature Museum at Grafton (186 Townshend Rd.; 802-843-2111; www.nature -museum.org), open year-round, puts the local environment in context with interactive exhibits. The museum also oversees **The Village Park**, a network of woodsy trails just behind the museum that is ideal for visitors who want a hike without a big time commitment. Pick up a trail map at the museum and look for shady gazebos for a picnic along the way. The Park, which has

Grafton covered bridge
SHANE HAGER

entrances at Townshend and Fire Pond Roads, is open year-round.

Food lovers should not even consider leaving Grafton without picking up a wheel of artisanal cheddar from the **Grafton Village Cheese Co., Inc.** (Townshend Rd.; 802-843-2221; www.graftonvillage cheese.com). Two of the company's cheeses were recently named among the top 100 cheeses worldwide by *Wine Spectator Magazine*, and other awards from top food and wine magazines literally cover its entrance wall. The two so honored are Grafton's Clothbound Cheddar and Grafton Premium Cheddar, but all the cheeses are made from dairy products from Vermont cows. Visitors can watch the cheesemaking process through a display window at the store, sample various products, and learn about what wines pair well with which cheese. The company, which had been in operation since 1892 as a cooperative, became defunct in 1912 when its facilities burned down. The Windham Foundation kicked the company back into gear in 1965, although the new version has a more artisanal, upscale feel than the original. The venture has been so successful that there is a second facility in Brattleboro, about a half hour away.

Nothing says Vermont like maple syrup, and the best place to stock up on a few bottles is at the source. **Plummer's Sugarhouse** (Townshend Rd.; 802-843-2207; www.plummerssugar house.com) sells all manner of locally produced syrup, maple candy, and maple cream, but visitors can take a tour of the sugarhouse and learn about the process of collecting sap and transforming it into syrup. If you needed a reason besides spring skiing to visit between mid-February and mid-April, also known as sugar season, you may see staff at the sugarhouse making syrup and offering free samples.

For a mix of souvenirs, from hand-blown glass to fruit preserves, stop in **Grafton Seasons** (Main St.; 802-843-2499; www .graftonseasons.com), in the town's repurposed Old Fire Station.

▪▪▪▪ WHERE TO STAY

The Old Tavern at Grafton (92 Main St.; 802-843-2231; www.old tavern.com) qualifies as much more than just a place to dine. In many ways the heart of Grafton, the tavern is also a 45-room inn that has been in operation since just a decade or so after the Revolutionary War. Notable guests who visited the inn read like a who's who in American history, from Ulysses S. Grant and Daniel

Webster to Teddy Roosevelt and Woodrow Wilson. A few famous writers, including Ralph Waldo Emerson and Rudyard Kipling, also paid the inn a visit back in the day. As the town began to decline after the turn of the century, however, those travelers who did make it to Grafton were looking for modern conveniences rather than drafty historic charm. The Windham Foundation revamped, insulated, and heated the Tavern so that it could welcome guests year-round, while retaining its original architectural details, including hand-hewn beams and period furnishings. Antique doesn't mean frumpy, however; the property is a member of the Small Luxury Hotels of the World, and guest rooms are discreetly Wi-Fi enabled and individually decorated.

In addition to the 11-room main property, the Old Tavern offers several guesthouses and four rental houses. The **Windham & Homestead** cottages across the street are also operated by the Old Tavern for guests looking for more privacy. **Barrett House**, **Tuttle House**, **White Gates**, and **Woodard House** are four rental houses that the Tavern runs, each of which can sleep from six to 10 people. They all have full kitchens and some feature working fireplaces. From $160.

The **By the River Bed & Breakfast** (460 Rte. 121; 802-843-2886) may not be Grandma's house, but it's the next best thing, complete with a bubbling brook and cozy fireplace. You'll get real syrup with your organic breakfast, a view of the river from your guest room, and a warm welcome from innkeepers Elise and Bill Brooks, who also offer yoga classes on request. From $135.

The **Inn at Woodchuck Hill Farm** (off Middletown Rd.; 802-843-2398; www.woodchuckhill .com), a few miles outside town, is another antique lovers' dream. Perched on 200 acres in a restored 1790s farmhouse, the inn has vast lawns, a gazebo, a picturesque pond, and even a wood-fired sauna. Guests can stay in the Main House, the Barn Suites, or— if you brought the gang—the Spruce Cottage. From $99; $400 for Spruce Cottage.

■ ■ ■ ■ WHERE TO CAMP

Tree Farm Camp Grounds (53 Skitchewaug Trail, Springfield; 802-885-2889), just over a half hour away, is open to tents and RVs. The sites are in wooded trails, and the grounds are open from May to November. $18.

■ ■ ■ ■ EATING OUT

The **Old Tavern** has gone all out with its cuisine, overseen by chef

David Smith. The menu changes seasonally, using organic and heirloom produce from its own kitchen garden, which is open for guests to tour. The restaurant also is part of the Vermont Fresh Network, which promotes locally grown and sustainable cuisine. From $19 to $32, but half plates are available.

The Daniels Café (802-843-2255) in back of the Tavern is a more casual option, and there is outdoor seating on sunny days. A soup and sandwich special with a drink will cost less than $10.

Grafton Grocery Market (Main St.) is the place to go for deli fare and drinks to go, including wine.

▮▮▮▮ SPECIAL EVENTS

Late May to early October: Cap off a perfect summer day at a free **Grafton Cornet Band Concert** (Town Common, 55 Main St.; 802-387-4145; www.graftonband .org), which, contrary to its moniker, presents music from a full band, with selections that can range from show tunes to rousing marches.

Memorial Day & July 3: **Grafton Ponds Outdoor Center** celebrates summer with kickoff festivities on Memorial Day weekend and the annual July 3 concert put on by the Vermont Symphony Orchestra, complete with fireworks. Plop down on the lawn or bring your own chair.

Late August to early September: **Exhibition at Grafton** (www.gnsgrafton.com) is a free juried art show that takes place every summer at various venues in town, showing off the works of some 50 professional East Coast artists.

▮▮▮▮ NEARBY

Three alpine ski areas—**Bromley Mountain, Okemo Mountain Resort, and Stratton Mountain**— are only about an hour away from Grafton. Each offers rental equipment, a variety of terrain for all skill levels, and parking. In summer, the mountains offer warm-weather activities, as well, including golf.

▮▮▮▮ RESOURCES

The Windham Foundation, 225 Townshend Road; 802-843-2211; www.windham-foundation.org

12 • LITTLE COMPTON/TIVERTON FOUR CORNERS, RHODE ISLAND

About an hour from Boston, Providence, and Cape Cod, and just over the Massachusetts border

We have all heard the old saw about how getting there is half the fun, but in the case of Little Compton and Tiverton Four Corners in Rhode Island, the saying holds true. These neighboring villages in Rhode Island's Sakonnet region are prettiest when taken in the context of their surroundings, like a painting in the perfect frame.

Comprised mostly of working farms, fishing docks, and vineyards, the region is tough to find—even with a GPS—and easy to miss on arrival if you don't slow down enough to appreciate the subtleties of its beauty. Instead of re-created villages with blacksmith shops and costumed guides, you will find authentic towns whose historical roots have blended seamlessly into their present-day lives.

This is not to say that there aren't any noteworthy historical sites or tourism amenities in Sakonnet, which loosely translated means "black goose." Little Compton, for example, was originally inhabited by the Sogkon-

nite Indians before being established as part of Massachusetts in the late 1600s. The first European settlers hailed from Plymouth, Massachusetts, but the land was eventually turned over to Rhode Island in the 18th century. Little Compton saw action in the Revolutionary War from the British, who occupied Newport, on the other side of the Sakonnet River Bridge.

The countryside in these parts is dotted with farm stands, where you will find yourself screeching on the brakes to buy heirloom tomatoes, overstuffed fruit pies, and just-picked sweet corn. Slow down as you approach Tiverton Four Corners, centered in an area so picturesque that it has been on the National Register of Historic Places since the 1970s. Seventeenth- and 18th-century architecture dominates the village, which boasts several historic buildings, from the **Grist Mill** to the **A.P. White Store**.

Grab a parking spot anywhere in the Four Corners area and begin your exploration on foot, poking around in the tiny shops that sell antiques, jewelry, pottery, and picnic food. For all its history, Tiverton is a little trafficky, so your best bet is to explore one side of the street at a time before bundling back in the car en route to Little Compton. Drive slowly, as you will likely find yourself stopping every few minutes along the way to visit a shop, take a picture, or sample local produce.

Once in Little Compton, you can park in the Commons, the town center organized around a village green. It offers a quieter visitor experience than Tiverton, but, to paraphrase Spencer Tracy when describing the slender build of Katharine Hepburn, "what's there is choice." If you are a history buff, stop at the **Wilbor House** (548 West Main Rd.) on the way into town, which dates from the 17th century and houses the Historical Society. The Society operates traditional Yankee events, like Cider Socials in the fall, and operates a museum

as well as a full schedule of talks and exhibits.

Or just poke around the town on your own; you can pick up local treats at the general store, wander through the green, and talk to the friendly locals about what they think you should see. Chances are, they will point you in the direction of Adamsville, also part of Little Compton, where you can pore over the antiquities—some kitschy and some elegant—at **Gray's General Store** (Main St., Adamsville), the oldest continuously run general store in the country.

Unlike some blockbuster New England destinations that require days to even scratch the surface—such as the Berkshires or the Vineyard—you can do Tiverton and Little Compton in a day and still have time to check out neighboring Wesport or Dartmouth.

■■■■ GETTING THERE (AND GETTING AROUND)

From Boston, take I-93 West to Route 24 South, then take exit 5

Farm in Tiverton

The Stone House, Tiverton

to Route 77 South. From this direction, you will reach Tiverton Four Corners first at the intersection of Neck Road, and in order to see most of the sights listed here, you'll need your car.

▊▊▊▊ WHAT TO SEE

Antique hounds will think they have died and gone to heaven in Tiverton, starting at **Antiques II at Four Corners** (8 Neck Rd.; 401-816-0864) and **Peter's Attic** (8 Neck Rd.; 401-625-5912) where you may find that farm table you have been dreaming of.

For pottery that you can actually use, like mugs, pitchers and candlesticks in cheerful, sherbet colors, stop in at **Roseberry-Winn Pottery & Tile** (3841 Main Rd.; 401-816-0010; www.roseberry winn.com), or stroll across the street to **Tiffany Peay Jewelry and Gallery** (3879 Main Rd.; 888-808-0201; www.tiffanypeay.com), where Peay, a transplanted New York artist, designs and sells jewelry in the shop and at the Stone House Spa in Little Compton.

The Four Corners Arts Center (3852 Main Rd.; 401-624-2600), in the 18th-century Soule-Seabury House, is a nonprofit that promotes the arts with theatrical productions, films, education, and exhibits. Summer visitors should check out the annual exhibit of sculptures, sprinkled on the lawn, not that you are likely to miss it. Next door, **Gallery 4** (3848 Main Rd.; 401-816-0999) is a cooperative store that houses the Silk Road Traders, Susan Freda Studio, and Wanderer Imports for everything from kilim rugs to embroidered dresses.

Other art galleries include the **Donovan Gallery** in the Arnold Smith House (3895 Main Rd.; 401-624-4000; www.donovangallery .com), which features the works of several artists, and **The Richards Gallery** (3964 Main Rd.; 401-624-3331) in the Mill Pond Shops, which exhibits the artist's own works. The **Amy C. Lund Handweaver & Handspinner** shop (3879 Main Rd.; 401-816-0000) is the place to go not only to buy textiles but also to watch the process from weaving to the finished product.

In the Commons, wander through the common cemetery, where with a little sleuthing you will find the grave of Elizabeth Alden, whose parents arrived from England on the *Mayflower*, making her the first European baby born in New England. You can also have a look at the **Town Hall** (40 Commons), which used to be a schoolhouse, and the **Brownell Library** (44 Commons).

Bird lovers and history buffs know that it isn't a black goose for which this area is famous, but rather the Rhode Island Red rooster, the state's official bird. The rooster was said to have been bred in nearby Adamsville in the 19th century, bringing fame and even a measure of wealth to the region because of the bird's superior qualities as a breeder. Check out the rooster monument in Adamsville (Main Rd.), believed to be the only one of its kind in the United States.

■■■■ WHAT TO DO

Go hiking in the 50-plus-acre **Emile Ruecker Wildlife Refuge** (Seapowet Ave., Tiverton), an Audubon Society refuge teeming with birds that abuts the Sakonnet River. There is an easy 1½-mile walking trail that wends through the marshes and woods. Download a trail map at www.asri .org.

Explore the many bike routes in the region, including a loop that links Little Compton and Tiverton. Either bring your own bike or rent one at the **Village Bike Shop** (678 Main Rd.; 508-636-0525) in nearby Westport, Massachusetts, which also offers guided group rides of the region several times a week in season.

Spend an afternoon on the water courtesy of **Osprey Sea Kayak Adventures** (489 Old County Rd.; 508-636-0300), also in Westport, where you can take guided eco- or adventure tours or even wine tours that include tastings at the Westport Rivers Vineyard.

If you would rather let someone else do the piloting, spend a day with **Sakonnet Charters** (401-474-2405; www.sakonnetcharters .com), which runs group and charter excursions out of Sakonnet Harbor in Little Compton. Up to six people can kick back and relax on one of two classic sailboats for a day of fishing, a sunset cruise with a lobster dinner, or even a multiday outing.

Go horseback riding at **Roseland Acres** (594 East Road; 401-624-8866), where you can choose from trail rides or lessons in an indoor ring.

Enjoy an old-fashioned hayride, pick your own pumpkins, or select a fresh-cut Christmas tree at **Pachet Brook Farm** (4484 Main Rd.; 401-624-4872). Why does everything grow so well in this region? Find out at

Peckham's Greenhouse (200 West Main Rd., Little Compton; 401-635-4775), a seaside farm stand that dates from the 1800s, or **Young's Family Farm Stand** (260 West Main Rd., Little Compton).

For a quirky way to spend a few hours on a sunny afternoon, pay a visit to the **Butterfly Farm** (409 Bulgarmarsh Rd., Tiverton; 401-849-9519), where you can see hundreds of butterflies and learn about how to plant the right kind of garden to attract them. The farm is open in summer except when it rains.

▪▪▪▪ WHERE TO STAY

The **Stone House** (122 Sakonnet Point Rd.; 401-635-2222; www.stonehouse1854.com) in Little Compton is a former private club that reopened in 2009 as a resort on the waterfront. The property benefited from a National Register history renovation using green technology, and the result is elegant without being overly formal. Splurge on an overnight stay in the original house or adjacent tricked-out barn. There also is a full-service spa and upscale restaurant called Pietra, with a less formal pub in the works. From $365.

The **Edith Pearl** (250 West Main Rd.; 401-592-0053) in Little Compton is a historic and pet-friendly B&B. There are public rooms galore if you want to mingle with other guests, a wraparound porch, and period furniture. From $175.

The **Paquachuck Inn** (2056 Main Rd., Westport Point; 508-636-4398; www.paquachuck .com), perched on Westport harbor, even has its own fishing dock. The 170-year-old property offers an above-average breakfast, views of the water and a cozy, Old New England ambience, complete with harpoons and whalebones in the lobby. From $125.

▪▪▪▪ WHERE TO CAMP

Horseneck Beach has an on-site campground, and you can reserve a spot online through www.reserveamerica.com. $15.

▪▪▪▪ EATING OUT

The Commons Restaurant (48 Commons; 401-635-4388) in Little Compton may look like a diner from the outside, but the menu is surprisingly varied, with everything from calamari and lobster to steak. The wine list is tiny, but the prices and friendly atmosphere will win you over. Try the johnny cakes for breakfast with stone-ground cornmeal and real maple syrup, and opt for an outside table in warm weather. From $4.99.

Provender (3883 Main Rd.; 401-624-8084) in the historic building that once housed the A. P. White General Store in Tiverton is the place to go for a fresh take on deli sandwiches with cute names like the Freudian Slip (Black Forest ham, garlic and herb cheese, and spinach) and the Mama Mia (turkey, roasted red peppers, and tomatoes). Get lunch to go or linger at one of the few tables over ice coffee, cleverly served with cubes made from coffee. From $6.95.

The **Milk & Honey Bazaar and Food Shop** (3838 Main Rd.; 401-624-1974; www.milkandhoney bazaar.com) is a gourmet choice for picnic food, particularly the dozens of artisanal cheeses and other charcuterie items.

The Four Corners Grille (3841 Main Rd.; 401-624-1510), also in Tiverton and open year-round, is a sit-down restaurant with everything from steak to seafood, served with wine. From $7.95.

The Last Stand (374 West Main Rd.; 401-592-0400) in Little Compton is a seasonal market serving sandwiches, panini, and salads using fresh, local produce. Save room for fresh pies and fruit crisps for dessert. From $7.25.

Back Eddy (Bridge Rd., Westport; 508-636-6500; www.the backeddy.com) is a popular waterfront eatery, known for littleneck clams, grilled swordfish, and native lobster. Market price.

Gray's Ice Cream (16 East Rd.; 401-624-450; www.graysice cream.com) got a nod from *Gourmet* magazine for their frozen treats, but the full parking lot out front tells the real story.

■■■■ NEARBY

Perhaps one of the most surprising features of Little Compton and its environs is that the land is viable for growing wine grapes, according to the owners of **Sakonnet Vineyards** (162 West Main Road, Little Compton; 401-635-8486). The 50-acre vineyard

Christmas tree farm

Little Compton and Tiverton have their own beaches, but for a full-on, it's-all-about-the-beach experience, head to **Horseneck Beach State Reservation** (www.mass.gov/dcr/parks/southeast/hbch.htm) in Westport, Massachusetts. This is one of the most popular of the all the Massachusetts parks, thanks in part to its huge size—the reservation measures almost 600 acres—and its gorgeous two-mile stretch of sandy beach and sheltering dunes. You will see people windsurfing here all summer, and there are all manner of activities available here, from boating ramps to fishing and bird-watching.

has been in business since the 1970s after owners deemed the climate and soil to be not unlike that of the Loire Valley in France and the Rhine region in Germany.

The vineyard, which produces some 30,000 cases each year, offers tours to visitors and hosts wedding and other special events. What even many locals don't realize is that the vineyard is a stop along the Coastal Wine Trail (www.coastalwinetrail.com), which runs along the coast from Cape Cod and the Islands into Connecticut. There are seven vineyards in all, and each year the group celebrates the beginning of the season with a kickoff event at one of the vineyards that features local cheese makers, bakers, and farmers showing off their wares to the sounds of live music and merrymaking. The event sells out early, perhaps because of the promise of wine and beer samplings on hand.

You can pick up a Coastal Wine Trail map from any of the vineyards and use it to plot out a wine tasting and sightseeing itinerary, but for a real *Sideways* experience, plan to spend at least two or three days on the trail.

▌▌▌▌ SPECIAL EVENTS

May to July: Kick off the summer season at the annual Four Corners Garden and Herb Festival in May on the lawn of the Soule-Seabury House with crafts, produce, and, of course, flowers. Or take in the Summer Bazaar, an international fair trade craft fair that takes place in the same spot in July.

Early June: The Friends of Tiverton Libraries Annual Library Street Fair (401-625-6796) features a flea market, bake sale, appraisals of antiques, and activities for the kids.

Mid-July and August: The Open Studio Tour for South Coast artists is a free event during which local artists throw open their doors to the public. Works include everything from paintings and sculpture to jewelry and glass pieces.

Late-July, early August: The Little Compton Antiques Festival takes place on the grounds of the Sakonnet Vineyards (W. Main St., Little Compton; 508-674-9186)

▌▌▌▌ RESOURCES

Little Compton Historical Society, 548 W. Main Rd. Little Compton, RI 02837; 401-635-4035

Tiverton Historical Society, 3908 Main Rd. Tiverton, RI 02878; 401-625-5174

Tiverton Town Hall, 343 Highland Rd.

13 • LITTLETON, NEW HAMPSHIRE

At the border of the White Mountains and the Connecticut River off I-93

Some of New England's prettiest towns and villages were born as resort destinations, attracting vacationers almost as soon as they were settled, either because they boasted lakes, oceans, ski mountains, or simply fresh mountain air. Not so Littleton, a charming town in northern New Hampshire that is, in some ways, the geographical equivalent of *The Little Engine That Could*.

Perched on the edge of the Ammonoosuc River, Littleton was founded in the late 18th century by residents who were there not to take the waters, but to work in the Littleton Grist Mill, which for years was the pulse of the town's industrial and economic growth.

Like many other former mill towns in New England, Littleton fell into hard times in the intervening years, but here is where the story differs. Rather than quietly devolve into a depressed ghost town, Littleton pulled up its socks and willed itself into a thriving tourism destination that goes all out to honor its humble past.

It is especially fitting that the

Littleton Grist Mill (8 Mill St.; 603-444-7478), which once gave the town its lifeblood, was also the source of its reinvention, thanks to the efforts of local residents who undertook to restore the mill in the late 1990s. With the help of photographs and other artifacts, renovators were able to duplicate the details of the original mill and several adjacent buildings, turning them into bustling shops and a free museum.

Today's visitors can while away an entire afternoon at the riverfront complex, which boasts such original architectural touches as wide-plank floors and a cedar shake roof. Watch the video on the second floor about the history of the renovation and the renaissance of the town. The jewel in the crown of the restoration is an actual gristmill, which grinds grain just as it did hundreds of years ago, and which you can see from an observation area inside the mill or from the deck outside. On the first floor, visitors can buy artisanal products, like specialty stone-ground whole-grain flours, to take home. The mill also sells cereals, old-fashioned sodas, organic snacks, and maple syrup, and they even throw in some recipes so that shoppers will use their products to their best advantage.

Antique lovers will have to be dragged out of **Saranac Street Antiques** (141 Main St.), which recently moved to its new digs in the old Masonic Temple building in the town center. A cavernous space, the shop boasts three floors jammed with furniture, art, and china. Store owners will deliver, but if you don't see what you want, they will look for it in their off-site warehouse.

■■■■ GETTING THERE (AND GETTING AROUND)

Littleton is about a three-hour drive from Boston; five hours from New York and an hour and a half from Concord, New Hampshire. From Boston, drive north on I-93 to exit 41 to Route 18. You can take a bus (www.concord coachlines.com) to Concord from Boston's South Station in just over an hour and a half.

Once there, park the car and leave it for an on-foot exploration of the town.

■■■■ WHAT TO SEE

With all this can-do spirit, it is perhaps no surprise that the most famous statue in town is not that of a bearded and serious-looking town father but rather of **Pollyanna** (Littleton Public Library, Main St.; 603-444-5741), the irrepressible young optimist who was the heroine of books, a movie, and even a Broadway show in the years since her creation in 1913. The author, Eleanor H. Porter, was born and raised in Littleton, and the bronze statue that was unveiled in 2002 is an

Restored grist mill and covered bridge

Pollyanna statue in Littleton

enduring symbol of the affection her character still manages to inspire even among hard-boiled cynics. Visitors are encouraged to touch the foot of the statue, which holds pride of place in the town center, for good luck.

From here, you can continue your exploration of Main Street, which, if you squint, resembles a movie set, thanks to the preponderance of turn-of-the-century architecture. The local Historical Society, housed in the **Littleton Community House** (120 Main St.), preserves town records and arranges such events during the year as the Cemetery Walk in October, complete with local residents recounting the town's history in character.

The **Littleton Opera House** is being earmarked as a venue for future performance events and films, but in the meantime, the exterior architecture alone is worth the visit. Or catch a movie at **Jax Jr. Cinemas**, with its neon sign. The theater's history goes all the way back to its earliest incarnation in 1920, and in 1941 the movie premiere of a Bette Davis film, *The Great Lie*, brought the star and her entourage to the town.

For a step back in time of another kind, head over to **Chutters Candy Store** (43 Main St.), which bills itself as having the world's longest candy counter at a whopping 112 feet. Candies, some of which you probably haven't seen since you were a child, are color coordinated in glass jars, and patrons are encouraged to take a bag and work their way from one end of the counter to the other. The shop also sells souvenir items, but we suspect you'll be too busy sampling the homemade fudge to notice.

Next door is the **Glass Goddess Stained Glass Studio** (21 Main St.; 603-444-6778; www.glass goddessstainedglassstudio.com), where local artisans will create a customized work based on your design, or you can browse through the objects on display.

Visitors can forgo the candy altogether and head instead to **The Healthy Rhino** (106 Main St.; 603-444-2177) for natural and organic fare.

Stop for a latte and a pastry from the King Arthur Bakery at the Corner Cafe at the **Village Book Store** (81 Main St.), where staff will help you find bestsellers or search for out-of-print books, games, or CDs.

▮▮▮ WHAT TO DO

Work off the gumballs from Chutters strolling along the easy half-mile **Riverwalk**, which starts near the mill and wends its way

*Historic
Thayers Inn*

through the adjacent covered bridge and along the Ammonoosuc River. Outdoor enthusiasts can try a longer walk at **The Dells**, a park just over a mile from downtown off Rts. 302 & 10, with a pond and picnic sites, as well as maintained walking paths.

There is a wider network of trails—75 miles in all—that links Littleton with neighboring towns like Whitefield and Bethlehem. The trails, which are maintained year-round by **Littleton Off-Road Riders,** are available for hiking, mountain biking, and horseback riding in warm weather and cross-country skiing, dogsledding, and snowmobiling in winter. Visitors who use the trails can make a voluntary donation of $10 a year to their upkeep.

For a glimpse of the area's prehistoric past, not to mention stellar views of the town of Littleton

and the Presidential Range, strap on your hiking boots and climb **Kilburn Crag**, just outside town on Route 18. You can also enjoy water sports at **Moore Reservoir**, also off Route 18, for an afternoon of paddleboats and fishing or tee up at the 18-hole Maplewood Golf Resort at **The Inn at Maplewood**, a late-19th-century resort in nearby Bethlehem (www.maple woodgolfresort.com).

In summer, enjoy that quintessential small-town New England experience, a summer concert in a gazebo in **Remich Park** (603-444-6561), which operates a summer music series on Friday evenings. Or take a 15-minute drive to the **Colonial Theatre** in Bethlehem (2050 Main St.; 603-869-3422) for concert series, live theatrical performances, lectures, and films.

If your itinerary includes an overnight stay, consider finishing your day with a microbrew beer

Winter sports are big in the White Mountain area of New Hampshire, and while you won't find Alpine skiing right in town, there are plenty of ski areas nearby. **Cannon Mountain** is only about 15 minutes away by car, while **Burke Mountain** (www.skiburke.com) in Vermont is about a half hour away. **Bretton Woods** (Rte. 302; 800-314-1752 or 603-278-1000; www.mountwashingtonresort.com), New Hampshire's largest ski area, and **Loon Mountain** (60 Loon Mountain Rd.; 603-745-8111 or 800-229-LOON; www.loonmtn.com) are also only about a half hour away, which means that skiers can be on the slopes when the lifts open and still be back in Littleton in time for dinner.

In the fall, the thing to do for visitors who love to sightsee from behind the wheel is to hit the **Kancamagus Highway**, a scenic 35-plus-mile route that runs from Lincoln, New Hampshire, through the White Mountain National Forest. Most popular during leaf peeping season, the ride takes about an hour, but if you don't mind not being the only one on the road, the views are worth it, or go in summer for a more serene experience.

in the tavern—some selections vary by season—at the **Italian Oasis Restaurant & Brewery** (106 Main St.; 603-444-6995), and stay for Italian fare, steaks, or stone-fired pizza in the restaurant or on the patio in season.

▮▮▮▮ WHERE TO STAY

Thayers Inn (111 Main St.; 603-444-6469; www.thayersinn.com), a 40-room hotel front and center in Littleton's downtown, is named for one of the town's most prominent citizens in the mid-19th century. The property, now on the National Register of Historic Places, offers guest rooms with period furnishings, Wi-Fi, and a seafood restaurant and tavern. $79.95 to $159.95.

The Beal House Inn & Restaurant (2 W. Main St.; 603-444-2661; www.thebealhouseinn.com) has changed hands several times in recent year, but the property was recently reopened after an extensive renovation. This 1833 farm is now a 9-room inn with a restaurant and piano bar. From $109.

The Hampton Inn Littleton (580 Meadow St.; 603-444-0025; 866-579-0037; www.littleton hotel.com) at the far end of town has an indoor pool and plenty of packages that bundle in tickets to nearby attractions along with accommodations. From $169.

The Maple Leaf Motel (150 West Main St.; 888-513-5323 or 603-444-5105; www.mapleleaf motel.com) offers plenty of bang for your buck with 13 rooms equipped with refrigerators—some also have kitchens—an outdoor heated pool, and a picnic area. The property, which is within easy walking distance of the town center, is run by motorcycle enthusiasts. From $59.

■ ■ ■ ■ WHERE TO CAMP

Camping is available at the **Littleton/Lisbon KOA Campground** (2154 Rte. 302; 603-838-5525; www.littletonkoa.com), where a site won't break the bank and the amenities include a heated swimming pool and mini golf. About $30 for a tent site.

■ ■ ■ ■ EATING OUT

Miller's Cafe and Bakery (16 Mill St.; 603-444-2146; www.millers cafeandbakery.com) near the Riverwalk is the place to go if you want to grab lunch on the deck overlooking the river. Choose a cappuccino and pastry, dig into a fresh grilled panini, or ask staff to pack up a picnic to go. Sandwiches from $7.99.

Bailiwicks Restaurant, Wine & Martini Bar (111 Main St.; 603-444-7717) in the Thayer Hotel serves dinner or Sunday brunch, or you can stop in for a drink after a long day of sightseeing. $8.95 to $12.95 for lunch; $29.99 for dinner.

Littleton Diner (145 Main St.; 603-444-3994; www.littleton diner.com) a fixture in town since the 1940s, offers a real dose of nostalgia, thanks to eat-in options, like roast turkey dinner, bread pudding, and rhubarb pie, that would have been at home on our grandparents' table. Take-out also is available, and breakfast is served all day. $2.99 to $7.99 for lunch; $6.99 to $13.49 for dinner.

Chang Thai Café (77 Main St.; 603-444-8810) serves Thai cuisine for lunch and dinner with fresh ingredients in a trendy setting. From $6.99 for lunch; $10 for dinner.

■ ■ ■ ■ NEARBY

Head northeast to the town of Milan for a day of rafting with **North Woods Rafting** (off Rte. 16; 603-449-BOAT; www.northwoods rafting.com). The company offers guided whitewater rafting and inflatable kayak tours for individuals and groups, or you can rent equipment for a self-guided outing.

The North Country Center for the Arts just over 20 miles away in Lincoln (off I-93; 603-745-6032;

Robert Frost may be most associated with Vermont, but in fact, it was the little town of Bethlehem, New Hampshire, only about 15 minutes from Littleton, that drew the poet laureate to the White Mountains. Frost came to the mountains to escape his allergies as much as to find inspiration in the scenery, and nowadays visitors can experience his legacy at **The Frost Place** in Franconia, about 30 minutes from Littleton. Part museum, part nature center, the farm is a nonprofit center that houses some first editions of the poet's works and offers a half-mile nature trail marked with plaques containing poems Frost wrote while living in the area. The center also fosters the work of up-and-coming poets and houses a poet-in-residence every year.

www.papermilltheatre.org) puts on musicals through its Mainstage Theatre program every summer and runs a year-round art gallery.

If you really just came for the views, hop on the **Cannon Mountain** aerial tramway (www.cannonmt.com) at Franconia Notch State Park, for a 10-minute ride that takes passengers to the 4080-foot summit for views all the way to Canada. There are walking trails at the top, an observation deck, and visitor facilities.

Cross the border into Vermont to the 100-year-old **Fairbanks Museum & Planetarium** (1302 Main St., St. Johnsbury; 802-748-2372; www.fairbanksmuseum.org) on the Main Street Historic District, where the Victorian building alone is worth the half-hour trip. The exhibits range from

natural history collections and planetarium shows to an Eye on the Sky Weather Gallery.

▮▮▮▮ SPECIAL EVENTS

Late May to early October The **Local Works Farmers' Market** (Rt. 302 & Park Ave.) in nearby **Bethlehem**, which runs on Wednesdays and Saturdays, livens up the business of selling produce, crafts, and baked goods with live music.

Mid-June: If you are a real fan—or just looking for a mood lifter—time your visit to coincide with **Official Pollyanna Glad Day** (603-444-6158). The event takes place in front of the Library, and if the live music, film showings, and prevailing good mood don't move you, the free cake likely will.

June to October: Snap up fresh

eggs, honey, and maple syrup at the Sunday morning **Farmers Market** on Riverglen Lane, where locals also show off their crafts and offer live entertainment.

▮▮▮▮ RESOURCES

Littleton Area Chamber of Commerce, 32 Main St., Littleton, NH 03561; 603-444-6561; www.littletonareachamber.com

14 • OLD WETHERSFIELD, CONNECTICUT

South of Hartford and about an hour and a half from either Boston or New York

New England boasts some of the finest re-created historic villages in the country, complete with homes brought in from elsewhere and costumed guides offering interactive glimpses into our past. Old Wethersfield isn't one of them.

Instead, this historic village bustles, albeit quietly, with the daily life of the 21st century in an Old World setting. There are some 300 historic houses in town, including dozens of pre-Revolutionary buildings, and visitors can have the fun of shopping, dining, and sightseeing among them. Old Wethersfield was the first permanent European settlement in Connecticut, and some of the houses have been turned into stores and B&Bs, while others are preserved as they once were and are open for tours.

Even without a formal museum visit, you can inhale the town's historic atmosphere just by strolling around in the very streets where George Washington and John Adams once walked. Set out on foot along Main Street for about a half mile toward the Cove, which once formed part of the Connecticut River before a storm in the late 1600s changed the course of the river and destroyed nearly all of the warehouses that once lined the waterfront. Here the 17th century maritime merchants who represented the heartbeat of the town's commerce housed their goods for trade. Stop in for a look at the one surviving Cove Warehouse (860-529-7656), dramatically perched over the water, or simply kick back and enjoy the sight of the yachts out on the water.

Locals in Old Wethersfield understandably are proud of the town's place in Colonial history, but there is another, darker side to its past that is no less fascinating. Although Salem, Massachusetts, gets all the attention, there were several witch trials in Connecticut in the 17th century, including a few public executions in town.

Leaf peepers flock to the area in the fall, and visitors will find plenty of nature in Old Wethersfield, including the 110-acre **Wethersfield Cove Park,** where you can play ball, picnic, or listen to concerts on the water.

■■■■ GETTING THERE (AND GETTING AROUND)

Old Wethersfield is about equidistant from Boston and New York off I-91. Take exit 26 and follow Marsh Street to the town center. Bradley International Airport in Hartford is about a half hour away.

There is plenty of street parking on Main Street, which you can use as a base for most of the sites in town. You will need a bike or car to get to the Eleanor Buck Wolf Nature Center and Mill Woods Park.

■■■■ WHAT TO SEE

For an overview of the town's history, pop into the **Keeney Memorial Cultural Center** (200 Main St.; 860-529-7656; www.wethhist .org), where parking is free and where information is available on how to make the most of your

visit, along with a map of historic sites. The building houses the Visitors Center and the Wethersfield Museum, and guides can help you plan your visit, which can include formal tours and self-guided explorations. Across the street from the Center is the **Webb-Deane-Stevens Museum** (221 Main St.), cared for by the local branch of the Colonial Dames. Visitors can opt to take the hour-plus tour or wander the pretty grounds in back on their own for free.

The **Eleanor Buck Wolf Nature Center** (156 Prospect St.; 860-529-3075) allows visitors to get an up-close look at a selection of animals and reptiles and hosts lectures and other events year-round. Admission is free, and the residents of the center include a friendly rabbit, as well as ferrets, snakes, and turtles. If the weather cooperates, you can access **Mill Woods Park** from the center and ramble along its 110-acre parkland on well-marked trails that wend over bridges and through

Old Wethersfield Cove Warehouse

Anderson Farms Stand in Old Wethersfield

Favorite son Silas Deane was a member of the Continental Congress and was sent to France in 1776 as an undercover agent to gather support for the Revolutionary War. It was in Wethersfield that then-General Washington met with France's compte de Rochambeau a year later to hatch plans for the battle of Yorktown, and their meetings took place at sites that exist in the town to this day.

One of these sites is the **Webb-Deane-Stevens Museum** (211 Main St.; 860-529-0612; www.webb-deane-stevens.org), which comprises a cluster of historic houses and is open more or less year-round, with abbreviated hours in winter. For a real treat, try a candlelight tour, available select Saturdays in December, and don't miss the bedroom in the Joseph Webb house where, yes, George Washington once slept and worked. One of the most picturesque antique houses in town is the **Silas Robbins House**, a wedding-cake extravaganza on Broad Street that has recently been restored and transformed into a Bed and Breakfast Inn (mentioned under Places to Stay).

the forest. The park also boasts a pond that has been divided into two separate bodies of water: one that has been kept in its natural state and the other, which has been transformed into a clean swimming hole, complete with a little sandy beach and dock. There is also a dog park for Fido and a skateboard park for the kids.

Or rest your feet on one of the shady benches on **Broad Street Green**, where farm animals were once put to pasture and where Connecticut's Sons of Liberty rallied against the Stamp Act in 1765. There are two farm stands still operating on the Green, where locals and visitors alike can buy fresh produce, that have been handed down for generations.

Behind the historic brick **First Church of Christ** (250 Main St.; 860-529-1575; www.firstchurch.org), peruse the old-fashioned names carved on the gravestones in the **Ancient Burying Ground**, some of which date from the 1600s.

If you are curious about early American kitchen gadgetry, make time for the **Buttolph-Williams House** (249 Broad St.; 860-529-0612; www.ctlandmarks.org), operated by the Connecticut Antiquarian & Landmarks Society. In summer, you can visit **McCue Gardens** (47 Hartford Ave.; 860-

529-5976), where you can find everything from wildflowers to sturdy perennials.

▌▌▌▌ WHAT TO DO

To make the most of a short visit, consider joining a guided walking tour, offered by the **Visitors Center** (mentioned above). The mile-long **Walk Historic Wethersfield** tour offers an overview of the most important sites and events in the town, while the **Burying Ground Tour** helps visitors appreciate the art on the local gravestones in the town's oldest cemetery. The 1½-mile **Colonial Revival Walking Tour** takes a look at how the more modern houses in the town were inspired by historical architecture when designing their own houses. Tours are 90 minutes long, and maps are available at the center for visitors who want to take self-guided versions of the tours.

Free 90-minute guided tours also are available of the **Griswoldville Mill Sites** (131 Griswold Rd.; 860-257-1705; www.griswoldville.org) for a look at the importance of the mills in the town's manufacturing history.

Saddle up for English or Western riding lessons at **Meadowgate Farms** (250 Elm St.; 860-257-9008), where you can also arrange a pony party for the kids and their friends.

See the sights from a bicycle on the **Wethersfield Heritage Way Bikeway Path,** a 10-mile route accessible from Mill Woods Park. A future leg of the path will link with the green in the town center, but for now the path meanders past the Cove and the beginning of Main Street.

If you'd rather buy a piece of history than look at it, the **Clearing House Auction Galleries** (207 Church St.; 860-529-3344; www.clearinghouseauctions.com) is the place to vie for deals on antiques. Estate-sale and other items are displayed in 5,000 square feet of space and go on sale Wednesdays and Fridays. Or go retail at **Antiques on Main** (167 Main St.; 860-721-0663), for furniture and collectibles and ask about the award-winning quilts that are sometimes on display.

▌▌▌▌ WHERE TO STAY

Silas W. Robbins House (185 Broad St.; 860-571-8733; www.silaswrobbins.com), a sumptuous Victorian that was lovingly restored in 2007 by innkeepers John and Shireen Aforismo, now offers five guest rooms, each with a private bath, flat-screen TV, and Wi-Fi. From $195.

Chester Bulkley House (184 Main St.; 860-563-4236; www.chesterbulkleyhouse.com) is a five-room Greek Revival with period touches and a full complimentary breakfast. From $95.

The **Comfort Inn** (1330 Silas Deane Hwy.; 860-563-2311; www.comfortinn.com) offers straightforward accommodations for travelers who would rather spend their money on dinner or antique shopping. There are 108 rooms, free Wi-Fi, refrigerators and microwaves, and an indoor heated swimming pool. From $99.

▪▪▪▪ EATING OUT

J. Michaels Tavern in the Standish House (222 Main St.; 860-257-0700; www.jmichaelstavern.com) is a historic property that serves lunch, dinner, and Sunday brunch in an 18th-century setting. You can sit outside in fine weather or time your visit for a jazz night or wine tasting. From $8.95 for sandwiches; entrées $14.95.

Mainly Tea (221 Main St.; 860-529-9517; www.mainlytea.com) for a prix fixe lunch of soups, sandwiches, and salad, or reserve ahead for the afternoon tea buffet. The decor is flowery and charming, and there is a gourmet tea shop for visitors who want to take home their favorite brew. From $12.95.

The **Spicy Green Bean Deli** (285 Main St.; 860-563-3100; www.spicygreenbean.com) offers straightforward sandwiches and

salads, as well as Kooky Konkoctions, like roasted beans with garlic and hummus on focaccia. There is no corkage fee for weekend BYOB dinners. From $19.

The Village Pizza of Wethersfield (233 Main Street, 860-563-1513; www.villagepizzau.com) serves lunch and dinner. In addition to pizza, you can get traditional Italian fare such as veal marsala and eggplant parmigiana. From $9 for pasta; $12.25 for pizza.

The Main Street Creamery (271 Main St.; 860-529-0509; www.mainstreetcreamery.com), closed in winter, focuses on ice cream and frozen yogurts, but sandwiches and even doggie treats also are available. From $2.

▪▪▪▪ SPECIAL EVENTS

Late September: Another annual event geared around shopping is the quirky **Scarecrows along Main Street** (860-721-0663), when store owners get competitive over who can decorate the most inventive and charming scarecrow.

November: Off-season has its own appeal during the annual **Wethersfield Antiques Show**, held at the Pitkin Community Center (30 Greenfield St.; 860-529-7656), where visitors can get a jump on their holiday shopping as they browse among the wares

Old Wethersfield Cove

assembled by more than 40 antiques dealers.

■■■■ NEARBY

In the early 20th century, amusement parks were created along the railroad lines to lure traffic on weekends, and the oldest still in operation is also one of the most charming. **Lake Compounce** (271 Enterprise Dr., Bristol; 860-583-3300; www.lakecompounce.com) is about a half hour from Wethersfield. The park has all the requisite thrill rides—including the superlative Boulder Dash, a wooden roller coaster that tops out at 65 miles per hour, and the Saw Mill Plunge, a first-rate flume—there are also nostalgic touches you might not expect. The Trolley, for example, a restored open-air trolley from 1911, and the bright red Lake Railroad take riders around the scenic park, which is located, as its

name implies, right on the lake. There also is an antique carousel, one of the oldest in the country, a giant Ferris wheel, water rides, and a dizzying Sky Coaster for visitors without a fear of heights.

■■■■ LIT LIFE

More than one author has made Wethersfield the setting for a popular novel, and one of the best known is Elizabeth Speare, who wrote *The Witch of Blackbird Pond.* The children's book, which won the Newbery Medal in the late '50s, tells the story of a young girl during the Puritan era who was suspected by small-minded townsfolk of being a witch because she could both swim and read. The **Buttolph-Williams House** (249 Broad St.; 860-529-0612), the setting for part of the book, features a collection of period decorative arts and original architectural features.

Actor-turned-novelist Thomas Tryon grew up in Wethersfield, and devotees will recognize the town as the setting for some of his spooky novels, including his most popular, *The Other*, which was later made into a movie in the 1970s.

■ ■ ■ ■ RESOURCES

The Visitor Center, 200 Main St.; 860-529-7656; www.oldwethers field.com

The Wethersfield Historical Society, 150 Main St.; 860-529-7656

15 • SCITUATE HARBOR, MASSACHUSETTS

About 30 miles south of Boston off Route 3 South or take the new Greenbush commuter train from Boston's South Station and ride it to the end of the line

You see them every Friday afternoon in summer: caravans of cars inching along bumper to bumper, drivers leaning on their horns, as they head south from Boston to Cape Cod, clogging the Sagamore Bridge. Why not shave at least an hour off the trip by stopping instead in Scituate Harbor, one of several lovely beach towns only about 30 miles south of Beantown?

Scituate (a Native American word that means "cold brook," pronounced Sitch-oo-ut) has retained its fishing-village feel over the years, despite upgrades in its dining, shopping and entertainment venues. Locals are into boating here and the landscape in summer is a cheerful mix of beach houses on stilts along the marshy coast, sailboats with white sails bobbing in the blue waters of the Atlantic, and tiny shops that line the one main street that wends through the town to the tip of the harbor.

Restaurants run the gamut from trendy cuisine offering fine wine pairings to waterfront eateries that serve up whole-belly fried clams and savory fish chowder, preferably washed down with a local brew.

Summer is high season here,

Quarter Deck Gift Shop

Scituate Lighthouse

One of the most popular pieces of historic lore about the Scituate Lighthouse relates to the family of the original lighthouse keepers during the War of 1812, who are said to have been away overnight leaving two teen daughters—Abigail and Rebecca Bates—alone in the lighthouse. On spying a British warship in the distance, the sisters launched into a rousing roll call using a fife and drum, which supposedly frightened the sailors—who thought the sound was a call to arms to a defending army—into retreat. Although the veracity of this unlikely tale has been questioned, some historians believe it to be true.

and the town comes alive with locals and visitors looking to make the most of the warm weather. Store owners bring some of their wares outside, restaurants open their patios for al fresco dining, and locals can be seen at the waterfront gazebo looking out to sea.

Scituate boasts a handful of some of the prettiest beaches on the South Shore, from **Peggotty Beach** near the town center to **Humarock Beach** on the other side of the North River. Most of Scituate's beaches require resident parking stickers in high season, but you can avoid the hassle altogether by following Front Street as it wends its way to Cedar Point and the **Scituate Lighthouse** (Scituate Historical Society, 781-545-1083).

Park your car for free here and wander along the small beach at low tide, when you will likely find yourself alone with the seagulls. A small path along the water's edge offers picnic benches where you can sit and look out over the busy harbor. Bring a camera to snap a picture of the 50-foot lighthouse, which dates from 1811 and, in its day, served to not only keep ships from smashing up on the rocks but also keep watch over enemy vessels. The lighthouse is operated by a young local family, who live in the cottage at its base and who are happy to answer questions about the town's history.

▌▌▌▌ GETTING THERE (AND GETTING AROUND)

From Boston, take Route 93 to Route 3 South to exit 13, then follow Rt. 123 to Scituate. Or take the new **Greenbush** rail line from Boston's South Station to the last stop, an hour-long journey that offers picture postcard scenery along the way.

The train is about 2 miles from Scituate's town center and the beach is a hike, but you can bring your bicycle on the train on weekends. To reach the lighthouse, you will want a car.

▪▪▪▪ WHAT TO SEE

One of the newer attractions in Scituate is the **Maritime & Irish Mossing Museum**, (301 Driftway), open year-round on weekends, admission free for children under 18, which pays homage to the town's rich fishing history. There is plenty of information on local families and their ancestors, but even casual visitors can check out books, T-shirts, and gifts that depict Scituate's seaside roots. Located in a former ship captain's 18th-century home, the museum takes visitors through the tough life of the men who fished for Irish moss, a form of edible algae, as well as the shipwreck of the *Portland Gale*, which went down in the late 19th century.

The incongruous **Lawson Tower** (First Parish Rd.) is worth a visit for its odd dash of European castle elegance in a town mostly known for its traditional Cape and Dutch Colonial architecture. The tower, which was built by wealthy entrepreneur Thomas

Lawson in the early 20th century, is in reality a gussied-up water tower, but because it looks as though it was airlifted into town from Germany's Black Forest, it remains one of the area's most photographed structures.

You can also visit the **Little Red Schoolhouse** (43 Cudworth Rd.; 781-545-1083, www.scituate historicalsociety.org) for a peek at Colonial life and a chance to browse its gift shop. Or check out **Stockbridge Mill** (Country Way; 781-545-1083), which was built in 1640 and operated until the 1920s. Historical Society members hope the mill, which is being restored, will be operational and open for tours by summer 2010. Historical sites are open on select days in season, so be sure to call ahead.

Like many scenic seaside towns, Scituate has attracted artists for generations. The **Scituate Arts Association** (132 Front St., 781-545-6150) exhibits works—including paintings and photographs—by local artists. Pottery enthusiasts can visit **Rossman Pottery** (Salt Meadow Lane, 781-545-3171) where artist in residence Judy Rossman sells her wares and conducts classes and workshops.

▪▪▪▪ WHAT TO DO

Climb aboard a charter fishing boat via **Polar Bear Charters**

(781-963-8860), **Elizabeth Marie Sportfishing** (781-564-7154; emfishing.com), and **Labrador Charters** with Captain Dan Campbell (781-293-3115) for a day at sea. The fishing boats are lined up on the town dock, so just pick one you like the looks of. Excursions range from sportfishing to whale-watching.

Go shopping along the main street, where you can buy antiques at **Goodies II** (124 Front St.; 781-544-0010) or browse among the seascapes at the **Front Street Gallery** (124 Front St.). **Out of the Blue** (781-544-3800), in the same building, sells cuter-than-average hats, purses, T-shirts, and jewelry, while **The Welch Company** (132 Front St.; 781-545-1400) purveys gifts, candles, pottery, and linens in seaside colors.

Hit the links at **Widows Walk Golf Course** (250 Driftway; 781-544-7777; www.widowswalkgolf.com), where you can pit your skills against the par-72 course that was once a derelict gravel quarry—or take a lesson if you could use help with your swing. You can also go bird-watching here, keeping an eye out for purple martins and eastern blue-birds.

Decide for yourself who has the best ice cream: the two contenders are **Dribbles** (4 Brook St.), which has a walk-up window and few bistro tables and chairs, and **Scoops** (1 Mill Wharf Plaza) on the harbor.

▮▮▮▮ WHERE TO STAY

The Inn at Scituate Harbor (7 Beaver Dam Rd.; 781-545-5550; www.innatscituate.com) is a 29-room, newly renovated property in the harbor with fresh, beachy decor. Every room overlooks the water and Scituate Harbor, and

Lighthouse Beach

Humarock, known for its miniscule village and lovely white sand beach, is part of Scituate but—like the old joke—you can't get there from here. The two parts of the town were once connected, but when the North River changed course years ago, the two sections became separated by water. Visitors to Scituate who want to check out Humarock now have to drive to neighboring Marshfield first.

continental breakfast is served in the lobby. From $109.

Fairview Inn (133 Ocean St., Marshfield; 781-834-9144; www.thefairviewinn.com) nearby, which dates from 1874, offers a fresh, romantic design scheme and ocean views from each of its seven guest rooms. The Inn is also a restaurant and tavern with elegant, upscale dining and water views. From $175.

■ ■ ■ ■ WHERE TO CAMP

Wompatuck State Park (Union St., Hingham; 781-749-7160) has 262 campsites in the woods, as well as a boat ramp and miles of paved biking trails. Camping is available mid-April through late October. From $12.

■ ■ ■ ■ EATING OUT

Riva Restaurant (116 Front St.; 781-545-5881; rivarestaurant.net), on Scituate's main street, offers upscale Italian cuisine, including plenty of Tuscan dishes cooked up in an open kitchen. Reserva-

tions are only accepted on weekends, so go early on weeknights for a spot in the tiny dining room. From $18.

The Barker Tavern (21 Barker Rd.; 781-545-6533; www.barkertavern.com) is an institution in Scituate Harbor, thanks to its location in a lovingly restored 17th-century home. From the dining room to the less formal pub, the look is Old World, but the atmosphere is lively and fun. From $21.

Chester's Mill Wharf Pub (Mill Wharf Plaza; 781-545-3999) is in a renovated mill overlooking the harbor. There is a deck for al fresco dining in fine weather, and floor-to-ceiling windows in the dining room for when the weather doesn't cooperate. Try the clam chowder and award-winning lobster roll or sample the appetizers at the Raw Bar. From $5 for lunch; $7.95 for dinner.

P J's Country House Restaurant and Pub (227 Chief Justice Cushing Hwy.; 781-545-1340;

http://pjsrestaurant.com) offers a full menu with everything from oysters on the half shell to clams casino and crab fritters, as well as a pub menu for less expensive fare. Plan to stay for the weekly piano and jazz entertainment Wednesdays to Sunday nights. From $7.95 for lunch; $19.95 for dinner.

T.K.O Malley's Sports Cafe (194 Front St.; 781-545-4012; www.eat tkomalleys.com) is a huge favorite with locals, thanks to its outdoor patio dining in season and indoor dining room and sports bar. The seafood chowder is a perennial award winner at $4.95, and entrées start at $10.95.

▪▪▪▪ NEARBY

If you have time to scout out the area, drive north on Rt. 3A toward neighboring Cohasset. See big-name musical performances at the **South Shore Music Circus** (130 Sohier St., Cohasset; 781-383-9850, www.themusiccircus.org), although seats sell out, so book online first. Past headliners have included everyone from Tony Bennett and B. B. King to Melissa Etheridge and the Steve Miller Band. Or take the scenic drive along **Jericho Road** for a look at some of the area's most impressive oceanfront mansions, then shop for antiques or dine at one of the eateries that line Cohasset's main streets. Stop for baked goods at the **French Memories Bakery** (64 S Main St.), which wins raves for its varieties of croissants, baguettes, and pastries. Pick up provisions to go or sit at one of the bistro tables outside.

▪▪▪▪ SPECIAL EVENTS

Late May: S.H.O.R.E. Run (www .coolrunning.com) is a 5K run followed by a 2K walk that begins at Peggotty Beach. The event includes live music and other entertainment.

Early August: For a festival atmosphere, time your visit to coincide with **Scituate Heritage Days**, a cheerful weeklong outdoor festival held in early August every year. Events are quintessentially New England, from the pie social at the Harbor Methodist Church to the boat races, the blessing of the fleet, and oyster-shucking contest. There is even a shark-fishing tournament and, of course, hours of live music of various genres at the Scituate bandstand.

▪▪▪▪ RESOURCES

Scituate Chamber of Commerce, 248 Gannett Rd.; 781-545-4000; www.scituatechamber.org

URBAN
ESCAPES

16 • ROSE KENNEDY GREENWAY, MASSACHUSETTS

Downtown Boston between North and South Stations

While it is not really true that Boston's streets used to be cow paths, the urban legend persists, perhaps because it's the only logical explanation for the narrow, convoluted streets that wend through the historic city, seemingly without rhyme or reason.

Enter the **Big Dig** in 1992—known by locals as the Big Pig because of its notoriously bloated price tag—which was an engineering project designed to submerge the Central Artery and repurpose the reclaimed land above it. Several years and billions of dollars over budget, the project is finally more or less complete, much to the relief of weary Bostonians, for whom the sight of cranes had become a familiar backdrop on the horizon.

Probably the most visible symbol of the project is the soaring **Leonard P. Zakim Bunker Hill Memorial Bridge**, spanning the Charles River and held aloft by peaks of white cables reminiscent of the sailboats that ply the waters beneath. Already a landmark, the bridge is sure to hold pride of place among the city's best-selling postcards, along with Faneuil Hall and the Old North Church.

But for tourists eager to roam the inner city on foot, the new **Rose Kennedy Greenway**, which opened to much fanfare in October 2008, is the jewel in the crown.

The Greenway, which was named for President John F. Kennedy's mother, is a mile-long series of parks and walkways that not only bring 15 acres of natural beauty to a part of the city previously characterized by concrete, traffic, and exhaust fumes but also opens up some of Boston's prettiest neighborhoods to pedestrian traffic.

Far more than just a static park you can walk through, the Greenway is a venue for music and dance performances, temporary art installations, guided tours, and children's activities year-round, coaxing residents and visitors alike to get in the act. Best of all, the parks are linked to some of the Hub's most interesting neighborhoods—such as Quincy Market and the North End—making it easy for pedestrians to patronize local restaurants and shops in these areas. And although many of these walkways are as yet unshaded, the conservancy promises that, given time, the young trees that line the paths will grow and provide much-needed shade.

There are essentially four parks that comprise the Greenway, and while you can enter at any point, the full trek spans from Chinatown to the North End.

■■■■ GETTING THERE (AND GETTING AROUND)

The Rose Kennedy Greenway is in the heart of Boston a few blocks from both **North** and **South Stations** (www.mbta.com), but you can also access the park from the **Commuter Ferry** and from a number of subway (referred to by locals as the MBTA or simply "the T") stops, including Downtown Crossing and Government Center.

Technically, you can drive in Boston, but we don't encourage it unless you like to live on the wild side and don't mind paying through the nose for parking. Because there are so many access points along the Greenway, most visitors won't have to backtrack to their starting point in order to reach public transportation.

■■■■ WHAT TO SEE

Chinatown Park, the southernmost tip of the park, is a few blocks from South Station and the Chinatown T-station on the Orange Line. This part of Boston is known for its lively restaurants, and you can happily while away a few hours trying the local dim sum, as well as poking through

---

The Greenway is overseen by a nonprofit conservancy dedicated to maintaining the space and making the most of the new parkland.

While some projects are on hold—such as a permanent stage for theatrical productions—temporary stages along the lines of those found in New York's Battery Park are more likely in the coming years, according to conservators who have been working on the project since its inception. The idea is that there will always be something new to see on the Greenway, from a pumpkin festival in the fall and ice-skating in winter to outdoor markets in the warmer months.

the tiny shops that sell everything from embroidered slippers
and dresses to interesting food
items. The design of the walkway
and the gardens as well as the
activities in this part of the
Greenway reflect the Asian heritage of the area. Special events
and public performances can
range from tai chi instruction,
lessons on classical Chinese gardening, Chinese folk dances, and
martial arts demonstrations.

As you head north and cross
Essex Street, you will hit **Dewey
Square Parks**, made up of 4½
acres linking South Station and the
Financial District. This section of
the Greenway offers plenty of open
space dedicated to temporary
performance venues and grassy
areas to picnic, listen to jazz, or
just relax with a good book.

Dewey Square Parks is also the
site of the **Boston Public Market**,
which opened in the summer of
2009. The market sells locally
grown and organic fruits, vegetables, and fresh baked goods in
summer. Park conservators are
eyeing a permanent indoor space
for the market in future in the
North End, and in the meantime,
don't be surprised to see top
chefs making appearances at the
market to offer demonstrations of
their craft.

Modern art lovers can use this
section of the Greenway as a
jumping-off point to visit the
Institute of Contemporary Art
(100 Northern Ave., 617-478-3100,
www.icaboston.org), a dramatic
structure with cantilevered walls
overlooking Boston Harbor that
opened in 2006. This museum is a
far cry from the staid Boston art
exhibits of our parents' generation. In fact, the ICA was in the
news when street artist Shepard
Fairey, known for his "Obey"
series of graphics and his widely
seen rendering of President
Obama, was arrested for graffiti
on his way into the museum on
the night his works were being
celebrated within. The ICA showcases cutting-edge art installations, using video and other
media, and hosts dance performances, poetry readings, and a
lecture series. Be sure to save time
for lunch or coffee at the museum's **Water Café**, catered by
Wolfgang Puck, overlooking the
harbor.

Two of Boston's most popular
attractions are at the northern
end of the Wharf District—the
New England Aquarium and
Boston Harborwalk. The first
thing you will see on entering the
New England Aquarium (1 Central Wharf, 617-973-5200, www
.neaq.org) is the flock of African
penguins that take center stage
in a habitat in the middle of a
circular walkway. The walkway

Although it has been nearly 20 years in the making, the Greenway is admittedly still a work in progress. Conservancy planners expect to see the parks evolve organically in the coming years as locals and visitors begin to use the space and as new foliage begins to mature. That said, a number of permanent projects are on the drawing table, with their fate unknown until the vagaries of the difficult economy begin to settle down.

One such project is the **Boston Museum**, which insiders hope will open by 2013. The fate of the proposed ultracontemporary **New Center for Arts and Culture** (18 Tremont St.; 617-531-4610), originally scheduled for completion in 2012, is less clear. Earmarked for the parcel across from the Rowe's Wharf arch, the center would explore Boston's Jewish culture and its interactions with other local cultures through gallery exhibitions and performance venues.

winds around higher and higher through the building, flanked with marine animal exhibitions along the way. See anaconda, harbor seals, lobsters, and turtles, and be sure to check out the giant Ocean Tank, which simulates a Caribbean coral reef and houses tiger sharks, stingrays, and moray eels. Plan ahead if you want to see the live animal shows, especially the harbor seal training sessions and the popular IMAX films. The aquarium has its own subway stop on the Blue Line. HarborWalk, a network of walkways on the city's waterfront, is especially inviting along this new segment, which links the Greenway with the Aquarium and Long Wharf.

Faneuil Hall Marketplace
(www.faneuilhallmarketplace .com) is one of those rarities— a tourist attraction that locals also love. A cluster of indoor markets grouped around an outdoor cobblestone space, the marketplace in warm weather is chock-full of street performers, vendor carts selling everything from Red Sox gear to toys and gifts, and sidewalk-café-style restaurants with tables set for lunch under cheerful umbrellas.

Whether you love Boston history or just want to enjoy a cappuccino and a cannoli, the northernmost section of the Greenway will take you into the **North End**, Boston's Italian neighborhood and also the home of the **Paul**

Revere House (19 North Square; 617-523-2338; www.paulrevere house.org), which offers self-guided tours. At present, there is no direct connection from the Wharf Parks to the North End, but the proposed **Boston Museum**, which would face North End Park, would include a pedestrian suspension bridge linking the two. Proponents of the project also predict its dramatic glass exterior would become a city landmark, and the five-story atrium would

feature interactive panels depicting Boston's evolution over the centuries—including galleries dedicated to sports and politics.

▮▮▮▮ WHAT TO DO

Take a spooky tour of Boston's creepier past—from the Boston Strangler to the city's oldest cemeteries—Old Town Trolley offers **Ghosts & Gravestones Frightseeing Tours** (200 Atlantic Ave.; 617-269-3626; www.ghosts andgravestones.com) in the evenings from April through October. Costumed guides will regale passengers on the Trolley of Doom with haunted tales during this 90-minute ride, which brings the city's most unsavory characters to life—so to speak—by focusing on some of the most atmospheric parts of the city. The tours get booked up quickly, especially on weekends and on Halloween, so reservations are recommended.

For a real insider's view of Chinatown's changing character, from its earliest settlers to its thriving population today, join a guided 90-minute **Historic Chinatown Walking Tour**, which operates once a month from May through October from the **Chinese Historical Society of New England** (2 Boylston St.; 617-338-4339).

One of the most popular walk-

Boston's South Station

Greenway Chinatown Entrance

ing tours in Beantown is the 2½-mile **Freedom Trail** (www.the freedomtrail.org), which visitors can do on their own by grabbing a map at the information kiosk in the Boston Common and following all or part of the marked path on the sidewalk. For a more in-depth understanding of what you are seeing, book a guided Freedom Trail walk. Costumed guides will show you some of the most historic parts of the city and tell of events from the lead-up to the Revolutionary War in 1770 until 1820. The tours take in 16 sites, including the **Old North Church** of Paul Revere fame to the **Old Corner Bookstore** on School Street, where works by Emerson, Longfellow, and Alcott were once published.

On a hot summer day, **Boston Duck Tours** (617-267-DUCK; www.bostonducktours.com) offer a land-and-water view of the city aboard World War II—style amphibious vehicles that take in most of Boston's top sights. The patter is a little corny—drivers are called "conDUCKtors," and they will urge you to quack at pedestrians as you pass them by—but the itinerary takes in the tony shops on Newbury Street, the golden-domed State House, Copley Square, and historic Bunker Hill. The second part of the tour comprises a splashdown in the Charles River for a look both at the Hub and its neighbor, Cambridge, home of Harvard University and MIT. You can pick up a tour at the **Museum of Science** (1 Science Park) or the **Prudential Center** (known locally as "The Pru") in the Back Bay (53 Huntington Avenue).

■ ■ ■ ■ WHERE TO STAY

Boston Harbor Hotel (70 Rowes Wharf; 617-439-7000; www.bhh.com) is one of Boston's prettiest waterfront hotels, but before the Greenway, it was sandwiched between the harbor and the highway. Now the Mobil five-star property has easy access to the revitalized waterfront district for guests or visitors who want to sample the gourmet fare at the highly rated Meritage restaurant. There are more than 12,000 bottles of wine in the cellar, and the menu is a splurge, but small plates are available for those whose desire for variety doesn't match their budget. In summer, the Rowes Wharf Sea Grills Terrace is transformed into an outdoor movie theater. From about $370.

The InterContinental Boston (617-747-1000; www.intercontinentalboston.com) on Atlantic Avenue is right on the Greenway at Fort Point Channel, an area that is abuzz with new restaurants and residential lofts.

Fans of the *Cheers* television show often flock to **Cheers** (84 Beacon St., 617-227-9605, www.cheersboston.com) expecting the interior to be identical to that seen in the show. While the original bar, which was called the Bull & Finch Pub when it was first scouted by Hollywood executives in the early '80s, was the inspiration for the look of the show's set—and exterior shots appeared in the opening credits—the inside design was modified to fit the series action.

The glass exterior reflects the buildings around it, and the ultracontemporary interior includes three eateries: Sushi-Teq, RumBa, and the Provence-styled brasserie. From about $315.

Boston Marriott Long Wharf (296 State Street; 617-227-0800; www.marriott.com) offers a waterfront location that is only about a block from Faneuil Hall Marketplace and within easy walking distance of TD Garden, Boston's main venue for big-name concerts and sports events. The newly revamped property also has an indoor swimming pool and an upscale seafood restaurant called the Oceana. From about $249.

The Fairmont Battery Wharf (3 Battery Wharf; 800-257-7544; www.fairmont.com/battery wharf), which opened in January 2009, features 150 rooms near the Greenway and on the waterfront. There are indoor and outdoor dining venues—including the much-buzzed-about Sensing—

and water taxis to the airport. From about $329.

Nine Zero (90 Tremont St.; 617-772-5800; www.ninezero.com), a posh Kimpton hotel near Boston Common, is one of the next-generation properties that has catapulted Boston from boring to trendy. Open since 2002, the pet-friendly hotel has won nods and awards from top travel magazines, thanks in part to its hip, contemporary design and upscale service. From about $280.

XV Beacon (15 Beacon St.; 888-229-0684; www.xvbeacon.com) is one of Boston's hippest hotels. Adjacent to the State House—just steps from the beginning of the Freedom Trail—the property boasts quirky, modern decor with gas fireplaces and stainless-steel touches. Its signature restaurant, Mooo, routinely wins kudos for its menu and wine cellar. From $295.

▮▮▮▮ EATING OUT

The Barking Crab (88 Sleeper St.; 617-426-2722; www.barkingcrab

.com) at Fort Point Landing looks tiny from the outside, but there is an additional dining room in back with indoor/outdoor seating. The brightly colored decor is fun, and the mood is casual, but come early to avoid the crowds. A bucket of peel-and-eat shrimp at the bar, which is more than enough for two, will only set you back about $13; lobsters and catch of the day, market price.

No. 9 Park (9 Park St.; 617-742-9991; www.no9park.com) on Beacon Hill focuses on Italian and French fare, under the direction of chef Barbara Lynch, a James Beard Award winner. The menu is strictly gourmet, and the decor is muted and sophisticated. About $30.

The Gourmet Dumpling House (52 Beach St.; 617-338-6223) is a real find for specials like pork and leek dumplings at prices that won't break the bank. Most

entrées under $10.

Dick's Last Resort (Quincy Marketplace, 617-267-8080) is popular with teens and young adults who enjoy the mock rude service of the wait staff and the lively atmosphere. Menu items have names like Case O'King Crabs and Ride'm Cowboy Rib Eye. From $12.99 for dinner; $7.99 for lunch.

Taranta (210 Hanover St.; 617-720-0052; www.tarantarist.com) in the North End serves Italian/Peruvian fusion with an upscale twist. Try the espresso-encrusted filet mignon or the saffron butter—brushed grilled trout, and in summer ask for a table on the street (the floor-to-ceiling windows open up). From $27.

Mamma Maria (3 North Square; 617-523-0077; http://mamma maria.com) is a family-owned AAA four-star restaurant serving Tuscan specialties like roast rab-

The new Zakim Bunker Hill Bridge

The **Quincy Market Colonnade** is a food hall with a dizzying assortment of stalls from some of the area's best-known eateries. For fresh seafood, try **Boston Chowda** or **Boston and Maine Fish Co.**, tuck into Greek fare at **Steve's Greek Cuisine**, or forgo your diet at the **North End Bakery**, all represented in the colonnade. Set up like a gourmand's food court, the hall allows visitors to split up, order what catches their eye to go, then stake out a table in the center atrium—don't forget to look upstairs for a free table—or eat outside on one of the many park benches that line the marketplace.

If a sit-down restaurant is more your style, there are more than a dozen to choose from, including a branch of **Sam's Café at Cheers** (Quincy Market Bldg., www.cheersboston.com), a replica of the Beacon Hill pub that inspired the long-running TV show. One of the oldest and best known restaurants in the marketplace is **Durgin Park Restaurant** (North Market Bldg., 617-227-2038, www.durgin-park .com), where you can order platters of oysters and clams, chow down on boiled lobster, or indulge in a retro dish of corned beef and cabbage with a side order of Boston baked beans. Don't forget to leave room for a slice of Boston Cream Pie or Indian pudding for dessert.

bit and osso buco with 120 types of wine in a 19th-century row house. From $26.

▪▪▪▪ SPECIAL EVENTS

July 4: Visitors lucky enough to be in Boston over the July 4 festivities can take part in the annual **Boston Harborfest** (www .bostonharborfest.com), centered on Boston City Hall and Faneuil Hall. You'll find plenty of costumed actors reenacting historic events, live concerts at City Hall Plaza, and, of course, the traditional chowderfest, where local seafood restaurants compete for top honors and where all are invited to be part of the show.

December 31: Winter visitors can also get in on the fun by attending **First Night** (www.first night.org), during which locals bundle up and fete the New Year's Eve in style. Activities go on all day and night and include ice sculptures by world-renowned international artists, live musical concerts, dance, theater, and fireworks. For the final countdown to the New Year, crowds gather on the Boston

Common or in Copley Square, and the mood is festive enough to warm up even the most chilly winter night air.

▌▌▌▌ RESOURCES

Greater Boston Convention & Visitors Bureau, Two Copley Place, Suite 105; 888-SEE-BOSTON; www.bostonusa.com

17 • BURLINGTON, VERMONT

About three and a half hours from Boston

There was a time not so long ago when Burlington would not have made it onto anyone's must-see list. That was then. Today, the city boasts a revitalized waterfront district on Lake Champlain, a picturesque pedestrian-only city center and a lively and very funky arts and cultural scene. The renaissance, which began in the 1980s, also resulted in an explosion of venues for outdoor recreation and a host of pubs and high-end eateries.

Despite the city's reputation as a hotbed of left-wing thinking—the Green Mountain State is still sometimes jokingly referred to as the People's Republic of Vermont—some important businesses have started here, including Ben & Jerry's ice cream and Burton Snowboards. Burlington is also a college town, with the University of Vermont campus within the city limits and Middlebury College about a half hour away.

Although the city has a distinct urban vibe, visitors looking for some of that old-fashioned Vermont rural charm will find that here, too, and you won't have to look too hard. For one thing, although it is the state's largest city, Burlington is quite small at only about 40,000 inhabitants. For another, Lake Champlain is used mostly for recreation, which means that you won't see a lot of development along its shore. What you will see is a ring of mountain ranges—the Green Mountains and the Adirondacks, to be exact—as well as a bustling waterfront within easy strolling distance of the pedestrian-zoned downtown.

You know you're in a people-friendly city the minute you cruise into town, where the streets are easy to navigate and the parking plentiful. You won't need a GPS to find the Burlington Boathouse at the end of College Street, with its inviting boat dock and scenic views. Park across the street from the dock and hop on the *Spirit of Ethan Allen III* (802-862-8300; www.soea.com) for a mellow lunch cruise (other cruise times are available) that takes roughly the same route as Samuel de Champlain did when he explored the lake that is named after him some 400 years ago. To the accompaniment of live music, you'll glide by North Beach, a sprinkling of tiny islands, and even a handful of daredevil cliff divers as you cruise along the shoreline. Be sure to keep your eye out for Champ, Lake Champlain's version of the Loch Ness Monster. If you missed him, don't worry—his latest sighting has been immortalized on YouTube.

▮▮▮▮ GETTING THERE (AND GETTING AROUND)

Burlington is just over 200 miles from Boston off I-89 North to Route 2. The Burlington Airport is about 4 miles away, and you'll also need wheels to reach the city center from the Amtrak station (29 Railroad Ave.; 800-USA-Rail; www.amtrak.com). Ferry service is available from mid-June to mid-October from Burlington to upstate New York via **Lake Champlain Ferries** (1 King St.; 802-864-9804; www.ferries.com).

Once you arrive, you can park downtown and easily reach the waterfront and Church Street Marketplace shops on foot or by bicycle.

Or hop on the **Green Mountain Railroad** (800-707-3530; www.rails-vt.com) for scenic train rides to Charlotte and Shelburne.

▮▮▮▮ WHAT TO SEE

For a look at Burlington's lesser-known, edgiest art district, drive along Pine Street to the South End, where art galleries, cafés, and offbeat shops line the street on both sides. Stop in at **Pine Street Art Works** (404 Pine St.; www.pinestreetartworks.com), where owner Liza Cowan sells her

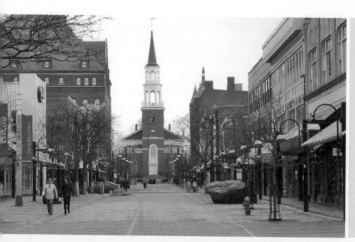

Church Street Marketplace, Winter

own works as well as paintings, ephemera, and other works of art by established local artists. Check out **The Lamp Shop** next door for a colorful collection of vintage lamps and save time for a coffee break at **Speeder and Earl's**. If you missed the Church Street retail location, visit **Lake Champlain Chocolates** (750 Pine Street; www.lakechamplain chocolates.com) for a free tour. In September, the Pine Street area becomes even more visitor-friendly with an annual **South End Art Hop**, when you'll experience fashion shows, art demonstrations, and live music.

Stop in the new **Echo Lake Aquarium and Science Center** (One College St.; 802-864-1848; www.echovermont.com), especially if you have kids in tow. You can wander through the museum in an hour or take all afternoon to enjoy the animal feedings and interactive exhibits, especially the Hurricane Simulator, which will leave your hair looking the worse for wear. Stay to learn the formation and ecology of the Lake Champlain Basin in a fun way, like donning goggles and "digging" for whale fossils or putting your face in the Turtle Face Tank, or simply stroll out onto the terrace to relax in deck chairs overlooking the water.

The Firehouse Center for the

Visual Arts (Church St.; 802-865-7166) showcases the work of local artists in a restored building in the heart of the Church Street Marketplace. Or nurture your inner artist at **The Robert Hull Fleming Museum** (61 Colchester Ave.; 802-656-2090; www.fleming museum.org) on the University of Vermont campus, with its impressive collection of fine art and ancient artifacts. For live music and theater, year-round, visit the **Flynn Center for the Performing Arts** (153 Main Street; 802-652-4500; www.flynncenter .org), with productions that range from the familiar to the cutting edge.

Shelburne Museum (6000 Shelburne Rd.; 802-985-3346; www.shelburnemuseum.org) is only a few miles outside town, and yet the outdoor attraction makes you feel as though you're in deep rural Vermont in another century. Some 39 buildings, many of which are authentic from centuries past, dot the rolling countryside. In addition to art galleries that boast paintings by Monet and Degas, works of folk art, and 19th-century quilts, the museum features a railroad station and even a steamboat—the *Ticonderoga*—that sits on the museum grounds as if tossed there by a giant wave. Best of all, if you are pressed for time, make

It stands to reason that an area as beautiful as Burlington would be a magnet for filmmakers, and in fact, there have been several movies made in the area in recent years. The 1999 Jim Carrey film *Me, Myself & Irene* was filmed partly in Burlington, as was the Michelle Pfeiffer ghostly thriller *What Lies Beneath*, released the same year.

the rounds in the free hop-on/hop-off trolley, complete with guided narration.

Shelburne Farms (1611 Harbor Rd.; 802-985-8686; www.shelburnefarms.org), also nearby, is a 1,400-acre working farm with walking trails, activities for the kids, and guided tours of the historic buildings and grand gardens overlooking the lake. The Farms serve as a venue for Mozart concerts in summer, as does the **Grand Isle Lake House** (www.grandislelakehouse.com), a former 1903 hotel on Lake Champlain Islands that is now part of the Preservation Trust of Vermont. Thanks to a causeway, you can reach the lake house by car.

▮▮▮▮ WHAT TO DO

Rent a kayak at **Umiak Outdoor Outfitters** (849 S. Main St.; 802-253-2317; www.umiak.com) for a self-guided excursion on the lake, or pick one up at the company's North Beach location during the summer. The company also offers guided tours of the lake and instructions for newbies.

Landlubbers can also enjoy the waterfront by renting a bike at the **SkiRack** (85 Main St.; 802-658-3313; www.skirack.com) for a ride along the extensive trails that circumnavigate much of the lake. There is a trail entrance across from the Boathouse that links to the Island Line Trail along the shore or as far as the Colchester Causeway, where you can make a day of it.

Eager to learn about Burlington's much-vaunted microbrew culture? **Burlington Brew Tours** (802-760-6091; www.burlingtonbrewtours.com) will take you around to four microbreweries, give you lunch at Al's French Fries or Beansies Bus, and offer you a whopping 18 to 23 beers to sample. Fortunately, the company also provides transportation, so you can indulge more or less guilt-free.

If you can tear yourself away from the waterfront, save some time to explore the **Church Street Marketplace** downtown. You can easily walk the few blocks to the pedestrian zone, where dozens of stores and restaurants line the four-block stretch, many in renovated historical buildings. In warm weather much of the life of the marketplace moves outdoors, with sidewalk cafés and performers entertaining passersby. Don't be surprised if you see street performers in the marketplace (okay, you probably won't see the semi-retired Phish, who got their start in the city, but that group of bedraggled singers on the corner might be their heirs apparent), especially during one of the musical festivals that go on year-round.

If the urge to shop franchise retail brands hits you, or the weather isn't conducive to wandering around outside, duck into the **Burlington Town Center Mall** (49 Church St.; 802-658-2545; www.burlingtontowncenter.com) also in the pedestrian zone, where you'll find everything from Ann Taylor Loft to Pottery Barn. Or save a bundle at the annual side-walk sale at the Mall and the Marketplace, which takes place every July. Nearly 200 stores participate with deals and discounts, and the city gets into the act by offering free parking for designated hours during the blowout. For a more back-to-nature shopping experience, try the **Burlington Farmer's Market** on City Hall Park, which takes place all summer long from May through October and where you can find everything from locally grown produce to handmade crafts.

■ ■ ■ WHERE TO STAY

The Willard Street Inn (349 South Willard St.; 802-651-8710; www.willardstreetinn.com) is an Old World brick Victorian B&B with flowery wallpaper, period architecture, and angled ceilings. New-fangled amenities are also abundant, such as free Wi-Fi. From $140.

The **Courtyard Burlington Harbor Marriott** (25 Cherry St.; 802-864-4700; www.marriott

Burlington Waterfront

Shelburne Museum

.com), overlooking Lake Champlain and near the Church Street Marketplace, is the city's newest hotel. The property overlooks the venue for the annual Jazz Festival, but is also walking distance from the town center. From $179.

The Essex Resort and Spa (70 Essex Way; 802-878-1100; www .vtculinaryresort.com) in nearby Essex is a splurge but well worth it for foodies in search of a seriously gourmet meal. Part culinary school, part destination hotel, the resort offers two restaurants: Butlers, which has won the *Wine Spectator* Award; and the more casual Tavern, with an outdoor patio. Many dishes are prepared from fresh ingredients grown on the grounds, and much of the waitstaff is made up of students from the Culinary Institute. The property just opened a full-service spa with a huge, 25-foot heated indoor lap pool, and also offers a catch-and-release casting pond, a rock course with zip-lines, golf, and tennis. From $219.

■ ■ ■ WHERE TO CAMP

The Burlington Campground at North Beach (www.enjoy burlington.com), within easy walking distance from the lake, is the perfect choice for campers who want to get away from it all and save a bundle on accommodations at the same time. Open May 1 through Columbus Day. $25 for a tent site.

■ ■ ■ EATING OUT

A Single Pebble (www.asingle pebble.com) looks small from the outside, but there are several floors and a full-service bar tucked inside. For the best deal on Chinese cuisine in town, try the $15 tasting menu at lunch, but be prepared to bring your appetite.

Leunig's Bistro (802-863-3759; www.leunigsbistro.com) on Church Street walks that fine line between high-end French bistro food and an unpretentious setting. Entrées range from a simple croque-monsieur to au poivre elk medallions. From $10 at lunch; $28 for dinner.

The Skinny Pancake (60 Lake St.; 802-598-3028; www.skinny pancake.com) on the waterfront is a creperie with savory and sweet offerings, as well as vegan and organic options. The restaurant also serves up crepes at its open-air cart at Church Street Marketplace daily. Starting under $10.

Magnolia Bistro (One Lawson Lane, 802-846-7446; www.mag noliabistro.com) serves lunch and one of the best breakfasts in town. A Sesame Tofu Scram and a Belgian Lime Waffle join the more traditional French toast and oatmeal dishes on the menu, which leans toward local organic produce. Starting under $10.

Rí Rá Irish Pub, (123 Church St.; 802-860-9401; www.rira.com) an Irish pub in a revitalized bank building on Church Street, is the place to go for a drink with friendly locals. You can also get pub and bistro food, and there is outdoor seating in season. $8 to $15 for lunch; $9 to $22 at dinner.

■■■■ SPECIAL EVENTS

Early June: The annual 10-day **Burlington Discover Jazz Festival!** (802-863-7992; www.discoverjazz.com) has been kicking off the summer season for more than a quarter century. The main venue is on the waterfront, but the fun spills out onto the street in the form of jam sessions, smaller concerts, and even themed cruise tours. The event is so popular that it essentially doubles the size of the city's population for the duration, thanks to such performers as Branford Marsalis and Diana Krall. Start looking at the Web site in May for the year's lineup of entertainers.

Early July: Time your visit to coincide with the **Champlain Burlington Waterfront Festival** (800-VERMONT; www.celebrate champlain.org), which marks the exploration of the lake with a riot of activities, from fireworks to live performances by local groups and well-known artists.

August to September: If your taste in festivals runs to quirky, check out the **Festival of Fools** in August or the **Outright Vermont Fire Truck Pull** in September, or fete the end of summer with the state's biggest event—the annual **Champlain Valley Fair** (www.cvexpo.org), with something for everybody.

October to February: Just because summer ends doesn't mean that the festivals don't keep coming. You can expect a costumed parade at Halloween and the much-ballyhooed arrival of Santa Claus in late November, but the centerpiece of winter festivities is **First Night Burlington** (www.firstnightburlington.com). Would-be rabble-rousers should take note that First Night is alcohol-free. The same cannot be said of the annual **Magic Hat Mardi Gras** (www.magichat.net) event in February, put on by the Magic Hat Brewing Co. and featuring floats, masks, and beads.

■■■■ NEARBY

Are you thinking of visiting Burlington in winter but worried you won't have enough to do? In addition to the cultural and dining possibilities mentioned above, keep in mind that the city is virtually surrounded by what locals call the "white necklace" of ski areas within an hour's drive. So bundle up for a day on the slopes at Bolton Valley, Jay Peak, Smuggler's Notch, Stowe, or Sugarbush, all of which have their own summer and winter activities and equipment rental operations.

■ ■ ■ ■ **RESOURCES**

Lake Champlain Regional Chamber of Commerce, 60 Main St.; 877-686-5253; www.vermont.org

18 • PORTLAND, MAINE

Technically a peninsula, Portland is on Maine's south coast.

The motto of Portland, Maine, "Resurgam" or "I will rise again," says it all. This trendy city on Maine's Casco Bay was nearly obliterated so many times in its long history that it is a wonder the early settlers didn't give up. Destroyed in the 1600s and during the Revolutionary War, Portland was immolated yet again in the "Great Fire" on July 4, 1866, probably from a rogue firework.

Certain geological advantages, however, most notably its thriving port, gave intrepid settlers impetus to rise again. Eventually, the city was prosperous enough to become the state capital for a dozen years in the early 1800s (many people think it still is, but in fact, that honor goes to Augusta).

Although the downtown area had its ups and downs throughout the 20th century, the last few decades have seen a wonderful renaissance, so much so that Portland now routinely ranks on lists of best places to live in magazine surveys and reader polls. New, avant-garde architecture sits adjacent to restored historic buildings, hipster art students mingle with local residents, and brewpubs are sandwiched in among high-end eateries and local hangouts.

Although the city has many attributes, if you had to pick just one, it would probably be its exploding arts scene. The presence of the Maine College of Art (522 Congress St.; 207-775-3052; www.meca.edu) has been a driving force in the evolution of the downtown Arts District, and this is a great place to begin an exploration of the city. You can take exit 6A off I-295, follow the signs to Congress Street, and either tour the school's meticulously restored Porteous Building, which houses the college's Institute of Contemporary Art, or just have a look from the outside at its elegant Beaux Arts exterior. In a case of beauty being more than skin deep, one of the attractions of Porteous is that it was renovated using up-to-the-minute green design techniques. Where an art college thrives, a world-class museum can't be far behind, and a case in point is the Portland

Museum of Art (7 Congress Square Plaza; 207-775-6148; www.portlandmuseum.org) just down the street. Thanks to its huge, redbrick facade with windows shaped like half-moons, you can't miss the facility, which dominates the city block.

Art may feed the soul, but visitors looking for more corporeal

The Old Port is a working port.

Shops along Commercial St.

nourishment will find enough bars and eateries in town—more than 200 at last count—to please even a finicky foodie. The Food Network gave Portland a top five nod for its cuisine in 2007, and nowadays the city has so many star chefs that they are tripping over each other. Follow your nose to the **Old Port** district and park on Commercial Street for a sampling of what's on the menu. The site of the city's first settlement, the Old Port now features warehouses transformed into shops, restaurants, coffee bars, and condos. Stroll along the length of the pier, where your senses will be assaulted by aromas from a myriad of cultures, from Mexican and Italian to fresh, local seafood caught just off the pier. Despite some yuppification, the architecture of the Old Port is beautifully preserved, thanks to its status on the list of National Register of Historic Places.

▎▎▎▎ GETTING THERE (AND GETTING AROUND)

Portland is just over 100 miles north of Boston, or about a two-hour drive. You can fly into Portland Jetport (www.portlandjet port.org), served by nearly a dozen airlines and a quick ride from downtown, or take a bus (www.concordcoachlines.com) from Boston or other points in

Portland's Rocky Coast

New Hampshire or Maine. One of the nicest ways to reach the city from Boston is via the Amtrak Downeaster (www.amtrakdowneaster.com), which takes just under two and a half hours and passes through some of the area's prettiest scenery.

The city is small and intimate, which makes it a great choice for visitors who like to do their exploring on foot, and it is close enough to Boston for an easy overnight—or even a day trip if you are feeling ambitious. There is plenty of on-street parking and relatively smooth traffic flow, which will seem like a dream to travelers used to negotiating Boston's intricate medley of downtown streets or New York's gridlock. The foot-weary can also hop a bus (www.gpmetrobus.com) to get around town.

▌▌▌▌ WHAT TO SEE

The **Charles Shipman Payson Building**, an extension of the Portland Museum of Art created by the I. M. Pei architectural group, boasts a collection that spans the 1800s to the present. The 19th-century American works are exhibited in restored original galleries on the first floor, and if you happen to love Winslow Homer, you are really in luck, as there are more than a dozen paintings by the artist on exhibit. The big-name European paintings, including works by Monet, Picasso, Renoir, Cézanne, and Magritte, are on the third floor tucked away from the elevator. Be sure to attend the **Sunday Morning Jazz Breakfasts** in April and May for food and music in the Museum Café.

If you happen to be in town on the first Friday of any month from 5 PM to 8 PM, you can join the **First Friday Art Walk**, when local galleries and museums fling open their doors and tempt you with wine and snacks to have a look at their creations. Best of all, because there are so many studios and galleries in town, even repeat visitors will find a different Art Walk itinerary to tempt them.

Stroll by the imposing granite **Custom House** (312 Fore St.) at the Old Port, which was built after the 1866 fire and is still in use today as the home of the Coast Guard. Adding to its authenticity, the area is still a working port serving the local fishing industry, as well as home to the Maine State Pier and the Casco Bay Lines ferry, where you can hop aboard a ferry for an outing to the islands that dot the harbor.

There are outdoor markets on the waterfront in season, or visit the renovated **Portland Market House** (www.publicmarkethouse .com) on Monument Square uptown for baked goods, cheeses, beers, and other fresh, local products.

Don't miss the cobblestone side streets leading up one block from Commercial Street to **Fore Street**, which runs parallel to the waterfront and where more shops and eateries will vie for your attention.

Performing arts thrive in the city, and theater buffs can find year-round productions at the **Portland Stage Company** (25A Forest Ave.; 207-774-0465; www .portlandstage.com) in the Arts District. For music, take in a performance at the **Portland Symphony Orchestra** (207-842-0800; www.portlandsymphony.com) at the intersection of Congress and Myrtle streets.

▮▮▮▮ WHAT TO DO

If you like artisanal beer, visit the 10-year-old **Shipyard Brewing Co.** (86 Newbury St.; 800-273-9253) on the waterfront, which offers tastings, hosts parties, and conducts tours. Or **D.L. Geary Brewing Company** (38 Evergreen Dr.; www.gearybrewing.com), whose owner, David Geary, learned the craft in Scotland and England before setting up shop in Portland in the 1980s. You can visit the shop or call ahead to arrange a tour. Or visit the **Casco Bay Brewing Company** (57 Industrial Way; 207-797-2020; www.cascobaybrewing.com), which specializes in lager and ale, including seasonal brews.

For a nostalgic trip along Casco Bay, hop aboard a steam train via the **Maine Narrow Gauge Railroad Co. & Museum** (58 Fore St.; 207-828-0814; www.mngrr.org), which runs daily on weekends from May to October and on weekends in the fall.

Hikers and cyclists love the **Harborwalk Trail**, which runs from East End Beach to Bug Light Park along the harbor and over the Casco Bay Bridge. If you are pressed for time, sample a portion of the walk starting at Commercial Street at the Old Port and crossing the bridge on foot.

Visit the islands in Casco Bay via ferry from the Old Port or by harbor cruise on a historic wooden schooner via the **Portland Schooner Company** (56 Commercial St.; 207-766-2500; www.port landschooner.com) at the Maine State Pier. There are two-hour sailings as well as overnight trips in the Bay, and the crew is knowledgeable about the sights and sounds of the area and their historic vessels, named the *Bagheera* and *Wendameen*. Or try a two-hour windjammer sail aboard the engine-free *Frances* via **Maine Sailing Adventures** (www.maine sailingadventures.net), which serves beer and wine along with narration about the region and its history.

▮▮▮▮ WHERE TO STAY

Old Port district hotels put you smack in the middle of the lively waterfront scene while being within easy access of downtown.

Portland Harbor Hotel (468 Fore St.; 207-775-9090; www.port landharborhotel.com) is a posh four-diamond property in the Old Port district. Recently renovated, the pet-friendly hotel offers a spa and fitness center and Starbucks in the lobby. From about $199.

Portland Regency Hotel & Spa (20 Milk St.; 207-774-4200: www .theregency.com), also in the Old Port, is in a preserved armory that dates from the late 19th century. Amenities includes the restored Twenty Milk Street dining room, a spa and fitness center, flat-screen TVs, and free Wi-Fi. From $139.

Hilton Garden Inn Portland Downtown Waterfront (65 Commercial St.; 207-780-0780; www .portlanddowntownwaterfront .hgi.com) features 120 guest rooms with fridges and microwaves. Rooms overlook the city or the waterfront. From around $118.

Can't leave home without your canine companion? Portland is one of the East Coast's most pet-friendly cities. Many local hotels and restaurants (deck dining only) welcome pets, and you can even take dogs on a number of harbor cruises and tours. Or drop off your four-legged friend at **Camp Bow Wow** (49 Blueberry Road; 207-541-WAGS; www.campbowwow.com), a day and overnight camp that even has Camper Cams so you can keep a virtual eye on your pet.

■■■■ EATING OUT

Consider hitting a couple of restaurants in search of the local specialty, the Italian Sandwich, which is a kind of sloppy foot-long sub with salami or ham, veggies, and salad dressing.

Hugo's (88 Middle St.; 207-774-8538; www.hugos.net) is presided over by one of the city's celebrity chefs, Rob Evans, winner of the 2009 James Beard Foundation Best Chef Northeast. With his ever-changing menu and particular attention to seafood, Evans puts a playful take on high-end cuisine, while keeping the ambience low key and unpretentious. From $15.

Fore Street (288 Fore St.; 207-775-2717; www.forestreet.biz) in the Old Port district is the brainchild of James Beard Award—winner Sam Hayward. The menu changes daily, using local ingredients in season. From $13.

Five Fifty-Five (555 Congress Street; 207-761-0555; http://fivefifty-five.com) showcases the talents of Steve Corry, named a Best New Chef by *Food & Wine* and featured in *Saveur* magazine. From $25.

Gilbert's Chowder House (92 Commercial St.; 207-871-5636) was voted Maine's Best Chowder by the readers of the *Maine Sunday Telegram*. The restaurant is open for lunch and dinner, or grab your order to go and enjoy a picnic by the water. From $4.50 for chowder; $9.95 for entrées.

Stop in for a bright-red steamed lobster or whole-belly fried clams at the **Portland Lobster Co.** (180 Commercial St.; 207-775-2112; www.portlandlobstercompany.com), and you'll find yourself sitting with as many locals as tourists. Market price.

■■■■ SPECIAL EVENTS

July: A **Weekday Music Series**, running consecutively in the Old Port and Arts Districts gives new meaning to TGIF with free Friday lunchtime concerts at noon, while **Movies in the Park** at dusk on Monday nights in Congress Square in July features films on a giant screen and provides ample space for picnicking during the show.

July to early August: Annual gatherings in other parts of the city include the **Alive at Five Concert Series** in Monument Square. Timed to draw locals after a day at work, the event offers live music and drinks at a beer garden set up by the Sebago Brewing Company on Thursdays from 5 PM to 7:30 PM.

October: If the culinary choices seem overwhelming, consider arranging your visit to coincide with the annual three-day **Harvest on the Harbor** event. A knockout food festival with wine and beer tastings, cooking demonstrations, and an open-air food market, the festival attracts several thousand people every fall. In addition to letting some of Maine's top chefs show off their expertise, the festival promotes the concept of high-end cuisine made from fresh, local ingredients. The venues are inventive and include a grand tasting on the harbor and a wine tasting aboard a vintage schooner. You can buy tickets online (www .harvestontheharbor.com), and be prepared to be carded if you look under 21. Or join the throngs at the Old Port Festival in June for an afternoon of street food, live music, and local art.

Late November: The good news for visitors in winter is that the city also makes noise during the holiday season with several annual festive events. A favorite is the **Tree Lighting** in Monument Square, which also marks the kickoff of free half-hour horse-drawn wagon rides on weekends, also from the square.

▪▪▪▪ NEARBY

Landlubbers can explore **Mackworth Island** in Casco Bay by driving to Falmouth just outside Portland, then taking the causeway to the island. Stretch your legs and get great views of the city and the boats in the bay by hiking the easy, mile-long trail around the island.

▪▪▪▪ LIT LIFE

Poet Henry Wadsworth Longfellow grew up in Portland, and his house (487 Congress St.; 207-879-0427G) was lovingly restored in 2002 before being opened to the public for the first time as a museum. You can tour the house, which is still filled with original furniture and household items, and meander through the garden. The house is open May through October plus select dates during the winter holidays. Be sure to download a two-for-one admission coupon at www.mainehistory.org. There also is a monument to the poet at the intersection of Congress and State streets.

▪▪▪▪ RESOURCES

Convention & Visitors Bureau of Greater Portland, 94 Commercial St.; 207-772-5800

19 • PORTSMOUTH, NEW HAMPSHIRE

About an hour north of Boston near the mouth of the Piscataqua River,
which forms a boundary between New Hampshire and Maine

If Portland, Maine, is the hipster artist in leather, then Portsmouth is her fresh-faced preppy cousin—no less interesting but with an ambience all its own. This is not to say that the city doesn't have its hip side—it does—but the overall vibe is that of a quintessential New England town that grew in size without losing its small-town feel. Residential areas boast some historic houses, many in soft pastel colors, while early-19th-century brick buildings characterize the downtown; the waterfront provides a picturesque backdrop.

No longer just a pass-through destination for Bostonians on their way farther north, Portsmouth has come into its own in recent years, capping off its renaissance with a nod from the National Trust for Historic Preservation, which named it one of a dozen "Distinctive Destinations" in 2008.

At first glance, it is immediately apparent that Portsmouth is an old city, even by New England standards. It was first settled by colonists in the mid-1600s, and while fishing has been a key component to the city's success, the bulk of its early industry—and even its identity—is all about shipbuilding. Revolutionary War naval hero John Paul Jones captained two ships built here, the Ranger and the America, and the Portsmouth Naval Shipyard on the other side of the river is the first in the country. The **John Paul Jones House** (603-436-8420), where the famous Scot lived while his ships were being built, is now a museum dedicated to his life.

Portsmouth is a nationally recognized success story, but its carefully preserved downtown is no accident, but rather the result of forward-thinking townsfolk who worked hard to stop ill-conceived plans to destroy some of its oldest neighborhoods. As recently as 50 years ago, the then-run-down riverfront section of the city, known as Puddle Dock, was slated for demolition. Local lore credits the town librarian for igniting a fire under the citizens of Portsmouth, convincing them to rethink the plan, and as a result, a living history project known as the **Strawbery Banke Museum** (Marcy St.; 603-433-1100; www.strawberybanke.org) was born. Nowadays the museum, which is open for visitors from May through October, is made up of 40-plus historic buildings, including 10 homes, each of which represents a different era in the city's history, spread out over nearly 10 acres.

What is unique about Strawbery Banke, particularly in contrast to other re-created historic villages you may have visited, is that this one is smack in the center of the city. Locals stroll past the antique homes and gardens on their way to work or to the park, visitors explore the grounds and learn about the daily lives of settlers in centuries gone by via horse-and-buggy rides, costumed guides demonstrate craft and baking skills of the era and reenact battles, and children play games and even do chores in the new Discovery Center.

Like all of the cities on our list, Portsmouth is a walking city, but here the access is especially easy, thanks to plentiful on-street and municipal parking for a retro price of only $1 an hour. Leave the car in a central location and set out on foot to explore downtown or stroll through **Prescott Park** on the waterfront, where dozens of varieties of flowers bring color to the summer landscape. Either way, bring your appetite, your love of history, and your appreciation of the arts to one of New England's most charming and no longer overlooked cities.

▮▮▮▮ GETTING THERE (AND GETTING AROUND)

By car, take exit 7 off I-95 from Boston, less than an hour away. The city does have its own airport, however—**Portsmouth International Airport** (36 Airline Ave., 603-433-6536)—which has the advantage of free parking and proximity to the city. You will need to splurge on a private plane or charter to use the facilities, however, as no regularly scheduled service is currently operating.

Train service via **Amtrak** (www.amtrak.com) will only get you as far as Exeter, Dover, or Durham, New Hampshire, but there is a direct hourly bus from Boston's Logan airport to Portsmouth (www.ridecj.com). Trolley service is available from the bus station to downtown hotels.

Once you arrive, park in a municipal lot and set out on foot to explore the city.

▮▮▮▮ WHAT TO SEE

One of the easiest ways to see some of Portsmouth's most impressive historic buildings and

Pastel antique buildings in Portsmouth

Strawbery Banke Museum

its waterfront is to download a map (www.portsmouthnh.com /harbourtrail) and stroll along the **Portsmouth Harbour Trail**, a self-guided tour that encompasses antique homes and historic landmarks. Or join a guided tour from the kiosk at Market Square on select days in season. Want to give your feet a rest? See the sights via 40-minute carriage tour (**Carriage Trails**; 603-431-2542) on Tuesdays and Thursdays in season, from the Strawbery Banke Museum.

Some of the antique houses sprinkled throughout the city include the **Jackson House** (76 Northwest St.; 603-436-3205), billed as the oldest wood frame house in New Hampshire and Maine, and the 19th-century **Warner House** (150 Daniel St.; www.warnerhouse.org), a brick mansion decorated in period furniture and boasting an original colonial wall mural. The Warner House has the distinction of being a site of one of the first lightning rods installed by Ben

Franklin in his quest to discover electricity. You can also stop and smell the roses in the grand garden of the **Moffatt-Ladd House** (154 Market St.; www.moffattladd .org) a Georgian mansion that also is a National Historic Landmark, or make your way to **The Hill**, a collection of restaurants and offices in historic buildings that were on the endangered list several decades ago.

European settlers weren't the only cultures that influenced this seafaring city. African slaves entered the country through its harbor, and the **Portsmouth Black Heritage** Trail honors their struggles via educational events and lectures. You can download a map from the Web site (www.pbh trail.org) for a self-guided tour or stop by the offices at the Governor John Langdon House (143 Pleasant St.; 603-431-2768) for the latest on events.

Stop in **Tugboat Alley** (47 Bow St.; 877-tug-alley; www.tugboat alley.com), a store that sells books, models, and gifts that range from the serious to kid-friendly Theodore Tugboat toys. "Gundalows," flat-bottomed cargo barges that once were a familiar sight in the bay, no longer navigate the waters (although you can see a replica in Prescott Park, mentioned below), but tugboats are still a familiar sight as they usher enormous tankers into the harbor.

Check out Congress and Market streets in the thriving downtown district among 19th-century red-brick buildings that have been transformed into sidewalk cafés and restaurants, one-of-a-kind boutiques, and art galleries. **Worldly Goods** (37 Congress St.; 603-436-9311), for example, sells American fine arts that have been fashioned into functional objects—such as vases, lamps, and clocks—while the **Three Graces Gallery** (105 Market St.; 603-436-1988) showcases the works of local artists in monthly exhibitions.

Stop in at the **Portsmouth Farmers' Market** (Junkins Ave.), held Saturday mornings in summer in the City Hall parking lot.

▪▪▪▪ WHAT TO DO

Hop aboard **Tug Alley Too** (47 Bow St.; 603-430-9556; www.tug boatalley.com) for an hour-and-a-half excursion on the river. This former working tug now takes passengers under the Memorial Bridge that separates New Hampshire from Maine, past the Portsmouth Naval Shipyard, several lighthouses, and forts, and along the Wentworth Marina. Guests are invited to bring a picnic or arrange for the tug staff to prepare one for you, and the romantically inclined can even get married onboard by the captain, who is also a justice of the peace. There are three sailings a day on weekends from May through October.

Try a narrated **Portsmouth Harbor Cruise** (Ceres St. Dock; 800-776-0915, 603-436-8084; www.portsmouthharbor.com), which offers several ways to enjoy Portsmouth's waterways. You can take an hour-long cruise aboard the 49-passenger *Heritage*, past lighthouses and mansions, or head out to open sea to the **Isles of Shoals**, a network of nine islands just 6 miles off the coast. Many famous and infamous travelers spent time on these historic islands, from Captain John Smith to bands of marauding pirates, but many contemporary visitors come for the bird-watching opportunities and for tours of the historic gardens on Appledore Island. There are evening cruises that show off the city's skyline at sunset, as well as seasonal fall foliage excursions that wend into the scenic Great Bay or the Cocheco River.

If self-powered exploration is more your thing, rent a kayak at **Portsmouth Kayak Adventures** (185 Wentworth Rd.; 603-559-1000; www.portsmouthkayak.com) for guided tours, instruction, or such specialty tours as yoga on the beach.

Get a handle on sea urchins, crabs, and other local sea creatures at the **Marine Life Touch Tank** (603-431-0260), a free interactive aquarium on the Isles of Shoals Steamship Co. dock. Operated by the Blue Ocean Society, the tank is open daily in summer, and naturalists are on hand to fill visitors in on the inhabitants of the tank.

Catch a glimpse of the claustrophobic life of a submarine seaman at the dry-docked **USS Albacore**, which has been transformed into a museum (600 Market St.; 603-436-3680; www.ussalbacore.org). In its heyday during World War II, the *Albacore* sank eight Japanese ships. Today's visitors can walk through the sub, learn about its history, and relive its battle exploits.

Tour **Redhook Brewery** (35 Corporate Dr.; 603-430-8600; www.redhook.com), where the $1 entrance fee will buy you a guided walk through the facility, samples of the brew, and a souvenir glass.

Take in a performance at **The Music Hall** (28 Chestnut St.; 603-436-2400; www.themusichall.org), where Suzanne Vega and the Doobie Brothers were recent headliners. You can also see films in the restored 1878 theater or take a guided tour of its new Beaux Arts lobby and trompe l'oeil decorated ceiling. Lecture series at the Hall are also popular. Past guests have included Barbara Walters and Dan Brown, author of *The Da Vinci Code*.

▪▪▪▪ WHERE TO STAY

The **Inne at Strawbery Banke** (314 Court St.; 603-436-7242; www.innatstrawberybanke.com) only has seven rooms, but the location is stellar and the ambience is historic. That said, guests won't have to sacrifice such modern niceties as private bathrooms and TVs. From $100.

Ale House Inn (121 Bow St.;

You can cool off at Portsmouth's 100-yard-long municipal swimming pool on Peirce Island (99 Peirce Island Rd.). The pool is open to nonresidents and offers a breathtaking view of the bay.

603-431-7760; www.alehouseinn
.com) in the historic Portsmouth
Brewing Co. building in the Market Square district offers a hip,
boutique hotel experience.
Amenities include a refrigerator,
free Wi-Fi, iPod dock, and flatscreen TV. From $129.

Wentworth by the Sea (588
Wentworth Rd.; 603-422-7322;
www.wentworth.com) is one of
the last remaining grand dame
resort properties in New England.
Now a Marriott property, the 161-
room, waterfront hotel is just a
few miles from downtown. Services include a full-service spa, a
golf course, and a waterfront
pool. Accommodations include
the Little Harbor Marina Suites
with full kitchens and private
balconies. From about $179.

The **Sheraton Harborside
Portsmouth** (250 Market St.; 603-
431-2300; www.sheratonports
mouth.com) is on the waterfront
a few blocks from Market Square.
The Sheraton has an indoor pool,
the Harbor's Edge Restaurant,
and a selection of artifacts in the
lobby that were uncovered during the hotel's construction in the
1980s. From about $150.

▪▪▪▪ WHERE TO CAMP

Shel-Al Campground (Rte. 1,
North Hampton; 603-964-5730;
www.shel-al.com) is near
Portsmouth and Hampton Beach

and has a playground and game
room for the kids. $27 per tent
site.

Wakeda Campgrounds (294
Exeter Rd., Hampton Falls; 603-
772-5274; www.wakedacamp
ground.com), which offers tent
sites and cabins in a woodsy setting. On-site features include
minigolf and a basketball court.
$32 per tent site.

▪▪▪▪ EATING OUT

Portsmouth's downtown area is
home to more bakeries than you
would expect to find in a few
square blocks. If sipping a
designer coffee over a luscious
dessert—while people-watching
from an outdoor table or window
seat—is your idea of heaven, you
are in luck. **Ceres Bakery** (51 Penhallow St.; 603-436-6518) just off
Market Square, serves up breakfast, lunch, and baked goods,
while **Popovers on the Square** (8
Congress St.; 603-431-1119) offers
a seasonal menu with a selection
of wines, irresistible pasties, and
popovers by the dozen. For a
more low-key take on the bakery
experience, stop by the **Works
Bakery Cafe** (9 Congress St.; 603-
431-4434) for a panini, fruit
smoothie, or frozen coffee drink.
Or check out **Café Espresso** (38
Islington St.; 603-334-3407),
where Hillary Clinton gave her
famous tearful response to a

sympathetic local's question during her campaign.

The **Rosa Restaurant** (80 State St.; 603-436-9715; www.therosa .com), a historic restaurant right behind Strawbery Banke, holds the distinction of being the first eatery in New Hampshire to serve alcohol after Prohibition. The menu is Italian American, with plenty of fresh seafood dishes, from Prince Edward Island mussels to garlicky calamari. From $6.99 for lunch; $8.99 for dinner.

The **Black Trumpet Bistro** (29 Ceres St.; 603-431-0887; www .blacktrumpetbistro.com) is in a former 19th-century warehouse in the old port section of the city overlooking the river. Opt for a romantic evening in the dining room on the first floor or head upstairs to the wine bar for live music with dinner. The menu is Mediterranean, and the wine list is extensive. From $16; small plates available.

The **Friendly Toast** (121 Congress St.; 603-430-2154) isn't your mother's breakfast joint. With its beyond-quirky decor, award-winning menu, and much-tattooed waitstaff, you will find everything from salads and burgers to smoothies and alcoholic drinks here. The real draw, however, is the inventive, served-all-day breakfast menu, which includes such oddball options as

French toast dripping with Grand Marnier and raspberry sauce and Almond Joy Cakes with chocolate chips and coconut. From $4.50.

The **Library Restaurant** (401 State St.; 603.431-5202; www .libraryrestaurant.com) is the place to go for a sizzling steak and a dose of history. Found in the Rockingham House, a red-brick mansion and former hotel dating from 1785, the restaurant's history involves a who's who of ex-presidents, from George Washington and Teddy Roosevelt to JFK. From $8 for lunch; $23 for dinner.

▮▮▮▮ NEARBY

Spend the day at **Hampton Beach** just south of Portsmouth on Route 1A. It was named Cleanest Beach on the Atlantic Seacoast and among the top five in the United States by the Natural Resources Defense Council. The water is warm by East Coast standards, and there are lifeguards in summer, as well as visitor facilities, parking, and even weekly fireworks in season.

Or, for a more secluded experience, bike out to **New Castle Beach**, where parking and restrooms are available at the adjacent Great Island Common. **The Seacoast Science Center** (570 Ocean Boulevard, Rye; www.sea coastsciencecenter.org) at Odiorne Point State Park just a few miles along the coast offers interactive exhibits, guided treks, and educational programs in a dramatic seaside setting. History buffs can check out the big gun mounts here that date from World War II. According to local lore, the guns were only fired once because they blew out the windows at Wentworth by the Sea.

▮▮▮▮ SPECIAL EVENTS

March: Sample several of the city's 250-plus restaurants off-season during the annual **Restaurant Week Portsmouth** (www.portsmouthchamber.org), when a multicourse meal will tempt your palate for rock-bottom prices.

May: Gardening enthusiasts can visit Portsmouth during the **Lilac Festival** at the restored Wentworth **Coolidge** mansion, down a dirt road overlooking Little Harbor (follow the signs). The site was named in part for the first English governor of the state, who brought lilacs—now New Hampshire's state flower—to the region.

Late June to late August: The **Prescott Park Arts Festival** (Marcy St.; www.prescottpark .org) has lured some 3 million visitors since the early 1970s. The festival covers all bases with theatrical productions (think crowd-

pleasing blockbusters like *Grease* and *Annie*); jazz, rock, and folk concert series; juried art exhibitions; dance performances; a whole menu of chowder and lobster feasts; and even a chili cook-off.

Early October: The **New Hampshire Fall Festival** (www.prescott park.org) has something for everyone with a mix of crafts, farm animals, garden tours, kids' activities, and live music. Bring your appetite for the chili cookoff, washed down with locally produced beer.

Early to mid-December: The Christmas Stroll at Strawbery Banke—complete with displays of Victorian ornaments and performances by the New Hampshire Symphony Orchestra—will take the chill out of a winter visit.

▮▮▮▮ LIT LIFE

Smuttynose Island, one of the Isles of Shoals, was the unlikely scene of several grisly murders in 1873, a story that inspired the novel *The Weight of Water* by Anita Shreve and a subsequent 2000 film with Sean Penn.

The **Portsmouth Naval Prison** on Seavey's Island, whose impenetrable castle-like exterior and location earned it the nickname "Alcatraz of the East," is famous for its connection with iconic movie actor Humphrey Bogart.

According to locals, Bogart worked at the prison when he was in the navy and was punched in the mouth by a prisoner, thus acquiring his famous lisp. The prison also served as the setting for the 1973 film *The Last Detail* with Jack Nicholson. Although no longer in use, the prison is not open for visitors, so you will have to be content with looking at it from afar.

▮▮▮▮ RESOURCES

Portsmouth Chamber of Commerce, 500 Market St.; 603-610-5510; www.portsmouthchamber.org

Portsmouth Historical Society, 43 Middle St.; 603-436-84333; www.portsmouthhistory.org

20 • PROVIDENCE, RHODE ISLAND

Just over 40 miles south of Boston as the crow flies

What do you say about a city that sets its river on fire every summer? Part art installation, and part quirky extravaganza, Water-Fire is just one of the ways Providence has reinvented itself from a gritty also-ran destination into its present incarnation as a trendy and thriving city. Some people credit the 1993 opening of the convention center, offering meeting planners a less expensive alternative to Boston, as a turning point in the city's transformation. Others point to T. F. Green Airport, which, thanks to ample parking and easy access, is increasingly appealing to travelers crazed by the years of snarled-up traffic around Boston's Logan Airport during the Big Dig. Or it could be Providence's impressive historic districts left intact over the years, not so much on principle, but because few organizations cared enough about the downtrodden city to raze and redevelop old neighborhoods. Whatever the reason, current residents now are proud of those old buildings—so much so that historic preserva-tion has been a key element in the city's recent development boom.

First-time visitors will likely be struck by the juxtaposition of old and new in Providence's revitalized downtown, particularly along the once-neglected river that runs through the city center. Formerly covered by what was supposedly the widest bridge in the world—a dubious distinction—the riverfront has been reimagined into Riverwalk, an inviting walkway with Venetian-style stone streets and small, arched bridges. At one end of Riverwalk is Waterplace Park, a people-friendly urban park with places to sit and watch passers-by, grab a quick picnic from a street vendor, examine eye-catching art installations, or burn off a few calories jogging.

The space is also used for a number of special events and celebrations, the most famous of which is WaterFire Providence (101 Regent Ave.; 401-273-1155; www.waterfire.org). The exhibition, for want of a better word, is basically a flotilla of 100 crackling bonfires that illuminate the river in summer to the accompaniment of ambient music. Crowds line Riverwalk or look down from the bridges to witness the spectacle, which was created on a smaller scale in 1994 by artist Barnaby Evans and has since expanded into a regular event.

If you arrive early and want to learn more about the installation, reserve a walking tour through the **Rhode Island Historical Society** (www.rihs.org) at 5:30 PM or stake out an outdoor table at Cafe Nuovo (1 Citizens Plaza; 401-421-2525; www.cafenuovo.com) for great views of the festivities. WaterFire was designed to be interactive, so don't be surprised

to also see performance artists juggling fire, spectators practicing salsa moves, and children running amok.

Providence also dazzles by day, and the good news is that many of the city's most appealing attractions are within easy walking distance of each other. **Brown University**, the **Rhode Island School of Design**, and **Johnson & Wales** are just three of the schools that make their home here, and the interplay between the schools and the city has been mutually enriching.

▮▮▮▮ GETTING THERE (AND GETTING AROUND)

From Boston, take I-95 N to exit 22. Or take the train to Amtrak Providence Train Station, which is a short, easy walk from the Water Place Park.

T. F. Green Airport, which wins kudos for being easy to get in and out of, is served by several low-cost carriers.

Once here, plan to walk just about everywhere unless you plan to visit Roger Williams Zoo, in which case you'll need a car.

▮▮▮▮ WHAT TO SEE

Bring your appetite and follow your nose to **Atwells Avenue**, where you'll pass under an entrance arch complete with a huge dangling sculpture of a

Providence River Walk

Swan Boats at Roger Williams Park

Diner Exhibit in Culinary Arts Museum

pinecone. You are now on **Federal Hill**, formerly the city's version of Little Italy, but now increasingly diverse with a cheerful mix of restaurants, boutiques, and art galleries. You don't have to be a foodie to love this quarter-mile strip of real estate, but be aware that you will trip over restaurants of various ethnicities on every block (see Where to Eat).

Would-be shoppers will find one-of-a-kind boutiques lining the streets of Federal Hill, like **Garbolino** (254 Atwells Ave.; 401-273-0080), a clothing store that was a mainstay of the neighborhood before it became cool, sandwiched in between hip art galleries like **Gallery Z** (259 Atwells Ave.; 401-454-884) and **Art Gallery at 17 Peck** (303 Atwells Ave., 401-331-2561). What you won't find here are franchise stores like Tiffany, Coach or Sephora (although all of those and more can be found at **Providence Place Mall** at Waterplace Park.)

Take the **Heritage Walk** on College Hill near the RISD Museum exit, a mile-long stroll that packs a wallop in terms of historic sites. You can pick up a map at the John **Carter House** (21 Meeting St.; 401-831-7440), but you won't need one to find the imposing **John Brown House Museum** (401-273-7507), a huge Georgian mansion with a sprawling lawn that takes up most of a block.

Keep walking and you will come to the beautifully restored **Old State House** (150 Benefit St.), where George Washington once dined and which now houses the **Rhode Island Historical Preservation & Heritage Commission**. The classic elegance of Benefit Street becomes funkier as you enter **Wickenden** and **Thayer Streets**, much- frequented hang-outs of RISD and Brown students in search of eateries, shops, and, of course, coffee drinks.

Johnson & Wales University is well known for its highly rated culinary program, and a happy by-product of that specialty is the quirky **Culinary Arts Museum** on Harborside Blvd. (401-598-2807; www.culinary.org). You will need a car to get there, but the short trek is worth it for its rotating exhibitions related to food, chefs, and kitchen gad-getry. Stroll through the decades as you pass kitchen vignettes that range from the open-hearth era through tenements to the 1950s and eventually to the microwave oven. Belly up to the bar in an 1833 stagecoach tavern from New Hampshire, pay homage to para-phernalia donated by famous chefs, and, best of all, end your visit at the just-plain-fun diner exhibit, much of which used to be in the private collection of Richard Gutman, museum direc-tor, author, and self-avowed obsessive collector of diner arti-facts.

In another example of col-lege/town partnership, **Trinity Rep** in the **Lederer Theater Center** (201 Washington St.; 401-351-4242;

The Greek Revival **Providence Athenaeum** (251 Benefit St.; 401-421-6970; www.providenceathenaeum.org), the fourth-oldest library in the United States and a listed National Historic Landmark, is a little intimidating when you first enter—it is a paying members' library—but come in anyway and look for the self-guided tour marked by place cards adorned with ravens. The raven emblem refers to Edgar Allan Poe, who is said to have met and wooed Sarah Whitman here over her parents' objections (and in this case, Mother may have known best), although the two never married. Notice the bust of Athena over the circulation desk, and check out the electrified gas fixtures and old card catalog filled with cards written on in the ele-gant, spidery handwriting of some of the first librarians. The upstairs has tiny alcoves just big enough for a single desk, which are said to be highly prized by Brown University students during exam time.

www.trinityrep.com) offers an MFA program for Brown University theater students. You don't have to be a student to attend a show, however, and the schedule is an intriguing mix of productions that range in tone from *The Importance of Being Earnest* to *Menopause The Musical.*

The theater scene in Providence is surprisingly rich, perhaps partly because as Boston's theater district exploded in the last few decades, so did its prices. Providence has had the luxury of sustaining many small venues for both popular and experimental theater. One to try is the **Rhode Island Black Repertory Company** (276 Westminster St.; 401-351-0353; www.blackrep.org), a 10-year-old organization about halfway between Federal Hill and the Riverwalk that produces thought-provoking plays, many by Pulitzer Prize—winning playwrights, as well as a range of educational and public programming.

Learn about the role of African American culture on Providence in the 19th century through the **Rhode Island Black Heritage Society** (65 Weybosset St.; 401-751-3490), which preserves and houses artifacts and offers lectures. If Broadway shows are more your thing, try the **Providence Performing Arts Center** (220 Weybosset St.; 401-421-2787; www.ppacri.org), housed in what was once Loew's Movie Palace in the 1920s.

Visit the 100-plus-acre **Roger Williams Park Zoo** (1000 Elmwood Ave.; 401-785-3510; www.rogerwilliamsparkzoo.org), named for the founder of the settlement that eventually became Rhode Island. You'll need more than a few hours to explore the park, especially if you want to take a ride on a swan-shaped paddleboat, rent a kayak at the **Dalrymple Boathouse** (401-421-8877), or let someone else do the piloting on a half-hour electric cruise boat ride. If you are really pressed for time, though, you can simply drive through the park on a scenic one-way loop that wends past the lakes and spacious greenery.

▮▮▮▮ WHAT TO DO

Book a ride with **La Gondola** (401-421-8877; www.gondolari.com) on a WaterFire night and find yourself gliding along the smooth water in an authentic Venetian gondola, (complete with professional gondoliers, although we can't guarantee any of them will sing) toward the hypnotic lights. Or bring a bottle of wine—the company kicks in with glasses, an ice bucket, and a fresh fruit platter—and relax on

The **Rhode Island School of Design's RISD Museum** (401-454-6500; www.risdmuseum.org) is not only a world-class art museum but also serves as a physical link from one of the most historic parts of the city to the modern downtown. You can still come in through the old Farago Wing door on Benefit Street, but it is more fun to walk down one block to the new entrance on North Main, where the wide-open Chase Center lobby is punctuated by a see-through shop/gallery filled with glass sculptures, jewelry, and other artworks created by faculty and alumni.

If you want to see projects curated by current students, skip the escalator and take the stairs to their dedicated exhibition space, which looks out over historic Market House, where Rhode Island had its own version of the Boston Tea Party. Or go right up to the new rotating exhibition space showcasing works by international artists, then take the glass bridge to the older part of the museum. Give yourself plenty of time to check out the collection, the extent of which is astonishing. There are more than 80,000 pieces of art at the museum, but only a tiny fraction are able to be on exhibit at any one time.

Exhibitions are organized more or less by century, but the arrangement is fresh, with paintings by such greats as Lichtenstein, Warhol, Hockney, Rothko, and Pollock juxtaposed with a mannequin sporting a bathing suit by '60s designer Gernreich and the iconic Zig Zag chair by Rietveld. Other greats include works by Cézanne, Picasso, and van Gogh and sculptures by Rodin and Degas, as well as one of Gilbert Stuart's iconic portraits of George Washington. Textiles, photography, and ancient art, including a tiny dragon from China and an enormous wooden Japanese Buddha, are among the other highlights. Don't miss the restored Main Gallery, with its arched high ceilings and streaming natural light.

the company's eco-friendly electric cruise boat, which also operate during WaterFire nights. Cruises and gondola rides depart from the Waterplace Park basin, and there is plenty of parking in the vicinity of the action.

See the city from the water via a **Providence Harbor Cruise** (200 Allens Ave.; 800-123-1234; www

.providencepiers.com) for a scenic history lesson that covers everything from Providence's Colonial history to its more recent rebirth.

Park for free and hop on the Art Bus at Regency Plaza (at the corner of Greene and Fountain streets) for **Gallery Night**, held the third Thursday of the month from March through November. A guide will be onboard to fill you in on the city's various art venues, and you are free to get on and off the bus from 5 PM to 9 PM.

■■■■ WHERE TO STAY

The **Mowry-Nicholson House Inn** (57 Brownel St., 401-351-6111; www.providence-suites.com) will likely be remembered for having housed Barack Obama's campaign headquarters for several weeks in 2008, but one look at its 1865 facade, and it is clear that the property had a high profile long before that. From $129.

The **Renaissance Providence Hotel** (5 Avenue of the Arts; 401-276-0010; www.marriott.com) was originally a Masonic temple that fell on hard times during the Depression and sat empty for decades before being transformed into a luxury hotel—although some of the graffiti from its fallow years has been incorporated into the decor. From about $179.

The **Providence Biltmore** (11 Dorrance St.; 401-421-0700; www.providencebiltmore.com) is a local landmark with 292 rooms and a central location. Best of all, a recent renovation has given the property a refreshed feel without taking away from its Old World charm. From about $143.

■■■■ EATING OUT

Al Forno (577 South Main, 401-273-9760; www.alforno.com) has garnered raves from famed restaurant critic Patricia Wells, and Ina Garten of Barefoot Contessa fame loves their five-cheese pasta dish. They don't take reservations, so be prepared to wait. Entrées from about $20. The owners recently opened a new restaurant called **Tini** (200 Washington St.; 401-383-2400), offering small plates in a small setting (the restaurant only seats 19 around a U-shaped table, but you can reserve ahead.) Small plates starting under $10. Either way, how could you resist chefs whose cookbook is entitled *On Top of Spaghetti . . .* ?

Gracie's (194 Washington St.; 401-272-7811) is known for its decadent desserts, like cherry almond gateau with Morello cherry sorbet, but don't overlook the dinner menu, with its emphasis on fresh, local ingredients. From about $25.

ZOOMA Bar Ristorante (245

Atwells Ave.; 401-383-2002) on Federal Hill serves updated Neapolitan fare, including antipasti, pizza, and plenty of pasta. From $10 for lunch; $20 for dinner.

Scialo Bros. Bakery (257 Atwells Ave.) has been in business since 1916 and is now, contrary to its name, run by three sisters. They whip up a mean dessert, with prices that vary from a few dollars for Italian cookies and biscotti to specialty cakes for $28.

Mediterraneo Caffé (134 Atwells Ave.; 401-331-7760; www .mediterraneocaffe.com) serves two-course prix fixe lunches and dinners with traditional Italian fare. Or jump into the lively nightlife scene with a distinct Euro-disco vibe. From $15.95 for lunch; $29.95 for dinner.

Lili Marlene's (422 Atwells Ave.; 401-751-4996) is a bar with a more low-key atmosphere, where you are more likely to mingle with locals. Pub fare from $5.

▪▪▪▪ SPECIAL EVENTS

Second Friday of Every Month: The RISD Museum (see sidebar below) livens up the atmosphere with **Music Fridays**, which combine exhibits with live music and a cash bar.

Early June: The annual **Federal Hill Stroll** encourages foodies to

spend the day sampling wares from local restaurateurs, shopping with special discounts, and listening to live music in the evening for a modest fee ($30 in 2009). The event is popular, so organizers suggest buying tickets online (www.pwcvb.com) beforehand.

July: **John Brown House Museum** is the site of the **Summer Concert Series**, which takes place every July (bring your own lawn chair).

▪▪▪▪ NEARBY

Do your sightseeing on a bicycle on one of the well-maintained trails that range from short and easy to all-day outings. The 5-mile **Fred Lippitt Woonasquatucket River Bikeway** runs from the Providence Place Mall and Lyman Avenue in Johnston. Or bike along the Narrangansett River on the nearly 15-mile **East Bay Bike Path**. You can also visit India Point Park in Providence and Independence Park in Bristol, a cute little town with waterfront cafés and great views.

▪▪▪▪ RESOURCES

The Providence Warwick Convention & Visitors Bureau, 144 Westminster Street, Providence, RI 02903; 800-233-1636 or 401-456-0200

MOUNTAIN
ESCAPES

21 • THE BERKSHIRES, MASSACHUSETTS

In Western Massachusetts, roughly 2.5 hours from both Boston and New York

Many of New England's premier mountain destinations offer cultural activities in addition to outdoor pursuits, but in the Berkshires, culture is the tail that wags the dog.

With its mixture of renowned art, music, theater and dance venues, and festivals, this is an area with serious appeal for a wide range of interests. The downside of all this charm is that the Berkshires attract crowds, which means that would-be visitors should do some preplanning to make sure their accommodations and even some of their activities are nailed down before they arrive, especially on weekends and holidays.

The first thing to realize when organizing your stay is that the Berkshires comprise a cluster of towns, most within a half hour of each other. Activities are scattered throughout the area, and because of their proximity, you can book your accommodations at any of them and still be within shouting distance of most top attractions. Some of the better-

known towns and cities include Lee, Lenox, Stockbridge, Great Barrington, Williamstown, Pittsfield, and North Adams, each of which has its own character.

Sip a cup of take-out coffee on the bench in front of the general store in quiet West Stockbridge, for example, and chances are every person who walks by you will greet you. In bustling Lenox, on the other hand, you will find more in the way of restaurants and shops, but you will also spend time jockeying for a parking place.

The population in the Berkshires is an interesting mix, as well, from well-heeled thirty-somethings and retirees, many of whom have second homes in the area, to New Age enthusiasts attracted by the famed **Kripalu Center for Yoga and Health** (www.kripalu.org) and aging hippies left over from the days of "Alice's Restaurant" in Stockbridge.

This area was once considered the mountain version of Newport, Rhode Island, where captains of industry would repair in spring and fall, moving on to the seaside in the full glare of summer. An astonishing number of dazzling mansions still exist in the Berkshires, some of which—like **Blantyre** (www.blantyre.com) and **Wheatleigh** (www.wheatleigh.com)—have been transformed into resorts, while others have been preserved as historical monuments and are open to the public.

For music lovers, the hot ticket in summer is **Tanglewood** (413-637-1600; www.tanglewood.org) in Lenox, where the programming ranges from classical to jazz and folk. Officially the summer home of the Boston Symphony Orchestra, Tanglewood also hosts the ultrapopular Boston Pops several times a year with conductor Keith Lockhart, as well as numerous guest conductors and performers. Past performers have included jazz performer Diana Krall, folk singer James Taylor, and Garrison Keillor, who has hosted the *Prairie Home Companion* live from the event. Seats in the Shed and the Ozawa Hall are prized, but many regulars would just as soon be on the lawn, where they can stretch out and listen to the music while gazing at the stars. Large screens will help you keep track of the action, and don't be surprised if your neighbors on

the lawn bring gourmet picnics with wine and real cutlery. You can do the same by ordering a picnic from the Tanglewood Café at least two business days beforehand and picking it up at the Main Gate or the Bernstein Gate on performance day. You can also rent lawn chairs at both gates.

It's a good idea to buy tickets online as far in advance as you can; in 2009 the Shed and Ozawa

The Sterling and Francine Clark Art Institute

View of restored gardens from The Mount, Lenox

Hall tickets for an August James Taylor weekend of concerts were sold out by mid-March. Traffic getting in and out of the venue is daunting, especially for block-buster events like the annual John Williams—conducted movie night, so plan to arrive early and wear comfortable shoes for the walk from the parking lot.

For an evening of interpretive dance, you won't find anything more cutting edge than a per-formance at **Jacob's Pillow** (358 George Carter Road, Becket; 413-243-0745; www.jacobspillow.org), on a 163-acre National Historic Landmark site. Ticketed perform-ances go on all summer with established and emerging dance companies performing every-thing from modern ballet to hip-hop and flamenco. If your budget is tight, take advantage of the 200-plus free events that go on all season, especially the popular Inside/Out performances that take place on an outdoor stage if weather permits, or inside a restored barn. Visitors can also get in on the act by watching rehearsals and participating in interactive performances and classes.

▮▮▮▮ GETTING THERE (AND GETTING AROUND)

The Berkshires are about a two-and-a-half-hour drive from Boston and New York. From Boston, it is an easy drive along the Mass Turnpike West (I-90) to Exit 2; I-90 East from Albany. You can also fly into the Albany Inter-national Airport about a half hour away or take Amtrak to the Albany Rensselaer train station.

Either way, you will want a car to explore the towns and villages of this picturesque region. The traffic can be intense in summer, and there is plenty of snow in winter, but the trick is to relax and give yourself ample time to get where you are going.

▮▮▮▮ WHAT TO SEE

Regional theater is sacred in this area, thanks in large part to the **Berkshire Theatre Festival** (413-298-5576; www.berkshiretheatre .org), which has been operating since the late 1920s. The BTF offers year-round productions that range from beloved classics, like *The Prisoner of Second Avenue* and *A Christmas Carol* on the Main Stage, designated a mem-ber of the National Register of Historic Places, as well as intrigu-ing works by new artists in the smaller Unicorn Theatre.

Fans of Shakespeare know that the works of the Bard were meant to be seen and not read, and one of the most enjoyable ways to do just that is via a performance by **Shakespeare & Company** (70

Jacob's Pillow

Kemble St.; 413-637-3353; www
.shakespeare.org), which is in the
process of re-creating Rose Playhouse, one of England's first the-
aters for plays and where some of
Shakespeare's works were performed in the 16th century. The-
atergoers can sit in a tent or on
the lawn with a picnic, or repair
to Josie's Place on-site for drinks
and victuals. The **Barrington
Stage Company** (30 Union St.;
413-236-888; www.barrington
stageco.org), which moved into
permanent digs in Pittsfield in
2007, is the place to see musicals,
from the blockbuster to the relatively unknown.

For the latest in new visual and
performance art, the Massachusetts Museum of Contemporary
Art—known to everyone as **MASS
MoCA** (413-MoCA-111; www.mass
moca.org)—is a testament to the
integral nature of culture in the
region. Located on 13 acres in a
repurposed 19th-century factory
building, the institute is smack in
the center of downtown North
Adams. There are nearly 20 galleries, one of which is the size of a
football field, indoor and outdoor
performance space, and an outdoor cinema, plus workshops for
artists to create their works on-
site. The Sol Lewitt exhibition is a
collection of wall drawings that
will be on view at MASS MoCA
until 2033.

Nineteenth-century European
and American paintings—from
Monet to Remington—are a key
element in the appeal of the collections at The **Sterling and
Francine Clark Art Institute** (225
South St.; 413-458-2303; www
.clarkart.edu) in Williamstown.
The institute expanded in 2008
with the new galleries at the
Stone Hill Center, open in summer, while the rest of the institute
is open year-round.

For a dose of nostalgia, visitors
might consider spending a few

hours at the **Norman Rockwell Museum** in Stockbridge (9 Glendale Rd.; 413-298-4100; www.nrm.org). There are special exhibits year-round, but the permanent collection is worth the trip, thanks to 367 of the artist's works, including some of his most familiar. In addition to the paintings, many of which graced the covers of the *Saturday Evening Post*, the museum also houses his studio and memorabilia.

▪▪▪▪ WHAT TO DO (IN SUMMER & FALL)

Hiking is big in the Berkshires, and trails crisscross the mountains, offering terrain for a variety of fitness levels. A place to start is the **Mount Greylock Visitors Center** (30 Rockwell Rd., Lanesborough; 413-499-4262) for information, maps, and weather information.

Brave the rapids with whitewater rafting along Zoar Gap on the Deerfield River. Suitable even for families, a guided daylong trip includes lunch and time for a relaxing swim. Try **Zoar Outdoor** (7 Main St., Charlemont; www.zoaroutdoor.com), which also offers new zip-line canopy tours.

Give your legs a workout and catch the view from Olivia's Overlook via rental bike. Rental outlets are widely available, including **Plaine's Bike** in Pittsfield (55 West Housatonic St.; 413-499-0294), which also rents skis and snowboards in winter.

In summer, **Jiminy Peak Mountain Resort** (800-882-8859; www.jiminypeak.com) in Hancock turns into a giant playground, thanks to the **Mountain Adventure Park**, complete with an Alpine Super Slide and a Mountain Coaster, both of which let you control your own speed. There is a Giant Swing—not to be attempted right after breakfast—and a ropes course navigated while in a safety harness. Take a ride to the summit in the six-passenger chairlift or test your mettle on the Rock Climbing Wall or the Euro-Bungy Trampoline or strap on a backpack for a hike through the mountain trails. You can also try lift-assisted mountain biking, designed for experienced riders only, and helmets are required.

▪▪▪▪ WHAT TO DO (IN WINTER)

Ski Butternut in Great Barrington (413-528-2000; www.skibutternut.com) is a great choice for newbies or visitors who are a little rusty, thanks to its simple, one-base layout and array of comfortable trails, some of which go all the way to the summit. There also are some advanced trails and a popular terrain park for those who like a little more challenge. If time constraints make skiing or snowboarding too much of a commitment, you can still enjoy the slopes at the **Tubing Center**, which has five dedicated lanes to keep the lines moving.

Fans of night skiing can squeeze in extra time on the slopes on Wednesdays through Saturdays at **Catamount Ski Area** (413-528-1262, 800-342-1840; www.catamountski.com) in South Egremont, which boasts a super-steep Catapult trail and a Terrain Park for intrepid freestylers and snowboarders. Beginners will have a field day here on several long cruising runs and a network of novice trails.

You can also night ski at **Bousquet Ski Resort & Summer Family Fun Center** (413-442-8316; www.bousquets.com) in Pittsfield, one of the oldest winter sports areas in the country, which also offers lift-assisted snow tubing.

Jiminy Peak Mountain Resort is a magnet for visitors in winter, thanks to 40 trails spread out over nearly 160 skiable acres and a new six-person, high-speed lift. You won't spend a long time in lift lines here, and fans of the mountain rave about the variety of terrain, which suits beginners and experts, and the top-rated terrain parks.

▪▪▪▪ WHERE TO STAY

The **Canyon Ranch** (65 Kemble St., Lenox; 800-742-9000; www .canyonranch.com) is the place to stay if you want to go luxe and get in shape at the same time. A stay at the resort, which can paper its walls with awards and accolades, is all about the spa and wellness facilities, as well as the setting, which is within walking distance of Lenox town center. A seven-night stay begins at $7,210, double, in summer.

Country Inn at the base of Jiminy Peak features 101 suites with free Wi-Fi, an outdoor heated pool and a day spa to work out those kinks after a day on the skis or bikes. From $129.

The **Red Lion Inn** (Main St., Stockbridge; 413-298-5545; www .redlioninn.com), a member of Historic Hotels of America, is the quintessential New England icon, with its wraparound porch and antique-filled public rooms. No two of its 108 guest rooms are alike, and the outdoor swimming pool is heated year-round. From $95.

The **Porches Inn** (231 River St.; 413-664-0400; www.porches.com) in North Adams is directly across from MASSMoCA. The elegant property is a mix of posh and Old World, with a heated outdoor pool, a gazebo, and access to walking trails. From $135.

The **White Horse Inn** in Pittsfield (378 South St.; 413-442-2512; www.whitehorsebb.com) is a newly renovated B&B with a cozy ambience and a great, central location in the area's biggest city. From $110.

■■■■ WHERE TO CAMP

The **Berkshire County State Parks Campground,** in the Mohawk Trail State Forest (Rte. 2, Charlemont; 413-339-5504), offers hiking trails, cabins, and plenty of facilities. Groups book up to six months ahead, so check ahead for availability. From $12.

The **Mt. Greylock State Reservation** (Rte. 7, Lanesboro; 413-499-4262) is for campers who like roughing it and prefer scenery over amenities. From $8.

■■■■ EATING OUT

Rouge (3 Center St.; 413-232-4111) in West Stockbridge serves up French bistro dishes, such as escalope of veal and steak au poivre. Sometimes lines form around the corner to get in, so reservations are a good idea. From $22.

The **Gramercy Bistro** (24 Marshall St., North Adams; 413-663-5300; www.gramercybistro.com) puts an elegant spin on European country food, with options like cassoulet, paella, and veal schnitzel. From $18.

The **Cranwell Resort, Spa, and Golf Club** (55 Lee Road, Lenox; 800-272-6935, 413-637-1364; www.cranwell.com) wins kudos not only for its wine list but also its commitment to using local ingredients. Try the prix fixe pre-theater menu in the Mansion restaurant for $38.

Blantyre (6 Blantyre Rd., Lenox; 413-637-3556; www .blantyre.com) features the sort of gourmet dining you would expect at a Relais & Châteaux property, complete with a vast wine cellar. There is a dress code, but the manor setting is worth putting on a tie for. Three-course prix fixe dinner for $125.

Pappa Charlie's Deli (28 Spring St.; 413-458-5969) in Williamstown is a great choice when you want to grab a bite without breaking the bank. Line up to order your favorite salad, sandwich, or wrap, each with such inventive names as the Olympia Dukakis or the Richard Dreyfus. Under $10.

The **Barrington Brewery & Restaurant** (420 Stockbridge Rd., Great Barrington; 413-528-8282; www.barringtonbrewery.net) for handcrafted beers and a chicken potpie. Sandwiches and burgers under $10.

■■■■ SPECIAL EVENTS

Early July to Mid-August: The Tony-winning **Williamstown Theatre Festival** (413-597-3400) has been an early stomping ground for actors Blythe Danner and Frank Langella, whose version of Chekhov's *The Seagull* was filmed for PBS in the 1970s. Nowadays, the company offers new and classic plays on several stages and serves as a training center for emerging talent.

July: The annual **Berkshires Arts Festival** (www.berkshiresarts festival.com) at Butternut draws some 175 artists and artisans, eager to show off their creations, including furniture, fine arts, and one-of-a-kind sculptures. Artists will be on hand to demonstrate their crafts in a mega-tent and in the base lodge, and be prepared for great food and live music.

Mid-July to early September: Shakespeare & Company offers **Lunchtime Shakespeare**, whereby visitors can preorder boxed lunches that they can eat on the terrace or in the Bernstein Theatre lobby before the 12:45 PM show.

Early August: The **Annual Zucchini Festival** in West Stockbridge is entertaining for kids, adults, and even the family pooch, thanks to a full schedule of races and games, a pet parade, and, of course, a best-zucchini contest.

▪▪▪▪ NEARBY

For a glimpse into the region's past, consider visiting **Hancock Shaker Village** (1843 W. Housatonic St.; 413-443-0188; www

.hancockshakervillage.org), in Pittsfield, which houses 20 historic buildings spread out over beautiful farmland. If pressed for time, don't miss the Round Stone Barn, and be sure to check out the beautiful simplicity of the Shaker furniture or participate in an interactive session with costumed staff.

▪▪▪▪ LIT LIFE

Anyone who has ever fallen under the spell of Edith Wharton should make time to visit **The Mount** (Rte. 7 & Plunkett St.; www.edith wharton.org), her home in Lenox. In addition to being a Pulitzer Prize—winning author, Wharton was passionate about architecture and garden design, and her home is a reflection of that interest. Join a guided tour of the recently restored gardens—to the tune of some $3 million—wander through the house, or attend special events and lectures. Save time for lunch or a cool drink on the terrace, where live music is played on summer evenings. No time to read *Ethan Frome* or the *House of Mirth*? Rent the Daniel Day-Lewis/Michelle Pfeiffer film *Age of Innocence* to get in the mood.

▪▪▪▪ RESOURCES

Discover the Berkshires Visitor Center, 3 Hoosac St., Adams; 413-743-4500; www.berkshires.org

22 • MANCHESTER, VERMONT

Just over 40 square miles in size, Manchester Village is tucked between the Green Mountains and stately Equinox Mountain.

Despite its frankly upscale ambience, complete with high-end designer shops and luxury spa hotels, it isn't that hard to imagine this pretty Vermont mountain village as it must have been in the mid-18th century. From the town green, which once served as pastureland for early settlers, to the lovingly restored architecture that gives the village its character, Manchester boasts a rich history and all of the charm that brings visitors to Vermont in the first place.

Over the years a number of U.S. presidents, including U.S. Grant and Teddy Roosevelt, stayed in Manchester, and thanks to a robust rail system that linked the town with New York and other urban areas, vacationers looking for clean mountain air and pretty scenery soon followed. By the end of the Civil War, the town was so well established as a desirable resort destination that Abraham Lincoln chose it as a family vacation spot. His son, Robert Todd Lincoln, built a summer home on 400-plus acres here in 1905, and the estate remained in the Lincoln

family for generations. Called **Hildene** (1005 Hildene Rd.; 800-578-1788, 802-362-1788; www.hildene.org), the estate is open to the public and features a farm, a formal garden, and 8.5 miles of walking trails. In winter, the paths become cross-country ski trails, and a pavilion adjacent to the Welcome Center is transformed into a warming hut and ski and snowshoe rental shop.

History aside, a huge draw for winter sports fans is Manchester's proximity to two of southern Vermont's best-known Alpine ski areas. **Bromley Mountain** (Rte. 11; 802-824-5522; www.bromley.com), only 6 miles away from Manchester Village, is the kind of family mountain that prompts skiers and snowboarders to wax nostalgic about their days on the slopes as children. Instead of a confusing spiderweb of trails and lodges, the mountain is built the old-fashioned way: around one base lodge, complete with roaring fire. Newfangled services are there where you need them, though, including a high-speed quad that gets skiers and riders to the summit in just six minutes.

There are plenty of wide-open novice and intermediate trails, but high-adrenaline junkies can find black diamond runs with names like Havoc and Pabst Panic, not to mention the two new freestyle parks. Bonanza on lower East Meadow was designed for beginners looking to ease into freestyling, while Exhibition Terrain Park offers intermediate and advanced terrain.

In all, Bromley offers about 175 acres of skiable terrain—80 percent of which is covered by snowmaking, and broken into 44 trails served by 10 lifts. Best of all, the mountain offers a sunny southern exposure, which keeps the slopes from getting too icy on cold winter days.

The other big downhill ski area nearby, **Stratton Mountain** (5 Village Lodge Rd.; 800-STRATTON; www.stratton.com), tends to be beloved by snowboarders because it was the first mountain on the East Coast to allow and even embrace the sport. That said, the newly revamped pedestrian-only base village has tilted the atmosphere toward a more upscale crowd, with high-end shops and restaurants and an expanded base lodge.

Stratton boasts some 600 acres of terrain in all, served by more than a dozen lifts, including a 12-person gondola. One of the newest runs is Easy Street, a three-mile, top-to-bottom trail for beginners, while glade skiers will find new challenges and obstacles, such as natural logs and rocks, strategically placed in the Emerald Forest glade. The mountain also offers several terrain parks and pipes for all skill levels.

Both mountains also offer activities in summer, ranging from horseback riding and fishing to hiking and biking on well-maintained trails.

Not everyone who comes to Manchester Village is interested in winter sports, and one of the most popular alternate forms of recreation is **outlet shopping**, which has the added advantage of being available year-round. There are dozens of big-name outlet stores (www.manchester designeroutlets.com) in the business district, called Manchester Center, where sawmills and a marble factory once stood, ranging from J.Crew, Coach, and Banana Republic to the more upscale Escada and Armani.

▋▋▋▋ GETTING THERE (AND GETTING AROUND)

From Boston, take Route 2 West to I-91 to Route 30 North. Manchester is about three hours from Boston, four and a half from New

York, and two and a half from Hartford. The closest airports are Burlington, Vermont, and Albany, New York, about 100 and 65 miles away, respectively.

The best way to get around Manchester is by car, but be prepared for heavy traffic in summer.

▌▌▌▌ WHAT TO SEE

Prominent buildings in town that lend to the fairy-tale atmosphere include the **Bennington County Courthouse** (Manchester Center; 802-362-1410) with its gold dome, and the **First Congregational Church** (3624 Main St.; 802-362-2709), not to mention the rows of beautifully maintained private homes along Route 7A.

For a dose of local culture, visit the **Southern Vermont Arts Center** (West Rd.; 802-362-1405; www.svac.org) a nonprofit gallery and educational institution on 400-plus acres. There are special and permanent art exhibitions in the galleries as well as performance space for shows that have ranged from the Duke Ellington Orchestra to Ballet Manchester.

For visitors looking to take home a work of original art, the **Tilting at Windmills Gallery** (24 Highland Ave; 802-362-3022; www.tilting.com) showcases works from local and international artists, while the **Artists' Guild** in the town center (802-362-

4450) is a cooperative that sells goods, from furniture to artwork, from local vendors.

Antique lovers can try Mark Reinfurt's **Equinox Antiques & Fine Art, Inc.** (3568 Main St.; 802-362 3540; www.equinox antiques.com) and **Millstone Antiques** (4478 Main St.; 802-366-9040; www.millstoneantiques .com), both of which specialize in fine furniture and art.

▌▌▌▌ WHAT TO DO

Try a **Full Moon Snowshoe Hike** from Stratton Golf Course to the Pearl Buck House, complete with hot chocolate and snacks, or try the trails behind the Equinox Resort (see Where to Stay). Rentals are available from the First Run Ski Shop on Stratton Mountain, and reservations are required (802-297-4230).

Go cross-country skiing at **Hildene** right in town or venture a little farther afield to **Wild Wings Ski Touring Center** (246 Styles Ln., Peru; 802-824-6793; www.wildwingsski.com) in the Green Mountain National Forest. Here you'll find groomed trails, rental skis and snowshoes, and a converted barn/warming room. The family-owned operation also offers yoga classes in the Peru town center.

Practice your figure eights at the Olympic-sized **Riley Rink** at

Hunter Park in Manchester (Hunter Park Rd.; 802-362-0150, 866-866-2086; www.rileyrink .com), along with rental equipment, snack concessions, and a warming room. Or skate at **Mill Pond** on the Stratton Village Common (1-800-Stratton), where you can warm up by a fire pit with games and hot chocolate on Saturdays and holidays.

Snowmobilers can book an hour-and-a-half or three-hour guided outing with **Equinox Snow Tours** between Bromley and Stratton (Rte. 11 & Rte. 30 junction; 802-824-6628; www .vermontsnowmobile.com), following trails through the Green Mountain National Forest and past local fauna and frozen waterfalls.

Horse-drawn sleigh rides are available at **Taylor Farm** (825 Rte. 11, Londonderry; 802-824-5690), a 180-year-old dairy farm that makes and sells varieties of Gouda using sustainable practices. Another option is **Horses for Hire** (893 South Rd.; 802-297-1468; www.horsesforhire.net), operated by Deb Hodis, who works the farm with her beagle sidekick. In addition to sleigh rides, Hodis also offers customized mountain trail rides.

Go shopping at **Orvis Retail Store** (4180 Main St.; 802-362-3750; www.orvis.com), one of the

American Museum of Fly Fishing

Manchester's historic Court House

oldest outlet companies in the country, which sells clothing, as well as camping and fishing gear.

Tempt your palate at **Mother Myricks Confectionery** (4367 Main St.; 888-669-7425; www .mothermyricks.com) for everything from hot fudge to artisanal butter crunch. Every New England village worth its salt has a great farm stand, and Manchester Village is no exception. The **Dutton Farm Stand** in the town center (802-362-3083) is open year-round and sells everything from apple cider to Christmas wreaths. Many of the specialty shops in Manchester sell maple syrup, but **Bob's Maple Shop** in Manchester Center (733 Richville Rd.; 802-362-3882) is a third-generation purveyor of the real thing, from syrup to candy.

See a play at the **Dorset Playhouse** (104 Cheney Rd., Dorset; 802-867-5570; http://dorset players.org), which showcases the works of new and established playwrights in a restored barn.

▌▌▌▌ WHERE TO STAY

The **Equinox Resort & Spa** (3567 Main St.; 800-362-4747; www .equinoxresort.com), is practically a destination unto itself, thanks to a menu of services that range from the frankly upscale to the quirky. The 195-room property, which has hosted some of the village's most illustrious guests since the mid-19th century, operates a British School of Falconry, a Land Rover off-road driving school and an Orvis fly-fishing school, for example, along with a par-71 golf course and full-service spa. The property completed a $20 million dollar renovation in 2008, adding, among other features, a **Falcon Bar and Chop House**, the former of which serves single-malt scotch or your favorite wine around an open-air fire pit. You can also tuck into a meal at the historic Marsh Tavern or enjoy a hearty breakfast at the Colonnade. From $229.

The **Barnstead Inn** (349 Bonnet St.; 802-362-1619) is a restored, mid-19th-century barn that has been transformed into a 14-room property, complete with outdoor

Making snow angels at The Equinox

swimming pool. From $99.

The **Brittany Motel** (Rte. 7A; 802-362-1033; www.brittany motel.net) has 12 rooms and views of green meadows dotted with cows and the dramatic mountains in the distance. The 12-room property also has DVD players in all the rooms and a DVD library. From $79.

The **Olympia Lodge** (Rte. 7A; 888-365-9674; www.olympia-vt .com) just outside town, offers 24 guest rooms, as well as tennis and a heated outdoor pool. From $75.

The 122-room **Inn at Stratton Mountain** (61 Middle Ridge Rd., Stratton Mountain; 800-stratton; www.stratton.com) is an ideal choice for those who can't wait to get to the lifts in the morning, although the four-season property also offers an outdoor heated pool in summer. Look for ski-and-stay deals during the winter season. From $69.

▪▪▪▪ EATING OUT

Mistral's at Toll Gate (10 Toll Gate Rd.; 802-362-1779) is pricey and posh, with a *Wine Spectator* award—winning wine list and high-end, seasonal fare. The menu, which, as the name suggests, leans toward French cuisine, routinely wins raves. From $25.

The **Reluctant Panther Inn & Restaurant** (39 West Rd.; 800-822-2331; www.reluctantpanther .com), a 2008 *Wine Spectator* award—winning eatery with a fine-dining menu, cooks up such dishes as foie gras and pheasant breast. Also an inn, the property also offers more relaxed pub fare for when you just want a panini or a pizza. Entrées from around $30.

Mulligan's of Manchester (Rte. 7A; 802-362-3663) serves up steaks, burgers, and seafood, livened up on weekends with music and dancing. From $10.

Al Ducci's Italian Pantry (133 Elm St.; 802-362-4449; www .alduccis.com) is the place to go for such specialties as ciabatta, fresh mozzarella, and cappuccino, all of which are also available for takeout. Many items under $10.

Ye Olde Taverne (5183 Main St.; 802-362-0611; www.yeolde tavern.net) has a more traditional New England menu, with chicken potpie and scrod and cranberry fritters. The ambience is colonial, Old World, with a fireplace and original, uneven floors. From $17.

▪▪▪▪ SPECIAL EVENTS

Late April: The **Emerging Poets & Writers Weekend** (The Old Forge building at The Rice House; 802-362-6313) offers a round of discussions and classes on how to unlock your inner writer.

Mid-June: In summer, the **Manchester Antique and Classic Car Show** (Dorr Farm, Rte. 30; www

.manchestervermont.net/car show) offers a chance to get a close look at cars that are as much works of art as transportation.

Early July to Mid-August: The **Vermont Symphony Orchestra** (800-VSO-9293) kicks off a summer concert series on the historic grounds of Hildene. Venues change yearly, so be sure to call ahead.

Early July to Mid-August: The six-week **Vermont Summer Festival Horse Show** (Harold Beebe Farm; www.vt-summerfestival .com) in nearby East Dorset is six weeks of equestrian competition for horse enthusiasts.

August: Serious bargain hunters not satisfied with outlet prices can hold out for the **Manchester Sidewalk Sales** in August.

▮▮▮▮ NEARBY

In August, check out the two-day Revolutionary War battle reenactment during **Ethan Allen Days** in Bennington's Colgate Park (1545 West Rd.), which commemorates the victory of Ethan Allen and the Green Mountain Boys over loyalists from New York. The Park is also the venue for the two-day **Shires Maple Festival** in July, which pays homage to all things relating to the maple sugar

industry with wagon rides, a farmers' market, and food tastings from local suppliers.

The town of **Pawlet**, about 15 miles north of Manchester, offers a quieter take on Vermont life, with scenic bike trails and prettier scenery. In its heyday, however, Pawlet was a hotbed of Revolutionary activity and still retains its unspoiled charm.

▮▮▮▮ LIT LIFE

Writer Sarah Cleghorn, who lived in Manchester for much of her life, left her stamp on society through her poetry and her activism. A friend of Robert Frost, Cleghorn used her craft to shine a light on the injustices of her day and to promote pacifism. Although known primarily for her poetry, she also published a novel with the intriguing title *The Spinster: A Novel Wherein a Nineteenth Century Girl Finds Her Place in the Twentieth.*

▮▮▮▮ RESOURCES

Manchester and the Mountains Chamber of Commerce, 5046 Main Street, Suite 1, Manchester Center, VT 05255-3451; 802-362-2100, 800-362-4144; www .manchestervermont.net

23 • MOUNT WASHINGTON VALLEY, NEW HAMPSHIRE

About 130 miles from Boston; about 60 miles from Portland, Maine; and 85 miles from Portsmouth, New Hampshire

New England is loaded with beautiful mountain villages that claim to be equally appealing year-round, but this part of New Hampshire really delivers on that promise, with ski mountains, recreational lakes, and more than its share of picturesque villages and farms. The flip side of all this popularity is congestion, which can get heavy in peak vacation weeks in winter and most summer weekends, particularly in and around North Conway. The trick to enjoying the region is to sidestep the crowds or, when that is not possible, meet them head-on with a little preplanning.

Depending on how much time you have, you may want to incorporate visits to Jackson, North Conway, and Bretton Woods into your itinerary, particularly if you are fond of year-round outdoor mountain fun.

If you love cross-country skiing, make your home base in Jackson, a village with all the iconic features visitors want in a New England town—such as a covered bridge and a waterfall—

but which is also close to the action. Despite the fact that there are more than a dozen ski areas nearby and a whopping 150 places to stay, Jackson is still quiet enough to let you keep your sanity. There are nearly 150 kilometers of dedicated trails maintained by the **Jackson Ski Touring Foundation** (www.jacksonxc .org). You need to be a member of the Jackson Ski Touring Club, but memberships are available by the day.

It is worth noting here that the conditions for cross-country skiing—often tricky for resorts to maintain—are typically better in this region than at many competing areas. Locals attribute the good snow to what they call the "notch effect," referring to the climate conditions shaped by the famous notches or crevasses carved out by glaciers millennia ago, including the Franconia Notch, the Crawford Notch, and the Pinkham Notch.

Downhill skiing is available less than 10 miles in North Conway, which, despite some urban sprawl, is beautifully situated amid more than 700,000 acres of White Mountain National Forest. Simultaneously picturesque and commercial, the town bustles with enough shopping, dining, and attractions to keep visitors busy for days, while lightening their wallets considerably in the process. Unfortunately, traffic can snarl up at the intersection of Rts. 302 and 16, but visitors can avoid the worst of it by parking just off Main Street and exploring the village center on foot or via shuttle.

Make time to enjoy the view of the 107-year-old red-roofed **Mount Washington Hotel** from the summit of Bretton Woods ski area nearby. Over the years, the hotel has welcomed swarms of luminaries, such as Babe Ruth (who, as you can imagine, is revered in these parts), Thomas Edison, and even a few U.S. presidents.

Historic doesn't mean dull, however, and today's visitors will find plenty of young guests looking to ski or snowboard in winter or hit the links in summer, along with entire families who have been coming to the property for generations. Best of all, the resort offers both Nordic and Alpine skiing, as well as a full menu of warm-weather activities for adults and kids.

■■■■ GETTING THERE (AND GETTING AROUND)

By car, plan on about three hours from Boston's Logan Airport to North Conway, following Rt. 95 North to Rt. 16. The trip is about an hour and a half from Portsmouth, New Hampshire, on Rt. 16.

In North Conway, the **Village Trolley & Shuttle Service** (877-986-7267) links Cranmore Mountain Resort with several stops in town every half hour. Hikers can take advantage of the Appalachian Mountain Club's Hiker Shuttle (603-466-2727), which links the region's trailheads. Or climb aboard the **Conway Scenic Railroad** (Schouler Park, North Conway; 800-232-5251, 603-356-5251; www.conwayscenic.com) for an old-fashioned diesel train ride to Bartlett or Crawford Notch to see the fall colors. In summer, the nostalgia factor gets cranked up even more with the seasonal steam locomotive excursion from North Conway to the town of Conway nearby.

■■■■ WHAT TO SEE

Go fishing—or just cool your toes—in the **Jackson waterfall**, which cascades down the mountain alongside Carter Notch Road just past the covered bridge. The falls go on and on, and on hot days, you will see intrepid townsfolk splashing in the pools of water at the base of the falls, although we advise caution, as the rocks are slippery and swimming is prohibited in some areas.

Shopaholics looking to save a few bucks can spend a few happy hours in **Settler's Green Outlet Village** in North Conway, where the outlet shopping—there are about 60 shops in all—is an attraction unto itself. Shopping is tax free in New Hampshire, and the types of stores include everything from clothing and home goods to jewelry and toys. If you only have time for one store, check out **L.L.Bean** (1390 White Mountain Hwy.; 603-356-2100), where you can get everything from fleece jackets and winter coats to flashlights and backpacks. Check the return bin for rock-bottom prices on returned monogrammed items.

For an aerial view of the fall colors, take the round-trip **Summit Triple Chairlift Ride** to the top of **Attitash Mountain** (Rte. 302, Bartlett; www.attitash.com), where you can see all of Mount Washington Valley from the observation tower. You can also take the Wildcat Mountain Gondola Ride (603-466-3326; www.skiwildcat.com) for stellar views, or try a more adventurous approach to seeing the countryside on the Wildcat ZipRider, a

zip-line that operates year-round; weekends only in winter. For the uninitiated, zip-lining involves being strapped to secure cables and zipping from tree to tree.

Go for a drive along the **Mt. Washington Auto Road** along the Pinkham Notch for spectacular viewing of the valley below. Although be aware that you won't be alone, especially during leaf-peeping season.

Browse the **Jackson Farmers'**

Fishing at Jackson waterfall

Jackson covered bridge

Market (Snowflake Inn Field), held July through October on Saturday mornings. Here you will find everything from fresh produce and pottery to baked goods and goat cheese.

▪▪▪▪ WHAT TO DO (IN WINTER)

For Alpine skiing, it's hard to resist the convenience of **Cranmore Mountain Resort** (1 Skimobile Rd.; 603-356-5543; www.cranmore.com), which has its base area practically in the center of North Conway. Alpine skiers and snowboarders can tackle the 200 acres of terrain, and while the 2,000-foot summit is not nosebleed high, nearly a quarter of the trails are for advanced skiers. You can ski at night on Saturdays and Wednesdays, test your mettle at the Darkside Terrain Park, or, if you just want a little downhill fun without all the work—or you haven't gotten around to taking that first ski or snowboard lesson—you can spend a few happy hours at **Arctic Blast Tubing Park** near the base lodge.

Great Glen Trails Adventure Center (Pinkham Notch; www.greatglentrails.com) not only offers great cross country skiing but also operates unique SnowCoach tours in a nine-passenger, four-wheel-drive vehicle that ascends the Mt. Washington Auto Road in winter for great above-treeline views of the surroundings. Best of all, passengers can either take the SnowCoach back down or negotiate the trip via skiing or snowshoeing.

Cruise the terrain at **Bretton Woods** (Rt. 302; 603-278-3320) at the Mount Washington Resort, mentioned above, where you can sashay down the wide-open intermediate runs for which the mountain is best known or work out the kinks at the more than 60 miles of Nordic ski trails. You can also brave the new year-round treetop zip-line **Canopy Tour** at Bretton Woods, billed as one of the longest in the United States.

Bundle up under a pile of blankets and take a dogsledding tour (**Muddy Paw Sled Dog Kennel**; 603-986-0697; www.dogslednh.com) of the snowy countryside, where the mushers will sometimes let passengers drive the team.

▪▪▪▪ WHAT TO DO (IN SUMMER & FALL)

Take the Flying Yankee chairlift to the summit of **Attitash Mountain** on Rt. 302 and plummet down the mountain on an Alpine Slide, billed as the longest in the United States, or use the handbrake for a slower, more scenic ride. Attitash also offers lift-assisted mountain biking with access from the summit to 5 miles of advanced terrain.

Explore the countryside on horseback with guides at Attitash or **Black Mountain Stables** in Jackson (603-383-4490). Saddle up for an afternoon of horseback riding at **Gunstock** (11A Gilford; 603-293-4341) from mid-June through mid-October. Kids 8 and up are welcome, and reservations are a good idea. You can also stop by **Northern Extremes Canoe & Kayak** (Rt.16, North Conway, 603-356-4718) to gear up for excursions on the area's many waterways.

For a day of sunbathing, swimming, and hiking, stake out a spot at the 118-acre **Echo Lake State Park** (off Rt. 302, Conway), where you can swim at a family-friendly beach or climb or drive to Cathedral Ledge for views of the Saco River. There is no camping, but the park is just 2 miles from North Conway's town center.

On a really hot day, try the **Mount Washington Cog Railway** (800-922-8825/603-278-5404), a three-hour ride in an antique steam train to the summit of Mount Washington, the highest peak in the Northeast, a near-vertical climb that will have you hanging on to your seat to keep from tipping backward. Be sure to bring a jacket even on hot summer days, as it has been known to snow in July.

■ ■ ■ ■ WHERE TO STAY

Eagle Mountain House (Carter Notch Rd., Jackson; 603-383-9111; www.eaglemt.com) could be forgiven for taking itself too seriously—it is listed by the National Trust for Historic Preservation—but instead the atmosphere is relaxed with an emphasis on fun. There is cross-country skiing

Conway Scenic Railroad station

from the back door, tennis and golf in warm weather, and several eateries, including Highfield's for champagne brunch. From $69 in low season; $129 in summer.

The **North Conway Grand Hotel** (Rte. 16 at Settlers' Green Outlet Village; 603-356-9300, 800-655-1452; www.northconway grand.com) offers 200 rooms with kitchenettes, indoor and outdoor swimming pools, and direct access to the outlets. Summer packages from $129.

The **Inn at Thorn Hill & Spa** (Thorn Hill Rd., Jackson; 603-383-4242, 800-289-8990; www.innat thornhill.com) has been completely rebuilt and now routinely receives "best of" awards from travel and wine publications. The property features fireplaces, antique furnishings, spa facilities, and regular wine-pairing dinners. From $169.

The **Inn at Jackson** (Main St. and Thorn Hill Rd.; 603-383-4321; www.innatjackson.com) is a 14-room property with views of Pinkham Notch and quick access to the cross-country trail network. Unwind at day's end in the outdoor hot tub and tuck into the free country-style breakfast and afternoon snacks. From $119.

▮▮▮▮ EATING OUT

Horsefeathers in North Conway Village (2679 White Mountain Hwy; 603-356-6862; www.horse feathers.com) is an institution among repeat visitors to the area, with its cheery, funky atmosphere. They don't take reservations, so be prepared to wait with a beer or two, and consider ordering the Great Garlic Toast, doused with garlic and butter. From $9.55.

The **Stonehurst Manor** (Rte. 16, North Conway; 603-356-3113, 800-525-9100; www.stonehurst manor.com) for wood-fired pizza and other specialties. From $10.95 for pizza; $28.95 for Stonehurst Wellington.

The **Wentworth Inn and Restaurant** (1 Carter Notch Rd.; 877-689-9879, 603-838-3282) is a Swiss-run inn with outdoor hot tubs and roaring fireplaces. The seasonal menu offers such entrées as cannelloni stuffed with Maine lobster and pinot noir—braised short ribs. From $21.

The **Shovel Handle Pub** in Whitney's Inn in Jackson is a converted barn where locals and visitors mingle over drinks and pub fare under the watchful eye of the moose mascot. Sandwiches from $8.95; entrées from $13.95.

Crepes Ooh La La (Rte. 16; 603-356-0244) is a new restaurant in North Conway with outdoor seating that serves made-to-order savory and dessert crepes, as well as homemade ice cream and fruit smoothies. From $3.

Lobster Trap Restaurant (West Side Rd.; N. Conway; 603-356-5578) serves steaks and Italian food as well as lobster specials. From $7.50.

▪▪▪▪ SPECIAL EVENTS

Late November: The annual **Jingle Bell Chocolate Tour** in Jackson village is a five-day extravaganza that includes sleigh rides through town, stopping at various eateries offering chocolate treats.

Mid-February: **Black Mountain** (www.blackmt.com), New Hampshire's oldest ski mountain, plays Cupid every year during the Valentine's Day Chairlift Speed Dating event. As its name implies, the idea is to encourage lovelorn skiers to mingle with like-minded souls on the slopes in hopes that they will find Mr. or Ms. Right. Local suppliers have gotten into the act by offering specials for the successful, such as the one-night package at **Whitney's Inn** in Jackson (357 Black Mountain Rd., Jackson; 800-677-5737, 603-383-8916; www.whitneysinn.com), which bundles in lift tickets, roses, and champagne.

July 4: **Independence Day Celebration** in North Conway's Schouler Park includes everything from live entertainment to fireworks.

Early to late October: The **Ghoullog Halloween Haunted Chairlift Rides** at Cranmore Mountain include a stroll through a haunted walkway filled with scary sights, as well as caramel apples and other fall treats. Stay for a drink at the Boo-Bonic Pub and Outdoor Beer Garden and check out the stellar nighttime views of Mount Washington lit up below.

▪▪▪▪ LIT LIFE

Some persistent rumors have it that the Mount Washington Hotel was an inspiration for Stephen King's megahit *The Shining,* but the real inspiration was reportedly the Stanley Hotel in Colorado's Estes Park. One whiff of the Mount Washington's elegant interior, not to mention the wraparound porch overlooking the mountains and a brand-new spa, puts the rumor to rest, anyway, as the ambience is much more like a Merchant Ivory film than a horror classic.

▪▪▪▪ RESOURCES

The Mt. Washington Chamber of Commerce; 800-DO-SEE-NH; www.mtwashingtonvalley.org

24 • SHAWNEE PEAK, MAINE

Two and a half hours north of Boston; one hour from Portland

No matter how much they love skiing or snowboarding, even the most diehard winter sports enthusiasts know they will have to put up with a lot during a typical day on the slopes. Parking miles away from the lifts and waiting for a shuttle bus while holding clumsy equipment has become the norm, as has standing in an interminable lift line at the base of the mountain. Add dodging out-of-control teens on the slopes and hunting for a table in a crowded base lodge, and you begin to sap some of the fun from an otherwise perfect day.

One solution is to scout out a lesser-known mountain popular mostly with locals, where the conditions and terrain belie its under-the-radar reputation. Also known as **Pleasant Mountain**, Shawnee Peak in Bridgton, Maine, about 20 minutes from the much busier North Conway, New Hampshire, ski areas, is one such mountain. Bridgton was founded in the late 18th century as a mill town, although nowadays summer boating and winter skiing are among its key industries.

While expert skiers who live for triple black diamond runs may not find enough challenge or variety here, most intermediate skiers will do just fine on its 40-plus trails served by five lifts. A family-owned mountain, Shawnee Peak nonetheless has some of the perks of a larger ski area, most notably a robust snowmaking system that covers nearly all of the terrain, which includes four glades and a newly expanded terrain park on the Main Slope. There is even a 400-foot half-pipe for the high-adrenaline among us, and at about $52 a day for an adult lift ticket—significantly less than some of the big-name resorts—visitors get plenty of bang for their buck. As at most ski areas, prices dip even more with multi-day or ski-and-stay packages.

The 70-year-old ski area—the longest-running in the state—has been enlarging its infrastructure in the last few years. Visitors will find plenty of breathing room on the slopes and a quick and painless entry into the lift lines, even on weekends and during peak vacation periods. Skiers and riders with limited time will appreciate the 20-year tradition of night skiing at Shawnee Peak, allowing even late arrivals to get in on the action.

Avoiding crowds is a little harder in the base lodge, but a new solar-paneled Great Room next to the cafeteria adds about 150 more seats and views of the slopes, thanks to floor-to-ceiling windows and an expansive cathedral ceiling.

And because Shawnee Peak is in one of Maine's prettiest lakes regions and just down the road from the cute little town of Bridgton, visitors can find plenty to keep them busy year-round.

▮▮▮▮ GETTING THERE (AND GETTING AROUND)

Shawnee Peak is about two and a half hours from Boston and about 35 miles west of Portland. Take the Route 302 West exit off I-93 North and follow it for about 50 miles to Mountain Road.

Once here, you will want your car to make the most of the area's attractions.

▮▮▮▮ WHAT TO SEE

Bridgton is a town in transition from an understated, sleepy little village to a full-fledged tourist spot. Yes, there is still a diner and a general store, but new entries

on the scene include arty clothing shops, art galleries, and funky food outlets.

Try the **Firefly Boutique** (82 Main St.; 207-647-3672) for mostly Fair Trade items, including jewelry and clothing, or visit **The Cool Moose** (36 Main St.; 207-647-3957) and the **Corn Shop Trading Post** (179 Main St.; 207-647-9090) for fun New England

Skiing free of crowds at Shawnee Peak
SHAWNEE PEAK

Kayak rentals at Sports Haus Ski & Sport Shop

products and gift items. You can also stroll through the **Bridgton Farmers Market** (15 Depot St.) on Saturday mornings for organic produce, baked goods, and fresh flowers.

Don't miss the **Civil War Monument** on Main Street commemorating the soldiers who fought for the Union during the war. Or, for an evening of retro entertainment, pack up some snacks and a pillow for the show at **Bridgton Drive-In Theatre** (Rte. 302; 207-647-8666). If the weather doesn't cooperate, catch a show at the newly restored **Magic Lantern** theater (9 Depot St.), which offers first-run and independent films, as well as Red Sox games in season in the Pub.

For a look at authentic Rufus Porter murals, check out the **Rufus Porter Museum and Cultural Heritage Center** (67 N. High St.; 207-647-2828), which celebrates the work of the famed watercolorist who spend his childhood in Bridgton. Porter, who also founded *Scientific American* magazine, rarely signed his murals, but this preserved home contains works signed both by the artist and his son, Stephen Twombly Porter.

The **Bridgton Historical Society Museum** (5 Gibbs Ave.; 207-647-3699) houses objects and archival information about the town, including its narrow-gauge railroad, and operates a restored 19th-century farm called **Narramissic** (Ingalls Rd. off route 107 in South Bridgton). Also known as the Peabody-Fitch Farm, the 25-acre property features the main house, the carriage shed, a barn, and a working blacksmith shop. There are events taking place at the farm all summer, including the **Woodworkers and Artisans Show** in July for craft demonstrations and a chance to buy such handmade products as jewelry, homespun wool, furniture, and canoes. In September, the historical society hosts events at the farm, including the **Harvest Supper and Festival**, complete with old-fashioned lawn games, live music, and dinner.

▮▮▮▮ WHAT TO DO (IN WINTER)

Nordic or cross-country skiing is big in the Bridgton area, and a favorite venue is **Five Fields Farm** (720 S. Bridgton Rd.; 207-647-2425) an apple orchard since the 18th century that has been operating cross-country skiing for the last 10 years. Rental skis and snowshoes are available on-site, and the groomed, one-way trail system wends wend through the orchards and along logging roads to Bald Pate Mountain. Guides and instruction are avail-

*Songo River
Queen in nearby
Naples*

able, or skiers can head out on their own. In the fall, visitors can pick their own apples—there are seven varieties—sample fresh homemade apple cider, and enjoy some of the best views in the area.

Carter's XC Ski Center, less than a half hour away off Route 26 in Oxford (420 Main St.; 207-539-4848; www.cartersxcski.com), offers 24 miles of groomed trails designed for beginner and intermediate skiers, as well as rentals and a snack bar.

Visitors with a need for speed can try snowmobiling on well-maintained trails that follow the town's old narrow-gauge railroad bed, pass through a covered bridge, or even climb Pleasant Mountain. Check out **Bridgton Easy Riders** (207-647-5255) for rental and trail information. Intrepid locals can be seen snowmobiling and cross-country ski-

ing on the area's frozen lakes, but the practice can be risky in the fickle New England climate, where even a day or two of warm weather can weaken the ice.

The **Lakes Environmental Association** or LEA (www.mainelakes.org) puts on a Full Moon Snowshoe Walk at Holt Pond in winter for a guided nighttime walk with like-minded enthusiasts, followed by hot chocolate. Participants must register ahead of time, but equipment is available if you don't have your own.

▌▌▌▌ WHAT TO DO (IN SPRING, SUMMER & FALL)

As appealing as the ski mountain is for visitors, Bridgton is buzzing with activity in the warmer weather, thanks to a menu of activities available on the mountain and at the adjacent lakes.

Moose Pond is directly across

from Shawnee Peak, and visitors can use a public boat launch to a day on the water, using gear from the **Sports Haus Ski & Sport Shop** (103 Main St.; 207-647-9528; www.sportshausski.com). Rent canoes, kayaks, water skis, and wakeboards by the day or take out a Sunfish or Rumba sailboat by the week. The store, which also has an on-mountain location (Rte. 302, Bridgton) for winter sports rentals, will deliver the boat or equipment to your location.

Highland Lake also has a public beach for swimming and tubing, as well as boating, and because powerboat use is limited, the atmosphere is serene and peaceful. Pick up a fishing license (www5.informe.org/cgi-bin/online/moses2/index.pl) and go fishing for trout, salmon, and perch, or try your luck at Long Lake or Moose Pond.

The LEA organizes a **Big Night Road Watch** to encourage volunteers to act as crossing guards to the frogs, salamanders, and other creatures that cross the roads at night as they migrate toward the wetlands.

If a simple **hike** is more your speed, there are several trails that begin behind the Shawnee Peak base lodge area, as well as a network of trails from the town of Denmark on Route 117 nearby

(207-647-4352). Your reward for hiking to the top of Pleasant Mountain is a panoramic view of the lakes and countryside below.

For walking of a different sort, play a round of golf at the 18-hole **Bridgton Highlands Country Club** (Highland Ridge Rd.; 207-647-3491; www.bridgtonhighlands.com), where nonmembers are welcome for a day on the links, a lesson, or an afternoon at the on-site tennis courts.

▪▪▪▪ WHERE TO STAY

East Slope Condos, which opened in 2006, provide Shawnee Peak's first ski-in/ski-out lodging options for the non-day-tripper crowd. The condos, near the base area on the side of the mountain that offers night skiing, offer high-end amenities at reasonable prices. Features include gas fireplaces, full kitchens, washers and dryers, and parking. Best of all, condo rentals include lift tickets for everyone. Three-, five-, and seven-night packages also are available. From $31.25 per person.

Noble House Inn (81 Highland Rd.; 888-237-4880; www.noblehousebb.com), overlooking Highland Lake, is a former private estate turned B&B. The elegant property touts its Wicked Good Breakfast and fresh cookies, as well as its romantic decor and ambience. From $125.

Bear Mountain Inn (866-450-4253; www.bearmtninn.com) in Waterford, Maine, is a four-season property set by a lake on 25 acres. Choose from guest rooms with shared baths to suites with fireplaces and Jacuzzis and even an eight-person, stand-alone post-and-beam house. Ski-and-stay packages include lift tickets to Shawnee Peak. From $110.

Or try **Highland Lake Resort** (Rte. 302; 207-647-5301; www.highlandlakeresort.com), which offers no-frills accommodations, but has its own beach on Highland Lake, free pedal boats and canoes, fishing, and tennis. From $85.

▪▪▪▪ WHERE TO CAMP

Lakeside Pines Campground (207-647-3935; http://lakesidepinescamping.com) on Long Lake offers 185 sites, picnic and laundry facilities, and beach access. From $24.

▪▪▪▪ EATING OUT

Base Lodge Café is one of several on-mountain eateries at Shawnee Peak, serving three meals a day and better-than-they-sound New England snacks like whoopee pie and fried dough. More substantial meals, like beef Stroganoff or fish and chips, also are available for the budget minded. The café, which also serves Starbucks coffee, is open all day until the lifts close. From $4.95.

Beth's Kitchen Café (82 Main St.; 207-647-5211; www.bethskitchencafe.com) serves breakfast and lunch, focusing on made-to-order salads, sandwiches, and pastries with fresh ingredients. Sit inside in the tiny café, or opt for outdoor seating under umbrellas by a babbling brook. From $6.25 for sandwiches.

Black Horse Tavern (8 Portland St.; 207-647-5300) serves drinks and pub food for lunch, dinner, and Sunday brunch. From $8.99.

The Good Life Market (Rte 302 & 85; 207-655-1196) not only sells deli products but also will whip up sandwiches and box lunches to go. From $5.50.

Ruby Food Chinese Cuisine (160 Main St.; 207-647-8890) serves eat-in or take-out Szechuan, Hunan, and Cantonese dishes for lunch and dinner. From $4.90.

▪▪▪▪ SPECIAL EVENTS

June: The **Antique Car Show** (207-647-4033) supports higher education through scholarships. In addition to showstopping automobiles, the event features music, refreshments, and, of course, prizes for the most fabulous set of wheels.

July: In summer, culture buffs can take in the **Art in the Park** show, held at Shorey Park on

Stevens Brook Mill Ponds near Highland Lake. Sponsored by **Gallery 302** (112 Main St.; 207-647-ARTS; www.gallery302.org), a year-round cooperative gallery showcasing the works of more than 60 local artists, the event includes paintings, pottery, and photography.

August: the **Annual Great Adventure Challenge** (207-647-8244 x15) is a charity event that involves 2½ miles of kayaking, 14 miles of biking, and a 2-mile dash up and down the mountain. The event, organized by Good Neighbors Inc., benefits adults with developmental disabilities in western Maine.

Mid-September: Visitors can take part in the **Loon Echo Hike n' Bike Trek**, an event that includes 25-, 50-, or 100-mile bike treks on terrain that gets tougher on the longer races, and a 6-mile hike along Pleasant Mountain. The event, which requires pre-registration well in advance, benefits local land conservation efforts. Post-trek festivities include live music, a cookout, and drinks at the Shawnee pub.

January: For one of the goofier events of the season, plan your stay around annual **Elvis on the Mountain Day**, where everyone is invited to hit the slopes in their best Elvis attire, then join an Elvis impersonator for après ski at Blizzard's.

Late January: Locals and visitors alike go all out for the 10-day annual **Mushers Bowl Winter Carnival** (www.mushersbowl .com), with events taking place at venues around the area. Join in the fun with dogsled rides, a broomball tournament, and free snowmobiling at **Highland Lake**, just down the road from Shawnee Peak near Bridgton town center; dogsled races, skijoring, and snowshoe hikes at Five Fields Farm; and free ice skating at the Town Hall Skating Rink (N. High St.), complete with free skates. Events take place concurrently at Shawnee Peak, including races and night skiing.

▮▮▮▮ NEARBY

Music, theater, and art are available in abundance at **Deertrees Theatre & Cultural Center** (Deertrees Rd.; Harrison; 207-583-6747; www.deertreestheatre .org), a nonprofit performing art center in nearby Harrison that operates a full roster of summer events. Past performances have included everything from jazz and blues to comedy troupes and cabaret.

Sebago Lake State Park, only about a half hour from Shawnee Peak (Rte. 302, Naples; 207-693-6231) is one of the oldest state parks in the country. There are some 250 campsites in the 1,400-

acre park, and facilities for boating, swimming, and fishing. From $15.

In August, **Point Sebago Resort** is the location of the annual **Maine Lakes Brew Fest** (www.lakes brewfest.com) with 25 to 30 breweries in attendance, each offering samples of their products.

Sunday River, less than an hour away in Newry, Maine (207-824-3000; www.sundayriver .com), is known for its vast terrain, excellent snow conditions, and visitor amenities.

In Naples, you can also take a two-and-a-half-hour cruise on the Songo River, passing through the authentic locks system, aboard the *Songo River Queen II* (851 Roosevelt Trail; 207-693-6861; www.songoriverqueen.net), a replica of a Mississippi paddlewheeler.

You'll think you're in the Wild West at the **Beech Hill Farm & Bison Ranch** (Route 35, North Waterford; 583-2515; www.beech hillbison.com) where you can enjoy a hayride, see the bison roam freely, and shop for gourmet steaks to take home.

■ ■ ■ ■ LIT LIFE

Stephen King chose Bridgton as the setting for his creepy thriller *The Mist*, which pits townsfolk against an unseen force that terrorizes the town. The story was later made into a movie with Marcia Gay Harden.

■ ■ ■ ■ RESOURCES

Shawnee Peak Mountain Resort, 119 Mountain Rd.; 207-647-8444

Chamber of Commerce, 101 Portland Rd.; 207-647-3472

25 • STOWE, VERMONT

About 200 miles from Boston, 325 miles from New York

Stowe has acquired the moniker "Aspen of the East," and whether or not you consider that a compliment depends upon your point of view. Despite its yuppie tendencies, this lovely village has created an intriguing blend of upscale and down-home attractions without obliterating the rural charm that draws visitors to Vermont in the first place. Best of all, while many New England resorts pretend to be year-round, Stowe really is, packing a wallop in winter as well as in the warmer May-to-October season.

In fact, ski fanatics who love **Stowe Mountain Resort** for its vertical drop—at 4,395 feet, Mt. Mansfield is Vermont's highest mountain—might be surprised to learn that the destination started out as a summer recreation area. City folk sweltering in the summer heat made their way to the Green Mountain Inn as early as the 1830s to spend their vacations in the cool mountain air.

That trend continues to this day, with a robust summer tourist trade that, on some days, threatens to take over the tiny village

streets. The historic village is charming, with more than 40 stores that dot Main Street and along Stowe Mountain Road, and foodies will think they have died and gone to heaven, thanks to a slew of tony eateries, ranging from pricey multiethnic cuisine to flapjacks served with local maple syrup. And it isn't your imagination that spas are huge in Stowe; the number of properties offering full-service spas is significant and growing. It is easy to get distracted by the stores and eateries in town, but the real fun is in the mountains, where active vacationers can inhale fresh country air and get an eyeful of calendar-worthy scenery at every turn.

Recently Stowe's reputation as a top-flight ski area got another boost with a much-ballyhooed mountain expansion program at **Spruce Peak**. The project, which includes posh ski-in/ski-out accommodations and a golf course, is scheduled for completion in 2010, but as of the time of writing you can already see the results of phase one, the brand-new **Stowe Mountain Lodge** (see

Where to Stay), which opened in 2008.

It's worth noting that while the expansion caused controversy, particularly among those who don't think Vermont needs more development, project planners worked with environmentalists to surround the new construction with conservation land. Their efforts paid off, according to the Audubon Society, which awarded the project the Audubon Green Community Award. The new base village will eventually have more shopping and dining venues, an ice-skating rink, and a performing arts center.

▊▊▊▊ GETTING THERE (AND GETTING AROUND)

The drive from Boston is about three and a half hours off exit 10 on I-89, and it is nice to have a car to make the most of the area. Vermont's Burlington International Airport is only about 45 minutes from Stowe, or you can hop aboard Amtrak for the scenic trip to Waterbury, about 15 miles

from Stowe, where a trolley meets the train for the last leg.

▊▊▊▊ WHAT TO SEE

Stowe's popularity as a winter resort has its roots in history, as witnessed by the **Vermont Ski Museum** in the old town hall (1 South Main St.), where visitors can check out vintage posters, photographs, and equipment—long, skinny wooden skis and scratchy woolen clothing, anyone?—from those early days.

For a taste of Vermont authenticity, the **Farmer's Market** (Mountain Rd.), across from the Stoweflake Resort, is a step back in time. Operating 10:30 AM to 3:30 PM on Sundays from mid- May to mid-October, the market showcases local products, from fruit pies and homemade root beer floats to organic soaps and handmade crafts. You can also expect live music and even a friendly sheep or two for the kids to pet.

Go shopping along Main Street and Mountain Road. Gourmet cooks or enthusiastic wannabes

Stowe's new Spruce Peak base lodge

Stowe Mt. Lodge great room

can check out **Stowe Mercantile** (Depot St. Bldg, Main St.), where locally made candies and candles vie for attention on the shelves with crafts and kitchenware. Or pick up Vermont-made folk art, crafts, and Christmas decorations at **Vermont Heritage Gifts & Crafts** (48 S. Main St.; 802-253-7507). At **Stowe Craft Gallery** (55 Mountain Rd.; 802-253-4693; www.stowecraft.com), the crafts and fine arts range from one-of-a-kind furniture to locally designed jewelry. If all you want is a pair of warm winter socks or a toy for a child, you can spend a happy hour browsing in **Shaw's General Store** (54 Main St.; 802-253-4040).

See the mountain views via the **Gondola Skyride** (Mountain Rd.), where you can hike along the summit or grab a bite at the food outlet. The ride runs from late June to mid-October.

▮▮▮▮ WHAT TO DO (IN WINTER)

Hit the slopes. Recent upgrades at **Stowe Mountain Resort** (5781 Mountain Rd.; 800-253-4754; www.stowe.com) include new trails, high-speed lifts, and a revamped novice area, bringing the total number of trails to 116, spread out over almost 500 acres. And while there is plenty of expert terrain, more than half of the trails are suitable for intermediates, which—let's face it—probably describes most of the skiing population.

Those who prefer high-octane thrills can try their moves at Stowe's half-pipe or freestyle terrain parks, while visitors who just want to work off that fondue can enjoy an afternoon cross-country skiing on miles of groomed trails.

Nonskiers and snowboarders— or just those who want a break

Topnotch at Stowe stables

from the slopes—can enjoy Stowe in winter with a whole menu of off-slope activities, from dog-sledding with a team of Siberian Huskies at **Peace Pups Dogsledding** or at nearby **Eden Dog Sledding** (1390 Square Rd., Eden Mills; 802-635-9070; www.eden dogsledding.com). Snowmobiling, ice skating, and snowshoeing also are available in Stowe.

▪▪▪▪ WHAT TO DO (IN SUMMER & FALL)

Listen to live music at **Stowe Performing Arts** (802-253-7792), which showcases the area's most scenic outdoor musical venues, including free concerts in the Stowe Gazebo to Music in the Meadow at the **Trapp Family Lodge** (see Where to Stay).

Enjoy live theater through the **Stowe Theater Guild** (67 Main St.; 802-253-3961; www.stowe theatre.com), which offers a summer season with productions for adults and children. The 2009 season featured *The Full Monty* and *Footloose*, as well as *Click, Clack, Moo*, for example, and evening shows allow plenty of time for a pre-theater dinner.

Explore Stowe's rustic beauty on foot or bicycle. The place to start is the **Stowe Recreation Path**, a 5+-mile trail that wends from the village through woods and meadows. Rent a bicycle at

AJ's Ski & Sports (350 Mountain Rd.; 800-226-6257) or **Pinnacle Ski & Sports** (3391 Mountain Rd.; 802-253-7222; www.pinnacle skisports.com), or, if you like touring with a guide, try **Peace Pups Bicycle Tours** (Lake Elmore; 802-888-7733; www.peacepups dogsledding.com). Guides will bring the bikes to your hotel, set you up with equipment and helmets, and help you plan a customized guided itinerary, complete with lunch or snacks.

If time permits, test your sense of direction at the **Percy Farm Corn Maze** (Stowe Mountain Rd., 802-253-4092) or grab a *Visitor's Guide Hiking Map* at your hotel or in town to explore the mountain trails on foot.

Canoeing and kayaking also are big in Stowe, with equipment rentals widely available, or you can try one of the offbeat river tours at **Umiak Outdoor Outfitters** (849 S Main St.; 802-253-2317). The 4-mile River & Spirits trip, for example, explores the Lamoille River via canoe or kayak, followed by a wine tour at the Boyden Valley Winery nearby. The company also rents kayaks and canoes and offers lessons and directions for visitors who want to head out on their own.

Visitors with a need for speed can try the lift-assisted 2,300-foot-ride **Stowe Alpine Slide** on

Spruce Peak from the third week in June through mid-October. While the slide is steep, riders can control the speed, and the slides move along a track, which means that you can enjoy an adrenaline rush without risking life and limb.

Those who like the idea of mountain climbing but need to brush up on their skills can try the new **Stowe Climbing Wall** (Stowe Mountain), open in summer and early fall.

As in most of Vermont, Stowe is surreally beautiful in the fall, particularly in peak leaf- peeping season, but be aware that tourists come from all over the world to see the sight. The hiking and biking options available in summer are great ways to see the blaze of fiery color, but you can also hop in your car and take the **Mt. Mansfield Auto Toll Road** for panoramic views of Lake Champlain and the surrounding mountain peaks for $23 per car. Bring your camera and a good pair of walking shoes and remember that for stays between the tail end of September through mid-October, you literally can't book your reservations early enough.

■ ■ ■ ■ **WHERE TO STAY**

Stowe Mountain Lodge (7412 Mountain Rd.; 802-253-3560; www.stowemountainlodge.com), is the jewel in the crown of the Spruce Peak project. The six-story, 139-room property offers a blend of modern and rustic decor, complete with such high-end touches as stone fireplaces, marble bathrooms, and goose-down feather beds. The real treat, especially after a long day on the slopes or a bicycle, is the 21,000-square-foot, three-floor wellness spa with his-and-her treatments. Dining includes Solstice for upscale Asian fare, and Hourglass for small plates, microbrews, and wines by the glass. From $435, but specials and packages are available.

Stoweflake Mountain Resort & Spa (1746 Mountain Rd.; 802-253-7355; www.stoweflake.com) takes the spa component of its identity very seriously. The 120-room property offers dozens of treatments, including ayurveda detox and wellness treatments, as well as scrubs and wraps using local ingredients. Unlike some of its competitors, this property eschews a minimalist look and celebrates its cozy New England character, with exteriors that look as though they were lifted directly from a Currier and Ives print. Accommodations are in the main house or in townhouses, or you can get a group of friends together and rent the four-bedroom Baraw Family Ski House with multiple fireplaces and four baths. Be sure to make time for dinner at the Wine Spectator award—winning Winfield's Bistro or, for more casual fare, Charlie B's Pub & Restaurant. From $249.

Topnotch at Stowe Resort and Spa (4000 Mountain Rd., 802-253-8585; http://topnotchresort .com), a 68-room spa property on 120 acres at the base of Mt. Mansfield, has also raked in its share of awards. The 35,000-square-foot Spa at Topnotch features solarium, waterfall, heated indoor swimming pool, and a whole menu of cutting-edge treatments. The hotel also runs a highly ranked Tennis Center—with indoor facilities for the winter season—and sleigh rides at the equestrian center. A free shuttle bus takes guests to the ski mountain, and rental gear is available on-site. Dining is at the ultramodern Norma's, where you can get scallops with sweet potato-mushroom risotto and edamame cappuccino, greens, and soups from the spa menu, or pumpkin soufflé, tarte tatin, or make-your-own s'mores for dessert. From $245.

The **Trapp Family Lodge** (802-253-8511; www.trappfamily.com) will seem familiar to anyone who has ever seen *The Sound of Music* and knows about the famous von Trapp family. You don't need to be a music fan to enjoy the 2,400-acre property, however, which features new mountain biking trails, a cross-country ski center, snowshoeing, and horse-drawn sleigh rides in winter and swimming, tennis, and summer concerts in summer. Try the Austrian-inspired fare and extensive wine list at the Dining Room, where dinner is served by candlelight to the accompaniment of classical harp music. From about $225.

■■■■ EATING OUT

The **Hàna Hibachi Steak House** (1128 Mountain Rd.; 802-253-8878; www.hanainstowe.com) offers a sushi bar and martini bar amid decor that gleams with wood and leather. From $27.95.

Mr. Pickwick's (433 Mountain Rd.; www.mrpickwicks.com) is the place to go for a hardy rack of elk or beef Wellington in an Old English setting. You can also wolf down bangers and mash (sausages with Cheddar mashed potatoes, for the uninitiated) or braised rabbit. From $17.

Blue Moon Café (35 School St.; 802-253-7006; www.bluemoon stowe.com) serves up lighter fare, featuring a menu of fresh, local ingredients that changes every week presented in a nouveau cuisine style. From $18.

Whip Bar & Grill at the Green

Mountain Inn (8 Main St.; 802-253-7301; www.greenmountain inn.com) boasts a welcoming après-ski scene, but you can also dine here on such specialties like Prince Edward Island mussels and roast duck. From $9.25 for a burger; $19.95 for an entrée.

▪▪▪▪ SPECIAL EVENTS

Mid-August: Sports and shopping aside, Stowe also boasts a robust arts and cultural scene, with festivals on tap year-round. A favorite is the **Annual Antique & Classic Car Meet**, complete with a classic car parade driven by costumed participants and even a selection of pricey autos for sale to well-heeled aficionados.

Early to Mid-August: Musical concerts keep evenings lively in summer, including the **Stowe Summer Music Festival**, a free event at various venues around town that features classical music performances

Mid-January: In winter, the air of festivity continues, especially during the annual **Stowe Winter Carnival** (www.stowewinter carnival.com), with ice sculptures, ski races, food, costumed parades, and fireworks to warm up the crowd.

▪▪▪▪ NEARBY

There are numerous factory tours within a few minutes' drive of Stowe, but we have a special fondness for the crowded but quirky **Ben & Jerry's Factory** (Rt. 100, Waterbury; www.benjerry .com). Watch the ice cream being made, sample the goods, and buy our favorite tourist T-shirts that read "Resistance is futile."

▪▪▪▪ RESOURCES

Stowe Area Visitors Association, Main St.; 877-GOSTOWE or 802-253-7321; www.gostowe.com